Challenges of Managing Information Quality in Service Organizations

Latif Al-Hakim
University of Southern Queensland, Australia

IDEA GROUP PUBLISHING
Hershey • London • Melbourne • Singapore

Acquisition Editor:	Michelle Potter
Senior Managing Editor:	Jennifer Neidig
Managing Editor:	Sara Reed
Development Editor:	Kristin Roth
Copy Editor:	Bernie Kieklak
Typesetter:	Jessie Weik
Cover Design:	Lisa Tosheff
Printed at:	Yurchak Printing Inc.

Published in the United States of America by
    Idea Group Publishing (an imprint of Idea Group Inc.)
    701 E. Chocolate Avenue
    Hershey PA 17033
    Tel: 717-533-8845
    Fax: 717-533-8661
    E-mail: cust@idea-group.com
    Web site: http://www.idea-group.com

and in the United Kingdom by
    Idea Group Publishing (an imprint of Idea Group Inc.)
    3 Henrietta Street
    Covent Garden
    London WC2E 8LU
    Tel: 44 20 7240 0856
    Fax: 44 20 7379 3313
    Web site: http://www.eurospan.co.uk

Library of Congress Cataloging-in-Publication Data

Challenges of managing information quality in service organizations / Latif Al-Hakim, editor.
    p. cm.
  Summary: "Incorrect and misleading information associated with an enterprise's production and service jeopardize both customer relationships and customer satisfaction, and ultimately have a negative effect on revenue. This book provides insight and support for academic professionals as well as for practitioners concerned with the management of information"--Provided by publisher.
  ISBN 1-59904-420-X (hardcover) -- ISBN 1-59904-421-8 (softcover) -- ISBN 1-59904-422-6 (ebook)
  1. Information technology--Management. 2. Information resources management--Quality control. 3. Database management--Quality control. 4. Service industries--Information technology--Quality control. I. Al-Hakim, Latif, 1946-
  HD30.2.C4716 2007
  658.4'038--dc22
                     2006019120

British Cataloguing in Publication Data
A Cataloguing in Publication record for this book is available from the British Library.

Challenges of Managing Information Quality in Service Organizations is part of the Idea Group Publishing series named *Information Quality Management Series.*

All work contributed to this book is new, previously-unpublished material. The views expressed in this book are those of the authors, but not necessarily of the publisher.

Challenges of Managing Information Quality in Service Organizations

Table of Contents

Section I: IQ Application in the Healthcare Industry

Chapter I
Eric Infeld, UnitedHealth Group/Ingenix, USA
Laura Sebastian-Coleman, UnitedHealth Group/Ingenix, USA

Chapter II
Latif Al-Hakim, University of Southern Queensland, Australia

Section IV: IQ Application for Research and Development

Foreword

In today's fast changing world, organisations generate enormous amounts of data, yet many are finding it difficult to use this data. Indeed it is estimated that more than 70% of generated data is never used. Decision-makers have access to much data but more than ever make decisions with sub-optimal data. The cliché "Drowning in data and starving for information" is so true these days.

Issues of information quality (IQ) problems in the organisation are not identified until it is too late. Few organizations treat information quality as a strategic issue, yet they make strategic decisions with often inaccurate, incomplete and outdated data.

There is however an emerging awareness that in the modern organisation one is required to make decisions very quickly in order to gain information superiority and competitive advantage. High quality data is critical in such situations. Equally, many organisations are also painfully aware of the significant costs of poor quality data. Consequently, there is a growing demand for IQ initiatives as organisations' awareness of the importance of their IQ increases.

Leading organisations must no longer treat data quality as a cost, but as a strategic issue that must be addressed. A variety of initiatives are becoming imperative to address real-time data profiling, cleansing, and matching, metadata management, new regulatory compliance requirements and so on. The real-time nature of e-business practices and processes today has made real-time profiling, cleansing and matching an important issue. The issue of metadata management has gathered attention because standards, definitions, and application metadata sharing are key to solving many IQ problems.

In tackling IQ problems, many lessons have been learned. It is well established that in improving data quality, organisations must treat IQ as a multi-dimensional concept beyond accuracy. Methods and tools for performing IQ assessments have been developed in practice. Understanding the systems, processes, and management practices of an organisation has become as important as understanding its data. Furthermore, many organisations have found that resolving their IQ problems is not a single-phase process, Rather it is a continuous process, where one solution may lead to new problems and employees at all levels must come together and to solve IQ problems.

Without a solid foundation of high quality data, dirty data can chip away at an organisation's ability to function effectively. An information quality initiative that is well defined within the context of an organisation may still encounter difficulties with implementation. The difficulties faced by organisations when executing their information quality initiatives include meeting data standards, handling secondary information, reconciling technology with general business IQ, integrating disparate disciplines, etc.

The book *Challenges of Managing Information Quality in Service Organisations* provides us with the unique opportunity to get an in-depth insight into the IQ issues facing organisations in the service industry. Information quality is a core business issue that is fundamental to the success of the contemporary Enterprise. Recently information quality has gained the status that it deserves in the research community and no doubt books such as this will also inform the communities of practice to enhance enterprise information orientation.

Andy Koronios, PhD
Adelaide
March 2006

Andy Koronios *received his PhD from the University of Queensland, Australia. He has extensive teaching experience both in the tertiary sector at undergraduate and postgraduate, MBA, DBA and PhD level as well as in the provision of executive industry seminars. He has numerous research publications in a diverse area such as multimedia and online learning systems, information security and data quality, electronic commerce, and Web requirements engineering. His current research interests focus on data quality and the use of information in strategic decision-making. He is currently a professor and the head of the School of Computer and Information Science at the University of South Australia.*

Preface

OVERVIEW

There have been three major interrelated trends in global markets over the last three decades that have brought the concept of information quality (IQ) to the forefront of management attention. These trends are as follows:

- **Innovation:** The current era is associated with widespread and successive waves of technology-driven innovations in information and communication technologies (ICT). Technologies such as the Internet, electronic commerce, World Wide Web (www) and mobile commerce bring with them ubiquitous connectivity, real-time access and overwhelming volumes of data and information.
- **Information economy:** The world has experienced a transition from an industrial economy to an information economy. Data and information have become as much a strategic necessity for an organisation's well being and future success as oxygen is to human life (Eckerson, 2002). Almost every activity in which an enterprise engages requires data. Data are the critical inputs into almost all strategic and operational decisions of an enterprise (Eckerson, 2002; Redman, 2001).
- **Mandatary requirements:** Organisations realise that they must provide the quality information expected by their customers "or run the risk of legislation that forces them to provide such quality" (English & Perez, 2003).

ICT allows organisations to collect great volumes of data. Vast databases holding terabytes of data and information are becoming commonplace (Abbott, 2001). The literature emphasises that enterprises have far more data than they can possibly use. Yet, at the same time, they do not have the data they actually need (Abbott, 2001; Eckerson, 2002). Furthermore, the stored data and information may be obsolete, ambiguous, inaccurate or incomplete. In other words, enterprises have achieved "quantity" of data and information but not necessarily the "quality" of either (Pierce, 2005).

Poor quality of data and information can have a deleterious impact on decision-making and therefore on the overall effectiveness of an enterprise. Incorrect and misleading information associated with an enterprise's production and service provision jeopardises both customer relationships and customer satisfaction and ultimately has a negative effect on revenue. Poor information quality is not only prevalent in manufacturing and service organisations, it can also be at the roots of many issues of national and international importance which dominate the news (Reman, 2004). Table 1 illustrates some well documented problems associated with poor information quality.

Laws and regulations have been formulated in an attempt to protect customers who may pay the price for poor data and information in the form of higher costs of products or services (English, 2005). The Information Quality Act enacted by the US Congress in December 2000 is just one example of such legislation. Enterprises may face legal actions if they fail to provide data and information to match customer expectations. Strong agreement is found in the literature in relation to the need for high quality data and of information. But the questions remain: What is "data"? and What is "information"?

DATA AND INFORMATION

The word data is the plural of "datum." In practice, however, "datum" is rarely used and people use data as both the singular and plural form of the word (Webopedia, 2005). There is no unique definition of data. The term data is sometimes used interchangeably with information. Data may be defined as the raw material of information or as a collection of facts, concepts or instructions organised in a formalised manner suitable for communication or processing by human or automatic means (Google Web, 2005). In computing, data is regarded as information that has been translated into a form that is more convenient to move or process. It could be viewed as information converted to binary digital form (SearchTechTarget, 2005). Turban et al. (2005) provide the following commonly accepted view of the these terms:

- **Data:** Items about things, events, activities, and transactions are recorded, classified, and stored but are not organised to convey any specific meaning. Data items can be numeric, alphanumeric, figures, sounds, or images.
- **Information:** Data that have been organised in a manner that gives them meaning for the recipient. They confirm something the recipient knows, or may have "surprise" value by revealing something not known.

The above definitions clarify the relationship between data and information. They are consistent with the concept of information product (Ballou et al., 1998; Huang et al., 1999) in which information is a product of an information manufacturing system. The input for this information manufacturing system is data. Similar to a product manufacturing system, an information manufacturing system is hierarchical in that information output from a certain stage can be considered as data for the next stage of the information manufacturing system. From this perspective, the term information can be used to refer to both data and information (Strong et al., 1997). However, the reverse is not always applicable, that is, data collected and stored in a data warehouse cannot be considered as information, as these data are not yet organised and processed to give meaning for a recipient.

Earlier literature dealing with information quality (see for example, Strong et al., 1997) and more recent publications — such as some chapters in Wang et al. (2005), use information quality (IQ) and data quality (DQ) interchangeably. While information quality as the quality of the information product implies data quality or the quality of its raw material data, the reverse is not always true. Whilst there is justification for speaking about "information and data" as a reference to a product and its raw material, emphasising and iterating terms such as "data quality and (or) information quality" or "DQ/IQ" as shown in some recent published literature, (see for example, Pierce, 2005), may create some confusion. Good IQ implies good DQ and poor DQ causes poor IQ. However, a good DQ may not necessarily lead to good IQ. Poor IQ may be caused by errors within the processes of transforming data into information. A researcher or analyst may collect accurate, complete and timely data but may conclude from them poor quality information. IQ implies DQ and the term information quality reflects both information quality and data quality. The focus of authors speaking only about DQ is primarily on the issue of data as a raw material, for example on issues related to quality of data for data warehousing. The editor of this book has successfully oriented the authors of this book to use DQ when their research is oriented to data only and to use IQ when they deal with both IQ and DQ. The work of authors researching in IQ either implies DQ or their research is applicable also to DQ.

DIMENSIONS OF INFORMATION QUALITY

Evans and Lindsay (2005) stress that quality can be a confusing concept. They provide two main reasons for this assertion: (1) people view quality using different perspectives and dimensions based on their individual roles, and (2) the meaning of quality continues to evolve as the quality profession grows and matures. Similar to product quality, IQ has no universal definition. To define IQ, it is important to comprehend both the perspective from which IQ is viewed and its dimensions. The Cambridge Dictionaries Online (2005) defines perspective as "a particular way of considering something" and dimension as "a measurement of something."

Individuals have different ways of considering the quality of information as they have different wants and needs and, hence, different quality standards which lead to a user-based quality perspective (Evans & Lindsey, 2005). This perspective is based on the Juran definition of quality which defines quality as "fitness for intended use" (Juran & Godfrey, 1999). Thus, information and data can be regarded as being of high quality if they are fit for their intended use in operations, decision-making and planning (Redman, 2004). Other related IQ perspectives are "conformance to specifications" and "meeting and exceeding consumer expectations" (Evans &

Table 1. Examples of some documented problems associated with IQ

Field	Problem	Reason	IQ Dimension
Space Industry	The spacecraft launched by NASA on 11 December 1998 to observe the seasonal climate changes on Mars was lost upon arrival at the planet on 23 September 1999.	It is found that the "root cause" of the loss of the spacecraft was the "the failed translation of English units into metric units in a segment of ground-based, navigation-related mission software" (Isbell & Savage, 1999). The IQ problem here is the use of two different types of information obtained from two measurement systems.	Consistency of representation, compatibility, coherency.
Mine Safety and Health	On July 24, 2002, miners working underground in the Quecreek coal mine in Western Pennsylvania (USA) accidentally broke into an adjacent abandoned mine, which unleashed millions of gallons of water and trapped nine men for three days.	The report of the Mine Safety and Health Administration (MSHA) found that the primary cause of the water inundation was use of un-dated information obtained from old mine map (MSHA, 2003).	Timeliness, free-of-error.
Bosnian War	On May 8, 1999, NATO forces accidentally bombed the Chinese Embassy in Belgrade.	The bombing instruction was based on outdated data. The data regarding the movement of the location of the Chinese Embassy in 1996 was undated in the NATA database and their maps (Lehrer, 1999).	Timeliness
Legal System - Death Penalty	In March 2000, a Judge acquitted Mr. Green from the 1992 murder of a Starke woman. Mr. Green became one of 21 inmates released from death row in Florida (Kestin 2000).	A study conducted by Columbia Law School found that during a period of 23 years, the overall rate of prejudicial errors in the American capital punishment system was 68% (Columbia News, 2000). The three most common errors are: (1) incompetent lawyers (37%); (2) suppression of evidence of innocence (19%); and (3) faulty instruction to jurors (20%).	Accuracy, believability, coherency, completeness, ease of understanding, relevancy, reputation.
Terrorism	On September 11, 2001, a series of terrorist attacks destroyed the twin towers of the World Trade Center and severely damaged the Pentagon.	The 9/11 Commission Report depicted a failure to effectively share terrorism warning information and to link the collective knowledge of the agents in the field of national priority (The 9/11 Commission Report, 2004).	Coherency, objectivity, value-added

Table 1. continued

Weapons of Mass Destruction	The United States government asserted that [the former Iraqi dictator] Saddam Hussein had reconstituted his nuclear weapons program, had biological weapons and mobile biological weapon production facilities, and had stockpiled and was producing chemical weapons.	The final report of a special commission confirms that "not one bit of it could be confirmed when the war was over." The Commission concludes that "our study of Iraq found several situations where key information failed to reach those who needed it" (Commission WMD, 2005).	Timeliness, free-of-error, completeness, coherency.
Health - Surgery	Two women with the same first name attended a hospital in the same day to have a breast biopsy. One had breast cancer. One did not. The woman with the breast cancer died after nine months.	It was discovered that the biopsy information results had been mixed up. The woman with the breast cancer died after nine months and the patient without breast cancer had endured months of chemotherapy and was minus a breast (Pirani, 2004).	Accuracy, interpretability, free-of-error, conciseness of representation,
Industry - Refinery	On 23 March 2005 the BP Texas City refinery in USA suffered a huge blast. The blast claimed 15 lives and injured 170 (BBC, 2005a).	The interim report into the tragedy has found that failure to follow the proper procedure (which is one type of information) contributed to the explosion, that is, IQ problem.	Accessibility, ease of understanding, interpretability.
Finance - Share Market	On 9 December 2005, brokers at Mizuho Securities tried to sell 610,000 shares at 1 yen (0.8 US cents) each. The company had meant to sell one share for 610,000 yen -US $5,065 (BBC, 2005b).	Mizuho said the brokerage had purchased the majority of the phantom shares it sold, but the error has so far caused the company a loss of 27bn yen or US $21.6bn. It is announced that this chaos into Japan market trading was a result of a "typing error" (BBC, 2005b), that is, problem in information quality.	Free-of-error, interpretability, objectivity.
Media & Mine Safety	On January 2, 2006 an explosion at the Sago mine (West Virginia - USA) trapped 13 workers. Shortly before midnight in Tuesday, a statement that 12 miners had been found alive was made on several national TV stations and the broadcast prompted jubilant scenes as friends and relatives celebrated. But the euphoria was short lived. Just hours after the banner headlines announced that the 12 miners were safe, rescue workers found their bodies (Associated Press, 2006).	Only one miner out of the 13 miners survived. The sole survivor was taken to the hospital where doctors said his condition was critical. Ben Hatfield, president of mine owner, International Coal Group, blamed the earlier report on "miscommunication."	Accuracy, accessibility, believability, reputation.

Table 2. Definitions of the common IQ dimensions used in literature and their categories (adapted from several research works)

Dimension	Definition	Category		
		Wang and Strong (1996)	Wang et al. (1995)	Lee et. al (2002)
Accessibility	The degree to which information is available, easy obtainable or quickly retrievable when needed. Accessibility depends on the customer's circumstances.	Accessibility	Internal + External -Data/system related	Usable
Accuracy	The degree to which information represents real-world state.	Intrinsic	Internal -Data related	Sound
Amount of Information	This dimension measures the appropriateness of volume of information to the user or task at hand	Contextual	Internal/External -Data related	Useful
Believability	This dimension measures the user assessment of trueness and credibility of information.	Intrinsic	Internal/External - Data/system related	Usable
Coherency	This measures how information "hangs together" and provide one meaning to different users.	Intrinsic + contextual	Internal -Data related	Sound
Compatibility	The level to which information can be combined with other information to form certain knowledge.	Intrinsic + Contextual	Internal -Data related	Useful
Completeness	The degree to which information is sufficient enough to depict every state of the task at hand or the represented system, that is, assesses the degree of missing information.	Contextual	Internal -Data related	Sound
Conciseness of representation	The compactness of information representation.	Represent'nal	External -Data related	Sound
Consistency of representation	The degree of similarity and compatibility of information representation format.	Represent'nal	Internal -Data related	Sound
Ease of manipulation	The applicability of information to different tasks.	Intrinsic	Internal - Data related	Useful
Ease of understanding	The degree of comprehension of information.	Represent'nal	Internal - Data/ system related	Useful

Table 2. continued

Free-of-error	The degree to which information is correct. This dimension measures the number, percent or ratio of incorrect or unreliable information.	Intrinsic	Internal- Data/ system related	Sound
Interpretability	The appropriateness and clarity of information language and symbols to the user.	Represent'nal	Internal -Data related	Useful
Objectivity	This dimension measures the information impartiality including information is unbiased and unprejudiced.	Intrinsic	External -Data related	Useful
Relevancy	Relevancy indicates whether information addresses the customer's needs. It reflects the level of appropriateness of information to the task under consideration.	Contextual	External -Data related	Useful
Reputation	The degree of respect and admiration of both information source and information content.	Intrinsic	External - Data related	Usable
Security	It indicates the level of either restriction on access of information or appropriateness of information back-up - protecting information from disasters.	Accessibility	Internal/External - System related	Dependable
Timeliness	This dimension measures how up-to-date information is with respect to customer's needs or the task at hand. It reflects also how fast the information system is updated after the state of the represented real-world system changes.	Contextual	Internal/ External -Data/ system related	Dependable

Lindsay, 2005). While these perspectives capture the essence of IQ, they are very broad definitions and are difficult to use in the measurement of quality. There is a need to identify the dimensions that can be used to measure IQ.

IQ is a multidimensional. This means that organisations must use multiple measures to evaluate the quality of their information or data. Several researchers have attempted to identify the IQ dimensions. Wang et al. (1995) list 26 IQ dimensions, which in turn are classified into either internal view (design operation) or external view (use and value). Each of these classifications is divided into two subcategories; data-related and system-related (Wand & Wang, 1996). Wang and Strong (1996) conducted an empirical two-phase sorting study and provide the most comprehensive list of IQ attributes. Their list comprises 118 attributes. The 118 attributes are reduced to 20 dimensions, which in turn are grouped into four categories: accuracy, relevancy, representation and accessibility. Wang and Strong (1996) re-examine their four initial categories and re-labelled the first two categories and the four categories to become: intrinsic, contextual, representation, and accessibility. It should be noted here that Wang and Strong using the term DQ (rather than IQ) to represent both DQ and IQ. Recently, Lee et al. (2002) developed a two-by-two conceptual model for describing IQ. The model comprises 16 dimensions, which are classified into four categories: sound information, dependable information, useful information and usable information. Table 2 provides definitions of the most common IQ dimensions used in the literature and illustrates their categories. The last column of Table 1 links the IQ problems with IQ dimensions.

STRUCTURE OF THE BOOK

Theories and methodologies are no longer enough for achieving their purpose without the ability to convert these theories and methodology into practice. "Ability to convert" is what organisations are really requiring. Such ability can be considerably enhanced by providing real case studies and applications. This book aims to deal with the application of information quality in various industrial service sectors including healthcare, banking, the postal system, and research and development. The book will provide insights and support for:

- Professionals and researchers working in the field of information and knowledge management in general and in the field of IQ in particular, and;
- Practitioners and managers of manufacturing and service industries concerned with the management of information.

The book provides 12 case studies and applications organised into four sections. The following is a brief description of each section and the chapters including in them.

Section I:
IQ Application in the Health Care Industry

The first section of this book presents two chapters that contain the results of case studies conducted in health care organisations.

The first chapter "Galaxy's Data Quality Program: A Case Study" by Eric Infeld and Laura Sebastian-Coleman discuses a case study of the data quality program implemented for Galaxy, a large health care data warehouse owned by UnitedHealth Group and operated by Ingenix, USA. The chapter presents an overview of the program's goals and components. It focuses on the program's metrics and includes examples of the practical application of statistical process control (SPC) for measuring and reporting on data quality. These measurements pertain directly to the quality of the data and have implications for the wider question of information quality. The chapter provides examples of specific measures, the benefits gained in applying them in a data warehouse setting, and lessons learned in the process of implementing and evolving the program.

The second chapter in this section is "Information Quality Function Deployment" by Latif Al-Hakim, who maps the information quality process and finds that the control constituent of the process comprises two types of factors: IQ dimensions and IQ indicators. The latter forms an information performance measure known as "information orientation" that measures the capability of an organisation to effectively manage and use information. This chapter stresses that the consistency between the two types of factors will improve the IQ function. Based on an actual information quality initiative occurring in an Australian hospital, the chapter employs a modified quality function deployment (QFD) procedure referred to as information function development (IFD) in an attempt to match IQ dimensions with the IQ indicators in order to identify the most important factors affecting the IQ function deployment.

Section II:
IQ Application in Banking, Real States, and Postal Industry

The second section of this book comprises three chapters that deal with the challenge of applying IQ in three service organisations: a bank, a real estate agency and a mailing centre. Personal information regarding names, addresses, and so forth, plays an important role in these selected organisations. The first chapter in this section is "Customer Investigation Process at Credit Suisse: Meeting the Rising Demands of Regulations" by Daniel Maier, Thomas Muegeli and Andrea Krejza, who depict how a combination of organizational and technical measures led to a significant information quality improvement in customer investigations at Credit Suisse, Zurich, Switzerland. The Investigation and Inquiries department of Credit Suisse has to handle approximately 5,000 client investigations per year. The investigation process has been very complex, time consuming and expensive. Several redundant query processes are needed to achieve satisfactory results. In the past few years, new regulatory requirements have led to a massive increase in the number of investigations to be performed. This case study describes how these requirements can be met by redesigning the process and building a data-warehouse-based application that automates most of the process. These two measures have significantly improved the customer investigation process, resulting in considerable cost and time savings for Credit Suisse.

The second chapter in this section "Assessing Mass Consumer Information Quality Requirements Using Conjoint Analysis" by Elizabeth M. Pierce demonstrates how conjoint analysis can be used to improve the design and delivery of mass consumer information products for real estate organisations. This chapter describes the steps in performing a conjoint analysis to assess information quality preferences of potential home buyers interested in using a real estate Web site to help them locate properties for sale. The author hopes that this tutorial will convince information systems professionals of the usefulness of conjoint analysis as a tool for discerning how to prioritize information quality requirements so that the resulting systems produce information products that better serve the needs of their customers.

The quality of name information has become an increasingly important issue as companies strive to implement customer relationship management (CRM) strategies in which the customer name plays an important role in the entity resolution process for data integration applications — ultimately impacting customer recognition systems. The third chapter of this section entitled "Applying Name Knowledge to Information Quality Assessments" by Kimberly Hess and John Talburt presents an IQ challenge in a mailing centre. It investigates applications developed and refined for assessing and improving the quality of mailing address information. This chapter discusses both theoretical and practical considerations in the approach, design, and administration of systems for assessing the quality of name information.

Section III:
IQ Application for Database Management Services

The third section of this book presents three chapters that consider issues related to database management services. The first chapter of this section is "Information Quality: How Good are Off-The-Shelf DBMS?" by Felix Naumann and Mary Roth, who study how well a typical DBMS meets the goal of providing a high-quality data storage and retrieval facility. The chapter draws on an established set of information quality criteria and assesses how well an exemplary DBMS fares. While quality criteria are usually defined for a set of data, the chapter extends, wherever possible, the definitions to the systems that manage this data.

In an enterprise setting, a major challenge for any data-mining operation is managing data streams or feeds, of both data and metadata, to ensure a stable and certifiably accurate flow of data. Data feeds in this environment can be complex, numerous and opaque. The management of frequently changing data and metadata presents a considerable challenge. The second chapter of this section "Management of Data Streams for Large-Scale Data Mining" by Jon R. Wright, Gregg T. Vesonder, and Tamraparni Dasu articulates the technical issues involved in the task of managing enterprise data. The chapter proposes a multi-disciplinary solution, derived from fields such as knowledge engineering and statistics, to understand, standardize, and automate information acquisition and quality management in preparation for enterprise mining.

The third chapter in this section "Metadata Quality Problems in Federated Collections" by Besiki Stvilia, Les Gasser and Michael Twidale presents a general model for analyzing and reasoning about information quality in large aggregated metadata repositories. It presents results from the authors' empirical studies of metadata quality in large corpuses of metadata harvested under Open Archives Initiative (OAI) protocols. The chapter presents a number of statistical characterizations of samples of metadata from a large corpus built as part of the Institute of Museum and Library Services Digital Collections and Contents project containing OAI-harvested metadata, interprets these statistical assessments and links to the quality measures. The chapter discusses several approaches to quality improvement for metadata based on the study findings.

Section IV:
IQ Application for Research and Development

The final and the fourth section of this book features four chapters that address issues enhancing research and development projects and initiatives. The first chapter of this section is "Analysing Information Quality in Virtual Networks of the Service Sector with Qualitative Interview Data" by Helinä Melkas. Public organizations, cooperatives and non-governmental organizations are forming networks, or entering into networks of companies. Tools for analyzing information quality in such environments have been lacking. In this chapter, a novel framework is introduced for analyzing information quality within information processes of complex organizational networks. The newly developed framework is operationalized within multi-actor, multi-professional networks offering safety telephone services for aging people. The analysis is based on data from interviews with professionals working in several service networks of different types and sizes in Finland. The information quality analysis framework helps in identifying information quality dimensions that are weak in a network. This analysis is usefully combined with an investigation of network collaboration that identifies weaknesses and strengths in network collaboration affecting management of information quality.

The second chapter of this section "Quality Measures and the Information Consumer" by Mikhaila S. E. Burgess, W. Alex Gray, and Nick J. Fiddian discusses the proposal for using quality criteria to facilitate information searching. It suggests that the information consumer can be assisted in searching for information by using a consumer-oriented model of quality. The chapter shows that quality measures can be used to focus information searches by achieving statistically significant changes in the ordering of the obtained search results.

Performing a traditional feasibility analysis based on return on investment, net present value, and so forth, may not capture the advantages of data quality projects: their benefits are often difficult to quantify and uncertain. In addition, they are mostly valuable because of the new opportunities they bring about. The third chapter of this section "DQ: Evaluating Data Quality Projects Using Real Options" by Monica Bobrowski and Sabrina Vazquez Soler presents a methodological framework to assess the benefits of a Data Quality project using a real options approach. The framework adequacy is validated with a case study.

Most authors use the terms data and information interchangeably, however, the purpose-focused, operations-research-based perspective requires considering data and information as two disjunctive sets of symbolic representations with common quality attributes but distinctively different quality problems. The fourth chapter of this section "Purpose-Focused View of Information Quality: Teleological Operations Research-Based Approach" by Zbigniew Gackowski supports this argument. The chapter demonstrates that a tentatively universal hierarchical result-oriented taxonomy of operations quality requirements can be defined for information quality, logical interdependencies among them can be identified, and subsequently a simpler economical sequence for their examination can be determined. The chapter has benefits for those who deal with information quality projects and initiatives.

REFERENCES

Abbott, J. (2001). Data, data everywhere — and not a byte of use? *Qualitative Market Research, 4*(3), 182-192.

Associated Press. (2006, January 5). Joy turn to grief for trapped miners' families. *South China Morning Post, LX11*(5). Hong Kong.

Ballou, D., Wang, R., Pazer, H., & Tayi, H. (1998). Modeling information manufacturing systems to determine information product quality. *Management Science, 44*(4), 462-484.

BBC. (2005a). Errors led to BP refinery blast. *BBC News*. Retrieved December 12, 2005, from http://news.bbc.co.uk/2/hi/business/4557201.stm

BBC. (2005b). Probe into Japan share error. *BBC News*. Retrieved December 10, 2005, from http://news.bbc.co.uk/2/hi/business/4512962.stm

Cambridge Dictionaries Online. (2005). Retrieved December 6, 2005, from http://dictionary.cambridge.org/

Columbia News. (2000). *Landmark study find capital punishment system "fraught with error."* Retrieved December 6, 2005, from http://www.columbia.edu/cu/news/00/06/lawStudy.html

Commission WMD — Commission on the Intelligent Capabilities of the United States Regarding Weapons of Mass Destruction. (2005). *Report to the President*. Retrieved November 12, 2005, from http://www.wmd.gov/report/report.html#chapter9

Eckerson, W.W. (2002). *Data quality and bottom line: Achieving business success through high quality data* (TDWI Report Series). Seattle, WA: The Data Warehousing Institute.

English, L. (2005). Information quality and increasing regulation. *News and Resources*. Retrieved December 2, 2005, from http://support.sas.com/news/feature/05may/iqcompliance.html

Evans, J. R., & Lindsay, W. M. (2005). *The management and control of quality* (6th ed.). Cincinnati, OH: South-Western, Thomson Learning.

Gates, B. (1999). *Business @ the speed of thought: Using a digital nervous system.* London: Penguin Books.

Google Web. (2005). *Definitions of data on the Web.* Retrieved November 30, 2005, from http://www.google.com.au/search?hl=en&lr=&oi=defmore&defl=en&q=define:data

Huang, K-T., Lee, Y.W., & Wang, R.Y. (1999). *Quality information and knowledge.* NJ: Prentice-Hall PTR.

Juran, J. M., & Godfrey, A. B. (1999). *Juran's quality handbook* (5th ed.). New York: McGraw-Hill, 2.2.

Isbell, D., & Savage, D. (1999). Mars climate orbiter failure board releases report: Numerous NASA actions underway in response. *SpaceRef.Com*. Retrieved January 28, 2006, from http://www.spaceref.com:16080/news/viewpr.html?pid=43

MSHA. (2003). *MSHA issues Quecreek investigation report.* U. S. Department of Labor: Mine Safety and Health Administration. Retrieved December, 6, 2005, from http://www.msha.gov/Media/PRESS/2003/NR030812.htm

Kestin, S. (2000). *State's death penalty error rate among highest in nation.* Retrieved on December 6, 2005, from www.helpvirginia.com/6-19-00.htm

Lee, Y. W., Strong, D. M., Kahn, B. K., & Wang, R. Y. (2002). AIMQ: a methodology for information quality assessment. *Information & Management*, 40, 133-146.

Lehrer, J. (1999). The wrong target. *Online News Hour.* Retrieved on December 6, 2005, from http://www.pbs.org/newshour/bb/europe/jan-june99/bombing_5-10.html

Pierce, E. M. (2005). Introduction. In R. Wang, E. Pierce, S. Madnick & C. Fisher (Eds.), *Information quality* (pp. 3-17*). Advances in Management Information System*, 1. Armonk, NY: M. E. Sharpe.

Pirani, C. (2004, January 24-25). How safe are our hospitals? *The Weekend Australian.*

Redman, T. C. (2001). *Data quality: The field guide.* Boston: Digital.

Redman, T. C. (2004, August). Data: an unfolding quality disaster. *DM Review Magazine*. Retrieved November 6, 2005, from http://www.dmreview.com/article_sub.cfm?articleId=1007211

SerachTechTarget. (2005). Data. *SearchDataManagement.Com Definition*. Retrieved November 30, 2005, from http://searchdatamanagement.techtarget.com/sDefinition/

Strong, D. M., Lee, Y. W., & Wang, R. Y. (1997). Data quality on context. *Communication of the ACM, 40*(5), 103-110.

The 9/11 Commission Report. (2004). *Final Report of the National Commission on Terrorist attacks Upon the United States — Executive Summary*. Washington, DC: US Government Printing Office. Retrieved December 6, 2005, from http://a257.g.akamaitech.net/7/257/2422/22jul20041147/www.gpoaccess.gov/911/pdf/execsummary.pdf

Turban, E., Aronson, J. E., & Liang, T. P. *Decision support systems and intelligent systems* (7th ed.). Upper Saddle River, NJ: Prentice-Hall.

Wand, Y., & Wang, R. Y. (1996). Anchoring data quality dimensions in ontological foundations. *Communications of ACM, 39*(11), 86-95.

Wang, R. Y. (1998). A product perspective on total data quality management. *Communications of the ACM, 41*(2), 58-65.

Wang, R. Y., Pierce, E. M., Madnick, S. E., & Fisher, C. W. (Eds.). (2005). Information quality. *Advances in Management Information System*, 1. Armonk, NY: M. E. Sharpe.

Wang, R. Y., Storey, V. C., & Firth, C. P. (1995). A framework for analysis of data quality research. *IEEE Transactions Knowledge and Data Engineering, 7*(4), 623-640.

Wang, R. Y., & Strong, D. M. (1996). Beyond accuracy: What data quality means to data consumers. *Journal of Management Information Systems, 12*(4), 5-34.

Acknowledgments

The editor is grateful to all those who have assisted him with the completion of this work. In particular, the editor would like to acknowledge his deepest appreciation to many reviewers for their time and effort. Amendments suggested by them were incorporated into the manuscripts during the development process and significantly enhanced the quality of the work.

The editor wants to thank Dr. Mehdi Khosrow-Pour, the executive director of Idea Group Inc., and Jan Travers, the managing director, who provided needed support and coordination. Appreciation also goes to Kristin Roth, Michelle Potter, and Sharon Berger who gave their time willingly to describe many issues related to the preparation of this work and share their experiences with me. A special thanks to the staff of the University of Southern Queensland for all of their assistance in seeing this work completed.

List of Reviewers

Laure Berti-Équille	Universitaire de Beaulieu, France
Monica Bobrowski	Pragma Consultores, Argentina
Mikhaila S. E. Burgess	Cardiff University, UK
Ismael Caballero	University of Castilla-La Mancha, Spain
Zbigniew J. Gackowski	California State University, Stanislaus, USA
Heather Maguire	University of Southern Queensland, Australia
Kimberly Hess	CASA 20th Judicial District, USA
Karolyn Kerr	Simpl, New Zealand
Andy Koronios	University of South Australia, Australia
Shien Lin	University of South Australia, Australia

Daniel Maier	Credit Suisse, Switzerland
Helinä Melkas	Helsinki University, Finland
Felix Naumann	Humboldt-Universität zu Berlin, Germany
Tony Norris	Massey University, New Zealand
M. Mehdi Owrang	American University, USA
Elizabeth M. Pierce	Indiana University of Pennsylvania, USA
Barbara Roberts	University of Southern Queensland, Australia
Mary Roth	IBM Silicon Valley Lab, USA
Ying Su	Tsinghua University, China
John R. Talburt	University of Arkansas at Little Rock, USA
Michael B. Twidale	University of Illinois at Urbana-Champaign, USA
Sabrina Vazquez Soler	Pragma Consultores, Argentina
Jon R. Wright	AT&T Labs - Research, USA
Zhenguo Yu	Zhejiang University City College, China
Suhaiza Zailani	Universiti Sains Malaysia, Malaysia

Section I:
IQ Application in the
Healthcare Industry

Chapter I

Galaxy's Data Quality Program:
A Case Study

Eric Infeld, UnitedHealth Group/Ingenix, USA

Laura Sebastian-Coleman, UnitedHealth Group/Ingenix, USA

ABSTRACT

This chapter is a case study of the data quality program implemented for Galaxy, a large health care data warehouse owned by UnitedHealth Group and operated by Ingenix. The chapter presents an overview of the program's goals and components. It focuses on the program's metrics and includes examples of the practical application of statistical process control (SPC) for measuring and reporting on data quality. These measurements pertain directly to the quality of the data and have implications for the wider question of information quality. The chapter provides examples of specific measures, the benefits gained in applying them in a data warehouse setting, and lessons learned in the process of implementing and evolving the program.

GALAXY'S DATA QUALITY PROGRAM:
A CASE STUDY

Very few people would need to consult a dictionary for a definition of "Galaxy." We understand the word refers to bigger-than-the-solar-system chunks of outer space or if we're talking about the Milky Way Galaxy specifically, the clouds, stars, planets, moons, rocks, meteors and dust that make up our corner of the universe. The dictionary is more specific and asks us to understand a "Galaxy" through data about it:

Galaxy, n. Any of numerous large scale aggregates of stars, gas, and dust that constitute the universe, containing an average of 100 billion (10^{11}) solar masses and ranging in diameter from 1,500 to 300,000 light years. (American Heritage College Dictionary, 1997)

While it's easier than trying to comprehend the entire universe, most people find it hard to keep straight in their minds — at least all at once — the stuff that makes up a Galaxy: gigantic aggregates and dust particles, distances measured in light years, and numbers over 100 billion. Still a physical galaxy is an apt metaphor for the Galaxy of this case study — UnitedHealth Group's enterprise data warehouse — which is also large, contains a wide range of objects of vastly different sizes, and is best understood through data about it. Like its physical counterpart, Galaxy — the data warehouse — is also constantly evolving.

The purpose of this chapter is to describe the data quality program we have begun to implement for Galaxy and to analyze lessons learned from applying theoretical assertions about data quality in a business setting. First, we will provide some background on Galaxy itself. Next, we will present a detailed description of Galaxy's current data quality program and how each of its components contributes to an overall view of the warehouse's data quality. Then, we will review factors within the business environment that enabled the program's development and lessons learned in applying data quality theory to Galaxy.

WHAT IS GALAXY?

Galaxy, UnitedHealth Group's 43-terabyte enterprise data warehouse, is among the largest data warehouses in the world. Launched in 2000 by UnitedHealth Group's Ingenix business unit, it has over 2,683 attributes across 14,286 columns in 467 tables. This data pertains to UnitedHealth Group's policyholders and their employees, health care claims, service patterns of providers, clinical data, and financial information pertaining to all of these. As a data warehouse, Galaxy makes data from more than 100 source input files from more than 25 distinct source systems (both internal to UnitedHealth Group and from external vendors) available in one central location and allows end users to pull together analyses from different parts of the business. Galaxy stores data in 11 subject areas: claim aggregation, claim financial, and claim statistical, customer, geography, lab, member, organization, pharmacy, provider, and product. The warehouse is constantly growing, in terms of both the amount and the type of data it contains. This growth presents a challenge because enhancements to the Galaxy carry with them the risk of changing existing processes that control the data.

Galaxy serves a wide range of purposes. These include business analytics — understanding how UnitedHealth Group is performing as a business — and financial reporting within UnitedHealth Group overall, as well as within individual health plans and business units. It is the source for a range of focused data marts, as well as for health care analytics — analysis of health issues, options for care, delivery of services. Galaxy data helps analysts understand how members use provider networks, how providers treat specific conditions, which treatments are effective, and which care options produce better outcomes. Ultimately the use of the data results in improvement of people's health and therefore quality of life through better health care delivery — one of UnitedHealth Group's overall business goals.

GALAXY'S DATA QUALITY PROGRAM: GOALS AND COMPONENTS

Galaxy's data quality (DQ) program began with a definition of "data quality" for Galaxy. Defined when Galaxy was launched, the DQ team's best practices read:

- Data errors in data warehouses and data errors in operational/transactional systems require different treatment. The data warehouse is not the place to fix errors passed to it. For lasting, effective solutions, errors should be fixed upstream — as close to the source as possible.
- First, prevent future errors. If data clean-ups are still needed, it focused them on pockets of critical data.
- Identify/detect root causes of errors and eliminate them. Research and experience show that root causes, while not always easy to find, are often relatively inexpensive and almost always highly effective to fix.
- In most industries, "clean-ups" have become habitual. It takes great effort to resist the pressures to continue this habit. Resistance is worth the effort.
- Correcting or cleansing in the data warehouse itself is enormously expensive and gives a false sense of security about the data.
- Seek exactly the right data for each purpose.
- Recognize that data represent a different asset category than technology (IT).
- Actively manage information chains. (Redman, 2001)

The basic approach to data quality was developed and honed through discussions with end users, who understand Galaxy's data through their particular business goals, and with data warehouse team members, who understand past issues, questions, and resolutions. The vision included a strategy for continual improvement of Galaxy's data quality.[1] From this strategy we implemented tactics: monitoring of business-critical quality indicators through clear metrics, reporting on these indicators, recommending and implementing preventative measures and process improvements, and demonstrating the impact of such changes through improvements in our metrics.

Galaxy's data quality program has three broad goals:

- First, ensuring that Galaxy's data meets business-defined quality standards. This includes defining, "discovering" and understanding what those standards are, recognizing that they will change over time, and flexibly responding to change (Lee, 2003).[2] Meeting this goal requires open communication with business users to assure that data continues to meet their needs.
- Next, monitoring Galaxy's data quality levels and communicating these levels to stakeholders on a scheduled basis. Ideally we would stop data problems before they ever enter the warehouse. While we cannot completely control our sources, monitoring via statistical process control (SPC) helps identify potential problems and reduce the need for downstream fixes. Communications to end users inform them first about how we measure data quality. Secondly, if data does not meet expected standards, users know it and know why as soon as possible.[3]
- Finally and most importantly, the program recommends and helps implement improvements to Galaxy's data quality and thus the warehouse's ability to contribute to UnitedHealth Group's business goals. Data quality efforts do not happen in a vacuum or for their own sake; they are part of the overall business purpose of the data warehouse.

The data quality program's current components align with and contribute to its goals. These include:

- Maintaining code and description (i.e., dimension) tables so that the data is complete and up-to-date and end users can rely on it for reporting purposes. The dimension tables contain data over which the data warehouse team exerts control and which can and should be current. All tables are reviewed at least annually.
- Reviewing the integrity of primary and foreign keys. Reviews, conducted annually, measure whether basic processes are working as expected.
- Monitoring and measuring key quality indicators through statistical process control. Monitoring allows early identification of issues with source system data or warehouse processes and allows the data warehouse team to limit the negative impact on end users.
- Reporting on key indicators, so that end users understand the condition of Galaxy's data, and the warehouse delivers data that meets business expectations.
- Recommending improvements based on these measurements so that insight about the warehouse's data improves its business value. To this end, we are in the process of improving the communications component of the program to strengthen the data warehouse team's ability to influence source systems and source system data.

The following sub-sections describe how these components work and identify lessons learned in implementing them.

Maintaining Dimension Tables and Reviewing the Integrity of Primary and Foreign Keys

The data quality team is responsible for assuring referential integrity between code and description (dimension) tables and fact tables. Galaxy contains over 530 code sets, which vary in size and complexity.[4] Some, like the gender code table, contain simple codes and descriptions of a few stable values. Others, like our diagnosis and procedure code tables, contain thousands of values with multiple sets of codes mapped in relation to each other. More importantly, Galaxy's code sets vary in their significance for Galaxy end users who use them for reporting purposes. Some receive a lot of scrutiny; if they are out-of-date, end users demand updates. Others are essentially orphaned. It is difficult to obtain definitions for unexpected values uncovered through data quality assessments.

On an annual basis, the DQ team compares all the values in the listings with the actual values that appear on the Galaxy tables where the codes are used. We have conducted an Annual Review of Code and Description Tables for three years. Its scope has grown each year. In 2003, it included 100 or so key tables including industry standard diagnosis, procedure, and revenue codes. In 2004 the review included all 530+ code listings and required comparisons to more than 700 columns in the database. It resulted in updates to more than 200 tables and listings. In addition to the annual review, the data quality team also makes monthly, weekly and quarterly updates to code tables with business mandated update schedules.

The annual Review is complemented through another annual data quality process, the baseline assessment of primary and foreign keys. Like the annual review, the baseline assessment tests referential integrity between columns in different tables. By comparing values as they appear on fact tables, we identify disjoints, research definitions for missing values, and update tables accordingly. We also assesses whether columns contain expected, business-logical values. For example, on a claim table, one would expect that the ratio of male to female, as determined through the gender code field, would mirror that of male to female on the member table. One would also expect a higher level of default values on a secondary or tertiary diagnosis code field than in the primary diagnosis code field. A recent change in the level of defaults on one of our columns alerted us to a change in business process that required Galaxy processes to be adjusted in order to accurately represent data from our sources.

Both the annual review and the baseline assessment draw on 6 Sigma methodologies.[5] Six Sigma is a data driven methodology for eliminating process defects or deficiencies. It uses rigorous data gathering and statistical analysis to measure outcomes — driving towards the near perfection of six standard deviations between the mean and the nearest specification limit. Many high-quality manufacturing

Figure 1. The codes in bold type — C1, MC1, and PDS — appeared on a data warehouse fact table but were not defined on the corresponding code table. Only one, MC1, was present on the fact table at a level above 4 sigma (.61%). However, when combined, the two that met the 4 sigma standard still accounted for over 170,000 rows on the table.

Sample Code	COUNTS	Percentage of total
	3638895	20.1660%
*EC	97459	0.5401%
AMC	31151	0.1726%
C1	108851	**0.6032%**
CMM	3786090	20.9817%
CMS	231646	1.2837%
CNV	468445	2.5960%
HPR	108355	0.6005%
MC1	152547	**0.8454%**
ONL	6491808	35.9763%
PDS	65250	**0.3616%**
PL*	1599787	8.8657%
PRS	1132867	6.2781%
UEP	131553	0.7290%
Total:	18044704	

companies operate at around 4 sigma (4 sigma = 6,210 defects per million; 6 Sigma = 3.4 defects per million).

Using simple row counts, we calculate percentages of individual values for all primary and foreign keys and investigate unexpected values that exceed 4 sigma (i.e., more than four standard deviations from the mean — or anything above .61% of the total row count). This is a very small percentage. However, on a large table, .61% can represent a number of rows large enough to impact specific analyses of the data. For example, as illustrated in the result set below (Figure 1), one code, "C1," was present on a fact table, but absent from our code table. It was populated on that fact table at .6032% — just below our threshold. Still 108,851 rows on the table had that code. Defining the code would eliminate the issue. As part of the assessment, we also investigated other questions regarding expected results, such as whether a 20% default level on a given attribute is aligned with the business uses and expectations for this code.

Like the annual review, the baseline assessment provides a measure of gross data quality. In 2003, the first year we conducted it, more than 97% of Galaxy's attributes met or exceeded the standard of 4 sigma — if they had unexpected values, these were at levels below .61% for 97% of columns tested. Results from 2004 were better: over 99% of tables met the 4 sigma standard. Only eight attributes of 1,247 did not meet this standard. Several factors contributed to the improved results. First, in the 2003 Baseline Assessment and the 2004 Annual Review, we identified and resolved a number of one-time issues in the code listings. Next, with regular monitoring in place, we have found and addressed discrepancies before they develop to the 4 sigma level. For example, we put in place automated DQ reports (discussed below under "Monitoring, measuring …") on several attributes we identified as not meeting 4 sigma in 2003 and improved processes associated with these attributes. Finally, in 2004 we were more efficient in our assessment and better understood both results and expectations for the data. Because our analysis was more complete, we were able to resolve more questions during the Assessment.

Lessons Learned: Maintaining Dimension Tables and Reviewing the Integrity of Primary and Foreign Keys

The process of reviewing tables and researching definitions makes clear that different business uses of data impact the perception of data quality. Very simply, listings differ in importance to end users. Importance is defined by the impact the codes have on specific business processes. End users scrutinize attributes they use in their reporting and ignore those they do not use. Attributes in which end users have a high stake can have very little "wrong" with them by objective measures and still be perceived as inaccurate if their errors have an impact on business processes. Yet, if there is a process in place to maintain them, and end users know the process, they are easier to maintain than tables of lesser importance to end users because end users will request updates. Tables in which few people have a stake can become badly out of date without anyone appearing to notice. In some instances, users have other sources for these codes and do not rely on the warehouse version. Because of this they also do not necessarily inform the warehouse that updates are needed.

The different levels of concern reflect the nature of data quality — quality is understood as "fitness for use" (Lee, 2003). If users are truly not concerned about a particular attribute, it is hard to "improve" its quality. Obviously, there will be very low return on investment in researching attributes that no one has a stake in. In some instances, it is questionable whether this information should be retained in the warehouse. However, in cases where users have developed work-arounds and rely on listings outside of the warehouse to understand data in the warehouse, there is an opportunity for improvement of both the quality of data in the warehouse and, through this, of the "reputation" of the warehouse. While the data quality team maintains the tables, improving their quality depends on source system representatives who provide definitions for use in the warehouse. Some representatives are simply more responsive than others. Their responsiveness depends their understanding of the downstream impact of their data. Communicating this information to them can improve responsiveness. Regular review contributes to this process.

While the primary purpose of our assessments is year-by-year measures of gross data quality (being able to state confidently that 99% of primary and foreign keys meet 4 sigma for expected values is a powerful metric), an additional benefit is the discovery of problems other than the ones directly under scrutiny. We have found indications of source system process changes that impact Galaxy's final loaded data, and evidence that codes themselves are being used differently from how they were originally documented. In these cases, we would not have been aware of changes in the uses of codes if we had not been looking at the data itself.

Once we had a clear process for conducting a comprehensive review of warehouse, the depth of analysis increased. For example, an initial challenge in the 2003 Baseline Assessment was simply keeping track of all the attributes we needed to check and then capturing basic information for follow up. For this we developed a simple spreadsheet and a process for storing result and capturing sets of similar issues. It sounds simple after the fact, but when we started it was not — especially since we were looking at over 1200 attributes. After the baseline, we identified ways the basic approach to tracking could be reused and improved. We applied lessons learned to the annual review and to the 2004 baseline. During subsequent baselines, we captured additional information, such as the relative volatility of listings. The large percentage of codes that do not change can be checked more rapidly than ones that frequently change. Subsequent reviews were more efficient because we focused on the most volatile codes. Currently we are automating baseline queries in order to report on the most volatile columns on a quarterly basis. This will enable us to keep these listings current and reduce the hours involved with the overall assessment.

Another example of efficiency gained through a repeated process involves listings in Galaxy's data dictionary. The dictionary, available to all UnitedHealth Group employees on the company intranet, contains definitions and metadata on all Galaxy attributes as well as valid value listings for code sets that are not maintained on tables in the warehouse. In 2004, we performed a comprehensive review of the listings. Some had not been reviewed since Galaxy was launched. Nearly 60% needed updates. Most were minor, such as identifying a default value. Because most of these codes are not highly volatile, in 2005 this percentage was significantly lower, around 6%.

Monitoring, Measuring, and Reporting on Galaxy's Data Quality

Another benefit of the information from the baseline is that it helps identify more sensitive measures on business critical attributes, for which we have implemented automated data quality reports. As discussed above, one of the successes of Galaxy's current data quality program has been the establishment of metrics through which we can communicate with end users about quality levels in the database. The Data Quality team publishes metrics on a quarterly basis and a per-load basis.

Both the baseline assessment and the annual review measure Galaxy's gross data quality. We report on these metrics quarterly. Reporting is straightforward, as seen in the sample below. For the annual review, we tell end users the number of tables reviewed and the total needing updates, as well as how many have been updated and how many are being researched so that updates can be made. The initial review takes place during the first quarter of the calendar year. Research extends into the second quarter.

Reporting on the baseline assessment is similar. It includes summary analysis of issues along with a graph illustrating how many columns and tables met 4 sigma and how many did not.

The third measure of gross data quality is the number of data issues reported and being actively resolved by the Galaxy's business analysts and systems engineers.

Figure 2. Results from the 2004 Annual Review of Code and Description Tables are summarized in a bar graph that displays the number needing no updates, those updated and those left to update. The graph is organized by Galaxy subject area.

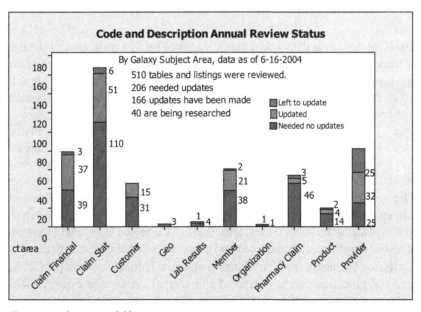

Note: Year-to-year data not available

Figure 3. Results from the 2004 Baseline Assessment are summarized in a bar graph that displays the number of attributes meeting 4 sigma and those below 4 sigma. The graph is organized by Galaxy subject area.

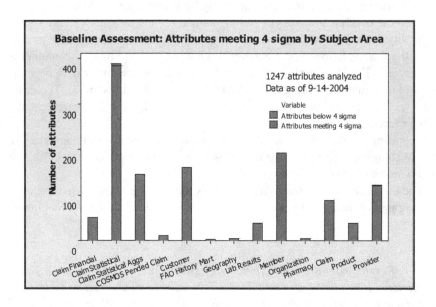

This measure draws on data in our change control/project management database, which tracks projects, issues, and source system changes. The data quality team uses the reports on trends regarding end user data concerns. "Issues" are identified by staff or end users and are considered "break/fixes," separate from enhancements or project requests. The published metric is a point-in-time snapshot that allows for a quarter-by-quarter comparison, organized by Galaxy subject area. Through it, end users see where issues are appearing and how the Data Warehouse team is addressing them. From this, users can understand their concerns in relation to the warehouse overall and also see progress on issue resolution in their subject areas.

Our gross data quality metrics are helpful in enabling end users to have wide view of warehouse data quality. However, the more sensitive, per-load metrics we have put in place for business critical attributes have allowed us to identify potential issues before they become apparent to end users. As noted above, our methodology for monitoring business critical attributes is statistical process control (SPC)[6]. SPC assumes that processes can be measured and normal variation is expected within them. Once a range of normal, "common cause," variation is identified, monitoring the processes identify unexpected or "special cause" variation. Using our existing

Figure 4. The Number of Issues Outstanding by Subject Area. The graph summarizes how resources are being used to respond to data issues identified by Galaxy end users.

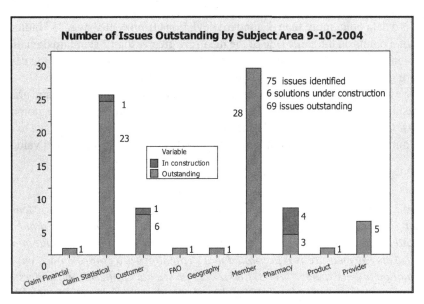

Note: Graph represents a point-in-time snap shot of data on September 10, 2004

data, we calculated the percentage of defaulted rows that was statistically expected per load cycle and established a working threshold of expected defaults. Depending on the attribute, default rows can be created through unexpected conditions in source data, limitations in how Galaxy processes that data, timing issues, or combinations of these factors. Each attribute's default threshold is expressed as a percentage of the total number of records loaded. As part of Galaxy's load processing, the automated program calculates the percentage of default rows and adds a row to a DQ table created to house this data. If the percentage exceeds the threshold, the data quality team receives an e-mail and begins investigating reasons for the unexpected level. If the percentage is within the expected limit, the team simply checks the table and obtains the information needed for the report. The threshold is housed in a separate code table, so that it can be adjusted as the expected level of defaults is impacted by process changes or by business demand. The program was built with an additional "emergency threshold." If the percentage ever reached this threshold, the load would be aborted.

The information in the report is presented in a control chart that allows end users to see changes in the pattern of the default level. We use the software tool Minitab to produce the actual chart. Minitab automatically calculates the upper and lower control limits and the mean. It includes additional statistical information, such as highlighting patterns that are statistically significant and could indicate special cause variation. For example, in the following chart, the points numbered "1" indicate there is a data point more than 3 standard deviations from center line; "5" indicates 2 out of 3 points on the same side of the mean are greater than 2 standard deviations from center line; and "6" indicates 4 out of 5 points on the same side of the center line are greater than 1 standard deviation from center line.

We began taking these measures in 2003 by running manual queries and graphing results on a control chart in Excel. In 2004, we implemented four automated reports. Currently, 40 automated reports are in place and standards in place to add them during the development process when analysis shows they will add value.

Figure 5. Control chart for default levels for one of Galaxy's key attributes, Member System ID on the Unet Claim Header table. After each weekly load of the database, the data about defaulted member system ids is circulated as part of a data quality report. This key measure is represented in a straightforward control chart, with an explanation about expected levels. End users can see data patterns and understand fluctuations and expected levels. The statistically determined upper control limit (UCL) — which indicates whether the process is under control, was 0.13247% in June 2004. The level at which data quality analysts investigate changes is slightly lower, at 0.12%.

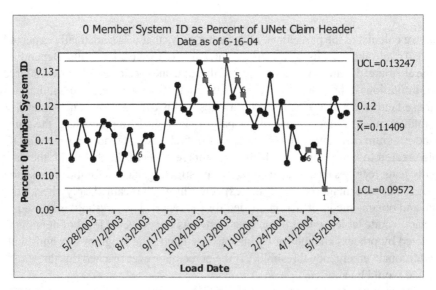

Note: Data quality threshold = .12%

One attribute we look at on several tables is the member system id. This number, assigned through Galaxy processing, uniquely identifies each member on our member table. It is used in a range of processes for other tables, as well as by end users in joins between tables. If source data is accurate and Galaxy processes function properly, then Galaxy will match members (people who receive services) to claims (financial and health information associated with those services). If member or claim data is missing or inaccurate, or if the processes do not function as expected, then the match process will fail and the member system id on the claim table row will be defaulted to zero. Default rows mean there are claims about which we have limited information — specifically, we will have paid for services that appear to be "unattached" to a member — and which cannot be joined to other data in Galaxy. We have similar system ids for providers and claims that are used in other matching processes. Member system id is especially significant because it is used on over 30 Galaxy fact tables.

Tracking defaults on business critical attributes has been an effective way to identify data issues before they have a large impact on the database. For example, in one instance (10/23/2003) when defaults exceeded the data quality threshold, we were able to identify that test data had accidentally been let into production warehouse records. We were also able to recommend and implement changes to the matching process that reduced defaults by improving the percentage of matches. In another, we discovered that a set of records had been loaded to the database twice.

Per-load key attribute reporting takes place 3-4 times a month, depending on Galaxy's load schedule. The data and supporting graphs are e-mailed to stakeholders within Galaxy. These reports are periodically augmented with progress updates on any issues that are being investigated. Per-load reports are also summarized in the quarterly data quality report to upper-level and senior management.

Lessons Learned: Monitoring, Measuring, and Reporting on Galaxy's Data Quality

One of the main purposes of Galaxy's data quality metrics is to assure end users that Galaxy processes are working as expected. The metrics also help build a common vocabulary around Galaxy data quality. In 2003, end users were concerned about default member system ids, but there was not a common understanding of how many records might be expected to default. Today there is, at least for the tables we monitor. More importantly, when data crosses data quality thresholds, Galaxy staff know it and can put action plans in place before end users "discover" a problem.

Once we established a particular kind of metric — in this case, presence of defaults — we had a better understanding of how to get the most out of our other processes, specifically the baseline assessment and annual review. During the 2004 baseline, it was very easy to identify additional columns that could benefit from monitoring via this basic DQ report.

Monitoring also contributes to improving data quality in other ways. As with the Baseline and Annual Review, through our per-load monitoring we have found issues we were not necessarily looking for (as in the example above, where we discovered we had loaded a set of records twice). Most importantly, monitoring allows for continuous quality improvement. Because we know what our quality levels have been and we have applied process improvements, we are able to use the same measure to demonstrate how quality has improved.

Implementing Improvements Based on Data Quality Findings

The ultimate goal of all components of the data quality program is to drive process changes that will improve the quality of the data in the warehouse. We have had some success in this area. Improvements in the DQ team's own processes have an impact on overall data quality. For example, we have added behind-the-scenes mapping tables to the Web application used to update our code tables. This reduces the amount of time spent on updates while increasing their accuracy and eliminating the risk of manual entry errors for a significant number of fields.

Figure 6. Control chart for Member System ID on the claim header table after the implementation of a change in the match process in July 2004. The change had a significant impact on the success of the match process and caused a downward shift in the overall level of defaults.

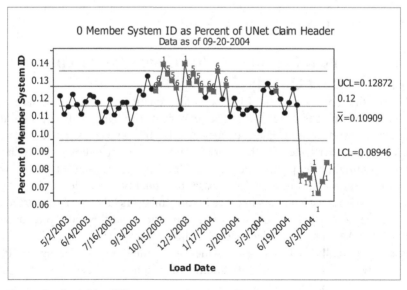

Note: Data quality threshold = .12%

Figure 7. Control chart for Member System ID on the claim header table from July 2004 to June 2005. The chart illustrates that the process has remained under control since the process improvement in July 2004. The mean has been reduced from 0.114% (see Figure 5) to .068%. The upper control limit has been reduced from 0.13247% to 0.08446%.

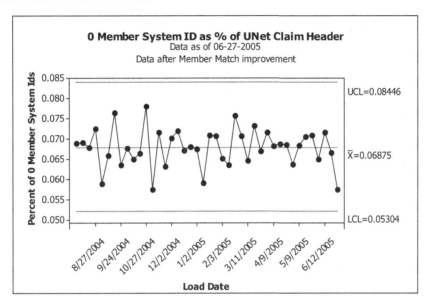

More important are changes in Galaxy's data processing. For example, DQ monitoring resulted in a project to improve the match process between our member and claim data. This eliminated some records that caused defaults. The result was a direct, measurable change in the quality of the data. The updated versions of the control chart for the percentage of default member system ids on the claim table illustrates the impact: the first (Figure 6) shows a significant drop in the percentage of default system ids on the claim table and therefore more records with full information; the second (Figure 7) shows that over time, the level of defaults remained lower and under control.

The improvement is even more dramatic on the Pharmacy Claim tables, where, in addition to the prospective change, we implemented a "one-shot" to update the existing data. The first graph (Figure 8) shows the trend before the process change. The second (Figure 9) shows the impact of the one-shot and the continuation of the lower percentage of default rows. The third (Figure 10) shows the new levels.

Figure 8. Control chart for Member System ID defaults from two source systems on the Pharmacy Claim table. This chart illustrates the levels while data quality analysts were monitoring the table, but before the data had been updated. The expected level of defaults was under 0.2%. Dramatic spikes mask smaller fluctuations within the data.

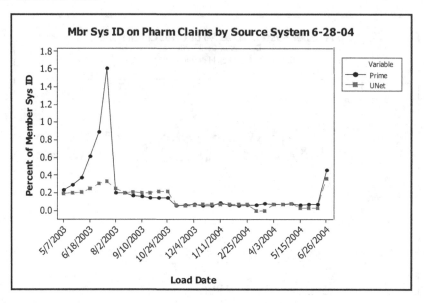

Lessons Learned: Implementing Improvements based on Data Quality Findings

The primary lesson learned during the implementation of improvements based on data quality findings is that a good measurement will speak largely for itself. When data and graphs are presented clearly and consistently, people understand what they are seeing. Still, measurements must continue after the changes are implemented to demonstrate that changes have lasting effects on the data's quality level.

SUCCESS FACTORS IN THE BUSINESS ENVIRONMENT

Galaxy's current data quality program, launched in summer 2003, focuses on ensuring that Galaxy's data meets business-defined quality standards. The data quality team is responsible for monitoring the referential integrity of codes and primary and foreign keys, monitoring, measuring and reporting on key attributes, and recommending process changes that will improve the overall quality of the data. So far,

Figure 9. Control chart for Member System ID defaults on Pharmacy Claim after the data have been one-shot to update defaults. Shown on the same scale as Figure 8 above, the chart has been completely "flattened" and the level is now significantly below 0.1% as opposed to being below 0.2% in Figure 8.

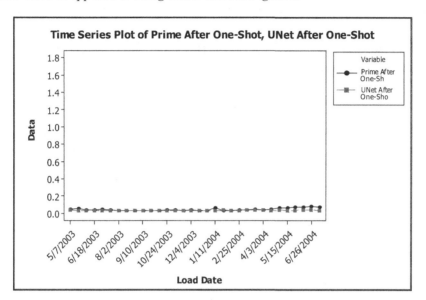

the DQ program is small but concrete and provides a firm foundation from which to identify potential process improvements for the database. It also allows end users to understand the warehouse's data quality in ways that are meaningful to their business needs. The program has been successful because business conditions were positive for its development. We had management support, we defined our strategy and executed its tactics — the most important of which was implementing clear metrics — and we built credibility and a common vocabulary by communicating regularly with stakeholders, through per-load and quarterly reports.

Management Support

Galaxy's management recognized the need for data quality and created a data quality role when Galaxy was launched. Through this position, a strategy was developed, based on best practices and theoretical models of data quality. This strategy recognized that data quality is subjective — dependent on the uses and users of the data. Because it also assumed that data quality begins at the source of the data, the strategy advocated root cause analysis and remediation of data quality issues. What was missing from the initial launch were data quality metrics that could be

Figure 10. The chart above illustrates the new levels associated with default system id values on our Pharmacy Claim tables. The levels have been cut in half. They are now well below 0.10%, whereas previously they had generally been around 0.2%. In addition, because the measure itself is now more sensitive to fluctuations, data quality analysts have been able to address the issues represented by the spikes.

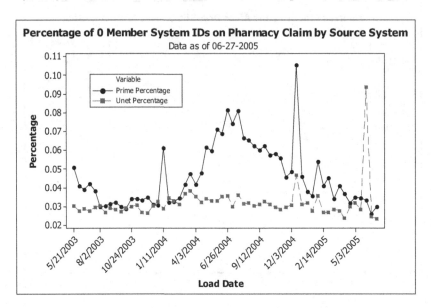

regularly communicated to end users. Among other things, such metrics mitigate the subjective elements of data quality by contributing to a common vocabulary, and through it a common understanding, about the quality of data in the warehouse. DQ metrics are the cornerstone of the current program.

While there was understanding of and strong advocacy for data quality principles within the data warehouse management team and higher up, other factors prevented the warehouse from getting a full return on investment from these at its launch. Primary was the immaturity of the warehouse itself. When Galaxy was launched, end user concerns centered on access. Once the access learning curve was ascended (both technically and by business users) end users were in a position to scrutinize Galaxy's data, and they did.

Strategy and Tactics

Implementing the program has been a lesson in the relation between strategy and tactics and what it means to have "management buy-in." Both common sense and management theory make it clear that you need a strategy before you can execute tactics. Without a strategy, tactical actions are simply actions — except by chance, they will lack the coherence needed to move a program forward in a consistent direction. However our experience shows that you also need successful execution of tactics for stakeholders (including management) to understand and be able to contribute to your strategy. For example, it is generally acknowledged that management buy-in on data quality strategy is a key success factor for a DQ program (Redman, 2001). Put this way, the goal seems to be to get buy-in. In fact, "buy-in" is not hard to get. No leader of a health information company is going to say that data quality is unimportant. However, support will fade, be forgotten, or become annoying if it is not sustained through concrete, meaningful results. Results come through execution of tactics. Ultimately, people fully support and contribute to strategy only when they see the results of tactics. This is a case where the "show don't tell" principle fully applies. In the case of Galaxy's Data Quality program, what we had to show were measurements that could demonstrate an improvement in the quality of the database.

The current program has the direct support of Galaxy management who recognized the benefits of incorporating data quality controls into Galaxy processes. Advocacy of statistical process control and 6 Sigma practices, recognition of the value and uses of metrics, and robust practice of reporting metrics up the chain of command also exists within the wider Ingenix management team. For example, the quarterly data quality report is one of four regularly published reports from data warehouse management. The others focus on database availability, usage patterns, and help desk service. These practices within the company enable the understanding and thus the value of the data quality metrics we have developed so far.

Developing Clear and Meaningful Metrics

With management support for the strategy, it was incumbent that we execute the tactics to fulfill the strategic goals. As emphasized earlier, the most important requirement was defining clear, understandable, meaningful metrics for the warehouse's data quality. The specific metrics, presented above, seem relatively simple and straightforward now that we have been using them for several quarters. However, determining an objective basis for these metrics took some work. It is worth reviewing the process through which we determined what to measure.

We began by drawing on our business partners' concerns about Galaxy data, our team's knowledge of data issues, and the issues tracked in our project management database. Many of these issues were originally reported by end users. We assessed potential measures based on impact to the database and ownership of data and processes. This allowed us to associate a set of measurable characteristics with each attribute we were proposing to monitor. To assess options, we used objective measures by answering a set of simple questions: How often does the attribute appear in the database? How often does it function as a primary or foreign key? How many help desk inquiries have been logged about it in the past 12 months? How often have we addressed an "issue" involving the attribute? Answers to these questions gave us an understanding of the "pain" caused when the attribute was not functioning as expected. We also defined the processes associated with the data: Does Galaxy "touch" the data and derive any part of it or is it obtained through a straight move from the source? We knew we could influence and improve processes internal to the warehouse, whereas we had limited, if any, influence over source system issues. Gathering this information on a group of attributes, we identified potential controls, compared them with some degree of objectivity, prioritized them, and proposed an initial set to our business partners. Within the proposal, we communicated the "whys" behind our recommendations by sharing the methodology by which we had compared options. We also rearticulated the choices as tactics within the context of the overall data quality strategy.

Looking closely at three of the attributes we measure will illustrate some of these considerations. As noted previously, the level of default member system ids on our claim tables provides an indicator of how well Galaxy matches members to claims. It appears 50 times in the database. In all instances it is a primary or foreign key. Since Galaxy was launched there had been a steady stream of help desk questions and problem reports regarding the attribute. In short, it caused a lot of end-user "pain." The member system id is an attribute internal to Galaxy. It is assigned through Galaxy processes and exists only in the data warehouse. If Galaxy is not able to match members to claims, it is a pretty clear indication either that we are getting unexpected data from the source, or that something is wrong with Galaxy processing. One of the other attributes, company code on our policy table, presents a different situation. This number is obtained directly from our source system and is not touched or changed once it gets to Galaxy. However, there are known timing issues with getting the information to Galaxy. These timing issues sometimes result in a level of defaults that is not acceptable to our business users. A third example, member system id on our Pharmacy tables is impacted by another factor, the completeness of data within files received from an external vendor. Monitoring this attribute measures not only Galaxy's success at matching, but also our vendor's ability to deliver complete and usable data.

Ultimately, the metrics we chose appear simple: we use control charts to track percentages of defaults over time and bar charts to report results of our assessments. What took work was defining and clarifying which metrics would effectively represent the state of the data in the database. The process was worth the time invested. We not only chose the attributes we would measure for our initial data quality reports, we created a methodology for identifying and evaluating additional metrics — in other words, we taught ourselves to fish. We can now use the matrix through which we evaluated the attributes to evaluate and compare any attributes we might consider monitoring. With this as a foundation, our systems engineer was able to write a generic, "lift and drop" program that can be implemented anywhere in the warehouse. We also now have an extensible approach to develop additional metrics for more complex data issues.

Building Credibility and a Common Vocabulary

In addition to having management support and clear and understandable metrics, the program has also succeeded thus far because we have worked hard to build credibility by communicating regularly with end users. This has had several important effects. First is that we are developing a consistent vocabulary about data quality. Our users now know that the 2003 Baseline Assessment results showed 97% of our tables met the 4 sigma standard for expected values. They understand that if the member match to claims is within statistical tolerance levels, then Galaxy processes are operating as expected. They also know that when an issue is discovered, Galaxy staff will take action on it. Secondly, they know to expect information on a regular basis. Regular communications were a key to building credibility. Though important, communication is not for its own sake. It is also a means for keeping stakeholders aware of how their data relates to, depends on and impacts other data in the warehouse. One lesson learned is that the more users know about the data, the better able they will be to use it. In such a case, the type of information is more important than the amount of information in managing expectations of data consumers.

Creator/Custodian/Consumer Relations

Academic discussions on different relations within data quality are helpful in shedding light on how different users and producers of data view quality from their individual perspectives (Lee, 2003).[7] In practice the lines between creators, custodians, and consumers are not as clear as they are in theory. Individuals and teams play multiple roles within this system and have different relations to the quality of the data and different definitions of data quality depending on the role they are playing. The model provides insight to these relations and definitions. For example, at first blush, the data warehouse team appeared to be "custodians" of data. But we also have an impact on the data — we are "creators." And we use the data — we are "consumers." We play an additional mediating role between creators and consumers — we are data "brokers."

One lesson learned was to use the knowledge gained from playing different roles. For example, a key element of the program was to have our house in order (i.e., we would start with elements of data quality that the data warehouse had control over and take seriously our responsibility to the data we create). In addition, we would be good consumers of the data (i.e., we would understand where it came from, why it might be in the condition it was in, and what we needed from it in order to use it for our purposes).

In addition, we would recognize that the custodial role is an active role. We needed to clearly define who had control over what aspects of the data, address issues that were in our control, and define impacts of issues that are not in our control, so that we could attempt to influence these. This understanding allows the creator/custodian/consumer paradigm to evolve into an accountability model, where each role feels a responsibility for the quality of the data. It also provides perspective on what to measure and how to report results.

WHERE WE ARE GOING

With the definition and regular publication of data quality metrics, the Galaxy DQ program broke through to a different level than it had previously existed on. However, the program is still relatively small and has not yet had the impact we want it to have. We will continue to monitor, publish, and act on findings and integrate data quality processes into the application development process. Future plans focus on developing additional levels of data quality assessment.

First, we will draw on baseline assessment results to put additional measures in place following the model (percentage of defaults) established for the first DQ reports. These additional reports will provide further controls on data elements that have been known to cause problems in the past. They will enable us to improve the baseline quality through statistical process control. We also want to develop additional "lift and drop" programs to monitor data levels: one that measures ranges, for example. Next, we will develop a second set of reports that gets at a more complex layer of the data, for example collecting data that allows us to find patterns in defaulted attributes. This second set of reports will automate the next layer of analysis. In instances where member system id has been defaulted, for example, one of the first things we look at is whether the defaults are associated with a particular policy number. Usually they are. Tracking these policy numbers allows us more quickly to identify the source of an issue. It will also provide information — patterns of behavior — for these numbers.

Next we will move forward on options to automate the processes for the baseline assessment and annual review. Currently these processes are labor intensive. When done initially, they treated all attributes in essentially the same way, despite differences in volatility and business significance. It was important to go through them "manually" in order to know the data and streamline the process itself. The next step is to automate in to order apply the process more fully where it will have the highest return on investment.

Finally, we will implement a process to analyze and address source system issues. This process includes standards for describing and tracking these issues, publishing metadata about them, and working together with source systems to address them. The process focuses on better managing expectations about data by educating end users and source system owners (consumers and creators). Its goal is to improve the data that comes into the warehouse by bridging gaps between creators (source systems) and consumers (end users).

REFERENCES

American Heritage College Dictionary. (1997). New York: Houghton Mifflin.
Lee, Y., Pepino, L., Funk, J., & Wang, R. (2003). *Journey to data quality.*
Redman, T. C. (2001). *Data quality: The field guide.* Woburn, MA: Digital.

FURTHER READING

English, L. P. (1999). *Improving data warehouse and business information quality: Methods for reducing costs and increasing profits.* New York: Wiley.
Loshin, D. (2001). *Enterprise knowledge management: The data quality approach.* San Francisco: Morgan Kaufmann.
Mitra, A. (1998). *Fundamentals of quality control and improvement* (2nd ed.). Upper Saddle River, NJ: Prentice Hall.

ENDNOTES

[1] The Galaxy DQ Program's intranet-published strategy focuses on business users of Galaxy's data.

While customers access Galaxy to meet a range of business needs, all users have a stake in the quality of information in the database. Galaxy's Data Quality (DQ) processes strive to improve Galaxy's overall data quality by identifying, recommending, and driving implementation of process improvements through ongoing monitoring and analysis of Galaxy and source data.

DQ takes an iterative approach to ongoing quality improvement. This approach includes:

- Identification and analysis of opportunities for improvement
- Prioritization of needs based on business criticality, and
- Implementation of directed measures to track, monitor, and report on data quality in Galaxy.

Working with business customers, DQ prioritizes opportunities for improvement based on:

- Business criticality — Data most important to business customers
- Impact on other Galaxy data — Data upon which SDW processes or downstream data are dependent
- Impact on downstream Galaxy users/applications — Measures to ensure Galaxy delivers quality data.

DQ takes a comprehensive approach to quality improvement through:

- Preventative measures to identify potential problems and reduce the need for downstream fixes
- Root-cause analysis to identify and remedy processes that create or allow for poor quality data.

These processes and criteria will help ensure that business customers have the high quality information they need to make sound business decisions.

[2]   The identification of DQ dimensions outlines the multiple ways the "quality" of information is understood. Many of these, such as the "accuracy," "objectivity," believability," and "reputation" associated with "Intrinsic DQ" are recognizably subjective. If quality is judged as "fitness for use," then ultimately all are subjective.

[3]   As noted in the text, Galaxy DQ methodology combines elements of Continuous Process Improvement (CPI) Total Quality Management (TQM), and 6 Sigma methodologies to improve data quality. These approaches share several characteristics:

- They are systematic and process-oriented and understand that quality outcomes result from interconnected processes within a system.
- They are customer-centered and rely on the customer to define what a defect or error is and what a quality characteristic is.
- They recognize that process improvement is a continuous, iterative effort and they seek to continually improve customer satisfaction.
- They recognize that analyzing the source of quality problems is necessary to overall quality improvement. That is, root-cause analysis, focusing on preventing future quality issues and reducing the need for "clean up" is necessary to bring about lasting and cost-effective solutions.

Customer-focus, root-cause analysis, and process improvement are primary components of the ongoing Galaxy Data Quality strategy and activities.

[4]   150 code tables updated manually through a Web-based application; 375 valid value listings in its data dictionary and maintained through our metadata repository; and 12 additional code listings on its intranet site.

[5]   The 6 Sigma method follows 5 basic steps:

1. **Define:** Identify critical-to-quality characteristics based on what the customer considers to have the greatest impact on quality and articulate why these are critical.
2. **Measure:** Define how critical-to-quality characteristics are understood and how they can be measured. Identify and remove "special causes" of

variance. Gather baseline performance data. Identify process performance gaps. Validate a system for measuring deviations.

3. **Analyze:** Determine key quality variables (i.e., conduct root-cause analysis). Identify chronic process problem areas.

4. **Enhance/Improve:** Determine acceptable/reasonable quality ranges and modify processes to ensure that quality is within these ranges. Solicit customer feedback.

5. **Monitor/Standardize:** Assess the impact of process improvements. Determine if root cause(s) have been reduced and eliminated. Put tools and processes in place to ensure that over time, data quality remains within ranges defined as acceptable to customers.

[6] Statistical process control is a methodology for improving quality through statistical monitoring. It originated in the manufacturing sector in the early 20th century. Walter Shewhart is considered the father of SPC. His student, W. Edwards Deming, developed the techniques that demonstrated the impact it could have on quality. Deming is also credited with introducing SPC to Japanese manufacturing after the Second World War.

One of the basic principles of SPC is that product defects may be attributed to "common cause" or "special cause" variation. Common cause variation is expected within a process. One goal of SPC is to reduce the range of variation through process improvements. Special cause variation is caused by outside factors. Another goal of SPC is to identify and eliminated special causes that have adversely impacted a process. If we understand "data as a product" (Lee, 2003), then the application of manufacturing techniques to measure quality makes sense. The challenge of applying SPC to data quality is largely in defining what can and should be measured.

Chapter II

Information Quality Function Deployment

Latif Al-Hakim, University of Southern Queensland, Australia

ABSTRACT

This chapter maps the information quality (IQ) process and finds that the control constituent of the process comprises two types of factors: IQ dimensions and IQ indicators. The latter forms an information performance measure known as "information orientation" that measures the capability of an organisation to effectively manage and use information. This research stresses that the consistency between the two types of factors will improve the IQ function. Based on a case study from the healthcare industry, the research employs a modified quality function deployment (QFD) procedure referred to as information function development (IFD) in an attempt to match IQ dimensions with the IQ indicators in order to identify the most important factors affecting the IQ function deployment. The research is in its initial stage and may include subjective results. However, the methodology used could be further enhanced for more impartial outcomes.

INTRODUCTION

Historically, information quality activities begin only after a disaster (Godfrey 2002). For example, 18 months after having a common bowel operation, an X-ray revealed a pair of 15cm surgical scissors, slightly opened, lodged between a patient's lower bowel and her spine. The hospital explained it did not count scissors after the surgery because they were considered too large to lose (Pirani, 2004). On another occasion, it was reported that two women with the same first name attended a hospital in the same day to have a breast biopsy. One had breast cancer. One did not. It was discovered that the biopsy results had been mixed up and the patient without breast cancer had endured months of chemotherapy and was minus a breast (Pirani, 2004). The woman with the breast cancer died after nine months. Though many factors contributed to these hospital errors, certainly one of these factors is related to quality of data or information that was received or generated. Prescription mistakes, mislabelled test samples and illegible handwritten patient data in paper forms, etc., make problems and errors associated with information quality the eighth leading cause of death in the United States, with the total cost of injuries related to medical errors exceeding US$17 billion a year (Hamblen, 2000). A recent international survey supported by The Commonwealth Funds finds that one-third (34%) of U.S. respondents with health problems reported at least one of the following four types of information quality errors: experienced a medical mistake in treatment or care; given the wrong medication or dose; given incorrect test results; or experienced delays in receiving abnormal test results (Surgicentre, 2005). The international survey shows that three of 10 (30%) of respondents experience medical errors in Canada, 27% in Australia, 25% in New Zealand, 23% in Germany and 22% in United Kingdom. In a survey of NHS trusts in England, the National Audit Office found that almost one million medical mistakes were reported in 2004-05, costing around 2bn Sterling. It is estimated that 200,000 mistakes went unreported. In regard to the number of deaths resulting from these mistakes, the survey concludes that "NHS simply does not know" (Carvel, 2005).

Poor information quality is not only prevalent in non-profit and business organisations, it can also be behind decisions at national or even international levels. The spacecraft launched by NASA on 11 December 1998 to observe the seasonal climate changes on Mars was lost upon arrival at the planet on 23 September 1999. It is found that the "root cause" of the loss of the spacecraft was "the failed translation of English units into metric units in a segment of ground-based, navigation-related mission software" (Isbell & Savage, 1999). This confusion over the design data led to the engineers incorrectly calculating Orbiter's entry into Mars's atmosphere (Pierce, 2005). Fisher and Kingma (2001) reveal that one main factor behind the explosion of the NASA space shuttle Challenger on 28 January 1986, and the shooting of an Iranian Airbus by the US Navy Cruiser USS Vincennes on 3 July 1988, was poor quality information. This is also the case with the allegations, in 2003, regarding the existence of weapons of mass destruction in Iraq (CBS News, 2005).

Information becomes a critical component of business operations (Sen, 2001). Today's technology allows business to collect and analyse "enormous volumes of information and manipulate it in different way to bring out otherwise unforseen areas of knowledge" (Abbott, 2001). The traditional focus on the input and recording of data needs to be offset with recognition that the systems themselves may affect the quality of data (Fedorowicz & Lee, 1998). Information technology (IT) advances can sometimes create problems rather than benefit the organization if information quality issues have not been properly addressed. Managers make decisions based on information available to them and most organizations have experienced the adverse effects of decisions based on information of inferior quality (Huang et al., 1999; Fisher & Kingma, 2001). Redman (2000d) estimates that the cost of poor information quality for an organisation is about 20% of its revenue. Dr. Redman emphasised that, "if we can free up that 20%, we can create an economic boom that will make the 1990s look like a depression!" The health care industry is noted for using leading-edge technologies that enable better cures and new scientific discoveries but has been slow in adopting technologies that focus on information systems to enable better management and administrative needs (Fadlalla and Wickramasinghe, 2004; Stegwee & Spil, 2001). Mandke et al. (2003 — in Fadlalla & Wickramasinghe, 2004) state that poor information quality is a major contributor to the large number of medical errors. Lorence & Jameson (2002) conclude that the quality of information maintained by health care organisations becomes a critical factor in the ultimate delivery of care. These authors emphasise the need for more rigorous system-based information quality assessment methodologies. The competitive advantage in hospitals is no longer based on using leading-edge technologies as such, but rather on how well the hospital manages its data and information produced by these technologies.

English (2002) observes that information quality researchers often focus their attention on information quality in isolation from the customers who use information or the systems that produce information. This chapter attempts to fill this gap. It identifies the dimensions of information quality (IQ) systems and attempts to match these dimensions with users' requirements incorporating information system (IS) performance indicators and measures. Based on a case study, this chapter uses quality function deployment (QFD) methodology with some modification. The research study is in its initial stage and may include subjective results. However, the methodology used could be further enhanced for more general outcomes.

QUALITY OF CARE AND INFORMATION QUALITY

Hospital executives face unprecedented challenges for survival under difficult economic conditions. One of these challenges is to improve service quality and specifically quality of patient care. Quality of care is about meeting the physical, psychological and social expectations of the patients who search for care. According to the American Institute of Medicine quality of care is "the degree to which health services for individuals and populations increase the likelihood of desired health outcome consistent with current professional knowledge" (Kupersmith,

2003). The notion of quality of care is further strengthened in this definition with the application of professional knowledge. The term "health service for the individual" in the definition is a reference to service quality as well as the link between service quality and patients (i.e., customers). In fact the link between quality and customers was established first in the health care industry as early as 1910. In 1910, the American surgeon Ernest Codman developed the concept of "end result idea" in hospitals. The concept requires the following: "Every hospital should follow every patient it treats long enough to determine whether the treatment has been successful, and then to inquire 'if not, why not' with a view to preventing similar failure in the future" (Codman, 1914 — quoted in NCBI, 2005). Unfortunately, Dr. Codman lost his staff privileges at the Harvard Medical School in 1914 when the School refused to endorse his plan for evaluating the competence of surgeons (Who Name it, 2005). Today, Dr. Codman is remembered as a guru for quality of care. The Ernest A. Codman Award was created in 1996 to showcase the effective use of performance measures and to encourage the quality of care. In the same year the Advisory Commission on Consumer Protection and Quality in the Heath Care Industry was established. The Commissions notes the following quality problems in hospitals (Advisory Commission, 1998):

•   **Avoidable error:** The report points out that too many Americans are injured and died prematurely as a result of avoidable errors. The report claims that "from 1983 to 1993 alone, deaths due to medical errors rose more than twofold, with 7,391 deaths attributed to medication errors in 1993 alone."
•   **Underutilisation of services:** The report claims that millions of people do not receive necessary care. It estimated that about 18,000 people die each year from heart attacks because they did not receive effective interventions.
•   **Overuse of services:** The claim was that millions of Americans receive health care services that are unnecessary.
•   **Variation in services:** There is a continuing pattern of variation in health care services, including regional variations and small-area variations.

Deming develops profound knowledge in quality and considers "variation" as "the chief culprit of poor quality" (Evans and Lindsay, 2005, p. 94). Deming observes that variation in quality characteristics exists in every process. Variation makes the process unstable and its outcome unpredictable because the variation that exists from one time period to the next is also unpredictable (Miller, 1998). Health care service is an information-based service (McLaughlin, 1996). Understanding the variation in information is the first step in reducing health care variation and then stabilising the health care process. There are major variations in the conclusions of clinical observations and their interpretation (James et al., 1994). In fact any health care quality considered above can be attributed to variation or what is referred to as "unwarranted variation" in health care delivery (Wennberg, 2002). The term "unwarranted" reflects the lack of necessary information or quality information to conduct health care processes. This suggests that information quality is a critical factor in decreasing variations in the health care industry. The recognition of data and information quality becomes a key area of both strategic and operations management in the health care industry (Lorence and Jameson, 2002). The Lorence & Jameson study also emphasises that there is a shift from traditional error-based approach to evidence-based data-driven medicine. This makes the measurement of quality of care based on data rather than intensive, personal interaction with patients. As such, "the quality of data maintained by organisations becomes a critical factor in the ultimate delivery of care" (Lorence & Jameson, 2002).

As a result of growing concern in relation to information quality, the Information Quality Act was enacted by the US Congress in December of 2000 (Copeland & Simpson, 2004). The Act requires Federal Agencies that disseminate important information to the public to address information quality of that information. In the fall of 2002, the Canadian Institute for Health Information (CIHI) initiated a data strategy program with the objective of developing a collaborative approach to promote a culture of data and information quality across the Canadian health care institutions (CIHI, 2005). Recently, the University of Arkansas at Little Rock, USA announced the first Master of Science program in Information Quality in collaboration with MIT IQ program (MITIQ, 2005). Nowadays, organisations must either provide "quality information expected by their customers or run the risk of legislation that forces them to provide such information" (English & Perez, 2003).

INFORMATION QUALITY

Meade and Sarkis (1999) emphasise that in an agile environment, skills, knowledge and information are no longer enough for achieving or enhancing competitiveness when lacking the ability to convert the knowledge, skill and information into products. "Ability to convert" is what companies are really relying on to achieve customer satisfaction (Al-Hakim, 2003). Such ability is the combined result of the two prerequisites of information process, that is, experience and technology. Ability to convert should be maintained via continual process improvement and learning. Wang (1998) takes a step beyond the work of Meade & Sarkis and finds an analogy between quality issues in product manufacturing and those in information manufacturing, and further asserts that information manufacturing can be viewed as a processing system acting on raw data to produce information products. Wang urges organisations to manage information as they manage products if they want to increase productivity.

Information is defined as "data that have been organised in a manner that gives them meaning for the recipient" (Turban et al., 2005). The definition is broadened to include "any communication or representation of knowledge such as facts or data, in any medium or form" (Copeland & Simpson, 2004). There are differences between product manufacturing and information manufacturing that can be classified under five main headings: intangibility, input, users, consumption and handling (Table 1). However, from the quality perspective, the differences listed in Table 1 will not affect the analogy proposed by Wang (1998) between products and information. However, the conventional view of information as analogous to a product has led many researchers, analysts and managers to concentrate on information quality hardware and software and costs associated with systems producing the information rather than how these systems actually meet the needs of the data and information to consumers (Pierce, 2005).

Customers view quality in relation to different criteria based on their individual roles in the production-marketing chain (Evans & Lindsay, 2005). Thus it is important to understand the various perspectives from which IQ is viewed. Like product quality, information quality can be viewed by information consumers from various perspectives: as "fitness for intended use," or as "meeting or exceeding customer

Table 1. Main differences between product manufacturing and information manufacturing

ITEM	DIFFERENCE
Intangibility	Product manufacturing system produces tangible, visible or physical products whereas information is intangible. The quality of product can be measured with physical measures such as design specifications. The measures for quality of information are subjective and mainly based on the user's opinion and expectation.
Inputs	Product process requires raw material, experience/knowledge, technology; while information process requires four inputs: data, experience, technology and time.
End user	The users of the end product are undefined in the former, whereas they are clearly defined in the latter (Sen, 2001). The user of an information system is part of the system, whereas products are produced away from the users.
Consumption	The raw materials used in information manufacturing are data which can be consumed by more than one consumer without depletion, not like raw materials in product manufacturing that can only be used for single physical products. Further, information can be produced and consumed simultaneously, while products need to be produced before consumption.
Handling	Unlike products, same data and information can be transported to an undefined number of consumers simultaneously via physical carrier (e.g., disk) or through an intangible way (e.g., e-mail). However, both information and products can be stored and inspected before delivery to the customers. This makes information quality similar to product quality but different from service quality as the service quality cannot be stored and inspected before delivery (Evans & Lindsay, 2005).

expectations." Sen (2001) emphasises the importance of applying total quality management (TQM) to the production of information. Sen argues that the zero defects goal of TQM becomes particularly relevant to data and information producing entities to avoid undesired consequences. Based on the principles of TQM, Wang (1998) and Huang et al. (1999) address total data management quality (TDQM). Further, Wang et al. (2003) emphasise the importance of having tools and techniques to manage the life cycle of the information product and stress the significance of developing a mechanism for producing the Information Product Map (IPMap), just like a blueprint for an assembly line that produces a physical product. Wang et al. (2003) introduce total information awareness. Further, Lee et al. (2002) develop a methodology for IQ assessment and benchmarking considering IQ dimensions that covers aspects of IQ that are important to information consumers.

IQ DIMENSIONS

Just like quality management of physical products, IQ has multiple dimensions. IQ dimensions refer to issues that are important to information consumers. Strong et al. (1997) group the IQ dimensions into four categories. These categories are: contextual, intrinsic, accessibility and representation (Table 2). These categories are widely acceptable in the literature (Li et al., 2003). However, there are no uniform lists for the IQ dimensions. The choice of these dimensions is primarily based on intuitive understanding, industrial experience, or literature review (Hung et al., 1999) and depends on the actual use of information. Good information for a specific user in one case may not be sufficient in another case. For instance, the Canadian Institute for Health Information adopts the following dimensions for data quality, namely: accuracy, timeliness, comparability, usability and relevance.

To achieve a useful conclusion from Table 2, each dimension can be considered as an indicator comprising several measures. For instance, "accuracy" can be used to measure the intrinsic dimension of the information, and so on for other measures mentioned in Table 2. However, there are no specified measures for each dimension, and the selection of appropriate measures may vary according to the situation and IQ environment.

IQ PROCESS

Langefors (1973, p. 248 — in Malmsjo & Ovelius, 2003) formulates the process of obtaining information to be $I = i(D, S, t)$, where I is the information obtained from the interpretation process i of data D, with pre-knowledge or user's life experience S at a certain time t. According to Langefors, a certain set of data could be interpreted differently by persons with different experiences or at different times. With the recent explosion of information technology, the absolute user's experience in most business

Table 2. Dimensions of IQ and their measures

Dimension	Implication/Definition	Dimension's Measures from Selected Literature				
		Delone & McLean (1992	Goodhue (1995)	Wang & Strong (1996)	Strong et al. (1997)	Jarke & Vassiliou (1997)*
Intrinsic	Information has quality in its own right.	Accuracy, precision, reliability, freedom from bias.	Accuracy, reliability.	Accuracy, believability, reputation, objectivity.	Accuracy, objectivity, believability, reputation.	Believability, accuracy, credibility, consistency, completeness.
Contextual	DQ must be considered within the context of the task.	Importance, relevance, usefulness, content, completeness, currency, sufficiency.	Currency, level of detail.	Value-added, relevance, completeness, timeliness, appropriate amount.	Relevancy, value added, timeliness, completeness, and amount of data.	Relevance, usage, timeliness, source, currency, data warehouse currency, non-volatility.
Accessibility	Information is interpretable, easy to understand and manipulate.	Useability, quantitativeness, convenience of access.	Accessibility, assistance, ease of use, location.	Accessibility, ease of operations, security.	Accuracy and access security.	Accessibility, system availability, transaction availability, privileges.
Representation	Information is represented concisely and consistently.	Understandability, readability, clarity, format, appearance, conciseness, uniqueness, comparability.	Compatibility, meaning, presentation, lack of confusion	Understandability, interpretability, concise representation, consistent representation, arrangement, readable, reasonable.	Interpretability, ease of understanding, concise representation, consistent representation.	Interpretability, syntax, version control, semantics, aliases, origin.

*Note: * Adapted from Lee et al. (2002); # Adapted from Turban, Aronson & Liang (2005)*

Figure 1. Inputs of information process

```
┌─────────────────────────────────────────────────────────┐
│  Traditional Information Process Formula                  │
│      I = i (D, S, t )                                     │
│  Developed Information Process Formula                    │
│      I = i (D, S, t, T )                                  │
│  Where:                                                   │
│    i = Reference to a process (i)                         │
│    I = Information obtained from interpretation of process (i) │
│    D = Data                                               │
│    S = Individual experience of the officer interpreting the data │
│    t = Time                                               │
│    T= Information Technology used                         │
└─────────────────────────────────────────────────────────┘
```

environments is no longer enough for the purpose of interpretation of data while relying on the developed technologies. Accordingly, data, experience, technology and time form prerequisites or inputs for the information process (Figure 1).

Input and Output

The formulation of Langefors (1973), and the addition of technology to Longefors's equation make information process definition more consistent with the requirements of product manufacturing systems if we consider the raw material in production to be equivalent to data in information systems. The constraints and environment required by the product system is part of the knowledge. In this regard, the information system requires additional input, that is, time.

An IQ system, similar to other quality systems, has inputs and outputs. The inputs to an IQ system are the prerequisites for the information process: data, experience, time and technology. The output of an IQ system is information with the focus on customer satisfaction.

IQ Process Mechanism

The IQ system involves the process of planning and administering the activities and functions necessary to achieve a high level of performance in the process of translating data into useful information. Process alone cannot achieve the performance intended from the process without the involvement of employees. Goldman et al. (1995) recognise the significance of employees as a company asset, and emphasise the importance of leveraging the impact of people and information for an agile enterprise. Evans and Lindsay (2005) show direct correlation between employees' satisfaction and customer satisfaction and argue that "people" are the only organisational asset that "competitors cannot copy; and the only one that can synergize, that is, produce output whose value is greater than the sum of its parts." Meade and Sarkis (1999) state that people are the most valued resources. It follows that the mechanism which converts the input of an IQ system to its output, that is, customer satisfaction, includes two main constituents: process and people. In an analogy with agile enterprise dimensions of Goldman et al. (1995), the leading mechanism for an IQ system is leveraging the impact of process and people.

IQ Process Control

To realise customer satisfaction, everyone should consider continuous process improvement as a key management practice (Evans & Lindsay, 2005). As part of this strategy, process and people are no longer enough for achieving the required output without the continuously improved procedures, policies and regulations that control the conversion process.

The dimensions of IQ are useful in ensuring coverage of the IQ concepts. They comprise measures that are useful to scale and benchmark characteristics of information, but are not as useful for deciding what to do to improve IQ (Lee et al., 2002). IQ dimensions should be based on the same principles of total quality for service or manufacturing which are listed by Evans and Lindsay (2005, p. 18) as:

1.   A focus on customers and stakeholders
2.   Participation and teamwork by everyone in the organisation
3.   A process focus supported by continuous improvement and learning.

These three principles should be supported by an organisational infrastructure, a set of managerial practices and a set of tools and techniques as shown in Figure 2. Infrastructure refers to the management systems to function effectively the IQ

Figure 2. The scope of information quality (Adapted from Evans & Lindsay, 2005)

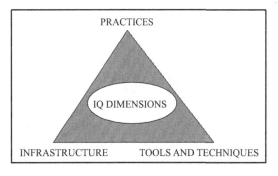

dimensions. Practices are the set of activities within infrastructures to achieve the IQ dimensions. The third principle, tools and techniques, refers to a wide variety of methods used to insure that practices are within the scope of IQ dimensions.

In other words, improving the quality of information requires an efficient tool taking into consideration practices in order to identify factors affecting information production infrastructure in addition to IQ dimensions. IQ improvement has, accordingly, two sets of elements. These are IQ dimensions and IQ factors. To be comprehensive, the IQ factors should measure the interaction of information users, information system outputs and technology. Factors significantly affecting the success of IQ systems are referred to as critical success factors.

This study relies on the research work of Marchand et al. (2000) in defining factors affecting the information process infrastructure (information system). These authors report a survey comprising 1,009 senior managers from 98 companies operating in 22 countries and 25 industries. Marchand et al. develop 15 competencies or measures (referred in their study as "dimensions") associated with effective information use. The measures are classified into three indicators: information technology practices (ITP), information management practices (IMP) and information behaviours and values (IBV). The indicators form an information performance measure referred to as "information orientation" or (IO), which measures a company's capabilities

Figure 3. Information orientation (IO) measures (Adapted from Marchand et al. 2000)

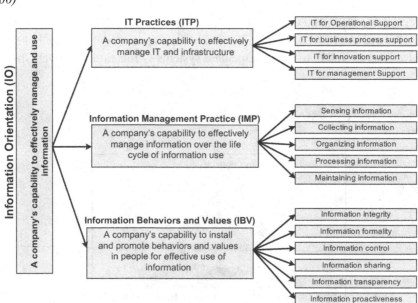

Figure 4. Environment of IQ system: input, output, mechanism and control

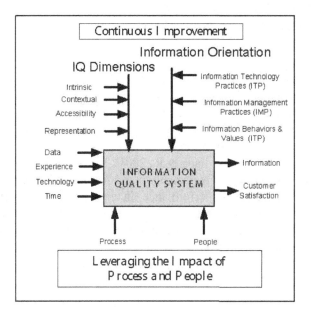

for effectively managing and using information. The three indicators are defined as follows (Marchand et al., 2000) (see also Figure 3).

- **Information technology practices (ITP):** This indicator measures a company's capability to effectively manage information technology applications and infrastructure to support operations, business processes, innovation and decision-making.
- **Information management practices (IMP):** This indicator is used to measure a company's capability to manage information effectively over the life cycle of information use. This indicator has several attributes including sensing, collecting, organising, processing and maintaining information.
- **Information behaviours and values (IBV):** This indicator reflects the company's capability to instil and promote behaviours and values in its people for effective use of information. The attributes of this indicator are integrity, formality, control, transparency, sharing and proactiveness.

However, the indicators and measures indicated by Marchand et al. (2000) are more useful at the macro analysis of the system and could be considered as an umbrella that may accommodate additional factors and measures at micro analysis of the system. For instance, the factors mentioned by Guynes & Vanecek (1996) could be used as sub-factors to determine the "organisation" measure of the IMP indicator in Marchand et al.'s work. Figure 3 illustrates the measures and indicators of Marchand et al. (2000). Figure 4 models the four constituents of the IQ system environment: input, output, mechanism and control.

Conflict of Interest

The mechanism of the IQ system process emphasises the importance of leveraging process and people. The term "people" in the mechanism of the IQ system process is a reference to two main stakeholder groups: IT technical staff and IT users. There is an apparent conflict of interests between IT staff and IT users, and "there is no prima facia priority of one set of interests and benefits over another" (Bedian & Zammuto, 1991 — in Jiang et al., 2001). IT staff look to the information technology system from their self-perception and learning experiences (Linberg, 1999). Users evaluate IS system performance "in terms of how well their needs are satisfied" (Jiang et al., 2001). Closer analysis of the user satisfaction reveals that the user requirements centred around the IQ dimensions: intrinsic, contextual, accessibility and representation. IT staff, on the other hand, deal with various aspects of information orientation (IO). Both IQ dimensions and IO form the control dimension of the IT system process. The two aspects of control dimension should complement each other, otherwise the IT system process cannot be controlled properly. Inferior results from any IO aspect may have a significant affect on IQ dimensions and accordingly, IO aspects form the technical factors influencing the IQ dimensions. In other words, IO aspects can be used to translate the user requirements into IT staff language. Such a translation can be effectively managed using the principles of a structured technique known as the quality function deployment (QFD).

INFORMATION QUALITY FUNCTION DEPLOYMENT

This research uses the principles of QFD in order to identify the deployable information functions. It considers both the IQ dimensions and IO measures in the same way the QFD using customers' requirements and technical requirements. The research integrates gap analysis technique using performance-importance analysis (Martilla & James, 1977). The modified technique is referred to as information function deployment (IFD). Below is a brief description of QFD, performance-importance analysis and IFD.

Quality Function Deployment (QFD)

QFD is a structured approach originated in 1977 at the Mitsubishi shipyard (Bosset, 1991) as a system to assure quality in manufacturing products. QFD is driven by what the customer wants and not just by technological innovation and is considered as a means translating the "voice of the customer" into specific, measurable product and process characteristics (Bosset, 1991; Han et al., 2001). It is defined as "a system for translating into appropriate company requirements at each stage from research and product development to engineering and manufacturing to engineering and manufacturing to marketing/sales and distribution" (American Supplier Institute, 1989). QFD differs from other quality tools in that it does not concentrate on protective activities such as inspection, but on understanding customer requirements and building them in. Accordingly, QFD is also a useful tool for assuring service quality. QFD enables the researchers or organisations to list within a matrix diagram "what" customer requirements and map them against "how" technical requirements should be developed to meet these requirements. The matrix diagram representing QFD is often called the "House of Quality" due to similarity of its shape to a house with various rooms and a roof. The construction of House of Quality comprises a number of rooms or cells which depends on the use and depth of analysis. The typical format of the House of Quality matrix is made up of eight major components or cells as shown in Figure 5. According to Evans & Lindsay (2005, p. 569) building the House of Quality for QFD requires six steps:

1.   Identify customer requirements, that is, preparing elements for cell 1.
2.   Identify technical requirements (cell 2).
3.   Relate the customer requirements to the technical requirements, that is, preparing the correlation matrix of cell 4.
4.   Conduct an evaluation of competing products or services (cell 6).
5.   Evaluate technical requirements and develop targets (cell 7).
6.   Determine which technical requirements to deploy in the remainder [remainder/} of production/delivery process (cell 8).

Figure 5. The House of Quality

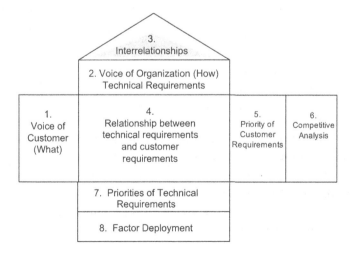

Figure 6. The iteration process of the House of Quality

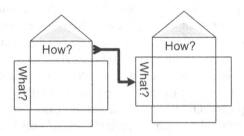

The QFD process is structured and could be iterated from macro to micro levels of analysis. The objective is to determine which technical requirements to deploy in order to meet customer requirements. The first QFD house of quality is on the aggregate level. Selected "how" or technical requirements from the first matrix become the "what" list of the second formulated house of quality. The technical requirements for the second House of Quality are more specific and with detailed descriptions of how the "what" list can be further developed as shown in Figure 6. Evans and Lindsay (2005) emphasise that the vast majority of QFD applications deal with the first and, to a lesser extent, with the second houses of quality.

Performance-Importance Analysis

This research integrates the performance-importance analysis with QFD. Importance-performance grit analysis was first introduced by Martilla and James (1977). The performance-importance grid includes four quadrants; high importance/high satisfaction, high importance/low satisfaction, low importance/high satisfaction, and low importance/low satisfaction. It was considered as an effective managerial tool but lost favour when more effective analytical methods developed with more powerful computers (Duke & Mount, 1996). The grid can be reduced to a tabular form with only two columns: the perception about the performance of a dimension (or a factor) and the expectation about importance of the dimension (Pitt et al., 1995). A gap between the perceived performance and the expected importance of a dimension may provide some indication about the criticality of the dimension (Al-Hakim & Xu, 2004). If the expectation of a dimension or a factor affecting information quality is high but the perceived performance of the dimension is low then the dimension should be treated as a critical one.

Information Function Deployment (IFD)

For the first house of quality, the IQ dimensions form the elements of "what" set while the elements of the "how" set are the IO measures. Because the IQ dimen-

Figure 6. The structure of the first House of Quality for IFD

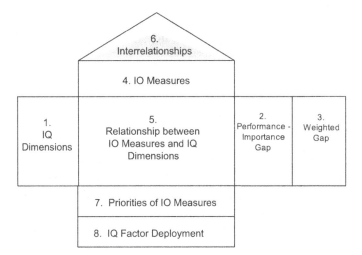

sions of the "what" set may not have the same weight, this research employs gap analysis between the perceived performance and expected importance to determine the weighting for each dimension in the "what" set. Priority of IO dimensions can be determined also using gap analysis. The research refers to this type of construction as the "information function deployment" (IFD). Figure 6 illustrates the structure of the first house of quality for IFD.

For building the house of quality for IFD, this research follows the following steps:

1. Identify IQ dimensions (cell 1).
2. Determine the performance — importance gap for IQ dimensions (cell 2).
3. Assign a weight for each IQ dimension and determine the weighted gap (cell 3).
4. Select IQ dimensions that significantly have wide weighted gaps.
5. Identify the IO measures (cell 4).
6. Find the correlation between IO measures and the selected IQ dimensions (cell 5).
7. Determine the weights of the IO measures and select the highest IO measures.
8. Determine the interrelationships between the selected IO measures and the others IO measures (cell 6).
9. Based on step 8, determine the weightings of all IO measures.

10.   From step 9 select the IO measures with the highest weightings.
11.   Deploy the selected IO measures (cell 8).

The best way to explain the previous steps is to deal with a case study directly.

CASE STUDY

An Australian hospital is presented in this chapter as a case study. The last five years have evidenced the movement of hospital management toward introducing quality concepts. For the purpose of this study, semi-structured interviews have been designed and 11 employees from the two stakeholder groups, IT professionals and IT system users, were interviewed. Three IT professionals, including an IT manager, were interviewed. Eight IT users were selected including two medical professionals, four nurses and two staff from the hospital registry office. The IT users were first interviewed and requested to consider each IQ dimension and rate the importance of the dimension to their work using a discrete Likert scale of 10 with increments in units of 1, being 1 the lowest and 10 the highest. Based on importance-performance analysis, the interviewees were requested to evaluate the expected importance of each dimension and their perception on the performance of the dimension as per their experience with the IT system using the same scale of 10.

One important issue that emerged during the discussion with the medical professionals was that the importance-performance gap difference for one dimension may not have the same weight for the same gap for another dimension, even though the two dimensions may have the same expectation rating. For instance, any gap difference for the "accuracy" dimension is very costly in comparison to a wider gap for other highly important dimensions. To achieve an adequate weighting for the gap analysis, this research study considers a scale of multiples of 3, that is, 81, 27, 9, 3, and 1, to weight the gaps. The gap weighting of 81 should only be assigned to a dimension in which a gap is absolutely not acceptable. The gap weighting of a dimension represents the average of gap weightings assigned by respondents for the dimension. The total weighting of a dimension is equal to the product of the gap by its gap weighting. There was a suggestion to allocate more weighting to the ratings of medical professionals' responses, but this suggestion was countered by the fact that most IT users are not medical professionals. Table 3 illustrates the responses of IT users in term of expectation, performance and gap weighting.

All IT users emphasised that the "accuracy" dimension of the IQ system was absolutely important and had a weighting of 27 allocated for its gap. However, the users stated that the IT system generated some inaccurate information resulting mainly from data collection or incorrect input. The medical professionals emphasised that the "relevancy," "completeness" and "timeliness" dimensions of IQ should be ranked as high as the "accuracy" dimension. The IT users did not assign a high rating for "believability," "reputation" and "objectivity" dimensions because these dimensions were already implied the integral framework of the "accuracy," "relevance," "completeness" and "timeliness" dimensions. The "value-added" dimension has a high rating with a high gap weighting. However, the IT users emphasised that this factor is a reflection of the association of "accuracy," "relevancy" and "timeliness." This information will have a value when it is accurate, relevant, and not out of date. "Security" is another dimension that received a very high rating and gap weighting by IT users. Apparently, the IT users are not fully convinced that their IT system provides a very high security level equivalent to their expectation. Nurses and registry staff stressed that accessibility and ease of operations were important dimensions and emphasised their gap weighting. All IT users emphasised the ar-

Table 3. IT users' responses on expectation, performance and gap weighting of IQ dimensions

Group	Dimension	Importance	Performance	Gap	Gap weighting	Total Weighting
Intrinsic	Accuracy	10	9.13	0.7	27	18.9
	Believability	7.5	7.5	0.00	7.5	0.00
	Reputation	6.63	6.5	0.15	7.5	1.13
	Objectivity	7.63	6.75	0.88	8.25	7.26
Contextual	Value-added	8	6.75	1.25	10.13	12.81
	Relevance	9.13	8.38	0.75	20.25	15.9
	Completeness	8.88	7.75	1.13	15.75	17.80
	Timeliness	8.88	7.5	1.38	11.25	15.53
Accessibility	Accessibility	6.88	6.25	0.63	8.25	5.20
	Ease of Operations	6.88	5.88	1.00	8.5	8.50
	Security	9	7.88	1.12	18	20.16
Representation	Understandability	6.13	5.25	0.88	5.25	4.62
	Interpretability	6.25	5.13	1.12	6.75	7.56
	Concise	4.75	4.5	0.25	5.25	1.31
	Consistent representation	6.75	6.34	0.41	5.25	2.15
	Arrangement	6.13	5.88	0.25	6	1.5
	Readability	3.38	3.38	0.00	3.75	0.00
	Reasonable	2.5	2.5	0.00	3.85	0.00

rangement and consistency dimensions of the IT output. Registry staff pointed to some difficulties in interpreting the information. Other dimensions received less rating and weighting. Either they are implied in other dimensions, irrelevant to the interest of IT users such as "reasonable" representation are or inapplicable such as with the readability dimension.

Table 3 indicates that the "security" dimension is the highest concern of the IT users (with total weighting of 20.16), followed by "accuracy." Other dimensions with high total weightings are "completeness," "relevance," "timeliness" and "value-added" dimensions. Considering the issues related to the "value-added" dimension stated above, this issue was dropped from further consideration.

For the purpose of IFD, the Information orientation (IO) measures of Marchand et al. (2000) could be considered as the technical factors for IQ dimensions. With the help of IT staff, the relationships between the selected IQ dimensions and the IO measures were identified (Table 4). The author of this research emphasises the subjectivity of these relationships. There is a need for more structured interviews with IT staff and more time to study carefully the definitions of the IQ dimensions and IO measures. Three symbols are used to identify the relationships. The symbol '●' is used to indicate a very strong relationship, '○' for a strong relationship and '◇' to denote a weak relationship. Weights of 9, 3 and 1 are assigned to the three relationships respectively.

Table 4 shows that five IO measures have weighting of 9 or higher. These measures are: operational, sensing, collecting, processing and maintaining measures. IT staff were requested to define the relationships between these high weighting IO measures and other IO measures. This step allows the determination of IO measures that should be selected together in order to achieve the required results. Table 5 illustrates the relationships between various IO measures.

Taking into consideration the weightings shown in Table 5, there only five IQ measures that have weightings of 20 or more. These measures are: sensing, collecting, integrity, sharing and transparency. It can be argued that the hospital management should pay more attention to theses five IO measures in order to achieve an improved information quality.

The selection of the five IO measures requires more analysis at the micro analysis level. The next stage of this research is to consider the five IO measures as customer requirements and to attempt to allocate the technical requirements for these IO measures. This is part of the future study.

CONCLUSION

Information quality (IQ) becomes a critical issue of hospitals' strategies and their ultimate delivery of care. This research maps the IQ process and defines its four constituents: input, output, mechanism and control. The research identifies two types of factors affecting the IQ process. These are the IQ dimensions and

Table 4. Relationships between selected IQ dimensions with IO measures

Dimension	Measure	ITP				IMP					IBV					
		Operational	Process	Innovation	Management	Sensing	Collecting	Organising	Processing	Maintaining	Integrity	Formality	Control	Sharing	Transparency	Proactiveness
Intrinsic	Accuracy					●	●		●		◇		◇			
Contextual	Relevance					●	●	◇		◇						
	Completeness						●	◇		○		◇				
	Timeliness					●			○	○			◇			
Accessibility	Security	●	○										◇	○		
	Weight	9	3			27	27	6	12	9	1	1	3	3		

Note:
Symbol '●' is to denote very strong relationship and has a weight of '9'.
Symbol 'o' is to denote a strong relationship and has a weight of '3'.
Symbol '◇' is to denote a weak relationship and has a weight of '1'.

Table 5. Relationships between various IO measures

		Weight - (Table 4)	ITP			IMP		IBV					
			Process	Innovation	Management	Organising	Processing	Integrity	Formality	Control	Sharing	Transparency	Proactiveness
ITP **IMP**	Operational	9									◊		
	Sensing	27		○	○			●	◊	◊	●	●	◊
	Collecting	27				◊	◊	●			◊	●	
	Processing	12			●					○			○
	Maintaining	9	○	○	○			○			●	○	
	Weight		3	6	15	1	1	21	1	4	20	21	4

Note:
Symbol '●' is to denote very strong relationship and has a weight of '9'.
Symbol '○' is to denote a strong relationship and has a weight of '3'.
Symbol '◊' is to denote a weak relationship and has a weight of '1'.

IQ indicators. IQ dimensions are classified into four categories. These categories are contextual, intrinsic, accessibility and representation. IQ indicators form an information performance measure referred to as information orientation (IO) which measures an organisation's capability to effectively manage and use information. IO is classified into three groups of indicators: information technology practices (ITP), information management practices (IMP) and information behaviours and values (IBV).

IQ dimensions could be considered as the information user's requirements while the IQ indicators are the technical factors affecting these requirements. Consistency between the constituents of IQ process control is critical for ensuring the performance of IQ process and for improving the process. This research attempts to match the IQ dimensions with the IQ indicators using a modified quality function deployment (QFD) procedure. The resulted modified procedure is referred to as information quality deployment (IFQ). IFQ can be used to identify the most important IQ dimensions that satisfy customers and to deploy technical factors affecting the identified IQ dimensions. An Australian hospital was selected as a case study and interviews were conducted with a number of information users and information system professionals. The study explains the procedure used in constructing the IFD matrix and identifying the most critical measures of IQ indicators that affect the performance of the IQ system. The study may include subjective results, as the research is in its initial stage. However, the methodology used could be further enhanced for more impartial outcomes.

REFERENCES

Abbott, J. (2001). Data, data everywhere — And not a byte of use? *Qualitative Market Research, 4*(3), 182-192.

Advisory Commission. (1998). *Advisory Commission's final report.* Retrieved November 6, 2005, from http://www.hcqualitycommission.gov/final/execsum.html

Al-Hakim, L. (2003). Web-based supply chain integration model. In J. Mariga (Ed.), *Managing e-commerce and mobile computing technologies* (pp. 183-207). Hershey, PA: IRM Press.

Al-Hakim, L., & Xu, H. (2004). On work alignment: Do IT professional think differently? In A. Sarmanto (Ed.), *Issues of Human computer integration* (pp. 291-320). Hershey, PA: IRM Press.

Bedian, A. G., & Zammuto, R. F. (1991). *Organisations: Theory and design.* Chicago, IL: Dryden.

Bosset, J. L. (1991). *Quality function deployment. A practitioner's approach.* Milwaukee, WI: ASQC Quality.

Carvel, J. (2005, November 3). More than 1m patients fall victim to mistakes in NHS hospitals. *The Guardian.* Retrieved November 6, 2005, from http://politics.guardian.co.uk/publicservices/story/0,11032,1607442,00.html

CBS News. (2005, April 26). *Iraq WMD hunt 'has been exhausted'.* Retrieved November 6, 2005, from http://www.cbsnews.com/stories/2005/04/26/iraq/main690922.shtml

CIHI. (2005). The CIHI data quality framework: June 2005 Revision. *Canadian Institute for Health Information.* Retrieved November 6, 2005, from http://www.cihi.ca

Copeland, C. W., & Simpson, M. (2004). *The Information Quality Act: OMB's guidance and initial implementation* (CRC Report to Congress, Updated September 17, 2004). Retrieved November 6, 2005, from http://www.ombwatch.org/info/dataquality/RL32532_CRS_DQA.pdf

English, L. (2002). Process management and information quality: How improving information production processes improves information (product) quality. In C. Fisher & B. Davidson (Eds.), *The 7th International Conference on Information Quality* (pp. 206-209). Cambridge: Massachusetts Institute of Technology.

English, L., & Perez A. (2003). Plain English about information quality: The information quality act: mandate for IQ. *DM Review.* Retrieved November 6, 2005, from http://www.dmreview.com/article_sub.cfm?articleId=6280

Evans, J. R., & Lindsay, W. M. (2005). *The management and control of quality* (6th ed.). Cincinnati, OH: South-Western, Thomson Learning.

Fadlalla, A., & Wickramasinghe, N. (2004). An integrative framework for HIPAA-Compliant I*IQ healthcare information systems. *International Journal of Health Care Quality Assurance, 17*(2), 65-74.

Fedorowicz, J., & Lee, Y. W. (1998). Accounting information quality: Reconciling Hierarchical and dimensional contexts. In E. Hoadley & I. Benbasat (Eds.), *Proceeding of Forth Conference on Information Systems* (pp. 9-11). Atlanta, GA: Association of Information Systems.

Fisher, C. W., & Kingma, B. R. (2001). Criticality of data quality as exemplified in two disasters. *Information & Management*, 39, 109-116.

Godfrey, B. (2000). Managing information quality — A critical process for most organisations. In *Proceedings of the 7th International in Information Quality*. Cambridge, MA: Massachusetts Institute of Technology.

Goldman, S. L., Nagel, R. N., & Preiss, K. (1995). *Agile Competitors and Virtual Organisations, Strategies for Enriching the Customer*. New York: Von Nostrand Reinhold.

Goodhue, D. L. (1995). Understanding user evaluations of information systems. *Management Science, 41*(12), 1827-1844.

Guynes, C., & Vanecek, M. (1996). Critical success factors in data management. *Information & Management, 30*(4), 201-209.

Hamblen, M. (2000). *Handhelds can help catch medical errors*. Retrieved August 10, 2005, from http://www.computerworld.com/printthis/2000/0,4814,44530,00.html

Han, S. B., Chen, S. K., & Sodhi, M. S. (2001). A conceptual QFD planing model. *International Journal of Quality & Reliability Management, 18*(8), 796-812.

Huang, K-T., Lee, Y. W., & Wang, R. Y. (1999). *Quality information and knowledge*. NJ: Prentice-Hall PTR.

Isbell, D., & Savage, D. (1999). *Mars climate orbiter failure releases report, numerous NASA actions underway in response* (Mars Polar Lander, Release 99-134). Retrieved November 10, 2005, from http://mars.jpl.nasa.gov/msp98/news/mco991110.htm

James, B. C., Horne, S. D., & Stephenson, R. A. (1994). Management by fact: What is CPI and how is it used?. In S. Horne & D. Hopkins (Eds.), *Clinical practice improvement: A new technology for developing cost-effective quality health care*. Washington, DC: Faulkner & Gray.

Jiang, J. J., Klien, G., Roan, J., & Lin, J. T. M. (2001). IS service performance: self-perceptions and user perceptions. *Information & Management, 38*(8), 499-509.

Kumpersmith, J. (2003). Quality of care in teaching hospitals: Executive summary. *Association of American Medical Colleges*. Retrieved August 15, 2005, from http://www.aamc.org/quality/surveys/start.htm

Langefors, B. (1973). *Theoretical analysis of information systems* (4th ed.). Studentlitteratur: Lund.

Li, N. Y., Tan, K. C., & Xie, M. (2003). Factor analysis of service quality dimension shifts in the information age. *Managerial Auditing Journal, 18*(4), 297-302.

Lee, W. Y, Strong, D. M., Beverly, K., & Wang, R. Y. (2002). AIMQ: A methodology for information quality assessment. *Information & Management, 40*(2), 133-146.

Linberg, K. R. (1999). Software developer perception about software project failure: a case study. *Journal of Systems and Software*, 49, 177-192.

Lorence, D. P., & Jameson, R. (2002). Adoption of information quality management practices in US healthcare organisations: A national assessment. *International Journal of Quality & Reliability Management, 19*(6), 737-756.

McLaughlin, C. P. (1996). Why variation reduction is not everything: A new paradigm for service operations. *International Journal of Service Industry Management, 7*(3), 17-30.

Malmsjo, A., & Ovelius, E. (2003). Factors that induce change in information systems. *Systems Research and Behavioral Science*, 20, 243-253.

Mandke, V., Bariff, M., & Nayat, M. (2003). Demand for information integrity in healthcare management. In *Proceedings of the 3rd International Conference on the Management of Healthcare & Medical Technology: The Hospital of the Future.* Warwick, UK: Warwick Business School.

Marchand, D. A., Kettinger, W. J., & Rollins, J. D. (2000, Summer). Information orientation: People, technology and the bottom line. *Sloan Management Review*, 69-79.

Martilla, J. A., & James, J. C. (1977). Importance-performance analysis. *Journal of Marketing*, 41, 77-79.

Meade, L. M., & Sarkis, J. (1999). Analyzing organisational project alternatives for agile manufacturing processes: An analytical network approach. *International Journal of Production Research, 37*(2), 241-261.

Miller, J. (2005). Information quality and market share in electronic commerce. *Journal of Services Marketing, 19*(2), 93-102.

MITIQ. (2005). *Masters in information quality at UALR.* Retrieved November 6, 2005, from http://mitiq.mit.edu/UALRMSIQ/

NCBI. (2005). *Ernest Codman's contribution to quality assessment and beyond.* Retrieved November 6, 2005, from http://www.ncbi.nlm.nih.gov/entrez/query.fcgi?cmd=Retrieve&db=PubMed&list_uids=2698445&dopt=Abstract

Pierce, E. M. (2005). Introduction. In R. Wang, E. Pierce, S. Madnick and C. Fisher (Eds.), *Information quality* (pp. 3-17). *Advances in Management Information System* (Vol. 1). Armonk, NY: M. E. Sharpe.

Pirani, C. (2004, January 24-25). How safe are our hospitals? *The Weekend Australian.*

Rampersad, H. (2001). 75 painful questions about your customer satisfaction. *The TQM Magazine, 13*(5), 341-347.

Redman, T. (2004). *First time, on time data quality.* Retrieved August 12, 2004), from http://www.dataqualitysolutions.Com/

Sen, K. (2001). Does the measure of information quality influence survival bias? *International Journal of Quality and Reliability Management, 18*(9), 967-981.

Stegwee, R., & Spil, T. (2001). *Strategies for healthcare information systems.* Hershey, PA: Idea Group.

Strong, D. M., Lee, Y. W., & Wang, R. Y. (1997). Data quality on context. *Communication of the ACM, 40*(5), 103-110.

Surgicenter. (2005). *Survey reveals U.S. leads other countries in medical errors.* Retrieved August 10, 2005, from http://www.surgicenteronline.com/hotnews/5bh39405091724.html

Turban, E., Aronson, J. E., & Liang, T P. *Decision support systems and intelligent systems* (7th ed.). Upper Saddle River, NJ: Prentice-Hall.

Wang, R. Y. (1998). A product perspective on total data quality management. *Communications of the ACM, 41*(2), 58-65.

Wang, R. Y., Allen, T., Wesley, H., & Madrick, S. 2003). *An information product approach for total information awareness.* Presented at the IEEE Aerospace Conference. Retrieved June 1, 2004, from http://web.mit.edu/tdqm/www/publications.shtml

Wang, R. Y., & Strong, D. M. (1996). Beyond accuracy: What data quality means to data consumers. *Journal of Management Information Systems, 12*(4), 5-34.

Who named it. (2005). *Ernest Armory Codman.* Retrieved November, 6, 2005, from Wennberg, J. E. (2002). Unwarranted variations in healthcare delivery: Implications for academic medical centres. Retrieved November 6, 2005, from http://bmj.bmjjournals.com/cgi/content/full/325/7370/961

Section II:
IQ Application in Banking, Real States, and Postal Industry

Chapter III

Customer Investigation Process at Credit Suisse:
Meeting the Rising Demands of Regulators

Daniel Maier, Credit Suisse, Switzerland

Thomas Muegeli, Credit Suisse, Switzerland

Andrea Krejza, Credit Suisse, Switzerland

ABSTRACT

Customer investigations in the banking industry are carried out in connection with prosecutions, the administration of estates or other legal actions. The Investigation & Inquiries Department of Credit Suisse has to handle approximately 5,000 client investigations per year. To date, the investigation process has been very complex, time consuming and expensive. Several redundant query processes are needed to achieve satisfactory results. In the past few years, new regulatory requirements have led to a massive increase in the number of investigations to be performed. This case study describes how these requirements can be met by redesigning the process and building a data-warehouse-based application that automates most of the process. These two measures have significantly improved the customer investigation process, resulting in considerable cost and time savings for Credit Suisse.

INTRODUCTION

Information systems (i.e., databases) are essential to support business operations, client relationship management processes (CRM) and management decisions. More and more companies are pursuing the trend of automating processes (Betts, 2001) and relying on complex and interrelated information systems. But poor data management can generate incomplete results, followed by wrong decisions that can have a negative impact for commercial organizations (e.g., wrong decisions lead to investment errors) and even for public institutions (e.g., terror attacks due to gaps in subject identification processes). It can also complicate and prolong workflows, leading to complex, time-consuming and costly work processes. According to Redman, poor quality data can generate costs of up to 20% of revenue for a typical organization (Redman, 2005), and poor data management is costing global businesses more than USD 1.4 billion per year (PriceWaterhouseCoopers, 2002). These facts reflect the importance of high data quality and the awareness of it as an increasingly business-critical issue. Furthermore, data quality can become a competitive advantage for businesses, for example, by improving marketing or customer satisfaction.

Spontaneously launched data quality management programs and other strategic corporate initiatives are usually not entirely successful, or fail because the data used to monitor and support organizational processes are incorrect or incomplete or otherwise faulty for a given application. As a result, "dirty data" can cause delays or even erase the potential of new systems and theoretically efficient workflows (Betts, 2001).

The term "data quality" (see also the chapter titled "Information Quality Function Deployment") describes the quality with respect to the relevance, the accuracy, consistency and reliability of the existent information. It defines how adequate our sense of reality is relative to a model. Knowledge about the quality criteria is the basis of working with data sets. As shown above, it is not always necessary to fulfill all the quality criteria. It may be sufficient to know only on which quality level the criteria have to be set. Usually, the criteria are already defined within a work process. In natural and social science, data quality is especially important, as the precision of the measuring and the amount of the data source are relevant for the acceptability of the final results. In contrast, business science calls for high data quality because the results lead to future statements and management decisions. In the past few years, several incorrect financial statements have resulted in economic scandals, caused not only by criminal backgrounds but also by poor data quality (e.g., Barings Bank). On the other hand, intelligence services collect a large volume of various pieces of information of different quality levels. The amount of similar information can be relevant for matches when exact data are unavailable. In other words, the more personal information a secret service collects about a relatively unknown searched person, the closer inaccurate data sets get to the reality of the subject in question. At any rate, awareness of the environment in which the data are processed (such as natural, social or business science, or intelligence service) already helps to define the quality criteria.

Nowadays, the banking industry is highly dependent on total information awareness to meet all external and internal requirements. Thirty years ago, it was usual for someone to simply open an account without today's common "know your client" policy and procedures. The name of a person could appear in different ways and aside from the basic recommendation, there was no standardized format for entering a name in a database. What is more, names transmitted verbally could sometimes be spelled in different ways (e.g., Silberstein, Silverstein, Silverstejn, Zylberstein, Zilberstain, Zylberstajn, Szilberstein, and so on). For example, a new client relationship could have been opened simply as "Mr. Silberstein" or "A. Silberstein." As a result, there are difficulties when matching names: "A." has endless possibilities (e.g., Albert, Abdul, Anthony but also Tony as the short version of Anthony) that can all refer to the requested entry in the database. Therefore, one of the top challenges concerning poor data quality is not only the heritage but also the inconsistency of personal name entries from an unfamiliar ethnicity or tradition (see the chapter entitled "The Challenge with Arabic Names"). Data quality in this sense does not describe a standardized form of information that is universally valid, but the amount of information about a subject. This is also the aim of customer investigation in the banking industry, described as follows (Klesse et al., 2004).

Customer investigations are common in the banking industry and are carried out in connection with prosecutions, the administration of estates or other legal actions. This chapter focuses on information quality in the customer investigation process (CIP) at Credit Suisse, a leading provider of comprehensive financial services worldwide. In 2003, Credit Suisse (not including Credit Suisse First Boston, Bank Leu and Neue Aargauer Bank) had over 2.6 million clients and 20,000 employees worldwide and had CHF 740 billion in assets under management. The bank has to handle about 5,000 individual customer investigation requests per year plus a varying, but steadily increasing, number of special embargo requests, such as the various terrorism-related search lists. The primary objective of the CIP is to find all the business relationships the bank currently has, or has had, with a certain customer or with individuals related to a certain customer. In the past few years, customer investigations in the financial industry have increased in importance due to the following external developments:

- **Risk management:** Banks are obligated by regulatory authorities and market developments to implement improved procedures for managing reputational, operational and legal risks. Reputational risk plays a major role in the banking industry, since the nature of its business requires the confidence of all stakeholders to be maintained. Operational risk can be defined as the danger of direct or indirect losses caused by the potential failure or inadequacy of internal processes. Legal risk is the risk that lawsuits, adverse judgments or unenforceable contracts adversely affect the operations or condition of a bank (Basel Committee on Bank Supervision, 2001). By implementing an effective and efficient CIP, banks ensure due diligence in identifying customers and understanding their business. This can reduce a bank's reputational and legal risks. The quality of the CIP also affects the operational risk of a bank, which in turn is important in the context of the New Basel Capital Accord, also known as Basel II (Basel Committee on Bank Supervision, 2003). By reducing the operational risk, banks are able to lower the required capital buffers for risk compensation.

- **Combating of terrorism:** Since September 11, 2001, many countries have issued anti-terror bills (e.g., USA Patriot Act of 2001 — US Government, 2001), which affect the banking industry. In addition to being unethical, having a terrorist as a customer increases the legal and reputational risks. All members of the Wolfsberg Group — an association of 12 global banks aiming to develop standards for the financial services industry — have committed to cooperate with government authorities in combating terrorism, to implement measures for identifying suspected terrorists quickly, and to support the Financial Action Task Force (FATF) Special Recommendations on Terrorist Financing (FATF, 2001; The Wolfsberg Group, 2002). The ongoing fight against terrorism is leading to a continuously growing number of customer investigation inquiries and a need to monitor transactions in order to detect those that appear suspicious. In addition, the increasing number of blacklists such as terrorist lists, the Office of Foreign Assets Control list (US Department of the Treasury, 2004), the FBI control lists, and so forth, have to be checked continuously against all customer information of a bank both to comply with the regulatory requirements and to avoid reputational or legal risks. Furthermore, it is necessary to check against other sanction lists (e.g., politically exposed persons) (The Wolfsberg Group, 2003), in order to be able to observe additional due diligence procedures. All these tasks need to be performed in addition to existing standard banking operations and must be executed in a timely manner.

- **Anti-money laundering:** Anti-money laundering laws and policies, which were adapted after September 11, 2001, are also leading to an ever increasing volume of customer investigation inquiries and a need for high quality investigations analyzing relations between individuals and organizations.

These developments are forcing banks to ensure a high quality CIP that enables preventive risk management and a swift response to the increasing number of legal inquiries. Therefore, the objective of this chapter is to present how Credit Suisse has improved and streamlined the process through organizational and technical measures. In order to give a structured and sound case description, an appropriate information quality framework based on a literature review is shown in the next section. The original CIP, its problems and the major challenges for process improvement are presented using this theoretical basis. In the subsequent section, the workflow of the revised and partly automated CIP is illustrated. The architecture and functionality of the supporting information system and the information quality improvements achieved are described in detail.

INFORMATION QUALITY FRAMEWORK

Several definitions of the terms "data quality" and "information quality" can be found in the literature, and these are often used synonymously. A standard information quality definition does not exist yet, but information quality is generally regarded as a multidimensional and hierarchical concept (Huang et al., 1999; Wang et al., 1995; Eppler & Wittig, 2000). Three different approaches can be distinguished for deriving and specifying quality dimensions (Huang et al., 1999; Liu & Chi, 2002). The *intuitive approach* proposes information quality attributes based on personal experience or on subjective insights about what dimensions or attributes are most relevant (cf., Wang et al., 1995; Miller, 1996; Redman, 1996; English, 1999). The *empirical approach* quantitatively captures the data consumer's point of view about what quality dimensions are important according to their tasks (cf., Wang & Strong, 1996; Helfert et al., 2002). The *theoretical approach* builds upon an established theory and proposes quality dimensions corresponding to this theory (cf., Ballou & Pazer, 1985; Te'eni, 1993; Wand & Wang, 1996; Liu & Chi, 2002). The major drawback of the intuitive and empirical approaches is the strong influence of the researcher's personal experience on the selection and deduction of information quality attributes and dimensions. The lack of a theoretical basis results in missing justifications and understanding of why and how certain information quality classifications and definitions are proposed. Therefore, this chapter adopts a theoretical approach for defining information quality. The information quality framework presented by Liu & Chi (2002) seems to be well suited for the purpose of a structured case description because their generic approach can easily be adapted to the characteristics of the case, and the proposed quality stages correspond to the different steps of the customer investigation process.

Figure 1 depicts the so-called data evolution lifecycle that is used by Liu and Chi as a theoretical basis to derive four data quality stages. The lifecycle characterizes the typical sequence of data evolution stages, consisting of data collection, organization, presentation, and application. First of all, data are captured (e.g., by observing or measuring real-world processes or objects). Then the data are organized according to certain structures (e.g., in file-based data stores or more sophisticated databases). After that, the data are processed and presented. Finally, the data are utilized for a certain application purpose which in turn can trigger further data capturing (Liu & Chi, 2002). At every stage of the lifecycle, specific techniques, methods, models or other approaches are applied, and these influence the evolution of the data. For example, data are organized in different ways depending on the modeling paradigm

Figure 1. Data evolution lifecycle and corresponding quality stages (Source: Liu & Chi, 2002)

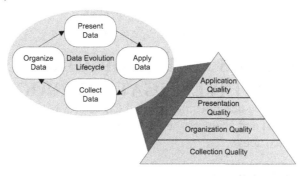

Figure 2. Data-oriented overview of the customer investigation process

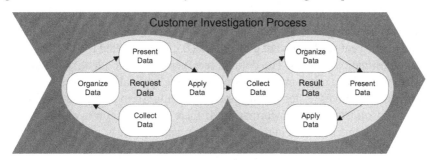

(e.g., relational or object-oriented) being used. Depending on the techniques, methods or models applied during the lifecycle, different errors may occur, and therefore different quality dimensions and attributes have to be measured. Accordingly, Liu and Chi introduce the concept of evolutional data quality consisting of the four quality stages: collection quality, organization quality, presentation quality, and application quality. The quality of data at earlier stages of the lifecycle contributes to that at later stages (i.e., the quality measure is accumulative) (Liu & Chi, 2002). Liu and Chi exemplify their evolutionary data quality approach by presenting typical root causes of poor data quality and deriving specific measurement attributes and models at each data quality stage.

For the purposes of this chapter, the concept of evolutional data quality is used to point out the information quality issues as well as the improvements in the customer investigation process at Credit Suisse. The process consists of two major phases. In the request phase, a new customer inquiry is placed, and in the reply phase, the results to a specific inquiry are produced (see Figure 2). Thus, the process consists of two connected data evolution lifecycles. First, data specifying the customer inquiry are processed. The application of the customer inquiry data triggers the second lifecycle, which handles the inquiry results. This two-phase structuring of the process is used throughout the chapter.

ANALYSIS OF THE ORIGINAL CUSTOMER INVESTIGATION PROCESS

The following section describes the original CIP as it was carried out within Credit Suisse in the past and analyzes the information quality issues according to the framework depicted above.

Activities and Workflow of the Original Customer Investigation Process

The CIP was initiated by an inquirer (e.g., external/government or internal person who requested information), who first had to identify one or more appropriate receivers or consignees for that specific inquiry (A). Having identified those, the inquiry was sent to all relevant consignees (B). This initiated the Credit Suisse internal investigation process. The defined receivers started to identify the departments that might have relevant information and were application owners or owners of information archives. After having obtained results from the departments, the receivers consolidated all the information. If there was no accurate result, further departments became involved in the same investigation process, and requests were repeated until the information collected was considered sufficient. The dossier with a summary of the final information was finally sent to the inquirer. This workflow was quite complex (for details see Figure 3) and time consuming for Credit Suisse, and required considerable coordination efforts on the part of the inquirer. The inquirer had to find an appropriate consignee for his request (B). Therefore, it was possible for him to have to trigger multiple redundant investigation processes simultaneously (C) if more than one receiver was identified. If multiple inquiries were sent by the inquirer, the dossiers received needed to be consolidated (D) before any action could be taken (E). Figure 3 below depicts the process steps 1-9 in the request and reply phases.

Analysis of Information Quality Issues in the Customer Investigation Process

The entire process can be broken down into two main parts: first, the distribution and processing of the inquiry itself ("request phase") and second, the processing of the inquiry results by the inquiry receiver ("reply phase"). Both of the phases have a unidirectional data flow. In the request phase, information flows from the inquirer

Figure 3. Original customer investigation process at Credit Suisse

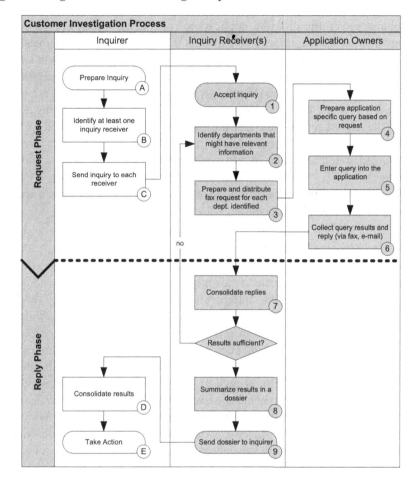

to the application owners, and in the reply phase it is collected from the application owners and consolidated by the inquirer.

Quality Issues in the Request Phase

During the acceptance of an inquiry (*collection quality*), the main problems were caused by *distributed responsibility* and the *coordination difficulties* of inquiries. To be on the safe side, an inquirer tried to identify one or more consignees for his information request. That led to *unnecessary redundant instances* of the process, since more than one department started the investigation and was searching for the information requested.

Since each investigation receiver could only guess who might have information concerning the inquiry and had only limited knowledge of the extent of the information stored in the different applications, unnecessary requests were also sent to application and/or information owners. Consequently, data sources that were irrelevant for the investigation purpose were covered as well. Further causes of potential organization quality issues were the many *media breaks* in the process, since most of the coordination in the process involved the sending of faxes, which on average led to about 40 faxes containing requests, lists and query results. Faxes containing the request sent to the application owners sometimes contained spelling errors in names, which often caused delays in the process. Furthermore, there was no standardized presentation quality and thus query results were delivered in many different ways.

Only experienced people were able to retrieve the relevant and requested information with this complex process.

Quality Issues in the Reply Phase

All these problems and their effects on overall information quality affected the information evolution lifecycle in the reply phase. Faxes or e-mails with query results were sometimes difficult to interpret or ambiguous for the inquiry receiver or contained insufficient information, which in turn affected *collection quality* in the reply phase. This could result either in a wrong decision at the end of the process or in a corrective iteration, which could become very costly and time consuming.

A major problem when consolidating the information and preparing the dossier concerned *information organization quality*. Information had to be consolidated manually, and relations between persons, companies and groups had to be detected by hand, which calls for a trained eye. In this task, *consolidation errors* as well as *relation detection errors* could occur (e.g., when two information records describing the same person or company were considered by mistake or when relations that did exist between persons and companies were not detected).

In particular, the long cycle time of the CIP could lead to outdated information or to an unacceptable latency for taking action. Investigations that were marked as extremely urgent could be processed only at the expense of quality, even if conducted carefully. The possible utilization errors included unnecessarily blocking a customer's account or an avoidable investigation of the customer by public authorities, potentially resulting in a dissatisfied customer. Table 1 summarizes the issues analyzed.

Table 1. Summary of potential information quality issues in the CIP

Collection Quality	Distributed responsibility and difficult coordination of multiple inquiries	Distributed responsibility often led to redundant investigation processes within Credit Suisse, causing an unnecessary workload.
	Redundant queries	Redundant CIP instances led to additional work for application owners.
Organization Quality	Coverage of irrelevant data sources, insufficient recall rate, media breaks	Distribution of inquiries via fax could cause misunderstandings. Even data sources not relevant to the inquiry were covered in an investigation for security reasons. Heterogeneous query interfaces of legacy application that were difficult to operate decreased the recall of relevant results.
Presentation Quality	Inadequate result presentation, media breaks	Query results were sent back from the application owners as they were, resulting in many inconsistently structured query reports.
Collection Quality	Insufficient presentation quality, media breaks	The fax containing query results were not always understandable, were ambiguous or could contain spelling mistakes. Typos could occur when reentering reply faxes for dossiers.
Organization Quality	Consolidation errors	Two people could wrongly be considered the same or persons, companies could be regarded as different although they concerned the same individual.
	Relation detection errors	Existing relations between individuals were not discovered or wrong/nonexistent relations were assumed between individuals.
Presentation Quality	Inadequate dossier structure	Dossier structure could be inadequate for the inquirer's purpose.
	Media breaks	Media breaks could lead to mistakes in the dossier.
Utilization Quality	Long investigation cycle time	Due to the process's long cycle time, the information could be outdated, or delays could occur in the inquirer's process. In very urgent investigations, a time/quality tradeoff had to be made.
	Quality issues in very urgent investigations	

SOLUTION

The Revised Process:
Reengineered by an Information System

Recent regulatory demands and political developments have led to a higher frequency of customer investigation inquiries and compliance checks. For example, after the terrorist attacks in the United States in 2001, a terrorist search list was suddenly generated to block cash inflows for terrorist organizations (according to the Patriot Act). Consequently, higher information quality and at the same time speed were needed to ensure that no accidentally blocked customer accounts or other inconveniences occurred due to quality issues in the CIP. Furthermore, the increasing workload of operational departments and the rising cost of the original process were not tolerable.

In summary, all these facts called for a fast and cost-effective investigation process delivering high quality information to enable preventive, proactive risk management and a swift response to legal inquiries. Fulfilling the new requirements as regards to information quality, cycle time and cost was feasible only with two large-scale organizational changes within Legal and Compliance as well as on the information system level. The *first* measure was the *organizational centralization and redesign of the CIP*. In conjunction with the second measure, a simplified and efficient process could be designed. The *second* measure taken was *automation of a large part of the CIP*. The automation of the process addressed the error-prone tasks of searching, analyzing and consolidating customer information and allows for preventive investigations of guaranteed high information quality.

Workflow of the Revised Customer Investigation Process

A central organizational unit, Investigations & Inquiries, was established within the Legal and Compliance department of Credit Suisse in order to avoid redundant investigation processes. It centralizes all activities concerning compliance management of legal inquiries and is responsible for customer investigations. Prior to the implementation of a new information system (investigation application), the customer investigation process had to be redesigned. It now consists of only a few activities (see Figure 4).

The Investigation Application:
A System Automating the Investigation Process

The investigation application was built in collaboration with the external company DeltaVista (http://www.deltavista.com), which provided expertise in address management and database search algorithms. This application acts as a single point of access for customer data that is relevant for investigations. It automates a large

Figure 4. Revised customer investigation process at Credit Suisse

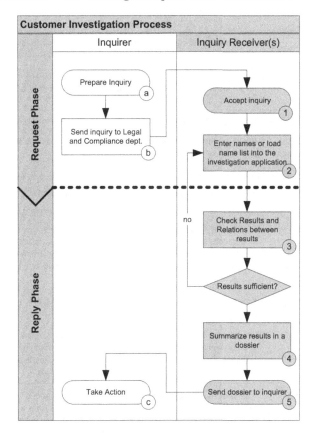

part of the CIP by providing two major functions: first, an *interactive search* mode and second, a *compliance check* function.

Description of the Functions Provided by the Application

Interactive search function. The interactive search function enables the user to find all information concerning a certain person and to explore that information interactively in a drill-down fashion. Since the person in question does not need to be an existing customer of Credit Suisse, the only identifying attribute is the person's name received from external address pools. Therefore, the investigation application was specifically designed to require only a person's name as input, although hit precision can be increased by entering further information like address, date of birth, an so forth. The investigation application then automatically searches all selected data pools (Table 2) for this customer name using a fuzzy search algorithm.

Table 2. Data pool content

Internal Data	
Credit Suisse Customer Information File	All Credit Suisse customers who are active or set inactive since 2001 who may have an account, safekeeping account, and so forth.
Authority to sign power of attorney	Information about who is authorized to sign on the behalf of a certain customer.
Consumer loans	Customers who have a consumer loan or a leasing contract.
Transactions over the counter (e.g., currency exchange)	Image Archive of documents, indexed with names of contract partners and/or proxy agents.
Safe-deposit box customer data	Persons who rent or rented a safe-deposit box, as well as location and type of safe-deposit box.
External Data	
Swiss addresses and company information (DeltaVista)	Address and company information integrated from a variety of official sources such as Yellow Pages, phone directories, registration offices and commercial data providers (e.g., Dun&Bradstreet, Orell Fuessli).
Bankruptcies (DeltaVista)	Persons and firms associated with insolvency proceedings.
Swiss Commercial Gazette (DeltaVista)	Commercial register (new entries, changes, deletions), bankruptcies, composition agreements, debt enforcement, calls to creditors, other legal publications, lost titles, precious metal control, marks, balances, public procurement, Infoservice, company publications.
World-Check Data (WorldCheck)	Names of individuals, firms, organizations, parties and groups that may cause a high risk in a potential customer relationship with the bank (e.g., politically exposed persons, persons associated with terrorist organizations and/or criminal organizations).

The application presents the search results in a list (Figure 5), sorted by hit probability.

To investigate the person or company further, an address detail view, a specific detail data pool view and a company detail view can be accessed. A special feature of all these detail views is the connection to further associated individuals. For example, the company detail sheet shows all owners or members of the Board of Directors of the company, and the address detail view shows other persons living in the same household, etc. This allows an investigation not only of the person or company searched for but also of persons or companies related to the name entry. Experienced staff in the Legal & Compliance Department of Credit Suisse use this function to find individuals who are or could become customers of the bank and may be associated with criminal groups or persons. By matching third-party information

Figure 5. List of search results delivered by the investigation application (fictitious data)

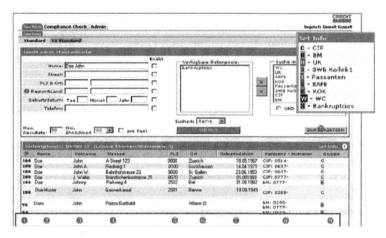

Figure 6. Report screen providing a detailed information summary on a result set entry (fictitious data)

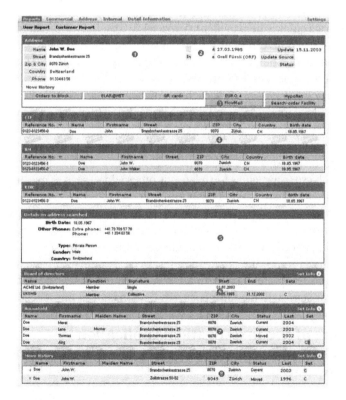

such as external data provided by DeltaVista with Credit Suisse data, the decision-making process can be faster and more accurate. In this way, unknown relationships between clients and companies can be detected automatically — information that may not be available by using only internal data.

Compliance check function. The compliance check function makes it possible to test all data pools against a complete list of names delivered by external regulators such as the OFAC (Office of Foreign Assets Control), UN (United Nations) or seco (Swiss State Secretariat for Economic Affairs). This function is used in connection with the prosecution of terrorists. A government member or a regulating body sends a list of names to Credit Suisse, and this has to be checked against the customer base. A simple name comparison is not sufficient for this task. Different spellings of the names and/or aliases have to be detected, and relations between the names on the list and active customers also have to be reviewed.

User Interface Design Considerations

In the design phase of the user interface, special attention was paid to the display of search results. Despite all the intelligence available in the system, the final decision on whether or not a result is relevant for the inquiry still needs to be made by a human being. Therefore, the result list needs to contain sufficient data to decide. If a closer look at the customer details and further investigation be required, then as little data as possible is needed to avoid confusion by overloading the screen. Color-coded icons quickly help to identify records with a link to Credit Suisse data, which is helpful if the investigator is also considering external data. All result list rows can be sorted: this helps to arrange the initial search results and facilitate the process of selecting relevant information.

In the *interactive search* mode used for normal inquiries, most of the work results from reproducing documents for a relationship identified to match an inquiry. In the *compliance check* module, where lists get processed, an effective clicks-per-result ratio is even more crucial. Lists such as sanction lists, terrorist lists or even lists of politically exposed persons tend to be much less accurate and comprehensive since additional search criteria such as birthdates or other addresses are missing in most of these kind of search lists. Individual inquiries are more accurate because this sort of inquiries are provided with additional search criteria (name, birthdate, addresses and others). When processed by the system, an obvious false positive match is the norm; a match that needs a closer look at the exception confirms that rule.

Bearing this in mind, the application has been designed to have a very low click-per-false-positive rate in order to allow high output. As a rule of thumb, the slogan "Think or start with the false positives first" has been introduced.

Architecture of the Investigation Application

The investigation application is based on two major subsystems: first, a data mart that is fed by the central Credit Suisse data warehouse, which delivers all the necessary internal data; second, another data mart containing external data as well as the matching and fuzzy search intelligence provided by DeltaVista. Since the data warehouse is an established system within Credit Suisse that collects data daily from over 300 data sources from Credit Suisse's legacy systems, most of the data sources needed for the investigation process were already available with sufficient quality and timeliness. Therefore, only a few additional external data feeds had to be developed (e.g., the integration of the register of politically exposed persons delivered by another third-party provider) (WorldCheck). Consequently, the internal data pools were easily integrated into the investigation application, as the implementation project only had to deal with a single data delivery interface. Using the data warehouse as a provider for internal data also ensures accuracy of the data delivered, since the data warehousing process within Credit Suisse has established closed loop data quality management (Winter et al., 2003). Also, data cleansing and consolidation is done within the extract, transformation and load (ETL) processes that load the data warehouse. A further benefit of using the data warehouse infrastructure is that scalability and stability of the application is high and the application is managed professionally by an operations and batch controlling department. Having standardized and automated secure feeds for both internal and external data means that the contents of the system can be expanded very effectively in a short time. This ensures that new requirements can be met if regulatory requirements change or a new application/version of the tool for other purposes becomes necessary.

The external and internal data are integrated during the ETL process of the dedicated data mart of the investigation application. A core concept used to integrate related data of persons or companies and to build probable relations that exist between the persons is the *address universe* described below.

Due to the sensitivity of the data stored in the application — based on Web technology and run on a server that is part of the Credit Suisse intranet — and the ease of retrieving data, the hardware runs in a secure environment. To cope with data-protection issues, access control to the system is regulated and restricted to a low number of specially designated investigators using a security logon certificate.

Core Concepts: Address Universe and Fuzzy Search

The investigation application is based on two core concepts contributed by DeltaVista. First, the so-called Address Universe is used to link people, customers and companies with each other. Second, a fuzzy search algorithm is used to search for names in the data pool to find an entry point for further browsing the data.

Address Universe. The Address Universe comprises all addresses stored for investigation purposes. It is used for linking related persons, groups and companies. Furthermore, it is the main index for searching the data to investigate. The Address Universe contains about 21 million addresses, of which about 13 million are from external sources. About 6 million older addresses represent the move history of the currently valid addresses. Often, data from internal data sources have an invalid or incomplete address. Therefore, a special consolidation process is used during the ETL process of the investigation data mart to connect internal addresses with similar external validated addresses. In this process, all new data are compared with existing names and addresses in the Address Universe, and a similarity metric is computed. If a certain similarity value is exceeded, the two addresses are considered as equal and are linked together. When an address is considered equal to an existing address in the Address Universe, the existing address is linked with the new data that are loaded into the investigation data mart. The link is stored in a special "connection table" to make the connection reversible. Additionally, a special "relation table" stores all known links between companies, people and groups (see Figure 7). These links may then be navigated by the user using the interactive search function. These relations are also extracted from operational systems and external data sources during the ETL process. There is also a special "declined relations table" that exists

Figure 7. Extract from the data model of the application — tables for linking addresses (fictitious data used)

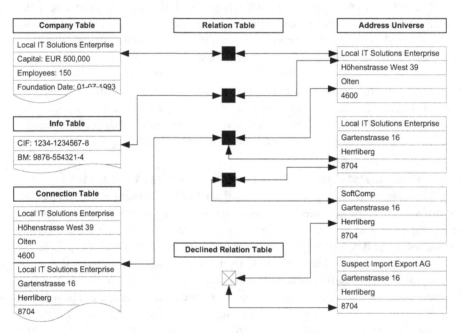

to store explicit non-links. This makes it possible to mark two persons or companies explicitly as non-related if this is for sure (e.g., if a Credit Suisse customer and a well-known terrorist have similar names but are certainly not affiliated with each other).

Fuzzy search. The traditional fuzzy search is based on the mathematical concept of fuzzy logic designed by Professor Lotfi A. Zadeh in 1965 as a means to model the uncertainty of natural language. He followed the idea that general statements are relative and also depend on someone's experience and level of understanding. Fuzzy logic is a superset of conventional logic that has been extended to handle the concept of partial truth. Following this concept, logical values between "true" and "false" are accepted to describe fuzzy amounts in a mathematical way. A fuzzy quantity then helps to build a smaller-sized graduation using an exact mathematical basic principle (Zadeh, 1965).

Using this theory in this case, the fuzzy search function simplifies the process of finding a name. Fuzzy logic returns the closest matches. But the simplicity of the principle results in inaccuracy caused by difficulties with fine-tuning the rules. In some cases, many non-relevant search results can occur. Therefore, it still is a time-consuming process for an inexperienced investigator, but an expert, on the other hand, can find an exact match much faster in this "data jungle."

Finding a name is not an easy task, especially when the correct spelling is unknown. This problem was already identified before sophisticated computer technologies flooded the market. One of the first approaches was patented by Robert C. Russel in 1918 for the US census. His approach was to reduce the syllables by codifying the names into four-digit codes. This method — called Soundex — is a combination of an alphabetical and a phonetic index. Despite the obvious limitations (four-digit codification, best suited for Anglo-Saxon name universe), Soundex is still very popular among database vendors. In most cases where a database system claims a phonetic search, the system uses Soundex.

An enhanced method — called "NYSIIS" — using a system of phoneticization of names as well, was invented on behalf of the New York State Identification and Intelligence System in the sixties (Taft, 1970). It avoids the major obstacle of Soundex by expanding the length of a converted name string to up to 10 characters and retaining the original position of a letter, but it too often fails to match non-Anglo-Saxon names. This code is quite popular among data miners.

Metaphone (or double metaphone) is the latest attempt to cover English pronunciation of names using a phonetic code algorithm. First introduced by Lawrence Philips (Verity) in 1990, then OpenSource community modified the code, calling it Double Metaphone. The major difference compared with the other phonetic codes is that there is no limitation in length for the result. But it is very Anglo-Saxon-centric and has some limitations for other names as well (Binstock & Rex, 1995).

Yet another approach uses the N-gram matching technique by drilling up groups of characters out of a string (Jurafsky, 2000). The matching then compares how many N-grams appear in a given search string. To find reasonable matches, it is recommended that other weighting criteria be used in the comparison process.

The retrieval functionality of the investigation tool is based on a combination of pattern matching and synonym lists to allow retrieval even if a name is slightly misspelled due to typing errors or has different official spellings (e.g., foreign people who have their original name and a German alias).

The problem of mismatched names can occur especially in cases where the external requester of an investigation has less information available than the bank (as official documents are required for the account opening process). This is a considerable problem in many investigations, especially when dealing with sanction lists, since it decreases the recall rates of the retrieved information (Lutz, 2001). To overcome this problem, the application implements the fuzzy search algorithm described above to index the name database in such a way that information about individuals with misspelled names is also retrieved. An important feature is that this works not only for German names but also for names in other languages and from a different cultural context (e.g., Arabic, Russian, or Asian names). If necessary, the algorithm can also be fine-tuned for a specific language. A customizable synonym search capability is available as well to leverage search capabilities.

The Challenge with Arabic Names

With Arabic and Asian names, for example, there is not only a problem of inaccurate data quality, but also a transcription problem. At the moment — due to the international political situation after 9/11 — a good understanding of Arabic culture and tradition as well as the Islamic movement is extremely important when matching the names of wanted people.

Knowledge of onomastics — science of words and names — is the key for an efficient work process in customer investigation. In some nations, a name had the power not only to identify someone's roots but also to protect him, giving him strength or immunity from disease. In Northern Europe, family names did not become common until the 12th century. Before this time, people were identified by only one name. When city populations started to grow and mobilization took place, people were soon given nicknames (i.e., a profession or a characteristic), followed by a provenance name for better identification. Later, these affixes were transformed into family names (for further details see the research results of the University of Leipzig, Onomastics section).

Particularly traditional Arabic tribe names show the lineage of a person in a concise way. The importance (political or religious) of someone is also represented in the length of a name: the fathers, grandfathers or even great-grandfathers name can be subsumed within someone's regular name. Usually, the given name was set at the birth of a child, but the nickname and ancestor's name were added later on in a person's lifetime. Ad-hoc recreated names are still traditional in Bedouin and rural regions, whereas in civilized regions perseverative names are common (Wild, 1982).

Today, a person's name has lost its historical significance in most western countries. However, in some cultures — such as in the Arabic culture — the full name still symbolizes the entire personality and heritage of a person who is often proud to have such a name.

In some Arabic countries, the government has started to adapt name spellings to western standards (first name/last name). In other countries, a three-way name is considered standard (Wild, 1982). This simplifies the process of entering a name in a database, but it does not make it easier to find a searched person. The name Mohammed can be spelled in only one way in Arabic letters but in over 200 ways in the Latin alphabet (Milstein, 2002). Prefixes and suffixes are sometimes used as a regular name (last name or first name), and sometimes they are even mixed within the given name. For instance, the name Abd al-Rahman can be both last name and first name. There are different ways of adding this name to a database. It depends not only on the system administrator's experience, but also the rules that are set for system inputs (Abdul Rahman, Abd Al Rahman, Abdurrahman and so on). Often there are endless variations of how to transcribe a name (Milstein, 2002). Some experts have tried (Achim Schlott-Kotschote, 2004), but there is still no official international standard for the transcription of Arabic names.

Terrorists in particular often take advantage of this well-known challenge with Arabic names. Their names, alternative names and aliases can appear with many different spellings in international search lists. Therefore, an investigator needs in-depth knowledge not only of the fuzzy logic of the system used but also of the culture, background and tradition of the searched subject. As shown above, a complete Arabic name can consist of many name parts that can be broken down only by experienced persons, and often it is still not clear which part is the first name and which is the last name. In this case, fuzzy logic can help to eliminate the problem of the position of the name part.

Assessment of the Impact of the Revision on Information Quality

The centralized entry point for investigation inquiries prevents redundant executions of the process. It also simplifies the procedure for inquirers, as they are offered a single point of contact that gives them consolidated information. The

Table 3. Impact of the measures taken on information quality

Collection Quality	Distributed responsibility and difficult coordination of multiple inquiries	Organizational centralization of the CIP effectively prevents unnecessary investigations.
Organization Quality	Redundant queries	Redundant queries are prevented; explorative queries for fine-tuning results do not affect operational systems or people from operational departments.
	Coverage of irrelevant data sources, insufficient recall rate, media breaks	The investigation data mart contains all relevant customer information. If additional data sources become relevant, they will be integrated into the data mart and become available for each investigation. The recall rate is improved by a fuzzy search algorithm and by explicitly stored relations between investigated subjects in the investigation data mart. Media breaks are eliminated through the automation of information retrieval.
Presentation Quality	Inadequate result presentation, media breaks	Automation of information retrieval eliminates this process step and the corresponding problems.
Collection Quality	Insufficient presentation quality, media breaks	Automation of information retrieval eliminates this process step and the corresponding problems.
Organization Quality	Consolidation errors	Automation of information consolidation during the ETL process of the investigation data mart eliminates most consolidation errors caused by manual consolidation.
	Relation detection errors	Automation of relation detection during the ETL process of the investigation data mart eliminates most relation detection errors. The table storing relations and explicit non-relations increases the reliability and reproducibility of investigation results.
Presentation Quality	Inadequate dossier structure	The investigation application provides standardized reports that can be used for creating the final dossier.
	Media breaks	The complete task of dossier assembly can be done electronically. Media breaks are avoided.
Utilization Quality	Long investigation cycle time	Automation and centralization of investigation know-how drastically shorten the process cycle time (from about 120 to around 20 minutes).
	Quality issues in very urgent investigations	High information quality is guaranteed through a high degree of automation and through data quality assurance during the data warehousing process. Investigation quality in urgent cases is much higher. However, quality issues may occur when the results presented by the investigation application are not interpreted carefully.

application automates the most error-prone tasks of the process (identifying and querying data sources, consolidating information and detecting relations), eliminates the media breaks and improves presentation quality by providing standardized reports for customer investigation. Table 3 summarizes how the problem categories affecting the information quality types were addressed by the process redesign and the investigation application.

Overall, the automation of the information preparation and retrieval process alone resulted in a cost reduction of approximately EUR 3.1 million (net present value calculation over five years). An investigation process cycle time could be reduced to one-sixth of the original duration. Furthermore, the short cycle time and the high degree of automation enable preventive investigations and can assist relationship managers in their customer due diligence procedures as well. Therefore, the measures taken can be considered effective and successfully implemented. The new requirements regarding customer investigations are fulfilled with the redesigned interactive search-supported process.

FUTURE TRENDS

To achieve fuzzy name matching, the current system uses a combination of both pattern matching and synonym lists. Despite the excellent operation, it is planned to test empirically whether an enlargement of the currently used synonym table would have a positive impact, and if better results would justify the potential negative impact on the system's response time. If this measure does not show the expected benefits or will eliminate the balance achieved between data, users and algorithms in the current system, indirect support of the user query could be considered by including a "query wizard" for an analysis of the query prior to execution in the system. As such a feature will only assist interactive users and will not be available for compliance checks, the decision needs to be evaluated properly.

CONCLUSION

This chapter depicts how a combination of organizational and technical measures led to a significant information quality improvement in customer investigations at Credit Suisse. First, the organizational centralization of responsibility for customer investigations concentrated the know-how necessary to interpret customer information and prevented incidents of costly redundant processes. In addition, the process was simplified for the inquirer as well as for the inquiry receiver. This simplification was made possible by a new application designed for customer investigations. This data-warehouse-based investigation application has proven its ability to boost the quality and speed of customer investigations. The increase in information quality and reduction in the cycle time of the process enable preventive investigations and proactive risk management, which has become necessary following recent regulatory developments. It has also turned out that both effects of the measures result in a significant cost saving.

The new CIP also meets the demands of taking the external developments described above (i.e., risk management, fight against terrorism, anti-money laundering) into account. The connections between subjects are not always obvious at first sight. By showing active relations as a result of the linked data sources, the investigation tool is able to highlight such connections.

Data have to reliable and often available immediately, but in the end a team with experts is still needed to exploit the entire functionality of this efficient system. Although the application was originally built to support the customer investigation process, it has the potential to be leveraged to support other banking processes as well.

REFERENCES

Ballou, D. P., & Pazer, H. L. (1985). Modeling data and process quality in multi-input, multi-output information systems. *Management Science, 31*(2), 150-162.

Basel Committee on Banking Supervision. (2001). *Customer due diligence for banks.* Basel: Bank for International Settlements.

Basel Committee on Banking Supervision. (2003). *Overview of the New Basel Capital Accord.* Basel: Bank for International Settlements.

Betts, M. (2001). Data quality should be a boardroom issue. *Computerworld.* Retrieved May 23, 2005, from http://www.computerworld.com/softwaretopics/erp/story/0,10801,66636,00.html

Betts, M. (2001). Dirty data. *Computerworld.* Retrieved May 23, 2005, from http://www.computerworld.com/softwaretopics/erp/story/0,10801,66618,00.html

Binstock, A. & Rex, J. (1995). *Practical algorithms for programmers.* Reading, MA: Addison-Wesley.

English, L. P. (1999). *Improving data warehouse and business information quality: Methods for reducing costs and increasing profits.* New York: Wiley.

Eppler, M. J., & Wittig, D. (2000). Conceptualizing information quality: A review of information quality frameworks from the last ten years. *Proceedings of 5th International Conference on Information Quality.* Cambridge, MA.

Financial Action Task Force. (2001). *Special recommendations on terrorist financing.* Retrieved May 23, 2005, from http://www.fatf-gafi.org

Helfert, M., Zellner, G., & Sousa, C. (2002). Data quality problems and proactive data quality management in data-warehouse-systems. In *Proceedings of BIT-World 2002*, Guyaquil, Ecuador.

Huang, K.-T., Lee, Y. W., & Wang, R. Y. (1999). *Quality information and knowledge.* New York: Prentice Hall.

Jurafsky, D., & Martin, J. H. (2000). *Speech and language processing: An introduction to natural language processing, computational linguistics, and speech recognition.* New York: Prentice Hall.

Klesse, M., Herrmann, C., Brändli, P., Mügeli, T., & Maier, D. (2004). *Customer investigation process at Credit Suisse: Meeting the rising demand of regulators.* Presented at the 9th International Conference on Information Quality (ICIQ 2004), Cambridge, MA.

Liu, L., & Chi, L. N. (2002). Evolutional data quality: A theory-specific view. In *Proceedings of 7th International Conference on Information Quality (ICIQ 2002),* Cambridge, MA.

Lutz, R. (2001). *The use of phonological information in automatic name screening.* Retrieved May 23, 2005, from http://www.las-inc.com

Miller, H. (1996). The multiple dimensions of information quality. *Information Systems Management, 13*(2), 79-82.

Milstein, S. (2002, December 30). Taming the task of checking for terrorists' names. *New York Times.* Retrieved May 23, 2005, from http://ygraine.membrane. com/enterhtml(live/Business/tunnel/ID_Terrorists.html

PricewaterhouseCoopers. (2002). *Global data management survey. The new economy is the data economy.* New York.

Redman, T. C. (1996). *Data quality for the information age.* Boston: Artech House.

Redman, T. C. (2005). *Navesink Consulting Group.* New York. Retrieved June 16, 2005, from http://www.dataqualitysolutions.com/index.shtml

Te'eni, D. (1993). Behavioral aspects of data production and their impact on data quality. *Journal of Database Management, 4*(2), 30-38.

Schlott-Kotschote, A. (2004). *Transkription arabischer Schriften.* Berlin: Klaus Schwarz Verlag.

Taft, R. L. (1970). *Name search techniques* (Special Rep. No. 1). Bureau of Systems Development, New York State Identification and Intelligence System, Albany, MA.

The Wolfsberg Group. (2002). *The suppression of the financing of terrorism — Wolfsberg statement.* Retrieved May, 23, 2005, from http://www.wolfsberg-principles.com

The Wolfsberg Group. (2003). *The Wolfsberg AML principles — frequently asked questions with regard to politically exposed persons.* Retrieved May, 23, 2005, from http://www.wolfsberg-principles.com

US Department of the Treasury — Office of Foreign Assets Control (OFAC). (2004). *Specially designated nationals and blocked persons (OFAC list).* Retrieved May, 23, 2005, from http://www.treas.gov/offices/enforcement/ofac/sdn/

US Government. (2001). To deter and punish terrorist acts in the United States and around the world, to enhance law enforcement investigatory tools, and for other purposes. In *H.R.3162.* Washington: US Government.

Wand, Y., & Wang, R. Y. (1996). Anchoring data quality dimensions in ontological foundations. *Communications of the ACM, 39*(11), 86-95.

Wang, R. Y., Reddy, M. P., & Kon, H. B. (1995). Toward quality data: An attribute-based approach. *Decision Support Systems, 13*(3-4), 349-372.

Wang, R. Y., & Strong, D. M. (1996). Beyond accuracy: What data quality means to data consumers. *Journal of Management of Information Systems, 12*(4), 5-33.

Wild, S. (1982). Arabische Eigennamen. In W. Fischer (Ed.), *Grundriss der arabischen Philologie Bd. I: Sprachwissenschaft*. Wiesbaden.

Winter, M., Herrmann, C., & Helfert, M. (2003). Datenqualitätsmanagement für Data-Warehouse-Systeme — Technische und organisatorische Realisierung am Beispiel der Credit Suisse. In E. Von Maur & R. Winter (Eds.), *Data warehouse management* (pp. 221-240). Wien: Springer.

Zadeh, L. A. (1965). Fuzzy sets. *Information and Control*, 8, 338-353.

Chapter IV

Assessing Mass Consumer Information Quality Requirements Using Conjoint Analysis

Elizabeth M. Pierce, Indiana University of Pennsylvania, USA

ABSTRACT

This chapter demonstrates how conjoint analysis can be used to improve the design and delivery of mass consumer information products. Conjoint analysis is a technique that market researchers have used since the 1960s to better understand how buyers make complex purchase decisions, to estimate preferences and importance ratings for product features, and to predict buyer behavior. This chapter describes the steps for performing a conjoint analysis to assess information quality preferences of potential home buyers interested in using a real estate Web site to help them locate properties for sale. The author hopes that this tutorial will convince information systems professionals of the usefulness of conjoint analysis as a tool for discerning how to prioritize information quality requirements so that the resulting systems produce information products that better serve the needs of their customers.

INTRODUCTION

For much of its history, the focus of the information systems (IS) field has been the automation of internal business operations and tracking metrics about the current state of an organization. Today this focus is broadening as an increasing number of firms view their information as more than just a collection of records or reports, but as assets to aid in tasks such as decision-making. Furthermore, many companies are now in the business of selling these information assets in a mass market environment. In order to successfully design, develop, and distribute information products to a multitude of consumers in a competitive environment, companies must take a serious look at how they market and manufacture their data-based merchandise.

Since the early 1990s individuals like Richard Wang, Yang Lee, Leo Pipino, and Diane Strong (Wang et al., 1998) have advocated that organizations adopt the notion that their data records and information products[1] are an end-deliverable that satisfies consumer needs, rather than some by-product of a computer system. Wang et al.'s (1998) approach recommends that organizations adopt four principles for managing information as a product:

1.   Organizations must understand their consumers' information needs.
2.   Organizations must manage information as the product of a well-defined information process that incorporates technology as well as organizational behavioral factors.
3.   Organizations must manage the life cycle of their information products.
4.   Organizations should appoint an information product manager (IPM) to manage their information processes and resulting products.

Organizations seeking to adopt these principles have traditionally turned to the total quality management (TQM) literature for guidance. Similar to a manufacturing system that uses an assembly line to convert raw materials into physical products, an information system can be viewed as an information manufacturing system that converts raw data into information products. The information product paradigm allows for proven TQM principles from manufacturing to be applied to the improvement of the design, development, manufacture, and distribution of information products. These classical TQM principles can be adapted to the improvement of information products through the undertaking of five tasks (Lee et al., 2006):

1.   Articulate an information quality vision in business terms.
2.   Establish central responsibility for information quality through the information product manager.
3.   Educate information product suppliers, manufacturers, and consumers.
4.   Teach new information quality skills based on the cycle of defining information quality dimensions, measuring information quality metrics, analyzing

root causes for information quality problems, and improving information products.

5.   Institutionalize continuous information quality improvement.

While the TQM literature provides much assistance in improving the quality of information products, the market research field also provides valuable insights because its knowledge base can help firms to better understand their consumers' information needs through the use of techniques for identifying customer-based quality requirements for products and services as well as the relative importance of these requirements. This is particularly important because unlike information systems of the past that were designed to support the needs of a few individuals within the organization, many of today's information systems must serve the needs of a wide range of customers external to the organization. The customer-based quality criteria for the information products produced by these systems should be balanced with other information product design constraints such as cost considerations, regulatory requirements, privacy restrictions, and standards such as uniform data formats in order to achieve an overall quality strategy for the information products.

A comprehensive information product quality strategy is the key to successfully improving and monitoring the quality of information products. The information product quality strategy should be part of the requirements analysis used to develop or modify the information system that will ultimately manufacture the information product. From the design of the conceptual model and system specifications through the database implementation, software engineering, and hardware selection and then on to quality assurance, acceptance testing, changeover, and finally the operation and maintenance phases, the information systems development group should be guided by the customer-based information product quality strategy. During the operation and maintenance phase of an information system's life, the information product manager will need to continuously monitor the system's output in order to assess how well the information products being produced by the information system are meeting the consumers' quality specifications and expectations. If the information product manager discovers gaps between the quality of an information product being produced and the consumers' quality criteria, then this signals that it is time to revisit the information product quality strategy and to implement changes in the information system that manufactures the information product. In addition, from the first contact with the consumer through the manufacture of the information product to any after-manufacture support, it is important for the information product manager to have precisely defined quality objectives for that information product. The design of the information product quality strategy should take into account the different needs of consumers so that the resources allocated to information quality can be used in the most cost-effective way (Christopher, 1998). The Appendix lists the areas that must be addressed when specifying the quality strategy for an information product(s).

The remainder of this chapter is organized as follows. The background section will explain the basic steps necessary to produce an information product quality strategy. The main thrust of the chapter will explain how one marketing technique known as conjoint analysis plays an important role in helping managers to formulate requirements for their information products quality strategy. The chapter then closes with a discussion of future trends and conclusions.

BACKGROUND

Before one can begin developing an information product quality strategy, it is important to express an overall vision of what role information quality should play in the culture and shared values of the organization, followed by a clear definition of the precise information quality objectives, especially as they relate to the overall quality mix of the organization. The information product quality strategy should then document the mechanisms by which these objectives will be achieved for a specified information product or set of information products. Besides expressing the vision, the culture, and the shared values of the organization as well as defining the scope of the business, this mission statement should provide guidance and direction to individuals in the firm as to the actions they should take. In particular, the mission statement should explain how information quality fits into the company's intended strategic positioning. Defining the mission statement requires the involvement of the firm's top management with input from those responsible for implementing the programs that will support the stated mission. The mission statement should be reviewed on a regular basis since a company's mission statement must be adjusted to reflect changes in the competitive environment (Christopher, 1998).

Although few examples of mission statements incorporating information quality exist, Albrecht and Zemke (1985) have summarized the prerequisites for a meaningful service mission statement which can be applied to the requirements for a successful information quality mission statement:

1.   It is nontrivial; it has weight. It must be more than simply a "motherhood" statement or slogan. It must be reasonably concrete and action-oriented.
2.   It must convey a concept or a mission which people in the organization can understand, relate to, and somehow put into action.
3.   It must offer or relate to a critical benefit premise that is important to the customer. It must focus on something the customer is willing to pay for.
4.   It must differentiate the organization in some meaningful way from its competitors in the eyes of the customer.
5.   If, at all possible, it should be simple, unitary, easy to put into words, and easy to explain to the customer.

Once the mission is well understood, the formulation of an information product quality strategy should follow these phases:

1. Identify information product customers and their quality dimensions.
2. Establish the relative importance of these quality dimensions for the information product.
3. Determine if "customer clusters" of information quality preferences exist. If customer segments exist with very different quality needs, it may be necessary to prioritize information quality objectives for the information product.
4. Based on the information collected for steps 1, 2, and 3, construct a customer-based information product quality strategy (see Appendix for an example).

Step 1 recommends that the information product manager begin the development of an information product quality strategy by identifying the customers for the information product in question as well as obtaining a list of quality dimensions that are important to these customers. The task of identifying customers who are the primary sources of influence upon the information quality specifications and expectations is crucial and often difficult. An information product may have customers both internal and external to the firm. In addition, an individual who receives an information product may only be acting as an agent for others. The information product manager will need to talk to both business and systems personnel to help discover exactly who uses (or who are potential users of) a given information product.

Once a representative set of information product consumers has been identified, the information product manager can use either interviews or questionnaires to elicit the significant quality dimensions that customers associate with the information product as well as the individual data components that make up the information product. Wang and Strong (1996) provide a hierarchical listing of 15 quality dimensions which are grouped into four major quality categories: intrinsic, contextual, representational, and accessibility.

- **Intrinsic quality:** This includes the dimensions of believability, accuracy, objectivity, and reputation. It implies that information has quality in its own right.
- **Contextual quality:** This includes the dimensions of value-added, relevancy, timeliness, completeness, and appropriate amount of data. It highlights the requirement that information quality must be considered within the context of the task at hand.
- **Representational quality:** This includes the dimensions of interpretability, ease of understanding, representational consistency, and concise representation. It addresses the way the computer system stores and presents information.

- **Accessibility quality:** This includes the dimensions of accessibility and access security. It emphasizes that the computer system must be accessible but secure.

Information product managers will find this list of data quality dimensions a useful starting point in engaging consumers in a discussion of the quality of an information product and its source data components.

It is important to keep in mind that the purpose here is to ensure that relevant and meaningful measures of quality are generated by the information product consumers themselves. Once the quality dimensions for the information product and its underlying data components are defined, the information product manager can proceed to step 2 to determine the relative importance of the information product quality dimensions. This step is necessary so that the information product manager can determine which consumers, source data components, and information quality dimensions to focus on when formulating a sound information product quality strategy.

Because customers will vary in their views as to which data components and quality dimensions are most important in determining a meaningful information product, the information product manager must devise the information product quality objectives depending on the customers' answers to these questions (Christopher, 1998):

1. From a customer's viewpoint, how important is a particular quality dimension compared to the other quality dimensions in the information quality mix? (e.g., for an information product consumer, how does the "time to access" the information product compare to the "ease of access"?)
2. Which basic data components and their associated quality dimensions contribute most to the overall customer satisfaction with the information product?
3. Which dimensions of information product quality are seen as priorities by customers when they make their choice of information product supplier?
4. Are customers relatively uniform in their quality preferences for an information product or do different customer preference segments exist? If different customer preference segments do exist, which segments are the most influential in determining the information product quality strategy? Once the first three questions are understood, this last question can be answered during step 3 using data-mining techniques like cluster analysis to assess if there are distinct information quality preference groups within the customer population.

To determine which information product quality attributes and source data components are most important, the product manager can employ several techniques: ranking, weighting, and tradeoff analysis (Christopher, 1998). The ranking technique is typically done by asking a representative sample of consumers to rank order a list of information product quality concerns from the "most important" to the "least important." The disadvantage of this technique is that it works poorly in situations where there are a large number of information product quality issues for the consumer to consider. It also does not give the information product manager a sense of the relative importance of the various information product quality dimensions for the various data components that make up the information product.

As an alternative approach, the weighting technique incorporates a rating scale. For instance, customers could be asked to place a weight from 1 to 10 against each of the information product's quality concerns according to how much importance they attach to that issue. The disadvantage of this technique is that most respondents will tend to rate most of the information product's principal data components and their associated quality dimensions as highly important, especially since this list of quality items was probably originally generated on the basis of their significance to customers.

The last technique, tradeoff analysis, or conjoint analysis as it is known in the marketing research field, is based on the concept of exchanges. The fundamental premise of this method is that people cannot reliably express how they weight separate quality aspects of an information product, but it is possible to "tease these out" using the more realistic approach of asking for evaluations of quality concepts through analyzing consumers' preferences when it comes to trading off one quality concern against another (Orme, 2004a). It is this technique that will be the focus of the rest of this chapter.

MAIN THRUST OF THIS CHAPTER

Conjoint analysis is a technique that has been applied to solving marketing problems such as understanding how buyers make complex purchase decisions, estimating preferences and importance ratings for product features, and predicting buyer behavior. The origins of conjoint analysis can be traced to work done in the sixties by mathematical psychologists Luce and Tukey, and in the seventies by McFadden, a 2000 Nobel Prize winner in Economics (Orme, 2004a). The main idea behind conjoint analysis is that respondents evaluate different product profiles composed of multiple conjoined features or attributes. Based on how respondents evaluate these combined elements, it is possible to deduce the preference scores that they might have assigned to individual components of the product that would have resulted in those overall evaluations. It is considered a "back-door" or decompositional approach to estimating people's preferences for features rather than an explicit or compositional approach of simply asking respondents to rate the various components.

A typical conjoint analysis study follows these six steps:

1. **Choose product attributes:** In the case of an information product, one needs to identify those features about which one would like to obtain customer preferences. These elements could pertain to the information product's content, presentation, storage, accessibility, usage, or services offered.

2. **Choose the values or options for each attribute:** For each characteristic under consideration, one must choose several options or levels for the consumer to compare. For example, suppose one would like to find out customers' preferences for the extent to which the source data for the information product has been verified, that is, the extent to which the source data provides an accurate representation of their real-life values. To describe the level of data verification, one might choose values such as "100% Verified," "75% Verified," "50% Verified," and "25% Verified." The choice of attribute options is typically under the control of the analyst, but the elements chosen should fulfill the following criteria (Orme, 2002):

    - Levels should be concise statements with concrete meanings: Ranges (e.g., Product costs between 3 to 5 dollars) and vague language (e.g., superior performance) should be avoided. One should try to use specific language to quantify as much as possible the exact meaning of each level.
    - Attributes should be independent. The meanings of the different attributes should not overlap.
    - Levels within each attribute should be mutually exclusive. For instance, if an information product can contain both data option A and data option B, then one should either specify two separate attributes (Data Option A or Not; Data Option B or Not) or one should create a single attribute whose levels describe all potential combinations of these features (Both Data Option A and B, Data Option A Only, Data Option B Only, Neither Option).
    - Attribute levels should cover the full range of possibilities for existing information products as well as information products that may not yet exist, but that the analyst wants to investigate.
    - Prohibitions should be used sparingly, or not at all. It is usually better to prompt respondents that they may see product attribute combinations during the interview that are not yet available in the market or that seem unlikely and to urge respondents to answer as if these information products were actually available today, than to simply prohibit such combinations.
    - The number of levels chosen to define an attribute can have a significant bearing on the results. It is a good idea to at least approximately balance the number of levels across attributes. Researchers in conjoint analysis have found that all else being equal, attributes with more levels tend to receive more importance from respondents than attributes with fewer levels. In addition, researchers have found it is best to limit the number of levels for quantitative attributes to no more than five.

- Attributes that cannot be adequately described in words should be represented via multimedia.
- The numbers of attributes being considered should be kept to no more than six. Researchers have found that when faced with too many attributes to consider, respondents often resort to simplification strategies to deal with the complexity.

3. **Define products as a combination of attribute options:** In this step, the analyst must define a collection of information product configurations based on the different attribute combinations. For example, suppose one wants to assess consumer preferences for an information product based on its cost to produce ($0.65, $1.25, $2.50), the time to manufacture it (1 day, 3 days, 5 days), and the accuracy of its data (100%, 90%, 80%). With 3 different attribute, each with 3 different levels, one can derive 27 different configurations for consumers to compare and rank according to their preferences. Each configuration represents a different combination of attribute options. For instance, one configuration of the information product may cost $0.65, take 5 days to obtain it, and is 80% accurate while another configuration may cost $2.50, take 3 days to obtain it, and is 100% accurate. Orthogonal design techniques are often used to reduce the number of product configurations to a manageable number for consumers to compare.

4. **Choose the form in which the combinations of attributes are to be presented to the respondents:** To find out how much consumers prefer an information product that possesses a certain combination of attribute levels, one can choose from several variations of conjoint analysis which differ depending on the style of presentation used to collect the preference data. These variations include the following (Orme, 2004b):
   - **Self-explicated approach:** Respondents rank the levels for each information quality attribute from most- to least-preferred and then assign an importance weight to each attribute. The self-explicated context puts emphasis on evaluating information products in a systematic, quality dimension-by-quality dimension manner, rather than judging the information product as a whole or in a competitive context.
   - **Traditional conjoint comparisons:** Respondents are presented with two or more different profiles for an information product and are asked to rank (or rate) the different profiles according to preference.
   - **Choice-based conjoint analysis:** Respondents are presented with two or more profiles for an information product and are asked to choose which profile they would use. Often this approach includes the option of choosing none of the above.

5. **Decide how responses will be aggregated:** In this phase one must decide if the response data collected should be examined individually, pooled (or averaged) into a single utility function, or broken into segments of respondents who have similar preferences.

6.   **Select the technique to be used to analyze the collected data:** One common and simple method for analyzing conjoint analysis response data is to use ordinary least squares to model how the different combinations of information product attributes influence the customer's preference ranking. For individuals wishing to obtain a more sophisticated analysis, the Internet can be used to locate software vendors who specialize in selling packages that execute more advance conjoint analysis algorithms on the collected data.

To illustrate these steps, consider the following example adapted from Joseph Curry (2004). Suppose the accounting department at XYZ Manufacturers wants to learn more about its customers' quality preferences for the invoices that it produces. From experience, accounting personnel know that their customers care mainly about three important quality features for this particular information product:

Table 1.

Accuracy of the Invoice	Time to Produce the Invoice	Cost to Provide the Invoice
100%	1 day	$0.65
90%	3 days	$1.25
80%	5 days	$2.50

Table 2. Accounting manager's rankings: Accuracy vs. time

		Time to Produce Invoice		
		1 day	3 days	5 days
Accuracy Of the Invoice	**100%**	1	2	4
	90%	3	5	6
	80%	7	8	9

Table 3. Accounting manager's rankings: Cost vs. time

		Time to Produce Invoice		
		1 day	3 days	5 days
Cost to Produce the Invoice	**$0.65**	1	4	7
	$1.25	2	5	8
	$2.50	3	6	9

- Accuracy of the invoice
- Time needed to produce the invoice
- Cost to provide the invoice

Accounting personnel further know that there is a range of feasible alternatives for each of these features as seen in Table 1.

Obviously, the ideal invoice would be 100% accurate, available in a single day, and only cost $0.65 to produce. However, it may not be possible to deliver an invoice that meets all those criteria. The accounting personnel will have to trade-off one information quality dimension against another, but what is the appropriate trade-off? To find out, the manager of the accounting department uses the self-explicated approach to rank his pair-wise conjoint comparisons of available trade-off choices as shown in Tables 2, 3, and 4.

Table 4. Accounting manger's rankings: Accuracy vs. cost

		Cost to Produce the Invoice		
		$0.65	$1.25	$2.50
Accuracy Of the Invoice	100%	1	2	3
	90%	4	5	6
	80%	7	8	9

Table 5. Accounting manager's utilities: Accuracy vs. time

		Time to Produce Invoice		
		1 day - 50	3 days - 25	5 days - 0
Accuracy Of the Invoice	100% - 100	150 (1)	125 (2)	100 (4)
	90% - 60	110 (3)	85 (5)	60 (6)
	80% - 0	50 (7)	25 (8)	0 (9)

Table 6. Accounting manager's utilities: Cost vs. time

		Time to Produce Invoice		
		1 day - 50	3 days - 25	5 days - 0
Cost to Produce the Invoice	$0.65 - 20	70 (1)	45 (4)	20 (7)
	$1.25 - 5	55 (2)	30 (5)	5 (8)
	$2.50 - 0	50 (3)	25 (6)	0 (9)

Table 7. Accounting manger's utilities: Accuracy vs. cost

		Cost to Produce the Invoice		
		$0.65 - 20	**$1.25 - 5**	**$2.50 - 0**
Accuracy Of the Invoice	**100% - 100**	120 (1)	105 (2)	100 (3)
	90% - 60	80 (4)	65 (5)	60 (6)
	80% - 0	20 (7)	5 (8)	0 (9)

Table 8. Summary of utilities for the manager of the accounting department

Accuracy of the Invoice	Time to Produce the Invoice	Cost to Provide the Invoice
100% = 100 Utilities	1 day = 50 Utilities	$0.65 = 20 Utilities
90% = 60 Utilities	3 days = 25 Utilities	$1.25 = 5 Utilities
80% = 0 Utilities	5 days = 0 Utilities	$2.50 = 0 Utilities

Table 9. Comparison of two quality strategies for an invoice

Accounting Manager	Invoice #1	Invoice #2
Accuracy of Invoice	100% = 100 Utilities	90% = 60 Utilities
Time to Produce the Invoice	5 days = 0 Utilities	1 day = 50 Utilities
Cost to Produce the Invoice	$1.25 = 5 Utilities	$2.50 = 0 Utilities
Total Utility	105 Utilities	110 Utilities

The goal of conjoint analysis is to figure out a set of values known as utilities for the different quality levels of invoice accuracy, availability, and cost so that when these values are added together for an invoice they reproduce the accounting manager's rank orders. These utility values can then be applied to an invoice quality combination to get an estimate of the accounting manager's preferences. Regardless of the technique chosen to obtain stable estimates of respondent utilities, most good conjoint studies collect 1.5 to 3 times more observations than parameters to be estimated.

Tables 5, 6, and 7 show one possible scheme for modeling utilities so that when these values are added together they reproduce the   manager's rank orders for the invoice's quality dimensions. Notice that there is some arbitrariness in the magnitudes of these numbers even though their relationships to each other are fixed. Once a complete set of utility values that capture a customer's tradeoffs are computed, they can be used to estimate a customer's preferences for an information product's quality mix (Table 8).

By applying the derived utilities in this example to two types of quality profiles for invoices that the accounting department is considering, the utility results for each quality profile are obtained (Table 9). Based on these results, one would expect the manager of the accounting department to prefer Invoice 2 over Invoice 1 because it has the larger total utility value.

It is important to keep in mind that these particular results only reflect the preferences of the manager of the accounting department. The accounting department should collect the responses from other individuals who have a stake in the quality of the invoices to see how their preferences compare to those of the accounting manager.

Although not explicitly categorized as information product studies, some researchers have already used conjoint analysis to investigate how to improve the delivery of online information. Dreze and Zufryden (1997) developed and applied a conjoint analysis based methodology to evaluate the design and the effectiveness of promotional content on the Web. For this study, the authors wanted to know how Web site attributes like choice of background, image size, sound file display, and the presence of celebrity endorsements might impact the effectiveness of the Web site as measured by the visitor's time spent per page, total time spent on the visit, and total number of pages accessed during the site visit. To collect their data for this conjoint study, the authors devised a randomization procedure whereby Web surfers were assigned one of 8 different Web configurations based on the Web surfer's IP address. Once assigned to a particular Web site configuration, the visitor's mouse click streams were tracked and logged. An analysis of the data provided evidence that certain combinations of Web site attributes were more effective then others in increasing the number of pages accessed and the time spent on the site.

In another study related to Web site design, Liechty, Ramaswamy and Cohen (2001) developed a menu-based form of conjoint analysis to study potential advertisers' willingness to pay based on additional services for content Web sites and searchable online databases. These additional services include items such as text, graphics, links to other sites, and audio messages. Approximately 360 advertisers participated in the study, completing a survey comparing sample menus of customized services and their specific prices. The analysis of the data was then used to devise an advertising pricing structure based on the different Web services offered.

Finally, Lipke (2001) demonstrated how conjoint analysis can even be incorporated into a Web site's programming to enhance the customer's buying experience through dynamic content delivery. Lands' End Web site personal shopper is a recommendation engine for customers who want help sorting through the retailer's large selection of clothing apparel. Customers visiting the Web site can fill out a brief survey which queries them on their preferred outfit preferences. Using conjoint analysis to scrutinize the responses, the Web site then presents the shopper with a list of suitable apparel options based on the customer's survey responses.

To demonstrate more explicitly how conjoint analysis can be used to evaluate mass consumers' tradeoffs for different information quality dimensions, consider the following scenario. Suppose a real estate agency is working on a project to improve their existing Web site. The Web site's main purpose is to encourage potential home buyers to search and view online information about available homes listed for sale. The real estate agency would like to know how the choice for different information quality dimensions might impact a potential home buyer's preference for using the realtor's Web site. In order to answer this question, the agency has commissioned a professor at a local university to perform a conjoint analysis study for a selected group of volunteers. It should be noted that although this example is hypothetical, it is based on a composite of actual online, real estate listings such as those found at www.indianapamultilist.com and online.indianagazette.com.

The first issue that the professor discusses with the realtors is which attributes and levels to focus on for the conjoint analysis study. For this example, the agency decides they would like to examine potential home buyers' preferences when considering these four information quality changes to their Web site.

- **Accessibility:** Accessibility refers to the extent to which data is available, or easily and quickly retrievable. The realtors would like to know if their listing of properties for sale should be accessible to the public or restricted to those individuals who have registered to access the site. Registration would be free, but potential home buyers would be asked to provide some account data (name, username, password required, other contact data like address and phone would be optional) and to answer a few questions about their purchase plans. The advantage of requiring registration is that it would provide valuable information to the real estate agency about potential home buyers and their needs. For potential home buyers seeking assistance, the registration would give them an opportunity to establish a dialog with the real estate agency. The disadvantage is that registration could discourage some individuals from visiting the Web site thus reducing the number of people looking at the advertised homes, a key factor in a successful, real estate listing Web site. Hence, the realtors are very interested in knowing how the presence of Web site registration might impact a potential home buyer's preference for using the Web site.
- **Relevancy:** This attribute refers to the extent to which the data is applicable and helpful for the task at hand. The real estate agency is curious as to how much information should be displayed about each property and the extent to which this additional information adds to a person's preference rating for the Web site. The real estate agency is currently considering two different types of profiles: basic property data versus extended property data. Both profiles would display information such as the property location, category (condo,

Table 10. Comparison of home information profiles

Basic Property Data	Extended Property Data

• Realtor Data (Name, Phone Number, Address, and E-mail Information)
• Property Location (Address, City, State, Zip code)
• Property Category (Condo, Single Family, Duplex, etc.)
• Home Style (A Frame, Ranch, etc.)
• Asking Price
• Current Status (Active, Sale Pending)
• Number of Bedrooms
• Number of Bathrooms
• A brief text description of home and property features such as the yard size, layout description, presence of a pool, eat-in kitchen, sun porch, etc.
• Photograph(s) of Property
	• Includes all the information available in the list of Basic Property Data
	• A fact sheet containing the following information:
	  o Total Square Footage of Home
	  o Lot Dimensions
	  o Total Acreage of Property
	  o Garage Type
	  o Number of Garage Stalls
	  o Fuel Type
	  o Sewer Type
	  o A/C Indicator
	  o Year Built
	  o School District
	  o Township
	  o Township/Borough Taxes
	  o School Taxes
	  o Zoning

duplex, single family, etc.), total bedrooms, total bathrooms, asking price, and a brief text description of key home and property features. However the Extended Home Data would also include a fact sheet with additional data about the property such as the type of heating system, annual taxes, square footage, and property acreage. Table 10 describes these two possibilities in more detail.

• **Value-added feature:** The real estate agency is also contemplating adding a new feature that would allow potential home buyers to take a virtual tour of the inside of the property and the surrounding neighborhood. The agency is hoping that this type of information would give them a competitive advantage over other realtors' Web sites. The agency would like to know how much value this attribute contributes to potential home buyers' preference ratings for the Web site.

Table 11. Search engine choices

Search Engine 1 Capabilities (Keyword Search)	Search Engine 2 Capabilities (Fixed Field Search)

• Select a property category from a list (condo, duplex, single family, etc.)
• Choose a distance (0, 10, 20 miles, etc.) from a city selected from a list.
• Select Price Range (Min and Max Price)
• Number of Bedrooms (Any, 1, 2, 3, etc.)
• Other descriptive home, property, and amenities data may be searched using any or all up to 4 keywords as well as an exclusion keyword.
	• For any quantitative data available on the home, one can enter a search range.
	  o Total Bedrooms (Min and Max)
	  o Total Bathrooms (Min and Max)
	  o Acreage Size (Min and Max)
	  o Total Square Feet (Min and Max)
	  o Garage Stalls (Min and Max)
	  o Year Built (Min and Max)
	• For any qualitative data available on the home, one can either select all values, one value, or multiple values from a list.
	  o Property Category
	  o City
	  o Style
	  o Township
	  o School District

• **Appropriate amount of data:** This attribute refers to the extent to which the volume of data is appropriate for the task at hand. In terms of the Web site, this will be determined by the type of search engine used to retrieve the list of properties matching the criteria that potential home buyers enter. For this study, the realtors would like to know if potential home buyers prefer one style of search engine versus another. One search engine under consideration allows for key word searches and a few fixed field searches such as the number of bedrooms, price range, geographic distance from a given city, and property type. The other search engine allows one to enter minimum and maximum ranges for any available numeric data values like price, number of bedrooms, number of baths, and drop down selections for any available qualitative data values like property type, city, and home style. A comparison of the two styles of search engines is listed in Table 11.

Table 12. Web site preference ratings from a single respondent

Registration Required (1 = Yes, 0 = No)	Type of Property Data Displayed (1 = Extended, 0 = Basic)	Virtual Tour Feature (1 = Present, 0 = Not Available)	Search Engine Type (1 = Fixed Field Style, 0 = Keyword Style)	Preference Rating (10 = Most Preferred, 0 = Least Preferred)
Yes (1)	Basic (0)	NA (0)	Keyword (0)	0
No (0)	Basic (0)	NA (0)	Keyword (0)	2
Yes (1)	Basic (0)	NA (0)	Fixed Field (1)	1
No (0)	Basic (0)	NA (0)	Fixed Field (1)	4
Yes (1)	Basic (0)	Present (1)	Keyword (0)	5
No (0)	Basic (0)	Present (1)	Keyword (0)	8
Yes (1)	Basic (0)	Present (1)	Fixed Field (1)	5
No (0)	Basic (0)	Present (1)	Fixed Field (1)	9
Yes (1)	Extended (1)	NA (0)	Keyword (0)	1
No (0)	Extended (1)	NA (0)	Keyword (0)	4
Yes (1)	Extended (1)	NA (0)	Fixed Field (1)	1
No (0)	Extended (1)	NA (0)	Fixed Field (1)	5
Yes (1)	Extended (1)	Present (1)	Keyword (0)	5
No (0)	Extended (1)	Present (1)	Keyword (0)	9
Yes (1)	Extended (1)	Present (1)	Fixed Field (1)	6
No (0)	Extended (1)	Present (1)	Fixed Field (1)	10

Having decided on a set of attributes and levels, the realtors are now ready for the professor to create the survey instrument and to begin collecting preference ratings for the different attribute combinations from a sample of volunteers. The professor designs a series of mock-ups, each one representing a different version of the Web site. For example, one mock-up depicts the Web site with public registration, the keyword search engine, basic home information, and no virtual tour feature. The professor interviews each volunteer, presenting them with a series of mock-ups and asking them to arrange the different Web site versions in order of preference. The volunteers rate each mock-up on a scale of 0 to 10 where 0 indicates no preference and 10 represents the highest level of preference. The results of the survey for one volunteer are presented in Table 12 .

To analyze the survey response for an individual volunteer, the professor specifies an ordinary least squares (OLS) model as follows: Model: Y (Preference Rating) = constant + b_1 Register + b_2 Home Info + b_3 Virtual Tour + b_4 Search Type + ε (error) where:

Register = 0 if publicly available, 1 if site registration is required

Home Info = 0 if Basic Property Data is provided, 1 if Extended Property Data is provided.

Virtual Tour = 0 if no virtual tour feature is available, 1 if virtual tour feature is available.

Search Type = 0 if Keyword Style Search Engine provided, 1 if Fixed Field Search Engine provided.

Table 13. Excel regression output

Regression Statistics				
Multiple R	0.99096715			
R Square	0.982015893			
Adjusted R Square	0.975476218			
Standard Error	0.494285527			
Observations	16			
ANOVA				
	df	SS	MS	F
Regression	4	146.75	36.6875	150.1627907
Residual	11	2.6875	0.244318182	
Total	15	149.4375		
	Coefficients	Standard Error	T Stat	P-value
Intercept	3.0625	0.276314009	11.08340473	2.62098E-07
Register	-3.375	0.247142763	-13.65607455	3.04832E-08
Home Info	0.875	0.247142763	3.540463772	0.004628944
Virtual Tour	4.875	0.247142763	19.72544102	6.19833E-10
Search Type	0.875	0.247142763	3.540463772	0.004628944

Using Microsoft Excel, the professor fits the model to the preference data for this particular volunteer. Table 13 contains the output produced by Excel. The Excel output reveals several important clues about this particular volunteer's preferences. The R-Square value reflects the proportion of variation in the preference rankings that can be explained by the regression model. In this case, the respondent has an R-square close to 1, an indicator of high internal consistency for this volunteer's survey responses.

The estimated coefficients associated with the independent variables represent the utilities or preference scores for the different levels of each attribute. Each coefficient indicates the magnitude and direction that attribute's setting has on the preference score assuming the other attributes are held constant. Note the negative utility of -3.375 for the presence of a registration requirement. For this respondent, all else being equal, a Web site that requires registration reduces this individual's preference rating by 3.375 compared to a similar Web site whose contents are accessible to the public. In contrast, the presence of a virtual home tour has a positive utility of 4.875. This indicates that all else being equal, this feature greatly adds to the Web site preference ratings for this respondent. The coefficients for the type of search engine (0.875) and extended home information (0.875) are smaller. They suggest that for this respondent there is a positive increase in preference for the type of search engine and choice of home data, but the respondent appears to already be fairly satisfied with the base options for these attributes so the increase in preference is less. The standard errors of the coefficients reflect how precisely this model is able to estimate the coefficients (i.e., preference scores). Lower standard errors are better. Note for all these attributes the p-value associated with the t-statistic indicates is quite small (less than 0.05 is considered significant), indicating that all these attributes have a significant effect on this volunteer's preference rating for the Web site.

If this individual is representative of the population at large, then the results of this analysis seems to suggest if the real estate agency wants to increase the preference rating of their Web site in order to increase visits to their Web site, then they should consider making the registration optional and adding the virtual home tour feature. The choice of search engine and property profile data also makes a smaller, but still significant contribution to the overall preference rating. In practice, most conjoint analysis involves the collection of preference data from many different respondents. By reviewing the preference data from a sample of volunteers, the professor can employ other analytical techniques such as cluster analysis to determine if the respondents are fairly uniform in their preferences or if specific customer segments exist. Within each segment, the preference model could be used to obtain preference forecasts for each customer group depending on the choice of attribute levels. These preference forecasts can help the real estate agency to design a real estate listing Web site with the broadest appeal to its potential home buyer population.

FUTURE TRENDS

Although conjoint analysis is well known in the marketing research field, the IS profession has largely overlooked this technique for improving the design of information products. Given the growing mass consumer information product industry, firms should look at conjoint analysis as a potential tool for better understanding the data preferences and choices of their target customers. While conjoint analysis has been used to study many different types of physical products and services, few examples exist in the literature of applying conjoint analysis to information products. More research is needed to develop a body of literature as to what works best when evaluating information consumers' preferences and choices using conjoint analysis. For example, information products have quality dimensions such as believability that are unlike any attributes found for a physical product or service. How should one capture this concept in a trade-off investigation with other dimensions? There are many different types of information products ranging from a simple report to a complex hypertext data warehouse. As the complexity of the information product increases, how does this affect the trade-off investigation? A conjoint analysis can be expensive to conduct. Can it be demonstrated that the benefits of an improved information product outweigh the costs and by how much? Such questions can only be answered through IS practitioners and academics applying conjoint analysis to the investigation of consumer preferences for a variety of different types of information products and sharing their findings with others.

CONCLUSION

For companies whose information products serve a mass audience, thoroughly understanding their customers' needs and desires is critical. This chapter serves as a primer for information professionals interested in learning more about how they can assess consumer preferences for information products using a tool that has been used successfully by market researchers to study consumer preferences for physical products and services. After providing a general background about conjoint analysis, the bulk of the chapter is devoted to a tutorial that demonstrates how one can conduct a conjoint analysis to study what feature(s) a customer likes about a given information product and how these desired attributes contribute to predicting the overall preference rating. The chapter concludes with a discussion of further research needed to establish this technique within the information product design literature.

REFERENCES

Albrecht, K., & Zemke, R. (1985). *Service America.* Dow-Jones Irwin.

Christopher, M. (1998). *Logistics and supply chain management* (2nd ed.). NJ: Prentice Hall.

Curry, J. (2004). *Understanding conjoint analysis in 15 minutes.* Retrieved May 27, 2004, from www.sawtoothsoftware.com.

Dreze, X., & Zufryden, F. (1997). Testing Web site design and promotional content. *Journal of Advertising Research, 37*(2), 77-91.

Lee, Y. W., Pipino, L. L., Funk, J. D., & Wang, R. W. (2006). *Journey to data quality.* MIT Press.

Liechty, J., Ramaswamy, V., & Cohen, S. (2001). Choice menus for mass vustomizations: An experimental approach for analyzing customer demand with an application to a Web-based information service. *Journal of Marketing Research, 38*(2), 183-197.

Lipke, D. (2001). Product by design. *American Demographics, 23*(2), 38-41.

Orme, B. (2002). *Formulating attributes and levels in conjoint analysis.* Retrieved August 21, 2004, from www.sawtoothsoftware.com

Orme, B. (2004a). *Conjoint analysis: Thirty-something and counting,* Retrieved August 21, 2004, from www.sawtoothsoftware.com

Orme, B. (2004b). *Which conjoint method should I use?* Retrieved August 21, 2004 from the www.sawtoothsoftware.com

Wang, R. Y., & Strong, D. M. (1996). Beyond accuracy: What data quality means to data consumers. *Journal of Management Information Systems, 12*(4), 5-33.

Wang, R. Y., Lee, Y. W., Pipino, L. L., & Strong, D. M. (1998). Manage your information as a product. *Sloan Management Review, 39*(4), 95-105.

APPENDIX

Components of an Information Product Quality Strategy (Christopher, 1998)

Examples of Pre-Transaction Elements

- **Written information product quality policy** (Is it communicated internally or externally, is it understood, is it specific and quantified where possible?)
- **Accessibility** (Is the information product manager easy to contact/do business with? Is there a single point of contact for discussing quality issues with the information product?).
- **Organizational structure** (Is there an information quality management structure in place? What level of control do they have over the information manufacturing process?)

- **System flexibility** (Can the organization adapt their information quality delivery systems to meet particular customer needs?)

Examples of Transaction Elements
- **Order cycle time** (What is the elapsed time from order to delivery of the information product? What is the reliability/variation?)
- **Data availability** (What percentage of demand for each information product can be met from currently stored data? What are the quality levels of currently stored data components?)
- **Order fill rate** (What proportion of orders for information products are completely filled within the stated lead time?)
- **Customer driven data quality requirements and requests** (What are the customer-driven data quality specifications and expectations for the information product and its data components?)
- **Other information product requirements and requests** (Are there any other cost, regulatory, or standardization considerations that should be factored into the design and manufacture of the information product?)
- **Order status information** (How long does it take the organization to respond to a customer query with the required information? Does the information product manager inform the customer of problems or do the customers contact the information product manager?)

Examples of Post-Transaction Elements
- **Call out time** (If a problem with the information product is discovered, how long before the problem is fixed?)
- **Product tracing/warranty** (Can the organization track the location of information products once they are delivered to the customer? Are information products properly archived or disposed of once they are no longer needed?)
- **Customer complaints, claims, etc.** (How promptly does the organization deal with information product complaints? Does the organization measure customer satisfaction with their response?)

ENDNOTE

[1] An information product is identified in terms of the raw, source data and semi-processed component data items required to manufacture it. The phrase, information product, emphasizes the idea that this item is determined by more than just its input data, but also by the procedures used to construct it. Examples of information products include sales orders, packing lists, shipping labels, and customer invoices.

Chapter V

Applying Name Knowledge to Information Quality Assessments

Kimberly D. Hess, CASA 20th Judicial District, USA

John R. Talburt, University of Arkansas at Little Rock, USA

ABSTRACT

An introduction to name knowledge and its application to information quality assessments through an expert system is discussed in this chapter. The quality of name information has become an increasingly important issue as companies strive to implement customer relationship management (CRM) strategies in which the customer name plays an important role in the entity resolution process for data integration applications — ultimately impacting customer recognition systems. As many applications have been developed and refined for assessing and improving the quality of mailing address information, the potential exists to affect a similar success for customer name information. This chapter discusses both theoretical and practical considerations in the approach, design, and administration of systems for assessing the quality of name information.

INTRODUCTION

As companies worldwide attempt to implement customer relationship management (CRM) strategies, they begin to understand their success is directly dependent upon the quality of the data (Huang, 1999). For this reason, these same companies are also adopting information quality management practices, such as total data quality management (TDQM) (Wang, 1998) and Six Sigma. These practices are guidelines for approaching and implementing measurable quality initiatives. Necessary requirements for improving information quality are to establish desired levels of quality (goals), measure actual quality, analyze failures, and implement improvements. In the case of CRM, name information quality along with address information quality can be seen as the foundation for building enduring customer-centric relationships.

Although companies often maintain many items of information about their customers, the poor quality of the core elements of name and address are often the roadblocks to the successful and cost-effective data integration. Traditionally, processes have focused on the address portion of customer contact information, motivated primarily by postage savings realized from the reduction of undeliverable mail and U.S. Postal Service discounts offered for presorting large mailings. Often processes that extracted address information from raw transaction data would simply aggregate and move any residual information into a name field with little or no name information quality processing. Organizations are now realizing that the name components must also be analyzed and improved to ensure accurate customer data integration (CDI).

The value of an enterprise's existing expertise on name information can be drawn from a variety of resources and leveraged throughout the enterprise by embedding it into knowledge-based-driven expert systems. These systems usually employ some combination of software capabilities, encompassing standard and comprehensive name knowledge reference tables (e.g., common names, vulgar names, standard abbreviations) and pattern analysis. If for no other reason, consolidating name knowledge across an enterprise into a standard assessment tool can be a huge step toward improving the consistency of name information and lessen the complexity of algorithmic resolution of name information in downstream processing. From a standard assessment, additional business rules can be developed and applied for determining the acceptable level of name information quality allowable in specific processing steps or applications. The knowledge exercised in the evaluation of name data utilizing an expert system can provide significant improvement in the overall results of processing from data integration to complex recognition solutions.

BACKGROUND

When the customer data management industry was primarily focused on direct mail marketing (DMM), postal delivery point validation, cleansing, and correction were elevated to a fine art, but minimal quality checks were applied to the name component — a mail piece addressed to "RESIDENT, 123 OAK STREET" was just as deliverable as one sent to "JOHN SMITH, 123 OAK STREET." With the current emphasis on customer relationship management (CRM) and its dependence on accurate and comprehensive data integration, the situation is very different. Organizations now realize that the failure to recognize customers and maintain a complete view of their accounts and interactions carries with it opportunity costs in terms of lost sales and customer turnover. However, even more serious problems with customer relationships can arise from the poor quality of name information, including negative publicity and litigation. A recent example is the much publicized case of a financial services company sending a mail piece addressed to "Palestinian Bomber" (Sandell, 2005). For these reasons, assessing and improving the quality of name information is increasingly as important as the quality processing of the address information. Unfortunately, quality assessment and cleansing of name information are immature. Far fewer tools and resources exist for determining the quality of name information than for address information. One reason for the lack of tools is because name information is not subject to the same standardization and regulation as postal delivery point information.

The universe of postal delivery points for the U.S. and most other industrialized countries is typically well-defined. Complete tables of delivery points, though large, are usually within the online, or at least, near-line storage capacity of medium to large-scale computing systems. Even though some standardization and pattern analysis may be required, the quality assessment and cleansing of address information is largely a table-driven exercise. When used in validation processes, these files can drastically increase the confidence of deliverability and significantly impact the overall value of address-based applications.

Unlike address information, names for individuals and businesses can be created at will, and are difficult, if not impossible, to compile into a comprehensive, finite source. Consequently, the assessment of a name information as valid or invalid carries a higher degree of uncertainty than for address information. Assessing name information quality is a more difficult and more subjective process requiring the collection and cross-referencing of name knowledge from a variety of sources. Likewise, assessment results must be interpreted by various users and applied in the context of their needs. Referencing the definition of quality as "fitness for use," the assessment of "Bob" as a nickname may indicate low quality for a data integration application and call for transformation to "Robert," whereas it may be considered high quality for a marketing application that relies on contacting the user by his "preferred name." As businesses continue to use multiple channels of customer contact, an increased priority exists for data integration solutions to be based upon high quality data. Considering that a customer's name and address information are the most commonly encountered items for customer identification, the application of name knowledge to the quality assessment of name information is a key component in the critical path for improving the quality of data integration and ultimately CRM applications.

NAME KNOWLEDGE RESOURCES

Data Resources

Several methods exist for gathering data to drive the assessment for name information. For example in the U.S., the registered names in databases such as the Census, Social Security Death Index, Fortune 500 Business List, and USPS standard business abbreviations maintained for data accuracy purposes are all sources of name knowledge. Various Internet sites maintain lists for vulgar words, phrases, and suspicious names. Prioritization of data sources by confidence can be helpful in applying business rules during the assessment process. Sources such as the Social Security Death Index file with factual and verifiable names would be considered a higher priority to validate name information, whereas names provided from corporate-specific solutions, which vary from customer to customer, should be incorporated only after research across multiple verifiable sources. In general, the reliability of self-reported name information is roughly proportional to what is perceived to be the gain to the individual reporting the information. For example, one expects reliability of information reported by Social Security claimants to be higher than that reported for Census purposes, but Census information to be more reliable than names reported to an Internet site seeking customer service feedback.

Frequencies associated with first name and last name usage can increase the assessment depth of knowledge for an expert name tool. Using frequencies and cross-source validation can help in negating errors from the data as well. Table-driven name assessment is dependent on the depth and breadth of supporting data used to apply analysis rules and assign reason codes based on these rule for user consumption.

Pattern Identification

Given the lack of a comprehensive name source for quality processing, application logic that relies entirely on validation of name information against tables (filtering) can produce a large number of false positives (i.e., valid name information that is labeled as suspect because it is not found in the tables). For this reason, most name assessment applications also incorporate some level of name pattern analysis to supplement table information. A simple example would be a name such as "M. SMITH" that illustrates a pattern where the first name is recognized as a single initial and only the second name word "SMITH" is validated through a table lookup operation. Although this approach can reduce false positives, it may also product false negative. A false negative is where invalid or suspicious name information is not detected by the application. Depending upon the sophistication of the analysis, a suspicious name such as "AL E. GADOR" might escape both pattern and table validation.

Identifying the most prevalent name patterns and forming definitions around each are key to ensuring the most comprehensive assessment is obtained. Obvious patterns such as special characters, numbers, single character, and missing vowels can be detected with simple rule sets and minimal supplemental table dependencies. Business words and offensive words in name information require more sophistication through reliance on multiple rule sets and tables along with well-defined return values to aid in the interpretation of the results for user-specific application. The granularity and depth of the assessment provided to the user increases his ability to make the best interpretation when multiple patterns are identified and distinguished in reason codes provided from the process. For example, the name information "J. AND MARY SMITH" may be associated with at least two patterns — one where a first name is an initial, and the other where multiple first names are given.

Many factors can influence the analysis rules related to patterns of name information including culture and ethnicity. For example, some common Asian names may appear be a variant of name information that would appear to be offensive, or at least suspicious, in American culture. Another example is the repetition of name words in Middle Eastern names, such as "ALI ALI," again a pattern not typically found in American names.

Other factors may be more granular and apply to characters within a name word, such as, where and which numeric characters might be valid in name information (e.g., John Doe, 3rd). Frequencies gathered from tables compiled to feed the assessment process can assist in determining how scenarios such as these should be handled. These are only a few examples of the hundreds of patterns that could be important in the various assessment applications. Overall pattern identification provides the context needed for users to obtain the most value from the assessment of name information.

As a rule, the complexity of pattern analysis is inversely proportional to the amount of table information available. In theory, if a complete set of name and name variant information were available, no pattern analysis would be required. However, this cannot be achieved in practice. Such a table, even if it existed, would be far too large for all but the largest available computing systems. A balance is needed between pattern analysis and table information with some tasks most easily handled through pattern analysis. For example, it is pointless to store all combinations of first name initials with all last name possibilities (e.g., A. DOE, B. DOE, C. DOE, etc.), when this can easily be handled through the pattern — "single letter followed by a name word."

However, in general tables are preferable over patterns because of the simplicity of application and maintenance. Rules tend to be more fragile and can produce unanticipated results when modified. For this reason, it is very helpful, in fact necessary, to have a large set of test data available to validate modifications to a name assessment system. A test set should exercise as many patterns and table entries as possible in an attempt to evaluate the positive and negative impacts of any modification.

Mining Internal Best Practices

In a large data management organization, many one-off solutions may be scattered throughout various teams and units that use a number of similar, if not identical, validation rules for assessing the quality of name information. Consolidating these efforts requires focus and may be a significant undertaking. Considerations must be made to the reliance of validation rules on the data sources and robust pattern identification. However, providing a common point to share accumulated expertise brings value as an organization-wide resource. The model of open-source software development can facilitate a centralized point of coordination for such an initiative.

One payoff for the effort in creating an enterprise standard assessment practice is that addressing errors in name information can, in many instances, decrease the amount of functionality and processing required for entity resolution or other data integration applications. Integration complexity can be reduced and integration accuracy increased by the degree to which name information anomalies are identified and corrected or discarded prior to the integration process.

For example, identifying a misspelling of a name along with a suggested (and presumably correct) version of the name could allow for much simpler entity resolution of "JOHN SMITH" for "JONH SMITH." The detection and correction of the misspelling prior to matching is an approach which minimizes the cases handled by functions in the matching process. Placing the quality assessment pieces from the data integration process into a separately maintained application can be beneficial for both the assessment and integration processes. Spelling variations like this can easily be generated by transposing letters in valid name information and confirming the transpositions do not "collide" with other valid name information. Many approaches for analyzing names can be leveraged in an enterprise to drastically influence the data quality realized across all touch points.

DESIGN CONSIDERATIONS

Performance Efficiency vs. Comprehensiveness

A design tradeoff, similar to the pattern analysis vs. table tradeoff discussed earlier, is processing efficiency vs. comprehensiveness of the assessment. Due to the nature of name information, some anomalies will lie outside of the logic and data utilized in a standard assessment. Even in a breadth-first approach, some percentage of records will require more than cursory examination. Overall computation effort can be reduced by first applying the assessment rules that are most likely to succeed, and only applying additional computational effort to the less common situations. For example in processing consumer name information (individuals), one expects to find that the majority of cases comprise two common names or two common names separated by an initial. These cases typically do not require further examination unless one of the name words also happens to be a clue in a name phrase of interest (e.g., JOHN Q. PUBLIC as suspicious). In other words, the 80/20 rule applies in that 80% of the cases can be handled through a simple assessment (e.g., all words are common names) leaving the complexity to the remaining 20%. Utilizing the U.S. Census data to filter common name words prior to applying more complex validation rules such as business, suspicious, or offensive is one approach to increasing processing efficiency while allowing for deeper assessment.

Even using the 80/20 rule, the designer knows how elaborate the processing steps will be and how far to take them based on the enterprise needs and resources available. Many types of analyses that could be applied may be computationally expensive, such as embedded word search (i.e., searching for particular substrings within name words) or trigram or even n-gram analysis (i.e., comparing all 3-character sequences in a name word to its expected occurrence within a name population).

Another consideration is the impact of table size. Larger tables may filter more cases at the first step, yet more time is required to access and search these. Smaller and more targeted tables are a more judicious choice of second step assessment logic. These considerations must be balanced by the decision to scale up the processing power and/or table capacity of the computing system. As hardware becomes less expensive and more efficient, scaling the computer system may offer the most cost-effective way to handle table comprehensiveness with efficiency. Options are growing to address this trade-off via highly distributed, highly parallel grid systems that provide orders of magnitude increases in both processing power and online storage over traditional server-based systems.

Standard vs. Custom

Even though an enterprise-wide assessment application for name information has great advantages for consolidating and preserving organizational expertise and promoting the uniform processing of name information, it does have its disadvantages as well. Foremost among these can be a lack flexibility to address different requirements within an organization. A name assessment system should appeal to users enterprise-wide, addressing a spectrum of needs from common name anomaly identification such as invalid characters or initials to the more complex, application-specific name variance rather than intrinsic quality.

If the shared assessment system is not configurable, the customization is limited to the granularity of the information provided as output (i.e., the reason codes reflecting the potential anomalies detected). Providing record-level reason codes offers users choices in filtering or selecting records via post-assessment business processing based on the requirements of their particular applications. For example, one user of the system might consider the detection of celebrity name information (BRAD PITT) a low quality issue whereas others working with a high-end retailer account might expect celebrity names on their files, thus ignoring these indicators.

The acquisition of name information from multiple sources often requires some level of customized assessment as well. Name information received by e-mail may require much more scrutiny than that received through a call center. Some of the issues surrounding diverse sourcing of name information are discussed further in the following section on optimistic vs. pessimistic approaches. A standard name assessment, including a wide scope and well-defined reason codes, creates the flexibility for interpretation, often minimizing the requirement for custom configuration and set up.

Considering customization through interpretation of a standard output may not be an acceptable solution in all organizations. Some organizations may choose to make the assessment system configurable within certain aspects. For example, the standard system may not consider "MERRY BAKER" as a name with a potential anomaly, but for another application, it may be a well-recognized, local business name. An alternative to writing a post-processing step to follow the standard application and also include the identification of "MERRY BAKER" with a reason code is to allow the user to supplement the table of business names in the standard application via runtime options.

The ability to customize the shared assessment system through changes in configuration must be balanced against the loss of uniform processing across the enterprise. If users have too much freedom to customize the application, they may not always understand the impact of their changes and, in the end, may actually contribute to the decrease in quality of name information. Additionally, demands for configurability over a large number of aspects of the application will have an impact on the complexity of the application, and ultimately on performance and maintenance of the application. To the extent in which the assessment system is configurable, a standard configuration should always be provided for users who do not have special requirements, or who do not or cannot introspect the implications of every configuration parameter.

Optimistic vs. Pessimistic View

An optimistic quality assessment system for name information assumes patterns or conditions identified in the input data are accidental or inadvertent (i.e., honest mistakes), such as errors introduced through typographical or data entry, or even from previous processing. In an optimistic system, name information not found to contain words or patterns related to these types of sources is assumed to be valid. On the other hand, a pessimistic assessment system assumes that some amount of error may have been intentionally introduced into the data and, in general, treats all name information as suspicious until proven valid.

Optimistic and pessimistic systems correlate somewhat to information sources. Some name sources, such as self-reported name and address data from the Internet, tend to have a larger percentage of intentional errors, such as "QUEEN OF DENIAL" or "TY TANNICK" (My, 1998) and call for a more pessimistic processing approach.

Information collected through more trusted sources, such as in-store point of sale, are usually safe to assess in a more optimistic fashion.

Even though one might assume a pessimistic or "better safe than sorry" approach is best, that is not always the case. Pessimistic approaches can be very costly in computation time because they typically containing analysis rules applying alternative analyses to the same name information. They also tend to produce more false negatives than the optimistic approach. A rule designed to catch the one in a million suspicious patterns, may also catch dozens or even hundreds of valid name examples. Pessimistic assessment systems require rigorous testing with large test sets in order to reach a balance between finding low probability anomalies and allowing similar, but valid names to pass without indication. Because of the low threshold of coupling between certain false positive and false negative cases, the tuning of pessimistic systems to optimal performance can be a very tedious, and sometimes, argumentative process.

AN EXAMPLE SYSTEM

Some of the choices and compromises described in this chapter are exemplified by a system called "NameCheck." NameCheck is a rule-based expert system that analyzes U.S. consumer names for specific patterns of words, characters, and symbols that may indicate a data quality issue and assists users in validation based on their particular quality thresholds. Ultimately NameCheck provides the user with information to make the final determination of the quality of data acceptable for their use. The following is a discussion of where NameCheck exists in the spectra of the three considerations of the previous section, performance efficiency vs. comprehensiveness, optimistic vs. pessimistic view, and standard vs. custom.

The NameCheck design opts for efficiency vs. comprehensiveness. Even though NameCheck currently runs in a highly parallel "pipeline" system where each record passes through multiple transformation operators, execution time is still an issue due to the sheer volume of records processed on a daily basis. In a production environment where file size routinely exceed 100 million records, small increases or decreases in efficiency are magnified in terms of overall run time. For this reason, NameCheck uses relatively small reference tables, approximately 40,000 entries, relying primarily on analyzing patterns built from these tables to discover potential name anomalies. The reference tables comprise name components, such as first name and last name, associated with specific knowledge used in assessing the quality of consumer name information. The graph shown below illustrates the effect on efficiency as the size of reference tables increases.

The graph in Figure 1 illustrates the impact that reference table size has on performance time.

Figure 1. Impact of reference table size on performance time

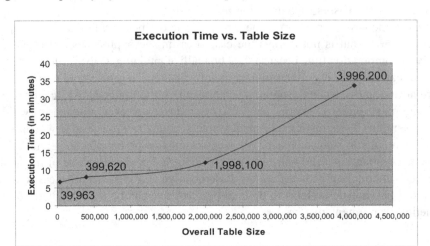

In terms of the design aspects discussed in this chapter, NameCheck is:

- Process efficient rather than comprehensive, primarily relying on pattern analysis over large tables,
- A standard system rather than configurable, users must rely on post-processes to add customization, and
- Optimistic rather than pessimistic, allowing many well-disguised suspicious names and names with unusual pattern to pass as valid.

The optimistic approach is to avoid the extra computational effort and large memory footprint required to detect many suspicious names, such as "BEN DOVER" (Sankey, 1996). Instead NameCheck focuses on the anomalies found more often in standard consumer name sources, such as, the identification of multiple names utilizing pattern analysis (JOHN AND ALICE SMITH), and missing surname information by matching to common name knowledge reference tables, such as "DIANE KATHRYN." Although optimistic on the whole, NameCheck does implement a few pessimistic rules to detect some of the more egregious offensive words, especially when embedded within other words.

Several of the pattern analysis rules in NameCheck are related to the use of special characters (i.e., commas, periods, virgule, etc.). It makes several assumptions around the meanings of these special characters that can affect the overall assessment of the name, especially in the case where the input is not pre-parsed into name components. For example, if a comma appears in a name after the first word an assumption may be made that the first word is the last name and the second word the first name rather than assuming that a comma has been erroneously introduced into the name. As similar scenarios play out the importance of balancing optimistic and pessimistic rules becomes more critical. When an initial assumption is based on an optimistic view, this may reduce the universe size for more complex analysis rules and alleviate the need for invoking pessimistic analysis rules for every record.

The decision to allow users to process name information that has not been pre-parsed mandates that NameCheck have some basic capability to parse names. It also exposes an interesting conundrum in the relationship between the quality of name information and name parsing. Low quality name information does not parse well, because most parsers rely on certain name clues that may be corrupted in poor quality data. At the same time, the detection of a pattern indicating potential anomalies may rely on knowledge of name components' context, implying the need for name parsing. The question then becomes which should be first, name quality assessment and improvement, or name parsing. For example, complexity can drastically increase when balancing such cases as multiple word last names. In the end, the best solution would be to fully integrate the two processes into a single process providing both.

The current version of NameCheck allows for three input options:

1. Pre-parsed including first and last name only
2. First, middle, and last names
3. Unparsed

Figure 2. An example system

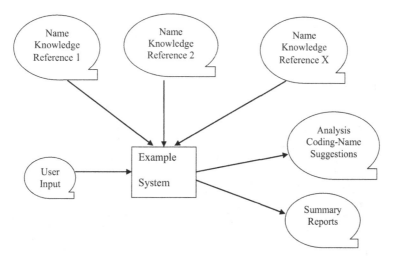

The system appends specific reason (pattern) codes on the record and also provides a "cleaned name," when applicable. The reason codes enable users to perform post-assessment analysis and apply additional custom, user-specific cleaning processes to the information.

An end-of-job report allows users to determine the overall quality of their file with summary statistics and examples of all types of patterns detected. The report also provides a complete breakdown of the reason codes, and a comparison of the number of common names expected (based on census information) to the number of common names actually found. Figure 2 shows the overall system design.

The multiple processing options available from NameCheck were developed to address users need to evaluate the quality of name information at different touch points in a multi-step process flow, where each step has different assessment needs and different levels of name parsing. The inclusion of name parsing logic in NameCheck was not an attempt to replace the highly robust name-parsing application used across the enterprise, but an attempt to include enough basic name structure analysis to allow the reasonable assessment of the quality of an unparsed input name. Regardless of the structure of the name information input, NameCheck is designed to provide a thorough evaluation of the consumer name field utilizing

Figure 3. User input, parsed   *Figure 4. User input, unparsed*

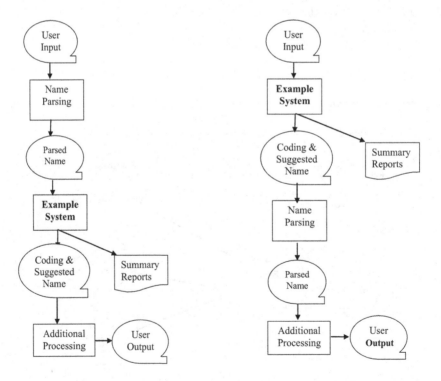

rules and reference tables inclusive of name context information to allow for pattern identification. With the flexibility of NameCheck the user can also choose to assess names at multiple points in their processing.

Figure 3 and Figure 4 illustrate multiple processing options available to users.

FUTURE TRENDS

The advent of highly distributed grid computing networks offering direct access to large volumes of data may offer some relief to the trade-off between comprehensiveness and performance efficiency. Large data grids now make it practical to access a enormous corpus of name reference information without a significant penalty in overall system performance (Thibodeau, 2004). For example, the U.S., Social Security Death Index contains approximately 74 million names (Beine, 2004). Even though it might require on the order of 100 grid nodes to maintain an online index of such an extensive amount of information, that is not a significant fraction of the capacity of several existing grids that operate with several thousand nodes. Both the grid computing and the open source initiative are evolving (Clement, 2005) overcoming many previous system development barriers. Open source is also an area where future development efforts could provide an avenue for extensive collaboration on the best approaches to assessing names and expediting enhancements. Users can choose to absorb others work with the continually functional updates and data available in the open source environment.

Another area is the need to assess the quality of name information on a global basis. The key to global processing is the ability to localize to specific languages and local name patterns. Although Unicode provides a solution for non-English character sets, handling analysis rules associated with non-U.S. naming patterns is more difficult. However, this is another area in which large-scale computing, such as grid computing, may provide a solution. Using the principle that pattern rules can be reduced by using larger name tables, the problem of localizing quality assessment of name information to different geographic areas may well be solved by simply indexing very large sets of valid name information into high-capacity grid systems. The expansion of name information assessments into global processing is mostly dependent on the name pattern identification and a basic understanding of special characters associated with a particular language or set of languages.

CONCLUSION

The increased need to assess and improve the quality of name information, particularly to facilitate customer data integration, can be challenging for any organization. However, the organizations that realized the need to elevate the quality of name information to the same level as address information have led the way in improving overall quality in the integration of their customer data through the development of systems capable of assessing and improving the quality of name information. As a result, these systems are now key components in the overall information quality management strategies of these organizations.

The challenges associated with the implementation of NameCheck were resolved through the consolidation of rules, data, and best practices throughout the organization. Along with leadership support and engaging users early in testing to show value and opportunity, NameCheck ultimately provides users with a comprehensive name data quality tool. As an integral part of an enterprise-wide information quality program, NameCheck has proven to benefit both to the organization and to the marketplace providing quantifiable evidence of name information quality assessment within the data accuracy and consistency dimensions of data quality (Campbell, 2003).

Future work includes:

- Building a configurable version of NameCheck that will allow users to enhance reference tables and to select and re-order priority of the reason codes application.
- Integrate NameCheck quality assessment logic with the enterprise standard, full-function name parser.
- Building a version of NameCheck that fully utilizes the online storage capacity of the grid environment, in particular, an index to all of the name information provided by Social Security Death Index.
- Extending the very-large data index version of NameCheck to prototype a quality assessment for non-U.S. name information, possibly a European language. The prototype will test the hypothesis that the pattern analysis can be made very thin using a very large corpus of names from the target geography.

REFERENCES

Beine, J. (2004-2005). The social security death index, a genealogy guide. *Online Death Indexes and Records*. Retrieved from http://www.deathindexes.com/ssdi.html

Britt, P., Compton, J., and Weinberger, J. (2004). *The 2004 Market Leaders CRM Magazine*. Retrieved from http://www.destinationcrm.com/articles/default.asp?ArticleID=4503

Campbell, T. and Wilhoit, Z. (2003). How's your data quality? A case study in corporate data quality strategy. In *Proceedings of the International Conference on Information Quality*, MIT.

Clement, B. (2005). Acxiom Chooses VA Software Solution to Bolster Open Source Initiative Driving Global Firm's Data Processing IT Environment. *VA Software.* Retrieved from http://www.vasoftware.com/news/press.php/2005/1518.html

Huang, K., Lee, Y. W., and Wang, R. Y. (1999). *Quality information and knowledge.* Upper Saddle River, NJ: Prentice-Hall.

My 3 C's. (1998-2005). *The name game.* Retrieved from http://www.psacake.com/silly.asp

Sankey, C. (1996-2000). Name Game. *Bodo's Lair.* Retrieved from the http://www.bodo.com/jokes/jname.htm

Thibodeau, P. (2004). *Software licensing emerges as grid obstacle computerworld.* Retrieved from http://www.computerworld.com/news/special/pages/story/0,5364,2565-93526,00.html

Wang, R. K. (1998). A product perspective on total data quality management. *Communications of the ACM, 41*(2), 58-65.

Sandell, C. (2005). *Credit card letter addressed 'Dear Palestinian Bomber', company apologizes for solicitation letter sent to california grocery store manager.* Retrieved from http://abcnews.go.com/US/Business/story?id=1059341

Section III:
IQ Application
for Database
Management Services

Chapter VI

Information Quality:
How Good are
Off-the-Shelf DBMS?

Felix Naumann, Humboldt-Universität zu Berlin, Germany

Mary Roth, IBM Silicon Valley Lab, USA

ABSTRACT

Commercial database management systems (DBMS) have come a long way with respect to efficiency and more recently, with respect to quality and user friendliness. Not only do they provide an efficient means to store large amounts of data and intuitive query languages to access the data, popular DBMS also provide a whole suite of tools to assess, store, manage, clean, and retrieve data in a user-friendly way. Some of these feature address database experts, others are targeted at end-users with little or even no database knowledge. The recent developments in the field of autonomic computing drive the ease-of-use even further. In this chapter we study how well a typical DBMS meets the goal of providing a high-quality data storage and retrieval facility. To this end, we draw on an established set of information quality criteria and assess how well an exemplary DBMS fares. While quality criteria are usually defined for a set of data, we extend, wherever possible, the definitions to the systems that manage this data.

THE QUALITY-IN-QUALITY-OUT PRINCIPLE

Arguably the most widespread architecture to store, manage, and retrieve structured data is the relational database management system (DBMS) architecture.

Starting with System R (Astrahan, 1979) of IBM, which evolved to the IBM DB2 database system, today there are many commercial systems storing petabytes of data. Other prominent examples are Oracle database,[1] Microsoft's SQL Server,[2] and MySQL.[3] Other data models, such as the object-oriented model or the hierarchical model are also widespread but not discussed here. The information quality provided by a database is not due to the data model itself, but to the system carefully managing the data. Thus, database systems with other data models enjoy the same information quality properties. Research and development for DBMS follows two main directions: scalability and usability. With the growing demand to store more and more data, databases systems have scaled in the hardware they use and in the software managing the data. Additionally, administrators of databases and end-users of the data demand more and more functionality that either adds value to the DBMS or makes its use easier. In this chapter, we analyze how well modern DBMS are able to meet user demands, or at least help database administrators (DBAs) meet user demands regarding their everyday work with the DBMS or applications built on top. Here, user demands are expressed as a set of information quality criteria taken from the empirical study of Wang and Strong (1996).

Information quality is a measure to assess the value of data to perform the task at hand (Wang, 1996). Other definitions mention fitness for use (Tayi, 1998) or user satisfaction (Delone, 1992). As DBMS are one of the most common means to generate, manage, and provide this data, it is worthwhile to examine how they influence the quality of the information they handle. This influence is both explicit within the core functionality of a DBMS and implicit through tools that help data providers, developers, managers, and consumers derive the most value from the data.

To examine DBMS with respect to the quality of information they are able to supply, we apply a large set of IQ criteria to DBMS as an entire system. Usually, IQ criteria are used to assess the quality of information, and not the quality of a system. Addressing this mismatch, we analyze not the DBMS itself, but its ability to provide high quality data. DBMS are not the sole source of high information quality, but they are designed to at least not diminish quality. While the well-known *garbage-in-garbage-out* principle holds for any system dealing with data, we postulate the *quality-in-quality-out* principle for modern, well-designed DBMS. For instance, if data is generated and inserted into a DBMS in a timely manner, a good DBMS will not unduly delay the accessibility of the data to users. Another example is the completeness of information: DBMS are developed to always return complete (and correct) answers to queries. Only if the stored base data is incomplete or incorrect will a DBMS answer with an inferior result. In this spirit we analyze several quality dimensions and provide details on if and how a typical DBMS meets IQ demands. In this chapter we ignore the issue of software quality and assume a DBMS that correctly implements the SQL standard and its added functionality.

Structure of this Chapter

In the following section we introduce IBM's DB2 database system as a typical representative of commercial DBMS. Additionally, we present three different roles that DBMS users acquire, each with different needs towards information quality and each with different demands on a DBMS. In third section we enumerate a comprehensive set of information quality criteria and discuss for each, if and how a DBMS used in different roles affects them. We conclude with a discussion of future work in the fourth section and a summary of our findings in the last section.

Database Management Systems and Their Users

A software product, such as a database management system (DBMS), is used by many different persons with different educational backgrounds, different IT needs, and, most importantly, with different roles inside an organization. These roles are the basis of our assessment of DBMS quality.

DB2 Universal Database:
A Typical, Off-the-Shelf Database Management System

Figure 1 illustrates a layered DBMS architecture that has evolved over the past 30 years of relational database technology evolution and is typical of most DBMS products in the marketplace. Requests to the DBMS are formulated in a semantically rich, declarative language and submitted via a command line or programming

Figure 1. A generic DBMS architecture

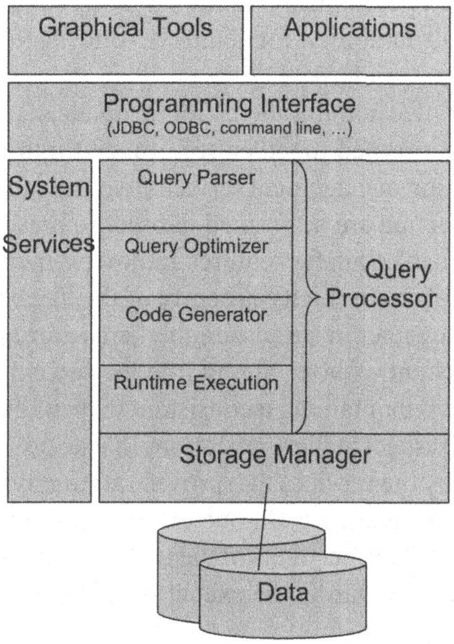

interface. SQL (Structured Query Language, [ISO, 1999]) has developed as the standard language for manipulating relational data, and interfaces such as JDBC and ODBC have evolved as the standard programming APIs by which SQL requests are submitted to the DBMS. Graphical tools, packaged and custom applications submit SQL requests through these programming interfaces. The maturity and wide adoption of these standards ensures that a wide variety of documentation is available to describe their use.

A query processor sits below the DBMS interface layer and executes requests to store and retrieve data as efficiently and robustly as possible. The query processor is made up of multiple components that work together to transform a declarative request for data into a series of executable steps that satisfy the request. The top level component is the query parser, which relies on a lexical analyzer and parser to interpret the request and populate a data graph that captures the semantics of the request. This data graph is passed to a query optimizer that analyzes the graph and explores several strategies for answering the request, eventually choosing the most efficient plan according to some criteria, such as to minimize response time, throughput, or resource utilization. Once a plan has been selected, the code generator generates code to implement the plan. The runtime execution engine executes the code, interacting with a storage manager to retrieve and combine the appropriate data to fulfill the original request.

The query processor handles not only requests to retrieve data, but it also handles requests to insert, update and delete data in the database. Such operations may be performed concurrently by multiple users. System services such as transaction management, concurrency control, logging, and recovery, maintain the *ACID* properties of a database that enable a DBMS to safely support concurrent query, insert, update, and delete operations by multiple users. ACID stands for atomicity, consistency, isolation, and durability (for details beyond the following brief descriptions of the properties see Graefe, 1993).

Atomicity refers to "all or nothing" behavior for database operations. Operations that must be logically performed together are grouped into *transactions*, and the DBMS provides transaction management services to ensure that either all or none of the operations of a transaction are performed in order to preserve a consistent view of data. For example, a bank transfer requires removing money from one account and adding it to another. The Atomicity property of the database ensures that if the operations are grouped together in a transaction, then a partial update — removing money from the first account without adding it to the second — will not occur.

Consistency refers to maintaining a consistent view of the data in the database both internally and with respect to the applications that access the data. Consistency is enforced by a DBMS by the services that provide atomicity and isolation. A committed transaction takes a database from one consistent state to another consistent state. For example, the two bank accounts of the previous example are in a consistent state before a transfer occurs. During the execution of the transaction, the database is temporarily inconsistent when the money is removed from one account but not yet added to the second account. However, after the transaction commits, the two bank accounts are again in a consistent state, with money successfully transferred from the first account to the second account.

Isolation ensures that concurrent users of a database will execute their transactions in isolation, and not interfere with each other's operations. For example, if Felix and Mary both initiate a transfer of funds for the same set of bank accounts, the DBMS's locking and concurrency services ensure that either Felix's transaction will execute to completion before Mary's, or vice versa. Thus, Mary will not see Felix's partial updates (e.g., the value of the account being transferred to), nor will Felix see Mary's partial updates.

Durability refers to the property that any transaction committed to the database will not be lost. Durability is maintained by the DBMS through logging and database recovery services. Logging records the state of database transactions, including whether they were committed, and database recovery restores a database to a consistent state in the event of a hardware or software failure. For example, when the transaction transferring money from one account to another is committed, the DBMS records enough information about the transaction, even in the event of a hardware failure.

Many of the challenges in information quality arise when integrating data from many, autonomous sources. Duplicates appear when a real-world object is represented in more than one source, information is "tainted" when integrated with data from an untrustworthy source, and completeness can be increased through integration. Simultaneously, much DBMS vendors have paid great effort to introduce integrating capabilities into their base DBMS product. These capabilities appear as data warehousing environments, as federated database management systems, such as IBM's Information Integrator, or as grid-enabled DBMS, such as Oracle's 10g database. In fact, many of the integrating technologies have become fundamental components of the DBMS. Thus, in the following discussions we include DBMS integration technology whenever applicable to the IQ criterion at hand.

Users that interact with a DBMS directly typically rely on two types of graphical tools. Such tools are either packaged with the database itself or produced by third party vendors. Administrative tools, such as DB2's Control Center or Oracle's Enterprise Manager are used to configure and maintain the database, including such tasks as defining database layout, governing user access to the data, monitoring performance, and scheduling backups to ensure the data is recoverable in the event of a failure. Application development tools, such as DB2 Development Center, Computer Associates Erwin Data Modeler, or Rational Rose, are used to create database artifacts that are used by applications, including such tasks as developing models of the data required for an application, or generating functions and stored procedures that encapsulate much of the data access logic for the application. In conclusion, large database vendors offer the same or similar base functionality, which is the focus of our research. We do mention DB2's additional functionality that is particular to information quality improvement.

Roles of DBMS Customers

An exhaustive analysis of DBMS use may identify a large population of DBMS users, each with distinct purposes and roles. Rather than address all of these roles, we focus our attention on three important DBMS customers (shown in Figure 2), each with different needs with respect to information quality and each with different means to improve IQ.

- **Administrator:** Database administrators are trained DBMS experts who install and maintain DBMS and accompanying tools. Their role is to manage the integrity, security, and overall performance of a DBMS system, including such tasks as scheduling backups and database reorganization activities, optimizing storage layout, tuning performance in response to application requirements, and managing user access to the data. Administrators often use the administrative graphical tools and command line interface shown in Figure 1 to perform their tasks.
- **Developer:** Application developers create software to support a particular business need. An application developer works with a domain expert to define the application requirements, architect a solution, and implement application code to meet those requirements. The application is typically composed of distinct software components that encapsulate the logic for a particular aspect of the solution, and application developers specialize in component areas. For example, an application that produces a daily report of business transactions might be composed of a component that runs queries against the database to retrieve the day's transaction information, a component that combines and summarizes the data according to specific business rules, and a Web-based interface that formats the information in an easy-to-read format. Application developers typically use application development tools and the programming interface illustrated in Figure 1 to implement their applications.
- **Business Manager:** A business manager relies on applications developed by application developers in order to make robust business decisions. The health and robustness of the database and the applications built on top are critical to the line of business; success and profitability often depend on the reliability and quality information produced by the applications. If a DBMS that stores order information is unavailable for several hours, business transactions cannot occur, and the business loses revenue. If data is corrupted by the DBMS or if information is computed incorrectly, the business may be subject to fines or penalties.

Figure 2. Three roles for DBMS usage

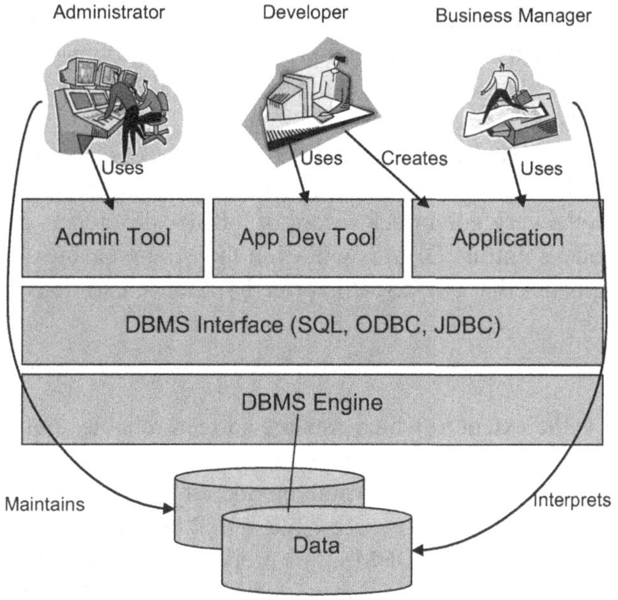

THE QUALITY OF DATABASE MANAGEMENT SYSTEMS

We analyze a set of information quality criteria from the perspective of the three distinct customer roles described above. There have been many attempts to collect and classify IQ criteria, most notably the empirical study of Wang and Strong (1996), in which the authors aggregated survey results to find a list of 15 IQ criteria. Here, the IQ criteria are ordered according to that classification, but we extended the set at appropriate places by several criteria that are of particular importance to DBMS users (and at which DBMS excel). For convenience, we quote the definitions of Wang and Strong (1996).

Intrinsic IQ Criteria

Believability

"Believability is the extent to which data are accepted or regarded as true, real, and credible" (Wang, 1996). In a sense, believability is the expected accuracy. Due to the ACID properties described earlier, DBMS faithfully report data as it was entered into the database. A main source for doubts in the accuracy of data is the difficult formulation of complex SQL queries. Thus, managers must rely on the ability of developers to correctly write and document queries that have the desired semantics. Research has developed methods to automatically detect dubious queries and subqueries and issue warnings to the developer (Brass, 2002). For instance, some queries always produce empty results because they contain mutually exclusive filtering predicates. Such techniques have not yet found their way into commercial DBMS.

However, given high quality data and a correct query (i.e., a query that reflects the semantics of the application), the produced query result is guaranteed to be correct. Through the very good track record of DBMS, developers and managers worldwide nowadays entrust DBMS with even their most business-critical data, proving a strong belief that DBMS will correctly produce and transform the data that is stored within.

Accuracy

"Accuracy is the extent to which data are correct, reliable, and certified free of error" (Wang, 1996). It is typically determined as the quotient of the number of correct values in a database and the overall number of values in the database.

With respect to the data as it is accessible, a DBMS always provides accurate answers to a query (in terms of DBMS, this property is called *correctness*). This IQ criterion best exemplifies the quality-in-quality-out principle of DBMSs. Correctness, and thus accuracy, is ensured by the use of checksums, locks and other methods of transaction processing. In particular, DBMS provide durability (the D in ACID), so that no data is lost. Since the main goal of a DBMS is to store data faithfully, vendors take great care to ensure the accurate insertion of data and the precise delivery of that data in response to queries.

General DBMS have no means to automatically correct inaccurate data. They do however provide some means to detect inaccurate data: Through the usage of pre-defined and user-defined types (UDTs), a DBMS verifies if a data value conforms to the syntactic definition of its type. Furthermore, administrators can implement triggers that perform certain actions and issue warnings when a possibly incorrect value, such as an outlier, is inserted into the database.

Objectivity

"Objectivity is the extent to which data are unbiased, unprejudiced, and impartial" (Wang, 1996). It is trivial to show that DBMS have perfect objectivity: The durability property of DBMS ensures that data entered into a database is not changed. Since DBMS are fully automatic machines and software, they are not prejudiced and are always impartial.

Reputation

"Reputation is the extent to which data are trusted or highly regarded in terms of their source or content" (Wang, 1996). Arguments similar to those for the Objectivity criterion also hold with respect to the reputation a DBMS conveys. In fact, there are occasions when the reputation of the DBMS increases the reputation of the data stored within. Major DBMS vendors, such as IBM, Oracle, and Sybase, have successfully marketed mature DBMS products for many years and have thus gained a high reputation. It should be noted that much of this reputation stems not from the quality of the data stored inside, but from ease of use, ease of maintenance, and marketing. IT managers have a tendency to trust data coming from a reputed DBMS more than from other less-renown IT products.

Contextual IQ Criteria

Value-Added

"Value-Added is the extent to which data are beneficial and provides advantages from their use" (Wang, 1996). Apart from simply storing data and retrieving data upon request, modern DBMS have many capabilities to add value to data. In Wiederhold (1997) the authors provide a list of features that DBMS (and in particular federated DBMS) may provide to add value to the base data. These features include simple aggregation of data, which most every DBMS is able to provide, search capabilities (such as those provided by DB2 Net Extender) to allow key-word searching, triggers to automatically react to certain events, etc. Many of the features listed there are directly provided by DBMS. For the rest, DBMS have standard interfaces so that third-party vendors can implement appropriate business intelligence applications on top of the DBMS. IBM's Information Integrator provides the ability to integrate multiple information sources within a single federated system, thereby directly providing value through integration, and indirectly through various capabilities for federated systems.

Relevancy

"Relevancy (or relevance) is the extent to which data are applicable and helpful for the task at hand" (Wang, 1996). DBMS can improve relevancy of data in with two techniques: the ability to declaratively select appropriate data and thus avoid redundant or irrelevant data, and the ability to access additional, remote data.

Using the declarative SQL language, developers can implement pre-defined views that select and filter data according to the application and according to the needs of the business manager consuming the data. SQL views can limit the set of columns of a data set exported and can limit the rows of the data set according to some filter predicates.

Using technology to federate multiple, heterogeneous and remote data sources, federated DBMS, such as IBM's Information Integrator, are able to greatly increase the amount of data accessible to the developer. Thus, developers are given more freedom to include relevant sources and improve relevancy (and completeness) in

124 Naumann & Roth

the final, integrated result: The percentage of relevant data compared to all available data can be increased.

Timeliness

"Timeliness is the extent to which the age of the data is appropriate for the task at hand" (Wang, 1996). Commercial DBMS provide several means to optimize the timeliness of data. At the database core level, DBMS ensure timeliness by making updates to the data visible immediately after the updating transaction is completed. High timeliness is jeopardized when same data is stored at multiple locations and then updated at only one location. Only after such updates are propagated to the other copies is the data once again up-to-date. Unfortunately, DBMS frequently duplicate data to ensure high response times. For instance, data accessed by a remote client is often cached at the client side. Another example is the deliberate replication of data at multiple clients. Finally, materialized views store pre-calculated query results from base data. In all cases, updates to the base data are not immediately reflected in the copies.

To improve timeliness, DBMS have implemented different schemes of update propagation, such as those available with DB2 Information Integrator Replication Server. Such replication offerings often support flexible latency characteristics for update propagation (continuous, event-driven, or scheduled), as well as transaction-consistent and table-at-a-time replication. Finally, there has been much applied research on the so-called view-update problem (Lehner, 2000).

Completeness

"Completeness is the extent to which data are of sufficient breadth, depth, and scope for the task at hand" (Wang, 1996). Usually, completeness can be measured as the number of records in a database, assuming that larger numbers are of higher utility (breadth). In Naumann (2004), we introduce a completeness definition that also accounts for the number of attributes of records and the number of (useless) null-values in database. The arguments to support our claim that completeness is well-accounted for by DBMS are similar to the ones for the accuracy criterion. In a sense, completeness is built-in in databases, and with respect to the data as it is accessible a DBMS always provides complete answers to a query. It must be noted that this interpretation of completeness relates to the data stored in the database and not to the data that is necessary or relevant for the application at hand.

Completeness is of great importance and particular difficulty when integrating multiple data sources. All modern DBMS provide flexible means to access remote data sources, either by supporting extract-transform-load (ETL) processes to fill data warehouses (materialized integration) or by providing federated access to remote sources at query time (virtual integration). Many ETL vendors, such as Ascential Datastage or Oracle Warehouse Builder supply advanced ETL tools that unburden administrators from programming individual transformations and instead allow them

Copyright © 2007, Idea Group Inc. Copying or distributing in print or electronic forms without written permission of Idea Group Inc. is prohibited.

to concentrate on the high-level definition of entire transformation processes. For virtual integration, extensive tooling exists to define so-called wrappers, which automatically translate and distribute queries to appropriate remote sources. The ability of wrappers to access sources of many different types and flavors (XML, Excel, flat files, other DBMS, Web services, etc.) help administrators improve completeness by wrapping all sources relevant to a particular domain (see for instance the DB2 XML Wrapper in Josifovski (2003a) and a tool to easily create one in Josifovski (2003b). For example, consider a typical insurance claim, which may include account information stored in a relational database, photographs stored in a content management system, and a police report received as an XML document. Virtual integration enables the insurance application to view all of this data as though it were stored and queried through a single interface.

Appropriate Amount of Data

"Appropriate amount of data is the extent to which the quantity or volume of available data is appropriate" (Wang, 1996). While selecting the set and amount of data that is *just right* for the task at hand is a difficult problem, DBMS help developers achieve this goal in two ways.

First, DBMS provide means to explicitly limit the amount of data returned through SQL extensions such as "FETCH FIRST N ROWS ONLY" in DB2 (for Microsoft SQL Server: "SELECT TOP N ... FROM ..." and for Oracle: "OPTIMIZER_MODE = FIRST_ROWS_N"). With this command the DBMS limits the number of rows returned to the data consumer. The technique improves latency (see below), addresses problems of limited bandwidth, and avoids users being overwhelmed by too much data.

Second, commercial DBMS place virtually no limit on the amount of data they can manage. The Winter Corporation lists some of the largest known database instances by different criteria, such as number of rows, size in Bytes, and so forth. (2003). According to that survey, the largest databases store close to 100 Terabytes of data and up to ½ trillion rows. In summary, large DBMS support appropriate amounts of data by providing capabilities to reduce the amount as much as desired and simultaneously allow the amount to be as large as necessary.

Latency and Response Time (New Criteria)

Latency is the amount of time from issuing the query until the first data item reaches the user. Latency is particularly important for end-users such as business managers. Instead of waiting for the DBMS to calculate the entire result of a query or to produce all pages of a report, modern DBMS have the ability to "fast-track" first results. Thus, users can browse the first part of a result. Further parts are either calculated on demand (saving execution cost if they are never needed) or calculated in the background (i.e., while displaying first results).

The most important technique to ensure good (low) latency is that of pipelined query execution. Data is sent through an execution pipeline, so that calculated results arrive at the user's application even while base-data is still being read (Graefe, 1993; and (Pirahesh, 1990). All modern DBMS are able to recognize a potential for pipelines for a given query and are able to execute the query in pipelined mode. Developers of applications are able to use certain functions, so that the applications also profit from low latency of the DBMS. For instance the getNext( ) function explicitly produces only the next subset of answers. Administrators can use DB2's SQL extension "FETCH FIRST N ROWS ONLY" to achieve low latency and also decrease query execution cost.

While latency measures the time until a first part of a response reaches the data consumer, response time measures the delay in seconds between submission of a query by the user and reception of the *complete response* from the DBMS. Response time is the main and often sole criterion for traditional database optimizers. In consequence there has been an enormous amount of academic and industrial research to improve response time of queries even over very large databases, much of which has been implemented in commercial DBMS. For lack of space, we refer the reader to surveys for query optimization for centralized databases (Graefe, 1993) and for distributed databases (Kossmann, 2000). While many of these optimization techniques must be installed and maintained by hand, recent work on autonomic computing lifts the burden of DBMS administrators. Automatic advisors, such as the Design Advisor of IBM DB2 Stinger, recommend optimal settings for many DBMS parameters, for instance regarding the use of indices and the use of materialized views (Zilio, 2004).

Representational IQ Criteria

Interpretability

"Interpretability is the extent to which data are in appropriate language and units and the data definitions are clear" (Wang, 1996). Interpretability is highly dependent on the interface that users have to the data. DBMS interfaces have two roles. One role is to *interpret* given data using metadata, such as the schema, constraints, etc. The other role of interfaces is to allow users *interaction* with the data, such as creating new data, reformatting data, and aggregating data.

Interpretation of data largely depends on the underlying schema, which can be well or poorly designed. DBMS support good schema design through visual tools, such as Computer Associate's ERWin Data Modeler. Also, DBMS provide multiple language support to improve interpretability. The main tools around DB2 are available in 15 different languages. Recent developments have given administrators and programmers more flexibility in schema design: Table and attribute names are no longer restricted to eight bytes, and user defined types (UDTs), user-defined functions (UDFs), and table functions allow development of specialized data items.

Interfaces for *interaction* with the data in a DBMS range from highly technical interfaces (SQL Query Language) to somewhat technical interfaces (query- and view-building tools, such as DB2 SQL Assist) to non-technical interfaces for business managers (report generators).

Understandability

"Understandability (or ease of understanding) is the extent to which data are clear without ambiguity and easily comprehended" (Wang, 1996). Thus, understandability measures how well a DBMS presents its data, so that the user is able to comprehend its semantic value. Standard DBMS query interfaces represent data in simple tables, using column names stored in the system catalog. Until several years ago, column names were restricted to eight characters in length, severely limiting the expressivity and thus understandability of the data. This has now changed and developers can give tables and columns more verbose names. Also, many third-party applications specialize in visualizing complex data.

One of the main concerns of DBMS administrators is to maintain efficient query response times to all queries. In particular, administrators are concerned with optimization of queries (i.e., finding an efficient execution strategy). DB2 provides an advanced visualization tool called Visual Explain, which graphically displays a query execution plan along with table sizes, join algorithms, filter selectivity and result size. Such visualization improves understanding of the data and the DBMS view of the data.

Visualization of query result data itself is not the focus of the DBMS, but rather of applications built on top. In consequence, business managers are rarely exposed to a simple tabular display of data directly from the DBMS, but instead use sophisticated tools that are able to additionally visualize data in other models, such as bar charts that more accurately reflects the business domain.

Representational Consistency

"Representational consistency is the extent to which data are always represented in the same format and are compatible with previous data" (Wang, 1996). Representational consistency from an administrator's point of view is accomplished through DBMS support of standard data exchange protocols, such as JDBC and ODBC, and standard data exchange formats, such as CSV (comma separated lists) and XML (Extensible Markup Language). These standards, which are supported by all DBMS vendors, allow fairly easy data exchange at the byte level among different data sources.

Achieving representational consistency in terms of the structure of the data as reflected in a schema is a far more difficult task. Two main research areas have dealt with the integration of heterogeneously modeled data: schema integration (see for instance Batini, 1986) and schema mapping (see for instance Hernandez, 2002). While schema integration attempts to generate a new integrated schema from different representations, schema mapping simply represents correspondences among heterogeneous schemas. The correspondences are then interpreted as data transformations that help achieve representational consistency among multiple data sources. Unfortunately, both approaches are not yet well supported in commercial DBMS. However, several prototypical tools with graphical interfaces for schema mapping are under development by vendors such as Clio at IBM Research (Hernandez, 2002) and Rondo (Melnik, 2003).

To conclude, achieving representational consistency is an extremely difficult task not yet well supported by DBMS and research towards semi-automatically solving it is only now underway.

Representational Conciseness

"Representational conciseness is the extent to which data are compactly represented without being overwhelming" (Wang, 1996). Data representation in most modern DBMS follows the relational model, which structures data into relations (tables) storing tuples (records) each having a set of attributes (stored in columns) (Codd, 1970). For many applications this is an intuitive and compact method to model data. In particular, through the process of normalizing tables, the representation can be rendered as compact as possible.

On the other hand, many applications have a more hierarchical view of data, so that an XML data model might be preferred. Most modern DBMS have some capability of storing and retrieving XML data, or even producing XML data from a set of tables through the new SQL/XML standard.[4]

As already argued for the Relevancy criterion, DBMS provide many means for developers to reduce the amount of data to some relevant and concise subset as needed for any particular application. Reduction is achieved by selecting relevant columns (called projection), filtering relevant rows (called selection), and summarizing data (aggregation).

Accessibility IQ Criteria

Accessibility/Availability

"Accessibility is the extent to which data are available or easily and quickly retrievable" (Wang, 1996). Availability of a DBMS is the probability that a feasible query is correctly answered in a given time range. Availability is a technical measure concerning both hardware, software, and their compatibility. Availability and accessibility are crucial features for large scale, mission-critical applications. For example, a DBMS server failure in the middle of a time-sensitive stock transaction or bank transfer could have an immediate effect on the core business.

DBMS have invested heavily in technology to achieve high availability. Centralized DBMS running on a single server have advanced in recent years to parallel DBMS and distributed DBMS running on multiple servers possibly distributed worldwide. Distribution opens the possibility of two means to achieve high availability: clustering and replication (Wright, 2003). Both clustering and replication exploit distribution to minimize the risk that DBMS software or hardware introduces as a single point of failure for applications that depend on the DBMS. DBMS clusters exploit features in the operating system on which the DBMS is deployed to automatically react to software or hardware failures. In the event of a failure, the DBMS cluster automatically engages a backup system to take over for the failed component. DBMS cluster technology achieves high availability for an entire DBMS system. It requires specific software and hardware to implement, and places restrictions on the distance and hardware over which it can be deployed. DBMS replication is an alternative technology for high availability. Replication allows an administrator to control the subset of data to be managed for availability, including what subset of the data to replicate, where to place replicas (including across platforms and over long distances), how to keep them up-to-date, and which replica to use to answer a particular query (Bourbonnais, 2004). DB2 Information Integrator Masala Replication Server, for example, supports multiple source/target topologies for replication, including 1-to-many, many-to-1, and many-to-many.

In addition to high availability features, DBMS provide a number of features to support user accessibility to the data managed by the DBMS. As shown in Figure 1, DBMS provide a number of different interfaces from visual to programming APIs to access data. Most standard DBMS APIs such as ODBC are fairly mature. However, DBMS vendors tend to keep up with current trends and technologies. For example, most DBMS vendors have developed tools to allow administration and user access to DBMS via a Web interface in a browser. Examples include IBM's DB2 Web Query Tool, Oracle's Application Server Portal, and Microsoft's SQL Server Web Data Administrator. In addition to flexibility with regard to interfaces, DBMS also provide features that allow administrators to customize user accessibility to data. Examples of such features include user authentication, object-level privileges, database views, and tools like DB2 Query Patroller that regulate database resource use by user-type.

To summarize, DBMS provide a number of built-in availability and accessibility features to provide reliable access to data at the time it is needed by the applications and users that depend on it.

Access Security

"Security is the extent to which access to data can be restricted and hence kept secure" (Wang, 1996). Security covers technical aspects, such as cryptography, secure login and so forth, but also includes the possibility of anonymization of the user and authentication of the DBMS by a trusted organization. Modern DBMS feature several abilities to ensure high security. First, the SQL standard specifies commands to GRANT and REVOKE detailed privileges to individual data objects, such as tables, views, functions, and so forth. Second, DBMS implement sophisticated authentication policies at servers and clients. Finally, DBMS vendors usually provide entire security tool suites ranging from security auditing and monitoring, intrusion detection, to privacy and security management tools.

Customer Support and Documentation (New Criterion)

Customer support is the amount and usefulness of human help provided to users either electronically or personally. Documentation is the amount and usefulness of (electronic) documents describing the DBMS and its functionalities and guiding customers during system deployment and application development. Business managers are usually not confronted with the DBMS themselves, but rather with applications on top, for which there exist separate support systems and documentation.

Administrators and developers: Large installations of DBMS are usually accompanied by agreements on technical support. The degree of support is available at different levels and costs. In addition to this explicit and contractually agreed-upon assistance, all vendors supply a multitude of resources to guide users. Questions to dedicated newsgroups are answered by experts; context-sensitive help systems are provided within the DBMS and online. Detailed documentation (IBM's Redbooks), tutorials, technical articles, white papers are available for download, user conferences, such as the International DB2 User Group conference (IDUG), are held regularly throughout the world, and reference implementations to common tasks are available for download, etc. In summary, customer support and documentation can be considered good, in particular for DBMS of large vendors.

FUTURE TRENDS

Many research papers have proposed to include data quality dimensions into the data model itself. Typically, extensions to the relational model are proposed. Wang and Madnick present the Polygen framework, which extends each data value with metadata about its origin (1990). The authors suggest how to extend operators of the relational algebra, necessary to manipulate and query the data, to accommodate and update the corresponding metadata. In a further extension of their work they allow for information quality metadata of many dimensions (1995). Again, the relational algebra is adjusted. More recently, Scannapieco proposed a similar extension to the XML data model (2004). Even more recently Widom has reiterated the importance of incorporating information quality aspects and proposed the Trio System, which includes accuracy and lineage information in the relational data model (2005). These and other projects have in common that they are merely suggestions or prototypical implementations at best and have not yet been implemented by major database management system vendors.

A second trend is the development of tools — most notably ETL tools — that are based on DBMS and enhance information quality. Such tools are mentioned throughout the chapter wherever applicable.

CONCLUSION AND DISCUSSION

In conclusion, DBMS are able to uphold the quality-in-quality-out principle postulated in this chapter. Table 1 summarizes our results by listing the most important techniques to uphold a quality level or to improve the information quality in criterion. We have distinguished features that are intrinsic or fundamental to relational databases and features that are common extensions to RDBMS distributions. The IQ advantages of the first set of features ("intrinsic DBMS capabilities") are automatic when using carefully and expertly configure databases. The advantages of the second set of features ("extended DBMS features") are common with most commercial DBMS but are tools that must be actively applied in order to achieve high quality data.

In several cases, DBMS are able to improve on the quality of the data within. Most notably, DBMS add value to data by providing many advanced value-adding services, such as aggregation, integration, etc., as mentioned by Wiederhold and Genesereth (1997). The powerful SQL query language supported by all DBMS and the vendor-specific extensions allow developers to manipulate data in many ways to enhance its quality: Selection and projections allows users to limit data to just the right subset improving relevancy, appropriate amount and response time. Tools at the metadata level, such as schema design and integration tools, improve representational consistency and conciseness, understandability and interpretability. Through their support of the ACID properties, algorithms at the database core ensure that data is not lost or tampered with, upholding criteria such as accuracy, completeness, and believability. The ability of DBMS to integrate data from multiple heterogeneous sources also improves completeness and relevancy of data. Finally, many usability tools to maintain and use DBMS improve security, support, and accessibility.

The only detriment to information quality imposed by the use of DBMS is the potentially limiting expressiveness of the relational model. DBMS data is modeled in relations using a set of attributes, while often a hierarchical or other model is the more natural way of expressing the structure of data. With the recent move of major DBMS towards support of the XML data model and the XQuery language, this disadvantage is already fading.

To summarize, it should come as no surprise that relational databases are able to uphold the *quality-in-quality-out* criteria described in this chapter. DBMS technology has matured over 20 years of development, and confidence in the reliability and robustness of the DBMS model is reflected in countless mission-critical applications deployed on DBMS systems today. The proactive improvement of information quality however must be left to improved processes, specialists and specialized applications.

Table 1. Summarizing effects of DBMS on IQ

IQ Criterion	Intrinsic DBMS capabilities	Extended DBMS Features	Summary
Believability	ACID properties		%
Accuracy	ACID, UDTs, Triggers, checksums	Outlier detection	%
Objectivity	Durability, "unbiased" machine		%
Reputation		Maturity of DBMS, reputation of DBMS	+
Value Added	Aggregation	Federation, integration, search, etc.	+
Relevancy	Powerful query language	Access to remote data	+
Timeliness	Update propagation for materialized views and replication		%
Completeness	ACID properties	ETL, Wrappers for heterogeneous data	+
Approximate Amount	Scalability to many Terabyte	First N Rows	%
Latency/ Response Time	Pipelining, advanced query optimization	First N Rows, autonomic computing	+
Interpretability	Language support, UDTs, UDFs	Visual schema design, query builders	+
Understandability	Metadata restrictions (8 char)	Query plan explanation for administrators, visualization tools on top of DBMS	–
Repr. Consistency	JDBC, relational data model	XML, schema integration tools, schema mapping	+/–
Repr. Conciseness	Relational data model, normalization, query language	SQL/XML	+
Accessibility	Distribution, replication	Web interfaces, portals	+
Security	SQL privilege management, authentication	Security auditing	+
Support/ Documentation		Phone and email support, tutorials, manuals, conferences, newsgroups	+

Note: – detrimental; % no effect; + beneficial

REFERENCES

Astrahan, M. M., Blasgen, M. W., Chamberlin, D. D., Gray, J., King III, W. F., Lindsay, B. G., et al. (1979). System R: A relational data base management system. *IEEE Computer, 12*(5), 42-48.

Batini, C., Lenzerini, M., & Navathe, S. B. (1986). A comparative analysis of methodologies for database schema integration. *ACM Computing Surveys, 18*(4), 323-364.

Bourbonnais, S., Gogate, V., Haas, L., Horman, R., Malaika, S., Narang, I., et al. (2004). An information infrastructure for the grid providing data virtualization and distribution. *IBM Systems Journal, 43*(4).

Brass, S. (2002). Semantic errors in SQL. In *Proceedings of the GI Workshop Grundlagen von Datenbanken*, Fischland, Germany.

Codd, E. F. (1970). A relational model of data for large shared data banks. *Communications of the ACM, 13*(6), 377-387.

Delone, W. H., & McLean, E. R. (1992). Information systems success: The quest for the dependent variable. *Information Systems Research, 3*(1), 60-95.

Graefe, G. (1993). Query evaluation techniques for large databases. *ACM Computing Surveys, 25*(2), 73-170.

Hernández, M. A., Popa, L., Velegrakis, Y., Miller, R. J., Naumann, F., & Ho, H. (2002). Mapping XML and relational schemas with Clio. In *Proceedings of the International Conference on Data Engineering (ICDE)* (pp. 498-499).

International Standards Organization (ISO). (1999). *Information technology — Database Language SQL* (Standard No. ISO/IEC 9075:1999).

Josifovski, V., Massmann, S., & Naumann, F. (2003). Super-fast XML Wrapper generation in DB2: A demonstration. In *Proceedings of the International Conference on Data Engineering (ICDE)* (pp. 756-758).

Josifovski, V., & Schwarz, P. M. (2003). Querying XML data sources in DB2: The XML Wrapper. In *Proceedings of the International Conference on Data Engineering (ICDE)* (pp. 809-820).

Kossmann, D. (2000). The state of the art in distributed query processing. *ACM Computing Surveys, 32*(4), 422-469.

Lehner, W., Sidle, R., Pirahesh, H., & Cochrane, H. (2000). Maintenance of automatic summary tables. In *Proceeding of the SIGMOD Conference* (pp. 512-513).

Melnik, S., Rahm, E., & Bernstein, P. A. (2003). Rondo: A programming platform for generic model management. In *Proceedings of the SIGMOD Conference* (pp. 193-204).

Naumann, F., Freytag, J. C., & Leser, U. (2004). Completeness of information sources. In *Information Systems*. Elsevier.

Pirahesh, H., Mohan, C., Cheng, J. M., Liu, T. S., & Selinger, P. G. (1990). Parallelism in relational data base systems: Architectural issues and design approaches. In *Proceedings of the International Symposium on Databases in Parallel and Distributed Systems (DPDS)* (pp. 4-29).

Scannapieco, M., Virgillito, A., Marchetti, C., Mecella, M., & Baldoni, R. (2004). The DaQuinCIS architecture: A platform for exchanging and improving data quality in cooperative information systems. *Information Systems, 29*(7), 551-582.

Tayi, G. K., & Ballou, D. P. (1998). Examining data quality. *Communications of the ACM, 41*(2), 54-57.

Wang, R., & Madnick, S. (1990). A Polygen Model for Heterogeneous Database Systems: The Source Tagging Perspective. *Proceedings of the 16th VLDB Conference*, (pp. 519-538), Brisbane, Australia.

Wang, R., Storey, V., & Firth, C. (1995). A framework for analysis of data quality research. *IEEE Transactions on Knowledge and Data Engineering (TKDE), 7*(4), 623-640.

Wang, R. Y., & Strong, D. M. (1996). Beyond accuracy: What data quality means to data consumers. *Journal on Management of Information Systems, 12*(4), 5-34.

Widom, J. (2005). Trio: A system for integrated management of data, accuracy, and lineage. In *2nd Biennial Conference on Innovative Data Systems Research*, Asilomar, CA. Retrieved from http://www-db.cs.wisc.edu/cidr

Wiederhold, G., & Genesereth, M. R. (1997). The conceptual basis for mediation services. *IEEE Expert, 12*(5), 38-47.

Winter Corporation. (2003). *The TopTen program*. Retrieved from http://www.wintercorp.com/VLDB/2003_TopTen_Survey/TopTenProgram.html

Wright, M. (2003). An overview of high availability and disaster recovery features for DB2 UDB. *IBM Developerworks*. Retrieved from http://www.ibm.com/developerworks/db2/library/techarticle/0304wright/0304wright.html

Zilio, D. C., Zuzarte, C., Lightstone, S., Ma, W., Lohman, G. M., Cochrane, R., et al. (2004). Recommending materialized views and indexes with IBM DB2 Design Advisor. In *Proceedings of the International Conference on Autonomic Computing* (pp. 180-188).

TRADEMARKS

- IBM, DB2, and DB2 Universal Database are trademarks of International Business Machines Corporation in the United States, other countries, or both.
- Microsoft is a trademark of Microsoft Corporation in the United States, other countries, or both.
- Other company, product or service names may be trademarks or service marks of others.

ENDNOTES

[1]   Oracle Database, www.oracle.com/ip/deploy/database/oracle9i/
[2]   Microsoft SQL Server, www.microsoft.com/sql/
[3]   MySql open source database, www.mysql.com
[4]   SQL/XML standard, http://www.sqlx.org/

Chapter VII

Management of Data Streams for Large-Scale Data Mining

Jon R. Wright, AT&T Labs - Research, USA

Gregg T. Vesonder, AT&T Labs - Research, USA

Tamraparni Dasu, AT&T Labs - Research, USA

ABSTRACT

In an enterprise setting, a major challenge for any data-mining operation is managing data streams or feeds, both data and metadata, to ensure a stable and certifiably accurate flow of data. Data feeds in this environment can be complex, numerous and opaque. The management of frequently changing data and metadata presents a considerable challenge. In this chapter, we articulate the technical issues involved in the task of managing enterprise data and propose a multi-disciplinary solution, derived from fields such as knowledge engineering and statistics, to understand, standardize, and automate information acquisition and quality management in preparation for enterprise mining.

INTRODUCTION

Witten & Frank (2000), Piatetsky-Shapiro et al. (1996), and others have noted that industrial *data mining* applications frequently require substantial effort in the activities that occur prior to the application of data-mining algorithms. These observations match very closely with our experience in working with real-world applications. We have been able to work with a telephony data-mining project over the past several years, and it has served as a test bed for our ideas and experiments on data quality. The project has visibility at all levels of the enterprise, and it provides us with access to complex data on a large scale. The monitoring methodology we have developed has largely been driven by our experiences in working with this application and therefore represents, in part, a response to practical needs. Fundamentally, the amount of data flowing into that project is at a scale that demands automated monitoring tools, or at least, machine-assisted monitoring of some sort. Our ideas, therefore, receive serious testing in the crucible of a real-world application, a facet occasionally missing from research projects. Certain aspects of the application are covered in more detail in a later section.

We find that perhaps 90% of the effort in a real-world data-mining project is spent in acquisition, preparation, management of data, and other related activities, with about 10% spent on analysis. Notwithstanding this fact, much of the research on data mining focuses on providing increasingly sophisticated analysis and discovery algorithms, typically relying on pre-existing databases, such as the World Wide Telescope (Gray, 2003). Consequently, the core practical issues involved in acquiring and managing data on a large scale have not received the attention they deserve.

Successfully managing data at scale, including preparation prior to analysis, is probably the key determiner of success on any practical data mining application. Typically, the most interesting data originates within the computer applications that support the core business processes of an enterprise. This data takes a variety of forms — transaction records, application logs, Web scrapings, database dumps, and so forth. The supporting computer systems, because of their critical role in the business, are nearly always off-limits to CPU and space-hungry data-mining activities, and there is no choice but to transfer the data to a computing environment that is more data-mining friendly. Because of the increased computer support and automation of the core business processes in the modern enterprise, the scale of data available for mining is both massive and growing. In addition, data-mining is sometimes the only window on important business processes within an enterprise. The *metadata* so essential in interpreting and understanding enterprise data can be of significant size in its own right. By necessity, both data and *metadata* evolve continuously with the changing business environment of the enterprise. Originally, it was thought that most problems could be solved through data warehousing but the scale and flexibility required by modern data-mining applications make this a less than efficacious and flexible solution.

Many of the key issues in data quality and information management have been described previously (Pipino, Lee, and Wang, 2002; Huang, Lee, and Wang, 1999). In particular, maintaining a high level of data quality is closely tied with data-feed management. In this chapter, we focus on tools and methodologies needed to implement data quality management techniques such as those discussed in these publications within the context of enterprise data quality management, from data gathering to data mining. We view the whole process as somewhat organic in nature, emphasizing the growth and evolution of data in a real setting.

The *mise en place* Problem in
Industrial Data Mining Applications

The term we use to designate the process associated with assembling, preparing, managing and interpreting data for the data mining process is *mise en place*, a cooking term, meaning "put in place," which describes the activities of measuring, chopping, peeling, and so forth, in preparation for the actual cooking process. In a similar fashion, enterprise data must be prepared for data mining. Such activities include: (a) assembling time-dependent metadata, (b) providing and managing a long-term repository for ephemeral data and metadata, so that longitudinal trends may be deduced, and (c) monitoring and improving the quality of the data. In many industrial settings the bulk of the effort for a data mining project focuses on these *mise en place* activities. Without these activities, meaningful data mining would be impossible (see Witten & Frank, 2000). Data preparation for data mining has also been addressed by Pyle (1999).

Our goals are to develop awareness for the important role these activities play, to standardize and automate preparation activities through supporting tools, methodology, and techniques, so that less effort is spent on preparation and more on data mining and to place these activities and data mining within the context of a continuous and evolving set of tools, processes and knowledge. Key techniques we are using to understand, standardize and automate this process are derived both from artificial intelligence and statistics, and include: knowledge engineering, planning, constraint management, and rule-based programming.

In the remainder of this chapter, we first frame the main challenges in data-stream management by discussing a data-mining application that we have worked with over the past several years. Next, we discuss some of the methods we have developed to detect missing and corrupted data in data feeds. Finally, we discuss some promising automation technology derived from artificial intelligence. A final section places all of these activities within the context of data quality and information management. The ultimate goal of our research program is to devise and promote techniques that reduce the time and effort for these activities, transforming the "one-of's" to *repeatable, automated processes and abstract general techniques.*

TELEPHONY DATA MINING

In this section, we will describe in broad terms a real-world enterprise data-mining application that illustrates the preceding discussion and focuses on the *mise en place* activities of data transfer, data integrity, and archiving. It is an application with which we have a lot of experience, and we'll refer to it simply as the Telephony Data Mining or TDM application. We will focus primarily on the problems and issues of managing the data feeds for this application. The TDM application is built on clustering technology using commodity hardware that was developed at AT&T

Figure 1. Three-tiered data stream architecture

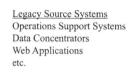

Legacy Source Systems
Operations Support Systems
Data Concentrators
Web Applications
etc.

Relay Stations
Vetting/Verification
Initial Replication
Relay/Transfer
Detection/Alerting
File Recovery

Compute Platforms
Data Integrity
Analysis/Discovery

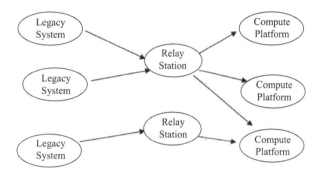

Research and is described in Hume and Daniels (2002). The clustering technology has some very interesting features in its own right, especially in terms of its ability to monitor and actively maintain the integrity of stored data on a large scale. It supplies the compute engine needed to execute analysis and discovery algorithms on that data.

Data transfers are managed using the three-tiered architecture shown in Figure 1. The source systems (shown on the left of Figure 1) are very heterogeneous, and many are mainframes. Because the mainframes run multiple applications, a single mainframe can generate more than one data feed, and, in addition, some of the source systems are concentrators for a much larger set of systems lying behind them. In many cases, data is generated automatically on a timed schedule, but some are generated from programs initiated by human operators in a data center. Typically, the source systems have enough temporary storage capacity to retain generated data on a short term basis — perhaps 48 hours — before deletion. This is important because if a transfer fails or is corrupted, there is a short window during which the data can be recovered.

We will not have much to say about the compute platforms shown in Figure 1, other than that they provide the resources for data analysis and are able to maintain the integrity of data within their domain. On the other hand, many interesting activities take place on the relay stations. When a file is first received on a relay station, it goes through a feed specific vetting process, among other things, making sure that file headers and contents match. Then the data is compressed, an initial replication of the data is performed, and the data is transferred to an appropriate compute platform. Replication is the fundamental tool used to maintain data integrity (see Hume & Daniels, 2002). We want to focus on two specific functions performed on the relay nodes: detection and alerting when there are problems in the stream of files arriving at the node, and taking action to recover data before it is lost.

Each data feed has its own characteristics. Some feeds send a fixed number of files per hour, 24 hours a day, every day of the year. Others send a variable number of files depending on the activity on the source system, for example, the transactions performed on some legacy system. This kind of data reflects daily, weekly, and seasonal cycles in addition to general upward or downward trends. Other feeds might send a fixed number of files but only on working days — in other words, no files are sent on weekends or holidays. Files can be sent in weekly, monthly, or quarterly cycles, as well as daily cycles.

Typically, human operators monitor the data feeds using a variety of ad hoc tools, and take some appropriate action when problems are detected. Frequency of monitoring varies, in part depending on the work load of the operators, and occasionally problems go undetected for a certain period of time. The task is complicated by the scale of the data passing through the relay stations. The TDM application receives something over 60 terabytes of uncompressed data per month from 100 or so sources. By applying good data compression we are able to bring the amount of storage required down to about 6 terabytes per month. Once data is compressed on the relay stations, it never exists again on disk in an uncompressed form. There are thousands of files received every month. One legacy system sends about 80,000 files per month, and most analyses of these data require the full set of intact files — in other words, missing data often invalidates the ability to do analysis.

THREE PRACTICAL PROBLEMS IN DATA-STREAM MANAGEMENT AND SOME PRACTICAL SOLUTIONS

Detecting Anomalies Using Statistical Ensembles and Agent Monitoring

A **statistical process control model**. Despite the amount of data flowing through the system, the TDM has a requirement of zero data loss. Therefore it is important to detect corrupted data, missing files, and other anomalies as early as possible, so data recovery can be initiated within the 48-hour window of opportunity. One of our goals is to automate the monitoring of data streams as much as possible. Monitoring or vigilance tasks are known to be a difficult problem for human operators (Davies & Parasuraman, 1982), and it makes sense for us to relieve the human operator of as much of this burden as possible. Statistical process control has provided a useful framework for thinking about data quality problems (Redman, 1996), and we have taken our lead from that literature. As an initial alerting mechanism, we built a simple univariate, nonparametric control chart for detecting holes in feeds — either due to missing files or due to smaller file sizes than usual. Smaller file sizes indicate data that has never been sent or data that got lost in transit.

For a single data feed, Figures 2 and 3 show the fluctuation in files received and the total file size by hour. That particular feed sends a fixed number of files per hour, but the size of the file is variable — it contains what are essentially transaction records that reflect variations in business activity. Figure 2 shows that file transmissions sometimes lag, and that a lower than expected number of files are received during some hours but that there is compensation in which the missing files are supplied during later hours.

Figure 3 clearly demonstrates a daily and weekly cycle in file sizes. The big spike corresponds to a large transmission that compensates for the data gap that just precedes it.

Figures 4 and 5 show the confidence bounds for a single daily cycle of files. They clearly show a daily cycle in activity, the high points of the two graphs reflecting the "busy" hours. We computed the predicted value and confidence bounds using metrics based on the median and the inter-quartile range over a stable period of time. Figure 4 shows a normal cycle where the file sizes received were within acceptable bounds of the expected values.

Figure 2. Hourly counts of files received over a one week period for a single data stream

Distribution of File Size

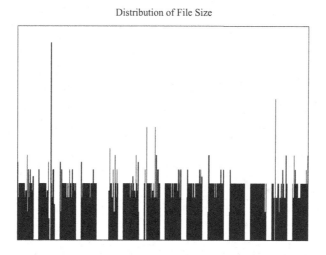

Figure 3. Total hourly file size received over a one week period for a single data stream

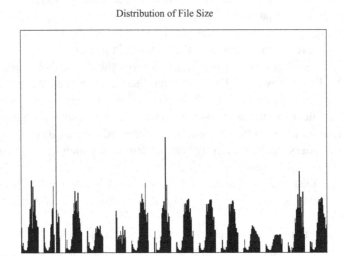

Figure 4. Control chart for a single day showing hourly counts of files received, median, and the 5ᵗʰ and 95ᵗʰ quantiles, and medians

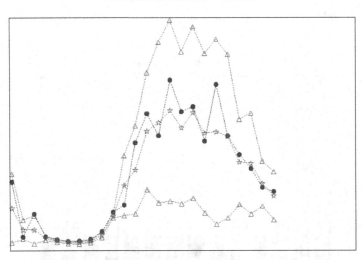

Note: •••Obs; ★★★Exp; ▲▲▲Upper; ▲▲▲Lower

Figure 5. Control chart for a single day showing hourly sums of file sizes for files received, medians, and the 5ᵗʰ and 95ᵗʰ quantiles

Error Bands on File Sizes — Abnormal

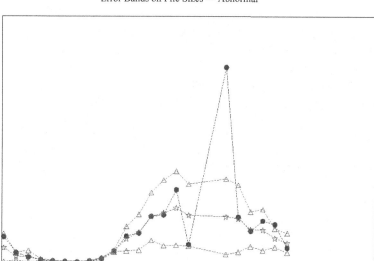

Note: • • •Obs; ★ ★ ★Exp; ▲ ▲ ▲Upper; ▲ ▲ ▲Lower

Figure 5 shows an abnormal day with two hours of light transmission followed by a spike of cumulative transmission. This is often due to problems with transmission links.

The two figures clearly indicate that an approach based on statistical process control would be appropriate. Using this paradigm, normal bounds are calculated from historical data and then alarms are generated when a data point goes out-of-bounds. Figure 5 is interesting in that it shows an out-of-bounds condition that is essentially a compensatory spike. It's part of the normal ups and downs that are representative of an internal corporate network, and not necessarily an abnormal condition because no data was lost. Alarming on that spike would be a false alarm. Avoiding false alarms or, at least, providing information that helps a human operator distinguish between likely false alarms and obvious hits is very desirable.

Statistical ensembles. To provide the human operator with better information to distinguish between hits and false alarms, we are currently experimenting with collections of statistical tests, called ensembles, to monitor the important data streams within the TDM application (Wright, Majumder, Dasu, & Vesonder, 2005).

Below is a sample ensemble for a single data feed consisting of six non-parametric tests. Each test is intended to give a slightly different perspective on the state of the data feed.

The six tests are:

1.   Hampel bounds
2.   Bounds based on 5th and 95th quantiles
3.   Bounds based on the 5% trimmed means of the log transforms
4.   3-sigma bounds of the log transforms
5.   Bounds based on 5% trimmed means
6.   3-sigma bounds

We calculate values for the six tests on the number of feed files received per hour and the total amount of data received during that hour. The bounds are calculated using a sliding three-month window of data, and the results are visually displayed using a simple graphical switchboard.

The Hample bounds and the trimmed mean tests were selected because they are well known to be robust with respect to contamination and are not influenced by a few outliers (Davies & Gather, 1993; Donoho & Huber, 1985). This is an important characteristic because, as noted above, outliers occur in the normal functioning of the data feeds, and it is important not to alarm unnecessarily. The two tests based on log transforms (tests 3 and 4) were selected because they will alert when there are truly large changes in data stream behavior. They are a red flag for the operator and they signal conditions that need to be responded to immediately. The 3-sigma tests have the advantage of being familiar to the engineers and operators of the TDM application. They provide the application engineers with a known basis for comparison with the other tests.

The **switchboard user interface**. The switchboard user interface for our example data stream is shown in Figure 6, and is based on real data collected during a week in which there appeared to be a significant problem with missing and corrupted data in the data stream.

The rows in the display show the results for the six statistical tests. Each time an out-of-bound value is calculated for one of the six tests, a point appears in the switchboard. The X-axis shows time in hours for the week. Early in the week, around hour 10, the value for the 5th-95th quantile test goes out of bounds, returns to normal briefly, and then goes out of bounds again consistently beginning around the 40th hour. Around that same hour, it is joined by several of the other tests. By the 48th hour, five of the six tests are going out of bounds with regularity, indicating that these are conditions that the operator needs to take seriously and respond to immediately.

Monitoring agents. We have implemented the alerting system by deploying what we think is best described as agents on the relay stations. The agents are

Figure 6. Switchboard user interface for data shown in Figures 2 and 3

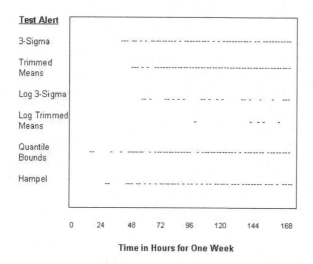

vehicles for implementing the ensembles of statistical and graphical tests we use to identify alarm conditions, and they pass back their results to a remote workstation where the graphical switchboard is displayed. Because the agents must run on nodes that do important work (i.e., the relay nodes), there is a requirement that they be computationally lightweight. For example, taking up a few percent of the CPU capacity of a node to perform monitoring tests is probably acceptable, but an agent that uses 20% of CPU capacity is not acceptable. The requirement to be lightweight constrains the kinds of statistical tests that an agent can perform. In addition, the output of the tests must be understandable and accepted by intelligent non-statisticians, and this places additional restrictions on the choice of tests. For the most part, we select simple non-parametric tests for our test ensembles. A more thorough discussion of statistical ensembles is contained in Wright, Majumder, Dasu, & Vesonder (2005).

Understanding System State

Lifecyle events. The complexity and scale of the data in our TDM application makes it difficult to understand the state of the system as a whole. We would like to have some simple measures that tell us something about the health of the system, whether data is in jeopardy of being lost because some portion of the overall system is not functioning properly. From the previous discussion, it should be clear that the framework we have discussed is file-oriented, and also that there are common events associated with each file. For example, all files are transferred from their source systems, vetted when they are received, consumed by applications, and eventually archived[1] when they are no longer needed for immediate analysis. These common events can fairly be described as a lifecycle.[2] We use these lifecycle events to describe the state of the system as a whole by counting files that have a specific event profile. The counts attributed to a specific event profile tell something about the overall state of the feed system.

Event profiles. As an experiment, we analyzed the profiles of a set of files associated with a single data feed. The four events that we mention here are Transmission Failure, Recompression,[3] Tape Replication and Consumed by Application. Note that in reality there are many more events that happen. For one thing, a file can be consumed by multiple applications. The interaction between applications can sometimes be inferred from these sequences, helping us to design a more efficient process.

In Table 1, we show a symbolic representation of the frequency of events and the number of files that exhibited that particular frequency of events.

The event frequency sequence is simply a count of the times each event occurred in the file's lifecycle. For example, the first data row indicates that there were 52,388 that had 0 transmission failures, 0 recompressions, were written to tape once and have not yet been analyzed or *consumed* by an application. This is a form of data reduction where we represent the sequence of events by a frequency of counts of the events. There is a loss of information (the exact sequence of events is lost as is the knowledge of the duration of the inter-event intervals), but the frequency counts help us compare the files based on event sequences in a simple manner. More complex analyses using point process methodologies are possible as well. The actual table is much larger — we skipped many rows (around 90) in the table — to make it possible to include a peculiar example. The last row is an instance of a file that experienced transmission failure 97 times! Fortunately there are not too many such files. A further examination of the file's history revealed that it was caught in a software glitch in the file transmission software that was soon fixed by the vendor of the software.

Automating Actions Using Plans

Borrowing from artificial intelligence. Monitoring and alerting on missing and corrupted data in data streams is just one side of the equation. In the current state of the art, anomalous conditions are presented to a human operator, and the human operator is expected to devise an appropriate action. Humans may always be in the loop somewhere, however, we are also interested in the ability to automatically respond to and repair abnormalities as much as possible. Effective automation is perhaps the most important factor in the ability to manage data at scale. We want to

Table 1. Multiple events in the life cycle of files

	Event Frequency Sequence	File Frequency
On Tape	0.0.1.0	52388
Replicated	0.0,2.0	16222
Replicated Consumed	0.0.2.1	7556
Recompressed On Tape	0.1.1.0	1848
. . . .	. . . .	. . . .
Failed Recompressed Replicated Consumed	97.1.2.1	1

be able to automate low and middle level tasks, but keep open the option to involve a human at the higher levels.

Artificial intelligence is the scientific discipline that tries to advance our understanding of the nature of intelligence by engineering autonomous agents capable of responding to their environment in a manner indistinguishable from human intelligence — the well-known Turing test (see Saygin et al. for a discussion of the Turing test's history). Many methods of building autonomous agents have been developed, some of which have been abandoned as their limitations in terms of developing a general intelligence became better understood. Nevertheless, some of these methods are of importance in a practical sense. One example is rule-based programming (Vesonder, 1996). Rule-based programming based on techniques developed in the artificial intelligence community are now used in business process automation (Minsky, 2004). In addition, some of the work in adaptive systems (i.e., Barto & Sutton, 1998) is beginning to appear in advanced and experimental systems design (Joshi et al., 2004). So there is precedent for technology developed in the artificial intelligence community leaking over and becoming utilized in systems design.

Planning systems. We believe that automated planning and AI planning systems are an underused automation technology that could become important in data-feed management. Weld (1999) describes the recent advancements in planning technology, including fast planners based on constraint programming and satisfiability algorithms. In our view, however, classical planning approaches are sufficient for many applications. Even when they are not, because we are mainly interested in applications rather than general intelligence, it is perfectly acceptable to develop and use a domain-specific planner. Therefore, relatively old approaches may work well enough, and the fact that they have not been tried so far represents a missed opportunity.

Following Nilsson (1980), a plan is a sequence of actions executed over a state-transition system that, when executed, leaves the system in a desired state. Each action is simply a specification of the preconditions required to perform the action and the consequences of performing the action. A logical formalism is typically used to represent system state and the preconditions and consequences of actions. A number of assumptions underlie the classical planning paradigm (Ghallab et al., 2004). One of the important assumptions is that the system is assumed to have no internal dynamics. At it simplest level, this means that the only way the state-transition system can change state is through actions taken by the planner. While this is obviously not true of the data feeds managed by the TDM application, we can pretend that it is true without much harm and still automate meaningful tasks that support the application in important ways. We will revisit this issue subsequently.

File archiving. An example that is relevant for data-feed management is file archiving. As we have discussed, the data used in a working application has a natural lifecycle, the last stage of which is archiving, after the data has been processed by all applications. In our TDM application, archiving to tape is accomplished with the help of a tape robot. The robot has six tape drives or *data transfer elements* (DTEs) and a large number of storage slots or *storage elements* (SEs). At any given time, the SEs contain a mix of blank tapes and tapes that have already been written. Software commands are used to transfer tapes between the DTEs and SEs (load and unload tapes) and to write data to tapes in specific DTEs. Using the tape robot, the steps required to archive a collection of files to tape are:

1.   Load a blank tape from an SE into an empty DTE.
2.   Compose the tape segments containing the set of files to be archived.
3.   Write headers to the tapes identifying the tape's contents.
4.   On the host systems where the files are resident, create the segments.
5.   Copy the segments to a host connected to a tape drive.
6.   Write the segments to tape.
7.   When the tape is full, verify that the tape was correctly written.
8.   Unload the full tape to an appropriate SE.

Each of these 8 actions can be represented by a plan operator. Planning then consists of applying operators in a state space search until the goal of having the original files on tape is reached. However, it's not the planner that concerns us per se, as we always have the fall back position of being able to write a domain-specific planner — it's the plan executor, the controlling system that executes plans.

Nilsson also describes a concise data structure for representing plans called a **triangle table**. The triangle table is the core of a simple plan execution system. To illustrate, we'll show a **triangle table** for a simple problem requiring three actions. Figure 7 shows the initial state and the goal state for the problem. We have two operators, one for unloading a tape volume from a DTE into an SE, and one for loading a tape volume from an SE to a DTE. We want to unload and load volumes such that Vol_0 is in Drive 0 and Vol_1 is in DTE 1. Although not the only solution, the goal can be reached with three actions shown at the top of Figure 7.

The **triangle table** for this solution is shown in Figure 8. Of course, we are only interested in the lower diagonal of the table. The columns represent the start state and the sequence of actions making up of the plan. Along the diagonal are the names or types of the actions. Consider the entry for the first action *Unload Volume*.

Figure 7. Example of a three-action plan showing initial state and end state for the tape robot

Actions: 1. Unload volume *Vol_1* from *Drive 0* to *SE 3*
2. Load volume *Vol_0* from *SE 1* to *Drive 0*
3. Load volume *Vol_1* from *SE 3* to *Drive 1*

	Initial State		End State
Drive 0	Vol_1	Drive 0	Vol_0
Drive 1	Empty	Drive 1	Vol_1
SE 1	Vol_0	SE 1	Empty
SE 2	Vol_2	SE 2	Vol_2
SE 3	Empty	SE 3	Empty
SE 4	Vol_3	SE 4	Vol_3

Figure 8. Triangle table for the example three-action plan

Start State	Action 1	Action 2	Action 3
Empty se1 Full dte0 vol1	**Unload Volume**		
Empty dte1	Full se1 vol1	**Load Volume**	
Full se2 vol0	Empty dte0		**Load Volume**
		Full dte1 vol1	Full dte0 vol0	**Goal State**

On the row to the left of that entry are the conditions in the start state that correspond to the preconditions for that action. In other words, storage element 1 is empty (represented by *Empty se1*) and data transfer element 0 (tape drive 0) contains a tape volume (*Full dte0 vol1*). The entries below the entry for *Unload Volume* contain the consequences of the action on which that later actions depend. In other words, some of the consequences of the *Unload Volume* action are preconditions for later actions. If we examine the entry for action 2, the first *Load Volume* action, we can see that it has two preconditions, one of which is satisfied by the start state (it's in the first column below *Start State*), and one of which is satisfied by a consequent of action 1 (it appears in the column below *Unload Volume*). The last row contains the elements of the goal state. If the consequent of an action fulfills an element of the goal state, that element appears in the last row.

Triangle tables are simply computed from the sequence of actions in a plan and descriptions of start and goal states. They provide a precise means of answering precise questions about where a plan is in terms of its execution. Data–mining- and data-stream-related tasks often require hours from start to completion — consider how long it takes to transfer 80,000 files among nodes. **Triangle tables** provide a useful basis for answering questions and issuing status reports about where a plan is in terms of execution, and for estimating time to completion. In addition, they contain key information about the dependency between actions. For example, the two *Load Volume* actions are independent of each other because there are no entries in the intersection of row and column for the two actions. On the other hand, both depend on the *Unload Volume* action because they have preconditions represented in the column for *Unload Volume*. Once *Unload Volume* is completed, the two *Load Volume* actions could theoretically proceed in parallel. In this case, they can't because tape robots are single threaded — they are only able to execute one command at a time. The parallelism can't be implemented because of limitations of the action system, not because of any inherent dependency between actions. Hence, triangle tables contain important information that is necessary but not sufficient to implement a plan execution system capable of parallel actions.

We can now discuss briefly how a triangle table can be used to soften the fact that the plan doesn't take into account that a system may have internal dynamics. For example, a human user could issue a command to our tape robot that changes its state while our plan is executing. Or the state of the tape robot could change while we are formulating our plan so that when the plan is launched the actual state is different from the initial state on which the plan was based. One method of dealing with this uses the notion of *highest matching kernel* or *HMK*. The *ith* kernel of a triangle table is defined to be all entries below and to the left of the *ith* column, including all entries on the *ith* row. By matching a triangle table against a description of the current state of a system, we can determine which entries are true and which are not at that specific point in time. The HMK is the highest numbered kernel for which all entries are found to be true in the current system state.

For example, kernel 2 in the triangle table shown in Table 2 has four elements: Empty drive_1, Full se_1 vol_1, Full se_2 vol_0, and Empty drive_0. If all four elements are true in the current state, kernel 2 is a matching kernel. If no higher numbered kernel is a matching kernel, then kernel 2 is the highest matching kernel.

Those entries are precisely those entries that are currently true and must remain true until the plan completes — because subsequent actions in the plan depend on them. By definition, the next higher kernel has some entries that are not true, and therefore actions must be performed to cause them to become true. Hence, the HMK identifies the next action that is eligible to be performed in the plan. Because the kernels of a triangle table overlap, a simple and efficient algorithm can be used to find the HMK given a state description and a triangle table.

By using the HMK to select the next action and taking sensor readings to update our state description after each action, we can run our plan executor in a loop and thereby handle certain kinds of internal dynamics. When the internal dynamics of the state transition system cause the state to change, this is picked up by our sensors and reflected in the current state description. Next, the HMK algorithm selects an appropriate action to apply regardless of what the previous action was. It may simply direct us back to some earlier action in the plan. If no HMK is found, we must re-plan with the current state description becoming the initial state of the new plan, otherwise, the selected action is performed. We simply continue until a goal state is reached.

The practical success of such a system depends such things as the rate of change due to internal dynamics, how fast the planner is (how much change takes place while a plan is being formulated), how likely actions are to fail, and a few other factors. Small-scale experiments with file archiving and file transfer have been successful using the approach described above.

CONCLUSION

In this chapter, we have proposed an important area of research in managing and mining constantly changing, large-scale information feeds in practical data-mining projects. Our TDM application gives us a close up look at the challenges of managing data in a practical setting where data must be transferred from source to destination at scale, and where zero or minimal data loss is a requirement. The task of data mining in such a setting offers challenges that are very distinct from traditional data-mining scenarios. Much of the ongoing work in data mining is analysis focused, and does not address the areas that seem to us the most problematic in a practical setting. The *mise en place* analogy is an accurate one. Most of the work in all the data-mining projects we have been associated takes place in the preparation stage, prior to analysis.

One element of future work is to address the issue of constantly morphing data feeds and the knowledge needed to parse and interpret these feeds. Data-mining systems are inherently *downstream systems* (Evans, 2004) sensitive to changes in the data introduced by the operational systems collecting and providing the data to the enterprise. Examples of such changes are the introduction of new products, repackaging of existing data or additions or changes to fields of existing data.

Our current framework can detect some of these changes by noticing changes to the frequency and size of the files. Notification and incorporation of these changes and less detectable changes requires frequent and lengthy interaction with Subject Matter Experts using traditional knowledge engineering techniques. Hendler (2005) has an excellent description of using the Web, or as he terms it the "semantic Web," for knowledge acquisition. His techniques are supported by a number of emerging Web standards such as OWL from the W3C. We plan to augment the change detection methods we have developed so far by actively mining the intranet for changes in the applications and data relevant to our feeds.

REFERENCES

Barto, A. G., & Sutton, R. S. (1998). *Reinforcement learning: An introduction to adaptive computation and machine learning*. Boston: MIT Press.

Dasu, T., Vesonder, G. T., & Wright, J. R. (2003). Data quality through knowledge engineering. In *Proceedings of the Conference on Knowledge Discovery and Data Mining*, (pp. 705-710).

Davies, D. R., & Parasuraman, R. (1982). *The psychology of vigilance*. London: Academic Press.

Evans, E. (2004). *Domain-driven design: Tackling complexity in the heart of software*. New York: Addison-Wesley.

Ghallab, M., Nau, D., & Traverso, P. (2004). *Automated planning: Theory and practice*. San Franciso: Morgan-Kaufmann.

Gray, J. (2003). Invited talk, On-Line science: The Worldwide telescope as a prototype for the new computational science. *Conference on Knowledge Discovery and Data Mining*, Washington, DC.

Huang, K. Y., Lee, Y. W., & Wang, R. Y. (1999). *Quality information and knowledge management*. New York: Prentice-Hall.

Hume, A. G., & Daniels, E. S. (2002, June 10-15). Ningaui: A Linux Cluster for Business. *Proceedings of the FREENIX Track: 2002 USENIX Annual Technical Conference*, Monterey, CA (pp. 195-206).

Joshi, K. R., Hiltunen, M., Schlichting, R., Sanders, W. H., & Agbaria, A. (2004, October 31-November 1). Online model-based adaptation for optimizing performance and dependability. In *Proceedings of the Workshop on Self-Managed Systems (WOSS 2004)*, Newport Beach, CA.

Minsky, Steve (2004, July). Business rules management: New business tools for innovation and accountability. *Business Process Trends*.

Nilsson, N. J. (1980). *Principles of artificial intelligence*. Palo Alto: Tioga Publishing.

Piatetsky-Shapiro, G., Brachman, R., Khabaza, T., Kloesgen, W., & Simoudis, E. (1996). An overview of issues in developing industrial data mining and knowledge discovery applications. In E. Simoudis, J. Han, & U. Fayyad (Eds.), *Proceedings of the Conference on Knowledge Discovery and Data Mining*, Menlo Park AAAI Press.

Pipino, L., Lee, Y., & Wang, R. (2002) Data quality assessment. *Communications of the ACM, 45*(4), 211-218.

Pyle, D. (1999). *Data preparation for data mining*. San Fransisco: Morgan-Kaufmann.

Redman, Thomas C. (1996). *Data quality for the Information Age*. Norwood, MA: Artech House.

Saygin, A. P., Cicekli, I., & Akman, V. (2000). Turing test: 50 years later. *Minds and Machines, 10*(4), 463-518.

Vesonder, G. T. (1996). Rule-based programming in the Unix System. *AT&T Technical Journal, 67*(1), 69-80.

Weld, D. S. (1999). Recent advances in AI planning. *AI Magazine, 20*(2), 93-123.

Witten, I. H., & Frank, E. (2005). *Data mining: Practical machine learning tools* (2nd ed.). San Francisco: Morgan Kaufmann.

Wright, J. R, Majumder, D., Dasu, T., & Vesonder, G. T. (2005). Statistical ensembles for managing complex data streams. In K. Matawie (Ed.) *Proceedings of the 20th International Workshop on Statistical Modeling*, Sydney, Australia (pp. 231-245).

ENDNOTES

[1]   Archiving is fairly involved requiring storage of both data and time-sensitive metadata.

[2]   The notion that data have a natural lifecycle was first pointed out to us by Andrew Hume.

[3]   New and better compression technology is made available on occasion. When that happens older files are recompressed to take advantage of space savings. Recompression changes certain key characteristics used to track files, namely file size and the md5sum of the compressed file. Recompression is therefore a key event in the history of a file.

Chapter VIII

Metadata Quality Problems in Federated Collections

Besiki Stvilia, Florida State University, USA

Les Gasser, University of Illinois at Urbana-Champaign, USA

Michael B. Twidale, University of Illinois at Urbana-Champaign, USA

ABSTRACT

This chapter presents results from our empirical studies of metadata quality in large corpuses of metadata harvested under open archives initiative (OAI) protocols. Along with a discussion of why and how metadata quality is important, an approach to conceptualizing, and assessing metadata quality is presented. The approach is based on a more general model of information quality for many kinds of information beyond just metadata. A key feature of the general model is its ability to condition quality assessments by context of information use, such as the types of activities that use the information, and the typified norms and values of relevant information-using communities. The chapter presents a number of statistical characterizations of samples of metadata from a large corpus built as part of the Institute of Museum and Library Services Digital Collections and Contents project containing OAI-harvested metadata, interprets these statistical assessments and links to the quality measures. Finally the chapter discusses several approaches to quality improvement for metadata based on the study findings.

INTRODUCTION

The usability and effectiveness of any digital library is clearly affected by the quality of its metadata records. Low quality metadata can render a library almost unusable, while high metadata quality can lead to higher user satisfaction and increased use. Consequently, digital library infrastructures should include effective quality assurance mechanisms of its metadata collections.

This chapter presents results from our empirical studies of metadata quality in large corpuses of metadata harvested under the Open Archives Initiative protocols. Along with some discussion of why and how metadata quality is important, we present an approach to conceptualizing, measuring, and assessing metadata quality. The approach we give in this chapter is based on a more general model of information quality (IQ) for many kinds of information beyond just metadata (Gasser & Stvilia, 2001). A key feature of the general model is its ability to condition quality assessments by context of information use, such as the types of activities that use the information, and the typified norms and values of relevant information-using communities. We present a number of statistical characterizations of analyzed samples of metadata from a large corpus built as part of the Institute of Museums and Library Services Digital Collections and Contents (IMLS DCC)[1] project containing Open Archives Initiative (OAI)[2] -harvested metadata. We link these statistical assessments to our quality measures, and interpret them. Finally, we discuss several approaches to quality improvement for metadata based on our findings.

Overview of Approach

This chapter presents a general model for analyzing and reasoning about information quality in large aggregated metadata repositories. The model has been developed using a number of techniques such as literature analysis, case studies, statistical analysis, strategic experimentation, and multi-agent modeling. The model along with the concepts and metrics presented in this chapter can serve as a foundation for developing effective specific methodologies of quality assurance in various types of organizations.

Our model of metadata quality ties together findings from existing and new research in information quality, along with well-developed work in information seeking/use behavior, and the techniques of strategic experimentation from manufacturing. It presents a holistic approach to determining the quality of a metadata object, identifying quality requirements based on typified contexts of metadata use (such as specific information seeking/use activities) and expressing interactions between metadata quality and metadata value.

We include findings from the statistical analysis and experimentation with an aggregated metadata collection built as a part of the IMLS DCC project that suggest general types and values for metadata quality metric functions. However, since quality metrics are context-sensitive, at this point these statistics provide only suggestive guidance for building such functions in general. Specific quality metrics and their value ranges can be only determined based on specific types of metadata and its local cost and value structures.

Background and Related Research

Libraries, archives and museums are some of the oldest institutions dealing with information. Their processes of adding value to information through selection, organization and access also include, explicitly or implicitly, the reasoning and decision-making about the quality of metadata and metadata tools (Landau, 1969; Taylor, 1986). Frameworks for measuring metadata quality and methodologies for identifying metadata quality priorities are proposed in Basch (1995). Quality assurance problems of on-line database aggregators are discussed in Williams (1990). In the spirit of Orr's systems theory view (Orr, 1998), Twidale and Marty (1999) propose an inexpensive technique of assessing and improving quality of a museum information repository through establishing a feedback link between information creators and users. There is a well-developed body of research literature on data and information quality assurance in management sciences and the database world. Wang and Strong (1996) discuss impacts of poor data quality and propose a framework of data quality dimensions. A methodology of assessing information quality through modeling information manufacturing systems is developed in Ballou et al. (1998). Strong and colleagues (1997) discuss a methodology for reasoning about information quality through process and task analysis. A comprehensive overview of information and data quality assessment tools and methodologies is given in Wang et al. (2003). Motro, Anokhin, and Acar (2004) and Naumann, Leser, and Freytag (1999) introduce techniques for quality-based evaluation of query results and source selection in a multi-database environment.

Existing research in information and data quality assurance provides a valuable knowledge base of methodologies, techniques and concepts for assessing and improving quality of information. However, for enabling effective and realistic quality assurance planning and/or simply justifying quality improvement spending, there is a need to connect the changes in an information object's quality to changes in its value and cost in some sound, systematic way.

In addition, one of the thorniest issues in the theory of information quality is how to account for the context-sensitive nature of information quality and value: the same information may have different kinds and levels of quality and value in different contexts of use. Studies of user information seeking and use behavior (Marchionini, 1990; Palmer, 1998; Sutcliffe, 2000) provide the anchor for a set of generic activities that can be used to establish "typified" contexts for (and types of) information use. We can construct more generic views of the cost, value, and quality of information in relation to these typified contexts. In addition, our current research draws on insights from manufacturing (Cook, 1997; Taguchi et al., 1989) to connect information quality to the cost and value of information and to account for how changes in cost and value over time influence (and are influenced by) information quality. Using these insights, we develop concepts, methods and software tools for modeling quality, value and cost structures of typified metadata objects and link them consistently with typified contexts of their creation and use.

Although in general the IQ research community has not shown much interest in metadata quality, the recent surge of large-scale digitization initiatives and adoption of campus-wide digital document repositories and archives by large academic institutions led a number of scholars to examine the issues of metadata quality and explore the consequences for quality of federated collections.

In a study of the use of the unqualified Dublin Core (DC)3 metadata element set by 82 data providers registered with the Open Archives Initiative, Ward (2003) found that the top five DC elements (in order: creator, identifier, title, date and type) accounted for 71% of all element usage. Furthermore just over half of the data providers used only the creator and identifier elements for approximately half of their overall usage, and the average number of DC elements used in the collection records was eight.

Dushay and Hillman (2003) examined another aggregated collection, that of the National Science Digital Library. They outlined four kinds of metadata quality problems found in the collection: (1) missing data; (2) incorrect data; (3) confusing data; (4) insufficient data. The authors note how certain elements can help serve particular search needs, and consequently that errors in those elements cause particular problems. In their case, the elements were resource type and format which would help in providing simple search limits. They found that: "In many cases, the entire collection consisted of materials in one format or of one type, and the missing information was deemed unnecessary for the collection's local purpose." Other errors noted were creator names repeated in the language element, type and format information interchanged, and various entries signifying or conveying no meaningful information.

Barton and colleagues (2003) reviewed metadata quality issues in a number of e-print archive and repository projects. They identified the following classes of metadata quality problems as most often cited and complained on in the literature: (1) spelling errors: (2) lack of authority control; (3) having no titles for non-textual objects, or having many titles for a composite object; (4) inconsistent and ineffective subject terms; and (5) inconsistent and ambiguous date information: does the date refer to the date of creation, the date of publication, or the date of conversion to digital form. Based on the reviewed literature they also pointed to the conflicting needs and consequent priorities of the local and global contexts of metadata creation and use. That is, local providers might not be motivated in explicating locally shared knowledge in their metadata records while that knowledge could prove to be critical to global users to successfully search. In addition, it was noted that while authors or subject specialists might possess with better understanding of the work or subject area, information specialists might have better understanding of the user needs.

Recently Bruce and Hillman (2004) explored the various dimensions of metadata quality, particularly in the light of their importance for aggregated collections. They noted that shared metadata may require additional quality efforts, and that the resource implications of this extra work. Especially as projects scale up, they might require more complex, precise and consistent metadata to identify objects unambiguously. Finally, they proposed a metadata quality assessment framework consisting of seven general dimensions: completeness, accuracy, provenance, conformance to expectations, logical consistency and coherence, timeliness, and accessibility.

While the above works provide a useful description of the quality issues of metadata aggregation, they do not to do deeper analysis of metadata quality problem incidents, their sources and activities affected. They fall short to develop a systematic framework of metadata quality assessment that could be reused and operationalized in many different contexts.

The chapter is organized as follows. First we introduce concepts and foundations of our approach. In addition, using an example of a typified information seeking activity, we explain how analysis of a given activity and its actions can be used for identifying relevant quality dimensions, and important tradeoffs between those dimensions and the types of quality metric functions. Next we present three models of quantifying the impacts of quality changes on the value of a metadata object. Following that we present some empirical observations and the results of statistical analysis of random samples from IMLS DCC aggregated metadata collection and interpret them through the methodology prism formulated in the earlier sections. And, finally we conclude the chapter with a summary of the proposed concepts and methods and identify the directions of future research activities.

CONCEPTS AND METHODS

The Oxford English Dictionary defines metadata as "a set of data that describes and gives information about other data." A more sophisticated definition would be defining metadata as an expression of specific knowledge about documents that enables some specific functions. Thus, in addition to being an information object itself, a metadata object serves as a tool that provides access to (and other services for) other information. For example, the report of the IFLA Study Group on the Functional Requirements for Bibliographic Records (1998) specifies a "typified" (Leontiev, 1978) set of information activities such as finding, identifying, and obtaining information, which bibliographic metadata records are intended to support. Differences in the quality of metadata records — assuming we could assess it — would lead us to predict to differences in the ability of that metadata to support the activities it should support. High standardization of metadata objects and availability of more or less standardized baseline representations may somewhat reduce the complexity of quality assessment, but they hardly eliminate it due to the contextual nature of information quality. In addition, metadata objects are generally complex, composite objects consisting of multiple components. Their structure ranges from schematic objects with multiple fields (e.g., Dublin Core, MARC) to complex knowledge networks (e.g., Semantic Web annotations such as DAML+OIL). As a result, we need a methodology that identifies contextual quality requirements for composite information objects and transforms them consistently into their composite (schema) and component quality requirements, as well as translating quality changes into changes of information value and cost.

We start with a framework of quality dimensions that can be used for assessing quality both at the composite and component levels. Following that, for effective reasoning about interdependencies among the quality dimensions and their impacts on aggregate quality assessments, we propose the use of quality curves modeled after the Taguchi value curves (Taguchi et al., 1989). Note that here and throughout the chapter we use a term aggregator to refer to this specific service type which collects metadata records from different OAI data providers and makes them available for gathering by others using the OAI metadata harvesting protocol (OAI-MHP). The records are expected to be using a common standard schema — Simple DC. Therefore, this particular aggregator does not integrate or aggregate information from different records through a mediated schema like some of the information integration services also known as wrappers do, though, as we will discuss later in the chapter, they still share a number of similar problems.

Metadata Quality Assessment Model

Almost as many different taxonomies of IQ dimensions have been proposed as there are writings about IQ. While these classifications differ in the granularity, detail, and naming of IQ dimensions, there are substantial overlaps among them. In the previous research (Gasser & Stvilia, 2001) we analyzed existing information, data, and metadata quality approaches, compiled a comprehensive taxonomy of IQ dimensions, and created a firmer and more unified theoretical foundation for them (see Appendix, Table 7). This taxonomy consists of 22 dimensions divided into 3 categories:

1. **Intrinsic IQ:** Some dimensions of information quality can be assessed by measuring attributes of information items themselves, in relation to a reference standard. Examples include spelling mistakes (dictionary), conformance to formatting or representation standards (HTML validation), and information currency (age with respect to a standard index date, e.g., "today"). In general, Intrinsic IQ attributes persist and depend little on context, hence can be measured more or less objectively.

2. **Relational/Contextual IQ:** This category of IQ dimensions measures *relationships* between information and some aspects of its usage context. One common subclass in this category includes the *representational* quality dimensions — those that measure how well an information object reflects some external condition (e.g., actual accuracy of addresses in an address database). Since metadata objects are always surrogates for (and hence bear a relationship to) other information objects, many relational dimensions apply in measuring metadata quality (e.g., whether an identifier such as URL or ISBN actually

identifies the right document, whether a title field holds the actual title). Clearly, since related objects can change independently, relational/contextual dimensions of an information item are not persistent with the item itself.

3. **Reputational IQ:** This category of IQ dimensions measures the position of an information artifact in a cultural or activity structure, often determined by its origin and its record of mediation.

Due to space reasons we use only a small subset from our entire set of IQ dimensions in the next section to illustrate the importance of metadata quality to an information seeking activity.

Activities and Metadata Quality Metrics

Studies have repeatedly shown that information quality assessments are contextual (Ballou et al., 1998; Strong et al., 1997). In order to measure the general quality of a metadata object: (a) we need to understand metadata creation and use activities, (b) we need to define procedures that transform attributes of metadata, its target objects (documents), and relevant contextual features into values for metadata quality, at both component and composite levels, and (c) we need to condition both of these by the activity or process context (Ballou et al., 1998).

In general, *metadata quality,* like *information quality,* can be defined as "fitness for use." A *quality dimension* is any aspect of quality. Hence, specific *metadata quality problems* arise when the *existing* quality level along some particular metadata quality dimension is lower than the *required* quality level, in the context of using that metadata to support a given activity (Gasser 2001). In general, metadata is generated based on the properties of a given information item and/or its information content by some surrogation process which itself uses a certain surrogation model or schema. The schema can be implicit or explicit like DC. However, one size does not fit all. The schema may not be complete or complex enough to match the requirements of all the activities the metadata object may be used. As a result, a metadata quality problem may occur at least at two different levels: (1) macro (schema), (2) micro (component) (Strong et al., 1997; Wand & Wang, 1996). To measure the quality gap we need to identify the specific information quality requirements for the activity on multiple dimensions and at multiple levels, measure the actual information quality value for the metadata objects on those dimensions, and compare them. Note that examining a metadata object and its schema alone may not be sufficient for assessing its quality on some dimensions, since all IQ dimensions except *Intrinsic* dimensions involve aspects external to a metadata object under assessment. These dimensions require analysis of the relationships and states of related objects and socio-cultural structures of user communities, and most importantly information activities of those communities. For anchoring the quality assessments of all three categories of dimensions we need to establish benchmarks/baseline representations meeting

Figure 1. Context sensitive metadata quality measurement

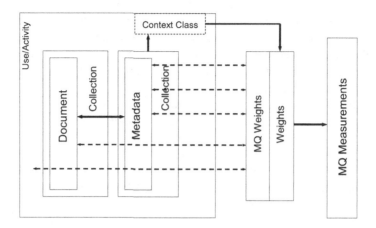

the minimum requirements of the activities and then produce an aggregate quality estimate for quality-based ranking. In Gasser and Stvilia (2001) we proposed using activity theory (Leontiev, 1978) and information/activity genres (Orlikowski & Yates, 1994) to establish generic, socially-justified quality and value structures for different types of information objects, and using them for constructing context-sensitive baseline representations and quality requirements. In addition, for more effective reasoning about the action-specific metadata quality requirements and tradeoffs we propose the use of quality curves adapted from Taguchi's value curves (Taguchi et al., 1989). In particular, we use 3 types of quality function curves. A Smaller is Better (SIB) curve is used when a decrease in certain quality dimension increases an aggregate quality of a metadata object. A Larger is Better (LIB) curve models a relationship when a larger value of the quality dimension leads to higher aggregate quality of the object. And, finally, a Nominal is Best (NIB) curve is used when the aggregate quality value for the object is highest when the quality dimension value is between too small and too large. Based on the type of a metadata object and the typified context of its use one can build a curve for each quality dimension at both macro and micro levels and define its critical and nominal values. For instance the general-case critical values of completeness for a Simple DC record can be set to 0 and 15 (the minimum and maximum numbers of distinct fields in the DC schema), while the nominal value may vary based on the types of activities the object is used in.

In summary then, a procedure for measuring metadata quality could be the following: (1) Analyze information creation and use activities: what actions are carried out within a given activity, what types of information tools, including metadata objects, are needed to provide the necessary functionalities for successfully accomplishing these actions; (2) Based on this analysis, identify macro (schema) and micro (component) functional requirements for a given type of metadata objects; (3) Based on the macro and micro requirements, construct a baseline data model; (4) Use the baseline model for measuring the quality of related metadata objects and identify quality problems; (5) Based on the measurement in the previous step assign quality rankings to the objects.

For effective metadata quality assurance, however, we also need to: (6) Decompose the macro-level quality problems identified in the step #4 into micro-level problems; (7) Measure the value and cost changes of quality improvement or degradation along a given quality dimension (value loss, user cost, lost opportunity cost, cost saving, etc.); and (8) Optimize quality assurance activities based on the criticality of metadata to the activity structure and resources available.

MODELING METADATA OBJECT QUALITY REQUIREMENTS BY ANALYZING INFORMATION USE ACTIVITY

To develop a model of the relationship between information quality of a metadata object and the information activities that comprise its context of use, we will consider a typified activity of information discovery: finding an information entity or FIND. We have chosen FIND as a representative type from the set of activities metadata is intended to support, as indicated in IFLA (1998).[4] While locating information can comprise several basic actions (e.g., select, locate, and obtain, in addition to find), for space reasons we only analyze the relationship between FIND and its quality requirements in this chapter. In addition, while there are many metadata schemes and formats in use, for this chapter we limit ourselves to DC metadata since it is a widely used standard for documents in electronic repositories and is the basis for the federated collections in our extended case study.

FIND: Finding an information entity. As with the other information activities not treated here, we conceptualize FIND as a set of actions heuristically selected from a space of possibilities. Note that FIND is an information access problem with at least two types of agents involved: information providers and information seekers. Each of these may have different metadata models, and the level of correspondence among them is an issue (Buckland, 1999; Wang & Gasser, 2005). The FIND process involves a collection of moves that includes (possibly in repetition and in varying order) the following: (a) a seeker establishes a space of possibilities to be investigated, initial criteria for success, and resource (cost) bounds; (b) the seeker (heuristically) generates descriptions of a set of candidate objects from this space using its own (sometimes ad-hoc and uncertain) metadata (e.g., structured or unstructured query terms); (c) the provider uses its own procedures (e.g., search routines) to provide its own corresponding metadata (e.g., search results) for the candidate set; (d) the seeker uses the provided metadata to comparatively evaluate the candidates, accepting and/or rejecting some of them, possibly accessing the entire source object (document); and (e) the seeker uses information from accepted or rejected candidates to reformulate the possibility space, its own metadata, the criteria for candidate generation, and the criteria for cost and success. The process terminates when the information seeker's final success criteria and/or cost bounds are met. Note that most of the process involves search, extraction, analysis, comparison of and inference over *metadata*, rather than over actual target documents.

Metadata has three purposes in FIND. First, an object's metadata is a surrogate or model (a representation) of that object in the possibility space. For the seeker, this metadata model may necessarily be unknown, guessed, or intelligently inferred. Ideally, metadata reduces the total amount of information that must be handled (model vs. full document) in the activity of FIND. Second, metadata limits and focuses attention to specific relevant, modeled attributes of the target object. This focus can make assessment more efficient, and can focus revisions in step (e), but if inaccurate, or does not match the complexity of a task under consideration, it may also degrade quality. Third, the typified or standardized aspect of metadata makes comparison of multiple candidates (e.g., across federated repositories) more efficient.

One key idea underlying our approach here is that information quality becomes critical (only) to the degree it affects the quality of activity *outcomes* (e.g., the quality of materials generated through the FIND activity, in this example). Metadata quality impacts FIND when any of the three metadata purposes given above is enhanced or compromised by metadata quality. This is true at the level of the composite metadata record taken as a whole, as well as at the level of each metadata component (e.g., Title, Creator, Identifier, etc., in DC). These impacts can be illustrated with the following suggestive examples, which are limited for space reasons:

Intrinsic

Automated generation, assessment, or comparison of candidates can fail if the metadata lacks *consistency*. Representing similar objects with the same metadata structure and vocabulary decreases variance in matching and leads to the reduction in the number of false positives and false negatives during search. The curves of semantic, structural and vocabulary consistency dimensions are of a LIB type. In general we can estimate that the more current a metadata object is, the more accurately it reflects the current state of a given information item. Consequently, for producing a partial ordering along the *currency* dimension, while all other variables remain fixed, one may not need to examine the original object or know its properties assuming that the most recent metadata object is of the highest quality. Both the currency and consistency dimension curves are of a LIB type.

Relational/Contextual

The information seeker's metadata model of information entities may not match the system or provider metadata model. The provider metadata schema or a single metadata record may not be *complete* enough to locate entities by the attributes the user intends to use. If the author name or subject word are missing in a metadata object and the user uses these attributes in search, the object will not be found and included in the set of relevant entities. A critical minimum point for the completeness dimension would be a data model containing no elements or attributes. A DC object with no elements filled is useless. The other extreme, theoretically, is an object containing an infinite number of elements which will not be useful either as *completeness* is often in conflict with *simplicity*. A completeness curve may be bounded by a simplicity curve and can be of a NIB type. Community specific nominal (optimal) values of completeness can be established through use analysis and experimentation.

High *naturalness* of metadata increases the chances of the overlap between the user and provider data models and consequently the effectiveness of search. For instance, using typified words in the surrogate title of an image increases the probability of the user choosing the same words in search. Naturalness is culture- and community-specific. Its curve is of an LIB type.

Inaccurate metadata can make an information object "disappear" and not be found in a search. In cases when partially accurate metadata is still useful for reducing a search space, the accuracy curve is of an LIB type. Indeed, when correcting all information errors is too expensive or impossible, Web search engines and other information systems take a "coping approach" and develop special procedures/algorithms to utilize partially accurate information (Twidale & Marty, 1999). However, some attributes can be less robust or tolerant with regard to inaccuracy than others. For instance, even a small inaccuracy can render an identifier element useless. For these types of metadata the accuracy dimension takes only binary type values: accurate or not accurate.

In certain cases when achieving high accuracy is too expensive, some *redundancy* can prove to be useful to increase robustness and reduce chances of search failure. For instance, if metadata is misspelled in one element of a DC record, but repeated in a correct form within the same or a different element, the item still will be found (Basch, 1995). Therefore, for FIND the redundancy curve is of a NIB type.

Increase in *volatility* increases the chance of metadata become invalid. For instance, 9-digit social security numbers (SSN) may not be valid identifiers once the US population exceeds 1 billion. Similarly, the relatively high probability of a female person changing her last name after marriage or divorce, in comparison to her DNA sequence, makes the DNA sequence a better quality identifier. However, there can be a tradeoff between *volatility* and *simplicity*. A personal name can be less complex to use than a SSN and a SSN itself is less complex than a DNA sequence according to the information theoretic measure of descriptive complexity (Cover &

Thomas, 1991). Therefore, the volatility dimension curve bounded by the simplicity curve is of an NIB type.

If the metadata object or any of its elements is not accessible for any reasons, it is of no use. There can be a tradeoff, however, between *accessibility* and *security*. If an increase in accessibility is achieved at the expense of security reduction, certainty of the information conveyed by metadata may suffer. Therefore, the accessibility curve is of the NIB type.

Reputational

Low *authority* or *believability* of metadata objects can lead to poor identification. The uncertainty about the provenance of a metadata object or its content may reduce its use or the collection as whole. This is especially true for an aggregated metadata collection where two or more records may refer to a same object (redundancy), but conflicting information in the date elements or the author elements may not allow the seeker to establish the correct identity of the object. On the other hand, if the information content conveyed by redundant metadata elements or records is confirmatory or "monotonic," an increase in redundancy may help in increasing believability. For instance, if there is no contradiction among the duplicate records, believability of the metadata gets increased. The authority/believability curve is of an LIB type.

Thus, the quality requirements for FIND may involve multiple quality dimensions. In addition, the interactions and interdependencies between these dimensions may result in significant tradeoffs. The following tradeoffs have been identified for FIND activity: *completeness vs. simplicity*; *volatility vs. simplicity*, and *accessibility vs. security*.

VALUE AND COST-SENSITIVE
QUALITY ASPECTS

In the previous section, using an example of the FIND activity we showed the importance of reasoning about metadata quality needs through a prism of the typified activities and actions in a domain. To come up with realistic quality assurance plans and targets, it is essential that one is aware about the activity and action-specific behavior of the quality dimensions and the tradeoffs among them. In addition, however, it is often necessary to quantify the effects of poor or good quality for justifying or making more effective investments in quality improvement.

In manufacturing, improving a product's quality means finding an optimal mean value for each quality-related attribute of the product and reducing the variance around the mean of each of these attributes. The target values for these attributes are calculated from the product's cost and user value structure. That is, the cost of improving quality of a given system attribute has to be met with an increase of product value, exemplified by an increase in cash flow (Cook, 1997). In digital library settings monetary metrics may not be directly applicable to metadata objects, however, one still can treat them as products and measure the increase in value from increased quality based on user satisfaction or increased use. Or, alternatively, one can measure the value loss caused by inferior quality (Taguchi et al., 1989).

Poor Quality as Value Loss

Consider a metadata object as an organizational asset and for simplicity assume that its value is equal to the cost of its creation measured by cataloging staff time and administrative overhead, even though the real value of the object may vary considerably depending of its context of use. If the average cost of an OAI DC record to an institution is $8, the record comprises 4 DC elements and the *identifier* information is inaccurate, then we may say that the value loss due the inaccurate identifier is $8 * 1/4 = $2. Obviously, if the *identifier* is the only element that may allow the user to find the corresponding information object, then the value loss due to poor quality is $8.

Likewise, one can design a function and calculate the total loss from all the quality deviations found in the collection. However, as we argued earlier, nominal (target) values as well as the ranges of tolerance may vary from one type of metadata to another. For instance, the allowable amount of inaccuracy for a DC identifier element can be 0, while a user may still find useful a *description* element with intrinsic quality deficiencies such as spelling errors. Similarly, the target values can be different from one domain to another. For instance, the target value of completeness for metadata objects used for academic library information may not be the same ones used in public libraries due to the different levels of complexity of typified activities carried out in these institutions. If for academic libraries the target number of distinct elements in a Simple DC record is N_d, the target total number of elements N_t and the collection shows the mean deviations (d_d, d_t) from these targets, then we can construct a loss function (F_{ca}) for completeness at the composite (schema) level as follows:

$$F_{ca} = k_a \times (d_d \times d_t)^2 / 2$$

Here k is similar to Taguchi's proportionality constant and can be measured as:

$$k_a = (L_d + L_t)/(\Lambda_d + \Lambda_t)^2$$

where L_d and L_t are the amounts of loss associated with the values of schema level completeness being outside of the tolerance limit; Λ_d and Λ_t are the tolerance limits of schema completeness with regard of distinct and total number of elements used. Similar functions can be constructed at the component level as well as for different types of organizations by using their domain/type specific values for the above variables.

Quality as Amount of Use

Compounded value and quality of a metadata collection, object or element can be also assessed by the number of transactions performed against it. According to Glazer (1993) value of information may increase in use. More frequently used metadata objects and metadata elements can become more valuable than less used ones. The amount of use on the other hand is determined by the needs of a user community and by the quality of the metadata. For instance, increasing completeness by adding additional metadata elements may enable new uses and increase the number of transactions. Consequently, the effects of quality changes can be quantified based on the decrease or increase in the number of uses.

The value of a metadata element can be a function of the probability distribution of the operations/transactions using the element. Likewise, the value of a metadata object can be assessed as an aggregated value of its individual element values. The ability of assessing and/or predicting the amount of use of an existing component and/or object, or the number of additional transactions enabled by the addition of a new component, can help in reasoning about quality-value-cost tradeoffs and spending quality improvement resources more effectively. For instance, the use statistics from Appendix (Table 5) rank *identifier* and *title* as the most highly used elements in the metadata records. Assuming that the providers of these records are at the same time one of the main consumers the metadata and their needs are reflected in the composition of the records, we may argue that *identifier* and *title* are the most valuable elements in this particular aggregated metadata collection. Another important source of establishing the value of metadata objects and elements can be a transaction log of component and object uses by the end users.

Quality as Effectiveness

To complete the picture of metadata quality assessment and reasoning, changes in a metadata object's quality need to be linked to changes in the cost of its generation and use. And, there are certain cost-generating factors that can be assessed objectively and linked systematically to the changes in quality. One of the simplest "cost drivers" which can be evaluated automatically is the number of metadata elements used and the length of each element. Creating a metadata object with many elements containing values comprising many bytes of information will require more cataloger time than generating a sparse object with a smaller amount of metadata in it. At the micro or component level the cost of using a DC *description* element in the object will be higher than the cost of using *identifier* or *type* elements (see Appendix, Table 5). In addition, creating metadata of a complex information object or an information object in a foreign language may require extra cognitive effort and time from the cataloger and result in a cost increase. Similarly, on the use side, the cost of using a metadata object can be affected by the number of elements it contains, the lengths of these elements and the complexity of metadata. Complexity or simplicity can be calculated as a normalized number of the words not recognized by a general purpose spellchecker dictionary. Thus, assuming that metadata elements do not convey duplicate information, one of the metrics of the cost-sensitive quality assessment or effectiveness of a metadata object can be as follows:

$$E = \sum_1^n e_i / \sum_1^n t_i$$

where e_i-s are the elements used; t_i stands for the average times needed to create or evaluate and comprehend the element and n is the total number elements in the object. The formula reflects the completeness vs. simplicity tradeoff discussed previously and suggests that reducing complexity along with maintaining the necessary level of completeness can be a target for cost-sensitive quality improvement activities.

QUALITY ASSURANCE

Effective quality planning involves exploring and analyzing the metadata production chain, that is, identifying processes, people, input/output interdependences, and quality controls (Ballou et al., 1998). Landau (1969) lists the following surrogation operations: selection, analysis, descriptive cataloging, subject indexing, classification, abstracting and editing. Modeling and analyzing quality assurance and value creation processes throughout these operations and linking them consistently with the use activities and actions, can help in enactment of appropriate control checks and triggers to prevent certain types of quality problems from occurring and make quality assurance decisions more sound and effective. Methods of metadata quality assurance through process control and preventive quality maintenance deserve their own separate treatment and won't be discussed further here. Instead, in this section we will give some of the suggestions on how an aggregator can improve metadata quality inexpensively.

What a Metadata Aggregator Can Do
to Improve Metadata Quality Inexpensively

In the federated information environments of interest in our research, metadata from a number of individual sources or collections is gathered together and normalized so it can be used uniformly for analysis and retrieval operations on the distributed collections under federation. Such federated or aggregated metadata repositories can pose quality challenges that may not be typical or pervasive for stand-alone metadata collections. These problems include: loss of context or loss of information — when the local contextual information from a local collection is lost or mapped ambiguously into a global schema; relational/representational problems such as "link-rot" and differences in update frequencies; changes in concept definitions and controlled vocabularies; misuse of standard metadata schema elements; variations in record completeness and use of controlled vocabularies; different domain models and definitions, abstraction levels and representation conventions; duplicate records and overlapping collections. These problems are not entirely unique to federated metadata collections; studies of them have been reported to some degree in the general data quality literature where the focus is on large integrated corporate databases and warehouses with more or less strong centralized attempts at quality control. However, federated metadata collections, such those in the IMLS/DCC project, rely heavily on volunteer cooperation among multiple metadata providers who are affected by local cultural, economic, and knowledge factors.

The quality of a metadata object is a product of the "quality assurance chain" which goes in parallel with the information production, supply and use chain (Williams, 1990). The scope of an aggregator's quality assurance activities is usually limited by its role in this process of division of labor, and the quality of an aggregated collection is largely determined by the metadata quality supplied by individual data providers. Nonetheless, the aggregator, informed by information seeking behavior studies, can still perform a number of actions to improve the metadata quality inexpensively.

The aggregator may not have leverages to influence the metadata creation processes of individual providers, but it still can influence the ways metadata is selected, aggregated, and presented. Earlier in this section we identified 3 models of how the effects of quality changes can be connected to value changes. The aggregator can use these models to improve the value of the aggregated collection. Specifically, the aggregator can: (1) reduce the value loss due to poor quality; (2) increase the collection value by increasing the number of its uses, and (3) increase the effectiveness of metadata objects.

The aggregator can significantly reduce value loss by simple data-scrubbing operations such as spellchecking or duplicate detection, which often can be done automatically. In addition, a collection's statistical profiles and data-mining tools can be used for identifying and correcting misplaced or invalid metadata entries inexpensively.

The aggregator can increase the pool of metadata users by generating supplemental metadata and enabling additional perspectives and contexts of uses. One can visualize the value of a metadata object as the sum of its values to local and global users: $V_m = V_l + V_g$. Often, individual data providers create metadata objects with only local users in mind and the presence of some shared, *a-priori* knowledge K is assumed due to their membership in the community. As a result the utility of including a metadata element E_i containing the same K or a subset of K can be zero or even negative if the cost of the inclusion of E_i is positive (Radner & Stiglitz, 1984):

$$U(E_i) = V(E_i|K) - C(E_i); \; (C(E_i) > 0 \cap V(E_i|K) = 0) \rightarrow U(E_i) < 0;$$

where U stands for Utility, V for Value and C for Cost. For global users, who are not the members of the particular metadata-generating community and may not share the community knowledge/information, $V(E_i|K)$ can be positive. However, since marginal information users for the local data provider are the local users, the local provider may lack incentives to improve quality that only benefit the global users and not the local ones, even in a short run. As a result, local resource providers may under-provide quality necessary for attracting non-local users. Therefore, the challenge the aggregator may face is to increase the value of a metadata object for the non-local users by inexpensive means and without decreasing its value to the local users.

Whenever possible, collection statistics and structural regularities of metadata objects can be used by the aggregator to infer pre-existing knowledge K, which was not included in metadata objects intentionally by local providers or was lost in conversion between different metadata standards. In that way the aggregator can mitigate some of the clarity/context loss problems mentioned earlier. The missing or new metadata can be also obtained from the original objects, if these objects are available to the aggregator and the metadata can be generated/extracted inexpensively, that is, automatically. Furthermore, the collection statistics can be used for generating or supplementing the metadata on individual collections, which combined with typified scenarios of metadata uses can be a substantial added value to the existing user communities, enable new uses and bring additional users to the aggregated collection.

The aggregator can increase metadata effectiveness by reducing unnecessary complexity or hide it and make it a lesser burden to the user by offering the view of the metadata that matches the user's cognitive capabilities and level of experience. At the information discovery activity level, one of the indirect measures of the quality of a metadata artifact can be average time the user spends to finish all the actions in the activity. Each metadata element can perform more than one function and each information action can be accomplished by utilizing more than one metadata element. However, some metadata elements are optimized towards certain functionalities and the cost of element use can be also different. Studies of information seeking behavior show that information seeking action trajectories and the choices of metadata elements for achieving a same goal may vary from one type of user to another (Sutcliffe et al., 2000). It has been found that novice users used fewer subject keywords and did more evaluation and comparison than expert users when searching for relevant articles (Marchionini et al., 1990; Sutcliffe et al., 2000). Consequently, some users may utilize a subject element more extensively while others may rely more on a description element for sense-making and comparison.

The different types of users choosing different metadata elements to accomplish the same goal can be explained by the different cognitive cost structures they may have for the same metadata element. For instance, the keyword vocabulary of an aggregated repository comprised of specialized vocabularies of the individual collections can be quite large and diverse (see Table 1). To memorize and use this

Table 1. DC elements ordered by their average information content or uncertainty (entropy) culculated from a collection of 154,782 OAI DC records, not normalized

Element	Total #	Unique #	Entropy
identifier	205,719	184,769	0.98
title	133,108	87,689	0.88
subject	304,661	80,702	0.71
source	29,537	11,008	0.68
description	153,088	59,523	0.67
creator	84,829	18,385	0.65
date	189,661	11,068	0.62
coverage	12,103	1,738	0.59
contributor	16,813	2,882	0.54
relation	80,629	3,115	0.35
publisher	114,305	3,347	0.35
rights	68,228	341	0.33
type	124,853	191	0.15
format	111,647	2,308	0.13
language	85,397	95	0.10

The standardized entropies are calculated as follows:

$$entropy = -\sum_{i=1}^{n} p_i Log(p_i) / Log(N)$$

where p_i is the probability of the i-th unique value for a given element and n is the total number of the unique values for that element.

vocabulary can require a significant cognitive effort (or incur a significant cost) from users doing cross-disciplinary research (Palmer, 1998) or novice users. Abstraction and reduction of complexity may help in reducing this effort by better aligning the user and the system models of information objects (Cole et al., 2002). However, it may come at the expense of a metadata object losing its discriminatory power and become less effective in reducing the search space. Certain techniques can make the tradeoff less crisp. For instance, by adding thesauri and ontology mappings, the aggregator can reduce the complexity of metadata and make it easier to use for novice users, while at the same time retaining the discriminatory power of domain specific subject keywords, which can be enjoyed by expert searchers or subject experts.

Finally, users can play an important role in the aggregator's quality improvement activities. Adding user feedback/error-reporting capabilities to the system can be an effective and efficient tool in increasing the collection's quality inexpensively by communicating the user dynamic quality needs to the aggregator (Twidale & Marty, 1999). While the producer/provider model of metadata quality can be more process-oriented, the user's perception of quality tends to be more product-experience-oriented mainly focusing on usability (Strong et al., 1997) — that is, whether a given information object and/or a system as whole is usable or not. Harnessing the user community power for error reporting can help in aligning these two models better by: (1) identifying metadata creation process errors, and (2) identifying user metadata quality needs at both composite and component levels. The aggregator can serve both as a quality improvement agent and as an intermediary by forwarding relevant feedback to an appropriate metadata provider (Williams, 1990).

CASE OF IMLS DDC
AGGREGATED METADATA COLLECTION

In this section we present some of the results of qualitative and quantitative analysis of random samples from an aggregated collection of OAI Simple DC records harvested as a part of IMLS DCC project, and interpret them using the concepts and procedures proposed in the earlier sections. In particular, we attempt to answer the following questions: (1) What are the quality problem types one may encounter using this metadata?, and (2) What are the types of activities affected by those problems?

At the time of the analysis the collection contained a total of 154,782 records (see Appendix, Figure 2) that had been harvested from 16 OAI data and service providers — academic and public libraries, museums and historical societies. A manual inspection of a random sample of 150 OAI Simple DC records using the Activity & Genre theoretic approach proposed in the earlier sections and the technique of Content Analysis (Bailey, 1994) identified six major types of quality problems: (1) lack of completeness, (2) redundant metadata; (3) lack of clarity; (4) incorrect use of DC schema elements or semantic inconsistency; (5) structural inconsistency and (6) inaccurate representation (see Table 2). All of the 150 examined records were incomplete. None of them used all 15 DC elements. 94% of the records contained elements with duplicate metadata. In addition, most of the date elements were ambiguous. Removed from the context, it was not clear to what date the information referred to: was it the date when a given photo was taken, donated, microfilmed or digitized? Using a single DC record for describing more than one object was another major source of ambiguity. Attempts were made to pack the descriptions of an original museum artifact and its multiple digital image objects (files) in a single DC record producing ambiguous mappings at the schema level. It was not clear to which object's attribute a given element referred to (see Figure 2). This inherent ambiguity of "Many-to-One" mapping was earlier discussed in Wand and Wang (1996). Incorrect use of the DC elements was also common. The most frequent

Table 2. Percentages of the DC records having quality problems (a random sample of 150 records from the population of 154,782 records)

Problem type	Incomplete	Redundant	Unclear	Incorrect Use of Elements	Inconsistent	Inaccurate Representation
%	100	94	78	73	47	24

Table 3. Quality problem type — dimension mapping

Problems Dimensions	Incompleteness	Redundancy	Clarity	Inconsistency	Accuracy
1. Intrinsic Completeness	x				
2. Intrinsic Redundancy/ Informativess		x	x		
3. Intrinsic Semantic Consistency			x	x	
4. Intrinsic Structural Consistency				x	
5. Relational Accuracy					x
6. Relational Completeness	x				
7. Relational Semantic Consistency				x	
8. Relational Structural Consistency				x	

misuse (or a possible workaround (Gasser, 1986)) was putting date information in a source element or using a description element for format information. Almost a half of the sample had consistency problems. Using different date formats was the most common problem as well as inconsistent structuring of records and the lack of vocabulary control. Finally, 24% of the records had representational problems in forms of broken identifier links and partially inaccurate representation of original object content.

After analyzing the contexts and patterns of quality incident occurrences we mapped them to 8 IQ dimensions from our IQ assessment framework (see Table 3 below). Note that the Incorrect Use of Elements and the Inconsistent problem clusters were combined into the higher level Inconsistency quality problem type.

In addition, the logical analysis of the sample records and modeling different scenarios (Carroll, 2000) of their use suggested that there are at least two kinds of information activities are more prone to metadata quality problems:

- **Representation dependent activities:** Whenever activity depends on how well an information repository's content *represents* some external situation, the correspondence between that representation and the underlying reality is a potential locus of IQ problems. Quality problems arise when there is an incomplete, ambiguous, inaccurate, inconsistent, or redundant mapping between a real-world state or object and an information system state or information object.

- **Activities that decontextualize information:** Whenever an agent removes information from the context in which it was produced — for example to aggregate information from a variety of original sources and integrate it into a focused collection supporting a specific task — the new context may change how information quality is assessed or understood. The analysis of the DC element use profiles of the individual data providers showed that each data provider's interpretation and usage of the DC schema was consistent within its collection, but different from the other data providers' interpretations. Assuming that those interpretations (local schemas) are known locally, it would be possible to search and retrieve their item-level metadata successfully. However, once placed into an aggregated collection, the success of finding and obtaining those metadata would depend (assuming that structured search was used) on the amount of commonality in the interpretations and usage across the aggregated collection which in the case of the IMLS DCC aggregated collection was reduced to a single element — identifier.

The results of statistical analysis corroborates the existence of quality tradeoffs suggested earlier. The analysis of a random sample of IMLS OAI DC records shows a strong negative correlation between Log (number of distinct DC elements per record) and simplicity (sample size = 1,000 records, population size = 154,782, the Spearman

Table 4. Quality problem type — activity type mapping

Activities IQ Problem Clusters	Representation Dependent	Decontextualizing Activities
Incompleteness	x	x
Redundancy	x	x
Clarity	x	x
Inconsistency	x	x
Inaccuracy	x	x

correlation coefficient -.684, significant at the 0.01 level, two-tailed). Simplicity, in this case, is calculated as 1 minus a ratio of the number of the words not recognized by MS Word spellchecker dictionary over the size of a record. Thus, there can be a significant tradeoff between completeness and simplicity/complexity.

Bade (2002) suggests that the size and complexity of metadata can be inversely related to its quality. Indeed, our analysis of the random sample of 150 OAI Simple DC records too shows a significant negative correlation between an aggregate quality problem rate, which is a simple normalized linear combination of the above-mentioned quality problem category scores for a given metadata object divided by the object's length, and a simplicity score (Spearman correlation coefficient -.434, significant at the 0.01 level, two-tailed). To our surprise, however, no significant correlation has been found between the aggregate quality problem rate and the normalized length of a metadata object (Spearman correlation coefficient .043, not significant at the 0.01 level, two-tailed). Interestingly enough, similar observations have been made in some of the software quality research projects. For instance, Troster (1992) found a strong correlation between the cyclomatic software complexity index and the number of defects/bugs in software. Although intuitive, the above observations once again emphasize the importance of reasoning about the quality tradeoffs. Generating completeness — simplicity and simplicity — quality problem tradeoff curves may help in predicting quality of metadata objects as well determining provider specific optimal levels of their completeness and complexity.

We mentioned earlier that the nominal or target values of a given quality dimension can vary from one domain to another and from type of metadata to another. Indeed, our analysis of a 2,000-record random sample from the aggregated collection showed that the number of distinct elements used in the records varied from a minimum of 2 elements to the maximum 14 with the mean equal to 7.62 and the standard deviation equal to 2.93. The total number of elements used per record also varied from the minimum 2 to the maximum 82 with the standard deviation 5.73 (see Appendix, Table 6). The results of the statistical analysis of the data also identified a significant correlation between the consistency of element use and the type of metadata objects and the type of data providers. Indeed, grouping by type of the same metadata records made the standard deviation of the total number of elements used to drop significantly (from 5.73 to 3.6), even for binary type values: photos and non-photos. Likewise, grouping the sample by the type of providers (public libraries, academic libraries, and museums) reduced the variance of the total number elements used per a metadata record from 5.73 to 4.5. Not surprisingly, academic institutions on average used more distinct elements per record: 13 vs. 8 used by public libraries. The metadata records generated by academic libraries on average were larger in size than the records generated by the other types of institutions. Indeed, clustering by the use of distinct DC elements, using the K-means clustering technique with 2 clusters, almost perfectly discriminated the public library records from the academic library records. Most of the public library records went into a cluster #1 with a center of 8 distinct elements (title, subject, description, publisher, date, type, identifier, rights) while the academic library records were placed in a cluster #2 with a center of 13 elements (title, creator, subject, description, publisher, date, type, format, identifier, source, language, relation, rights). Museum records in our sample were split almost equally between these two clusters.

Thus, implicitly or explicitly, public and academic libraries may use different subsets of the DC schema when generating metadata records based on the needs of their marginal users and cost structures. A realistic loss function needs to reflect these differences and use organization type specific baseline values. For instance, if for academic libraries the target number of distinct elements used in a DC record is 13, the target total number of elements 16 and the collection shows mean deviations (d_d, d_t) from these targets — 1.7 and 4.6, respectively — then we can construct a loss function (F_{ca}) for completeness as follows:

$$F_{ca} = k_a \times (d_{da} \times d_{ta})^2 / 2 = k_a \times (1.7 \times 4.6)^2 / 2 \approx 30.6 \times k_a$$

where k and N are defined in the same way as earlier. If bringing distinct element and total element completeness up to the nominal values at academic libraries costs on average \$8 per record and the tolerance limits are 10 and 13, then:

$$k_a = (8+8)/(10+13)^2 \approx 0.03 \quad \text{and} \quad F_{ca} = 30.6 \times k_a = 30.6 \times 0.03 = \$0.918 \quad \text{per record.}$$

Hence, if we assume that 100% of the records are incomplete and there are 50,000 records from academic libraries, then the value loss to the collection due to incomplete records can be estimated as \$45,900.

Inexpensive data quality improvement actions such as date, type and language element normalization can substantially reduce the element variance (noise) and make metadata object evaluation and comparison easier (Cole et al., 2002). Indeed, we found that simple spellchecking and normalization can reduce the variance of these elements more than in half. In addition, to further reduce cognitive cost of using the metadata records, we experiment with the use of subject thesauri allowing automatic query expansion during search.

CONCLUSION

In this chapter, we studied the problems of quality assurance in large federated collections of metadata objects. Random samples from the collection of 154,782 OAI Simple DC records have been examined to identify the types and severity of metadata quality problems. A general framework of information quality assessment proposed earlier in Gasser and Stvilia (2001) was used for identifying relevant metadata quality dimensions, developing metrics and linking them consistently with the quality problems encountered in typified information seeking and processing activities.

We found that developing an inventory of the mappings among metadata elements, metadata creation and use activities, quality dimensions and tradeoffs can allow more robust reasoning about metadata quality and apply limited quality improvement resources more effectively.

In addition, the results of the statistical analysis of the data has shown significant correlation between some of the quality dimensions such as completeness and the type of metadata objects and the type of data providers. However, whether these regularities are the results of the data providers using implicit genre/type based schemas when generating metadata objects or the byproducts of particular cataloging software conventions are open to question.

The research reported here does not yet explicitly consider user evaluations of information quality metrics or actual quality assessments by users. In future research we will also focus on user evaluations. We intend to use focus groups and surveys for establishing quality and value structures for different types of metadata objects and developing functions for measuring and translating objectively the changes of a metadata object quality into the changes of its value and cost.

The data evaluated in this research were structured standardized metadata objects created in formal institutions by trained specialists. To extend and refine the proposed model IQ assessment, we plan to apply it to different kinds of collections from different domains. In particular we have begun research that applies and validates the model on entire corpus of over 500,000 articles in the English version of Wikipedia — an open collaborative on-line encyclopedia project in which anyone can participate without prior vetting.

ACKNOWLEDGMENTS

This work was supported under grant # 04135 from the University of Illinois Campus Research Board and an IMLS National Leadership Grant. We thank Tim Cole and Sarah Shreeves for helpful comments and suggestions.

REFERENCES

Bade, D. (2002). The creation and persistence of misinformation in shared library catalogs: language and subject knowledge in a technological era. *GSLIS Occasional Papers, 211*. Champaign, IL: GSLIS, University of Illinois.

Bailey, K. (1994). *Methods of social research* (4th ed.). New York: The Free Press.

Ballou, D., Wang, R., Pazer, H., & Tayi, G. (1998). Modeling information manufacturing systems to determine information product quality. *Management Science, 44*(4), 462-484.

Barton, J., Currier, S., & Hey, J. (2003). Building quality assurance into metadata creation: an analysis based on the learning objects and e-prints communities of practice. In *Proceedings of the International DCMI Metadata Conference and Workshop*.

Basch, R. (1995). Introduction: An overview of quality and value in information services. In R. Basch (Ed.), *Electronic information delivery* (pp. 1-13). Brookfield, VE: Gower.

Bruce, T., & Hillman, D. (2004). The continuum of metadata quality: defining, expressing, exploiting. In E. Westbrooks (Ed.), *Metadata in practice*. ALA Editions.

Buckland, M. (1999). Vocabulary as a central concept in library and information science. In *Proceedings of the 3rd International Conference on Conceptions of Library and Information Science*, Dubrovnik, Croatia.

Carroll, J. (2000). *Making use: Scenario-based design of human-computer interactions*. Cambridge, MA: The MIT Press.

Cole, T., Kaczmarek, J., Marty, P., Prom, C., Sandore, B., & Shreeves, S. (2002). Now that we've found the "hidden web," what can we do with it? The Illinois Open Archives Initiative Metadata Harvesting Experience. In *Proceedings of the Museums and the Web 2002* (pp. 63-72).

Cook, H. (1997). *Product management: Value, quality, cost, price, profits, and organization*. Amsterdam, The Netherlands: Chapman & Hall.

Cover, T., & Thomas, J. (1991). *Elements of information theory*. New York: Wiley.

Dushay, N., & Hillman, D. (2003). Analyzing metadata for effective use and re-use. In *Proceedings of the 2003 Dublin Core Conference*, Seattle, WA.

Gasser, L., & Stvilia, B. (2001). *A new framework for information quality* (Tech. Rep. No. ISRN UIUCLIS - 2001/1+AMAS). Champaign, IL: University of Illinois at Urbana Champaign.

Gasser, L. (1986). The integration of computing and routine work. *ACM Transactions on Office Information Systems, 4*(3), 225-250.

Glazer, R. (1993). Measuring the value of information: The information-intensive organization. *IBM Systems Journal, 32*(1), 99.

IFLA Study Group on the Functional Requirements for Bibliographic Records. (1998). *Functional requirements for bibliographic records: Final report.* Münche: K. G. Saur. Retrieved from www.ifla.org/VII/s13/frbr/frbr.pdf

Landau, H. (1969). The cost analysis of document surrogation: A literature review. *American Documentation, 20*(4), 302-310.

Leontiev, A. (1978). *Activity, consciousness, personality.* Englewood Cliffs, NJ: Prentice Hall.

Marchionini, G., Lin, X., & Dwiggins, S. (1990). Effects of search and subject expertise on information seeking in a hypertext environment. In *Proceedings of the 53rd Annual Meeting of the American Society for Information Science,* Toronto, Canada (pp. 129-142).

Motro, A., Anokhin, P., & Acar, A. (2004). Utility-based resolution of data inconsistencies . In *Proceedings of the SIGMOD IQIS 2004 Workshop* (pp. 35-43).

Naumann, F., Leser, U., & Freytag, J. C. (1999). Quality-Driven integration of heterogeneous information systems. In *Proceedings of the International Conference on Very Large Databases,* Edinburgh, UK.

Orlikowski, W., & Yates, J. (1994). Genre repertoire: The structuring of communicative practices in organizations. *Administrative Science Quarterly, 39*, 541-574.

Orr, K. (1998). Data quality and systems theory. *Communications of the ACM, 41*(2), 66-71.

Palmer, C. (1998). Structures and strategies of interdisciplinary science. *Journal of the American Society for Information Science, 50*(3), 242-253.

Radner, R., & Stiglitz, J. (1984). A nonconcavity in the value of information. In M. Boyer & R. Kihlstrom (Eds.), *Bayesian models in economic theory* (pp. 33-52). New York: Elsevier.

Strong, D., Lee, Y., & Wang, R. (1997). Data quality in context. *Communications of the ACM, 40*(5), 103-110.

Sutcliffe, A., Ennis, M., & Watkinson, S. (2000). Empirical studies of end-user information seeking. *Journal of the American Society for Information Science, 51*(13), 1211-1231.

Taguchi, G., Elsayed, E., & Hsiang, T. (1989). *Quality engineering in production systems.* McGraw-Hill.

Taylor, R. (1986). *Value-added processes in information systems.* Norwood, NJ: Ablex.

Troster, J. (1992). Assessing design-quality metrics on legacy software. In *Proceedings of Proceedings of the 1992 Conference of the IBM Centre for Advanced Studies on Collaborative research* (pp. 113-131).

Twidale, M., & Marty, P. (1999). *Investigation of data quality and collaboration.* Champaign, IL: GSLIS, University of Illinois at Urbana - Champaign.

Wand, Y., & Wang, R. (1996). Anchoring data quality dimensions in ontological foundations. *Communications of the ACM, 39*(11), 86-95.

Wang, J., & Gasser, L. (2005). *A mutual adaptation model for information retrieval.* Submitted for publication.

Wang, R., Allen, T., Harris, W., & Madnick, S. (2003). *An information product approach for total information awareness.* Paper presented at the IEEE Aerospace Conference.

Wang, R., & Strong, D. (1996). Beyond accuracy: What data quality means to data consumers. *Journal of Management Information Systems, 12*(4), 5-35.

Ward, J. (2003). A quantitative analysis of Dublin Core metadata element set (DC-MES) usage in data providers registered with the Open Archives Initiative (OAI). In *Proceedings of the JCDL 2003.*

Williams, M. (1990). Highlights of the online database industry — The quality of information and data. In *Proceedings of the National Online Meeting.* Medford, NJ.

APPENDIX

Table 5. Use of Dublin Core elements (16 providers, 154,782 records)

Dublin Core element	% of repositories using element at least once	No. of records containing element	Total times element used	% of total records containing element	Average times used per record	Average element length (in characters)	Mode	Mode Frequency in %
Title	100.0	124,304	133,108	80.3	1.1	39.9	1	75.8
Creator	87.5	78,402	84,829	50.7	1.1	21.5	0	49.3
Subject	93.8	112,875	304,661	72.9	2.7	110.4	2	37.1
Description	81.3	73,298	153,088	47.4	2.1	104.1	0	52.6
Publisher	75.0	94,791	114,305	61.2	1.2	38.5	1	50.9
Contributor	62.5	10,158	16,813	6.6	1.7	47.0	0	93.4
Date	81.3	66,514	77,175	43.0	1.2	10.9	0	57.0
Type	81.3	118,419	124,853	76.5	1.1	6.6	1	72.5
Format	56.3	107,381	111,647	69.4	1.0	8.3	1	66.6
Identifier	100.0	154,113	205,719	99.6	1.3	84.4	1	71.5
Source	50.0	23,012	29,537	14.9	1.3	68.3	0	85.1
Language	75.0	85,201	85,397	55.0	1.0	3.3	1	54.9
Relation	43.8	48,356	80,629	31.2	1.7	95.6	0	68.8
Coverage	37.5	9,136	12,103	5.9	1.3	21.0	0	94.1
Rights	62.5	63,435	68,228	41.0	1.1	151.7	0	59.0

Table 6. Descriptive statistics (a random sample of 2,000 records from the population of 154,782 records)

	N	Minimum	Maximum	Mean	Std. Deviation	Mode	Mode Frequency
Total number of elements per record	2,000	2	82	10.45	5.73	9	0.2
Number of distinct elements per record	2,000	2	14	7.62	2.93	7	0.3

Table 7. Taxonomy of IQ dimensions (Source: Gasser & Stvilia, 2001 — IQ Assessment Framework)

	Dimension	Definition
Intrinsic	1. Accuracy/Validity	the extent to which information is legitimate or valid according to some stable reference source such as a dictionary, and/or set of domain constraints and norms (soundness)
	2. Cohesiveness	the extent to which the content of an object is focused on one topic
	3. Complexity/ Simplicity	the extent of cognitive complexity of an information object measured by some index/indices
	4. Semantic consistency	the extent of consistency of using the same values (vocabulary control) and elements for conveying the same concepts and meanings in an information object. This also includes the extent of semantic consistency among the different or the same components of the object
	5. Structural consistency	the extent to which similar attributes or elements of an information object are consistently represented with the same structure, format and precision
	6. Currency	the age of an information object
	7. Informativeness/ redundancy	the amount of information contained in an information object. At the content level it is measured as a ratio of the size of the informative content (measured in word terms which are stemmed and stopped) to the overall size of an information object. At the schema level it is measured as a ratio of the number of unique elements over the total number of elements in the object
	8. Naturalness	the extent to which an information object's model/schema and content are expressed by conventional, typified terms and forms according to some general purpose reference source
	9. Precision/ Completeness	the granularity or precision of an information object's model or content values according to some general purpose IS-A ontology such as WordNet

Table 7. continued

Relational/ Contextual	10. Accuracy	the degree to which an information object correctly represents another information object or a process in the context of a particular activity
	11. Complexity/ Simplicity	the degree of cognitive complexity of an information object relative to a particular activity
	12. Accessibility	Accessibility of information relative to a particular activity (speed, ease of locating and obtaining)
	13. Naturalness	the degree to which an information object's model and content are semantically close to the objects, states or processes they represent in the context of a particular activity (measured against the activity/community specific ontology)
	14. Informativeness/ Redundancy	the extent to which the information is new or informative in the context of a particular activity/community
	15. Relevance (aboutness)	the extent to which information is applicable and helpful/ applicable in a given activity
	16. Precision/ Completeness	the extent to which an information object matches the precision and completeness needed in the context of a given activity
	17. Security	the extent of protection of information from harm, unauthorized access and modification
	18. Semantic consistency	the extent of consistency of using the same values (vocabulary control) and elements required or suggested by some external standards and recommended practice guides for conveying the same concepts and meanings in an information object
	19. Structural consistency	the extent to which similar attributes or elements of an information object are consistently represented with the same structure, format and precision required or suggested by some external standards and recommended practice guides
	20. Verifiability	the extent to which the correctness of information is verifiable and/or provable
	21. Volatility	the amount of time the information remains valid
Reputational	22. Authority	the degree of reputation of an information object in a given community

Figure 2. IMLS DCC DC record example

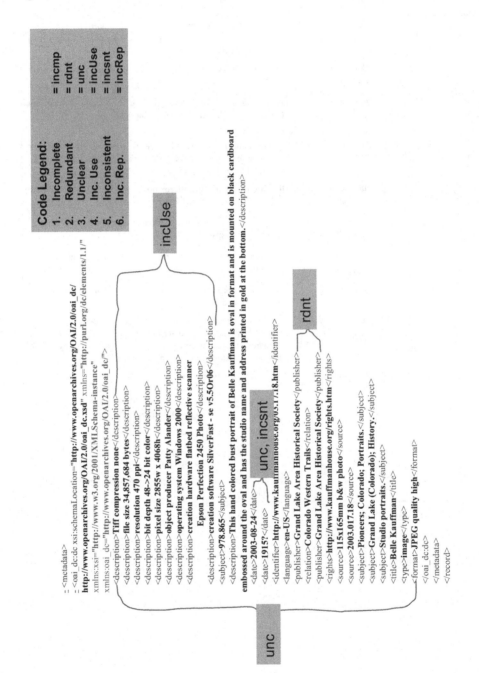

ENDNOTES

1   http://imlsdcc.grainger.uiuc.edu/
2   http://www.openarchives.org
3   http://www.dublincore.org/
4   By "typified" we mean activities that are cognitively, culturally and/or socially generic to some process, in this case information seeking and use as defined in IFLA (1998) and elsewhere. Our general approach is to use well-understood information-seeking use models as the foundation for identifying generic activities to be used in specifying metadata needs.

Section IV:
IQ Application for
Research and Development

Chapter IX

Analyzing Information Quality in Virtual Networks of the Services Sector with Qualitative Interview Data

Helinä Melkas, Helsinki University of Technology, Finland

ABSTRACT

In this chapter, a novel framework is introduced for analyzing information quality within information processes of complex organizational networks on the basis of qualitative data. Networking and virtualization call for new ways of looking into information quality. Public organizations, cooperatives and non-governmental organizations are forming networks, or entering into networks of companies. Tools for analyzing information quality in such environments have been lacking. The newly developed framework is operationalized within multi-actor, multi-professional networks offering safety telephone services for aging people. These services utilize well-being technology. The analysis is based on data from interviews with professionals working in several service networks of different types and sizes in Finland. The information quality analysis framework helps in identifying information quality dimensions that are weak in a network. This analysis is usefully combined with an investigation of network collaboration that identifies weaknesses and strengths in network collaboration affecting management of information quality.

INTRODUCTION

Discussions on information often focus on information systems, information technology, data warehouses and data mining, to mention a few examples. Information itself is the material that is essentially needed. The real goal of information quality is to increase customer and stakeholder satisfaction (English, 1999; Huang, Lee, & Wang, 1999). If internal users of information within organizations are treated as consumers of information, their performance and productivity will improve. Delivering quality information may be seen as a self-reinforcing process leading to improved company performance (Huang, Lee, & Wang, 1999).

Tools that have been developed for measuring and analyzing information quality (e.g., English, 1996; 1999; 2001; Huang, Lee, & Wang, 1999; Strong, Lee & Wang, 1997a; 1997b; Wang, 1998; Wang, Lee, Pipino & Strong, 1998; Wang & Strong, 1996) have mainly been utilized in individual organizations, often companies. Information transfer processes and management of information quality are challenging enough within one organization with clearly defined boundaries. Yet, we are witnessing a rapid increase in networking and virtualization among companies. Information-related issues require particularly urgent attention in these circumstances. Networking and virtualization do not concern companies only. Public organizations, cooperatives and non-governmental organizations are also forming networks, or entering into networks of companies. This tendency is seen, for instance, in the social and health care sector of the society, and in the utilization of new kinds of well-being technology. Challenges appear to be especially numerous there. Tools for analyzing information quality in such environments and on the basis of qualitative data have been lacking.

The objective of the chapter is to introduce a new kind of framework for information quality analysis within information processes of organizational networks on the basis of qualitative interview data — and to describe how this framework was operationalized within multi-actor networks that provide safety telephone services to aging people. Safety telephones and wristbands that enable a call for help by pushing just one button increase the possibilities of an aging person to continue to live in her or his own home even when there may be a need for assistance. Aging people usually wish to live at home as long as possible, and safety telephones are part of today's structure of elderly care in Finland. Safety telephones have also been called "safety alarm systems" (van Berlo, 1998) and "social alarm systems" (EN 50134-7, 1996).

According to population forecasts, one of four Finns will be over the age of 65 in the year 2030. The average life expectancy for a female child born in the 1990s was over 80 years, and for a male child 73 years, as compared to 75 and 65 years respectively for those born in the 1970s. The number of retired people will start to grow significantly after the year 2005. High pressure is placed on services of aging people of today, and the situation is not likely to get any easier or less problematic in the future. The case study context of the present chapter is thus timely and socially significant, as populations are also aging rapidly in other countries.

BACKGROUND

The quality of information cannot be improved independently of the processes that produced this information or the contexts in which information consumers utilize it (Strong, Lee, & Wang, 1997a; 1997b). One starting point in this chapter is that the same applies vice versa; contexts and processes of networks cannot be improved independently of the quality of information. Quality information is essential also because through the assessment of information, knowledge controls and guides decision-making and other processes in organizations (cf., English, 1999; Huang, Lee, & Wang, 1999; Miller, Malloy, Masek, & Wild, 2001; Pierce, Kahn, & Melkas, forthcoming).

Enterprise networks and information management systems are widely studied fields — but there is a very limited understanding of the information processes of networks of public and private service organizations in the literature. Virtual organizations, virtual enterprises and virtual teams within enterprises have been studied by many researchers in recent years (e.g., Duarte & Tennant Snyder, 2001; Handy, 1995; Holton, 2001; van Hout & Bekkers, 2000; Jarvenpaa, Knoll, & Leidner, 1998; Katzy & Dissel, 2001; Kayworth & Leidner, 2002; Kotorov, 2001; Lipnack & Stamps, 1997; Miles & Snow, 1992; Putnam, 2001; Rouse, 1999; van der Smagt, 2000; Voss, 1996). The kinds of multi-actor service networks that provide the field of operationalization in this chapter have barely been investigated. Some work has been done to assess effectiveness of public-sector service networks (cf., Provan & Milward, 2001), but information-related matters were not included among the effectiveness criteria. Very little work has been devoted to the requirements placed by the utilization of well-being technology on information processes, information quality and networking among different types of organizations — despite the growing societal weight of such technology.

The focus of the chapter is on content and quality of information. The chapter does not contain an investigation of information systems as such. Within the case networks, such an approach would not be meaningful due to the poor development state or even lack of information systems. The amount of information transferred is treated as background information only. Due to the objective of methodology development for network environments, the quality of the service provided to customers — aging people — is not systematically investigated.

NEW FRAMEWORK FOR ANALYZING INFORMATION QUALITY

Data produced by applying qualitative methods in the case networks were analyzed with the help of the new information quality framework. This chapter presents the way in which this operationalization was undertaken. Details of the data collection for the operationalization are described in the Appendix. The comprehensive results cannot be specified in a single chapter (see Melkas, 2004, for further details).

The information quality analysis framework is proposed as a tool to investigate the quality of the different types of information that are transferred in the case networks. Information quality is an essential slice of the whole of information management, but it may be overlooked due to, for instance, extensive attention to information systems — or various knowledge management initiatives concentrating overwhelmingly on utilization of tacit knowledge. The information quality analysis framework helps in identifying information quality dimensions that are weak in a network (or in an individual organization). The use of the framework is combined with an investigation of network collaboration that helps in identifying weaknesses and strengths in network collaboration affecting management of information quality. A very brief description only of the latter investigation is included in this chapter (for details, see Melkas, 2004).

Basis and Development of the Information Quality Analysis Framework

The information quality analysis framework was elaborated primarily on the basis of the studies of Wang and Strong (1996), Strong, Lee and Wang (1997a; 1997b) and Wang et al. (1998). Their data quality framework has been used effectively in industry and government, but they have also called for further research to apply the framework in specific work contexts. Wang and Strong's work (1996) provided most of the dimensions of information quality that were investigated. The new framework of analysis was structured so that six stages of analysis were discerned from the following summary of challenges of information management:

If the right piece of information from the right source and in the right format is at the right place at the right time and handled in the right way, action is relatively easy and predictable. (Adapted by the author on the basis of Lillrank, 1998, p. 7)

Combining the dimensions of information quality with the six stages of analysis provides an essentially novel way to assess information quality in complex network processes on the basis of qualitative data. Each stage of analysis represents a criterion for information quality that is key to the successful operation of a network.

Each criterion is then further broken down by information quality dimensions that are most relevant to that stage of analysis.

For each stage of analysis, appropriate dimensions of information quality were assigned from those listed by Wang and Strong (1996). For another branch of business with different operations, dimensions to be assigned for the six stages could be different. The starting point was that all the dimensions from Wang and Strong (1996) are included at each stage. However, that would make the analysis quite heavy. On the basis of the data collected, the author started to exclude dimensions from consideration. The data showed the necessary exclusions relatively clearly. Where there was unclarity, the dimensions were kept. The assignments were based on an assessment of the definitions of dimensions of information quality, aims of the six stages of analysis as well as the data collected (knowledge of the branch). In this phase, also a few "service-specific" dimensions were added (as described below). The result was the framework that is shown in Table 1, and subjected to testing and operationalization.

Table 1. The information quality analysis framework

Stage of Analysis	Information Quality Dimensions
Basis: the right source of information	Relevancy, timeliness, completeness Accuracy, objectivity, believability Accessibility, security
Component: the right piece of information	Relevancy, value-added, timeliness, completeness, appropriate amount of information
Content and instrument/ means: in the right form	Accuracy (including accurate coding of message), objectivity, believability, reputation Interpretability, ease of understanding, concise representation, consistent representation Ease of operation, traceability, flexibility
Timing: at the right moment	Timeliness, relevancy Appropriate velocity
Routing: in the right place	Accessibility, security Relevancy, value-added Traceability
Processing procedures: handled in the right way	Accessibility (intellectual and physical), security Interpretability, ease of understanding, concise representation, consistent representation Traceability, cost-effectiveness, ease of operation Authority of person handling, appropriate velocity, sustainability (costs and ethical aspects)

In the interviews, it became quite clear that collecting data from the interviewees for making the assignments would have led to meager and unreliable results. The interviewees from safety telephone services are not used to thinking about information at a conceptual level. Even at the practical level, these things are felt to be somewhat difficult to grasp. The case environment thus caused quite many special challenges. Developing a list of criteria for the assignments could even be counterproductive in environments, where the topic of information and information quality first need to be made visible.

It seems that criteria could be developed in future research at the level of an individual organization — or rather, a couple of organizations, where people would agree on the assignments in joint discussions, and the researcher would then document their reasons for the assignments and develop a list with the help of those. The persons would have to be knowledgeable about the topic of information quality. However, also "difficult" network environments need to be studied.

The word "right" in Table 1 means the opposite of wrong. It cannot be given a universal definition, as situations and contexts vary. The new framework was designed with the aim of taking into account context dependent variables as well as information as an output and a process. Within safety telephone services, the information that is given by a customer in an alarm call, for instance, transforms as the service process advances. This is the reason for not testing Wang and Strong's (1996) seminal framework of information quality as such. Their information quality dimensions have here been assigned in an innovative way to the different stages of analysis. This approach suits the particular characteristics of the case environment — but it is also flexible for use in other branches or organizations.

Adding Service-Specific Information Quality Dimensions

The "service-specific" dimensions that were added to the framework of analysis on the basis of the information on safety telephone services are the following:

- **To the stage of analysis "content and instrument/means":** for accuracy, an explanatory addition: accurate coding of message; ease of operation, traceability, flexibility
- **To "timing":** appropriate velocity
- **To "routing":** traceability
- **To "processing procedures":** for accessibility, an explanatory addition: intellectual and physical; traceability, cost-effectiveness, ease of operation, authority of person handling, appropriate velocity, sustainability (costs and ethical aspects)

Traceability, cost-effectiveness, ease of operation and flexibility are dimensions that were originally included in Wang and Strong's framework (1996) but which the authors later eliminated, because these dimensions could not be readily assigned to any category (intrinsic, contextual, representational and accessibility information quality). They were reintroduced here because of the author's assessment — based on the data collected — of their importance in safety telephone services.

Accurate coding of message was added to the stage of analysis "content and instrument /means" as an explanatory remark for accuracy. This is intended to reflect the occasional difficulty in interpreting customers' needs when an alarm call is received at a call centre. How the person on duty interprets the customer's message and transfers the information forward to the collaboration network may have a major impact on service quality. Interpretation is likely to depend largely on the call centre personnel's tacit knowledge and experience, but it is an issue that needs to be brought up in an information quality analysis.

Appropriate velocity is a concept that is related to both accessibility and timeliness, but it is felt to be insufficiently covered by them. Yet, it needs careful attention particularly in the context of safety telephone services. Appropriate velocity has to do with how quickly incoming calls are answered at a call centre, how quickly relevant service providers are called out to provide help, how quickly help is finally provided to the customer, how quickly changes in customer information are inserted into the customer database, and so forth. There may be definitions or guidelines as to how quickly help is provided — for instance, within half an hour — but the velocity dimension seems to require increasingly systematic attention with regard to all types of information.

The explanatory remark concerning accessibility — intellectual and physical — is intended to highlight the importance of handling information in a way that ensures intellectual accessibility within the often very heterogeneous collaboration networks of safety telephone services. As the networks may consist of representatives of many different professions in different localities and work environments, intellectual accessibility of customer or other types of information is not self-evident, even if physical accessibility (the extent to which information is available or easily and quickly retrievable) would not cause any problems (cf., Miles & Huberman, 1985). Intellectual accessibility is closely related to ease of understanding and interpretability but more wide-ranging, requiring a comprehensive consideration of collaborators' point of view and needs.

Authority of person handling has to do with confidentiality of health-related information. This matter is at a level different from the other dimensions. It is intended to highlight the importance of the security dimension and widen its sphere. As to sustainability, costs and ethical aspects require our consideration. Sustainability with regard to costs is connected to cost-effectiveness (the extent to which the cost of collecting appropriate information is reasonable), but concerns the whole of safety telephone services. In addition to the cost of collecting information, also the costs of storing and transferring information, the costs related to information systems, and the quality costs of missing, incomplete and incorrect information, inappropriate or inefficient services as well as of missing follow-up and assessment of customers' services should be taken into account. Sustainability with regard to ethical aspects has to do with overall practices and management of information processing in a way that ensures consideration of the customer's point of view. The precise ethical aspects have to be defined at the level of an individual organization and, where relevant, the collaboration network, depending on the exact type and combination of services. Therefore, no list of what the ethical aspects include is given here.

The Six Stages of Analysis

Stage 1

Analysis of basis contains an investigation of the sources of different types of information. In the case of, for instance, customer information, a certain amount of basic information is given for the call centre's database when a safety telephone is first subscribed. This is usually done by filling in a form that contains details on who subscribes (if different from the customer) and her/his contact information, customer's contact information, address for invoicing, some space for additional notes, information on customer's health condition, medication, technological aids (such as hearing aid), other related services (typically municipal home care) as well as near relatives and their contact information. These types of information are given by the customer only or by the person subscribing with/on behalf of the customer. Depending on the service system, the information may be supplemented by, for instance, municipal home care employees or telephone installers. The quality dimensions utilized in the analysis of basis are relevancy, timeliness, completeness (dimensions of contextual information quality), accuracy, objectivity, believability (intrinsic information quality), and accessibility and security (accessibility information quality) (for their definitions, see Wang & Strong, 1996). The quality dimensions utilized in the different stages of analysis overlap in many cases, but it is argued that an artificial separation would lead to an incomplete and misleading picture.

Stage 2

Analysis of component aims at finding out whether the right pieces of information are stored and transferred. This has to do with information quality dimensions such as relevancy, value added, timeliness, completeness and appropriate amount of information (dimensions of contextual information quality). If, again, the example of customer information is used, we can distinguish two different situations that place different demands. When an alarm call from a customer is received at a call centre, the right pieces of customer information to be transferred differ from those pieces that should/could be transferred when a new customer subscribes to the service, as background information to service providers — depending on demands for confidentiality and possible related expressions of consent by the customer.

Stage 3

Analysis of content and instrument implies an investigation of whether the information in question is transferred in the right forms. Dimensions of information quality to be investigated in this context include accuracy, objectivity, believability, reputation (intrinsic information quality), interpretability, ease of understanding, concise representation, consistent representation (representational information quality) and ease of operation, traceability and flexibility.

Stage 4

Analysis of timing focuses on whether the necessary information is available at the right moment. Timeliness and relevancy (contextual information quality) as well as appropriate velocity are the quality dimensions investigated.

Stage 5

Analysis of routing, again, focuses on checking whether the necessary information is in the right places. Dimensions such as accessibility, security (accessibility information quality), relevancy, value added (contextual information quality) and traceability are utilized in this context.

Stage 6

Analysis of processing procedures is directed at investigating whether the information in question is handled in the right way. Accessibility (intellectual and physical), security (accessibility information quality), interpretability, ease of understanding, concise representation, consistent representation (representational information quality), traceability, cost-effectiveness, ease of operation, authority of person handling, appropriate velocity and sustainability (costs and ethical aspects) are investigated.

RESULTS

Mapping of Information Flows

Before the framework of analysis can be applied, a mapping of information flows needs to be undertaken to find out about:

- Types of information that are transferred and stored
- Events (or types of information) that trigger an action or a process
- Which piece of information justifies which action
- How an activity triggered by an event proceeds in the network (organization)

Figure 1. The information quality (IQ) analysis step by step

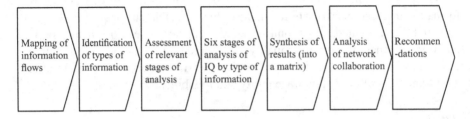

- Bottlenecks of information flows
- Logic of the network (organization) in organizing information processes

Such a mapping (including a graphical presentation of its results) is necessary for translating the interview and other case data into the set of stages of analysis and relevant information quality dimensions (see Figure 1 for a summary of the whole research methodology).

Types of Information within Safety Telephone Services

In this brief chapter, only the types of information that are transferred within safety telephone services can be discussed (for comprehensive results of the mapping, see Melkas, 2004). Discussions on information processes within safety telephone services centre round alarm information. The reason seems obvious — those information processes form the foundation for that service type. However, even safety telephone service professionals appear to concentrate overwhelmingly on alarm information, without giving the necessary attention to the other types of information (especially network information).

Information being transferred within the safety telephone service networks can be divided into four types: customer information, information related to alarm calls, technical information and information related to collaboration network (see Table 2). Table 2 reports examples from interviews — not a general, ideal state of affairs. The requirements for the precise contents of the different types of information vary somewhat across the different types of networks — depending on their environment and operations.

The four types were identified as the distinct types of information that are transferred in the networks. For instance, information that is given to the customer and near relatives at the time of installation of the safety telephone is of essential importance, but it is not transferred in the networks. Therefore, it is not included as such in the information quality analysis. Comprehensive frequency data on the transfer of the different types of information are not available for any of the case

Table 2. Types of information transferred within safety telephone services

Type of Information	Examples
Customer Information	Customer's contact information Condition of customer's health Customer's medication, technological aids (such as hearing aid), other related services Near relatives and their contact information Changes in the information mentioned Expressions of consent regarding information transfer
Alarm Information	Customer's name and address Reason for alarm call Basic information on customer's health Special remarks (e.g., especially poor hearing) Information on near relatives if they should be informed in case the customer is hospitalized Information on visits and actions by safety helpers
Technical Information	Broken appliance Need to change battery of appliance Disconnection and connection of appliance Service needs (e.g., related to thunderstorms)
Network Information	Organization of operations Changes in organization of operations Contact information of collaborators and changes in it Feedback from customers Feedback from collaborators

networks. It can be estimated that there are differences in the transfer of (1) customer information and (2) network information. The importance of transferring the latter kind of information namely depends on the type of network. For instance, in an internal system of an institution offering sheltered accommodation, the personnel knows the customers and deals with alarm calls, so there is no need to transfer network and customer information.

Detailed survey data are available on the reasons for incoming alarm calls for one of the case networks. Those are cited here to give an idea of the percentages of typical reasons. The figures can be considered fairly representative for safety telephone services in general. In the survey, 80% of all the alarm calls were related to technical faults, needs to change batteries, test alarms, needs to have social contact, causeless alarms and false alarms. These usually do not lead to sending help to the customer. In only 0.4% of the calls, the call centre personnel called for urgent ambulance transportation. Other kinds of helpers were called for in 14.3% of the cases (such as visiting nurse or near relative) (Molander, 2003).

Identification of Relevant Stages of Analysis

Taking into account many different types of networks and types of information might lead to chaos in the application of the information quality analysis framework, unless the investigation is further systematized beforehand. This systematization is an iterative and cyclical process based on an understanding of the service branch, study visits and interviews. Weighting is based on the interview data, but it is not a mechanical process for which numerical criteria could be shown. The systematization was done by assessing the relevance of each of the six stages of analysis by network and by type of information (Table 3).

The starting point was that all six stages are undertaken. Excluding some stages in the case of, for instance, technical information is not contradictory to the intention to investigate information processes. The systematization shows which analyses are meaningful. For instance, an analysis of basis is not meaningful with regard to technical information. Information on a broken appliance is relayed automatically (or sometimes by the customer, a near relative or a care professional). There does not seem to be anything problematic in the sources of such information, in any kind of a network.

In this investigation, the amount of data was so large that a prior systematization was vital before the detailed analysis. When applied in an individual organization, irrelevant parts of the information quality analysis framework could be identified in joint discussions without anyone filling in a table first. Even there, however, a similar matrix to that in Table 3 could be developed by unit or department — particularly in bigger organizations. This can also help in giving the appropriate weight to the different types of information. Certain types may be seen as self-evident and omitted in planning, although they contribute to the transfer of other types of information. Particularly in heterogeneous multi-actor service networks such as those investigated here, employees are not very knowledgeable about the different types of information.

Table 3 implies that differences in relevance mainly depend on the type of information. There are not many differences between the types of network within safety telephone services. The only environment with clear differences was institutions offering sheltered accommodation. After thus identifying the natural restrictions, the actual analysis on the basis of the framework could start. The six stages of analysis were undertaken by analyzing the interview data with the help of the information quality dimensions assigned for the different stages. Going through the comprehensive analysis with the six stages is beyond the scope of this chapter. Only one brief example, discussion of timeliness of the sources of customer information

Table 3. Relevance of analyses by type of network and type of information

Type of network	Type of information	Analysis of basis	Analysis of component	Analysis of content and instrument	Analysis of timing	Analysis of routing	Analysis of processing procedures
Nation-wide network (company operated) (1)	Customer	3	3	2	2	3	3
	Alarm	0	3	3	3	3	3
	Technical	0	0	0	3	2	0
	Network	2	3	3	3	3	2
Municipal network (3)	Customer	2	3	2	2	2	3
	Alarm	0	3	3	3	3	3
	Technical	0	0	0	3	2	0
	Network	2	3	3	3	3	2
Sheltered accommodation (cooperative or foundation operated) (2)	Customer	1	2	2	2	2	2
	Alarm	0	2	2	2	2	2
	Technical	0	0	0	2	2	0
	Network	1	1	1	1	1	1
Private customers (non-governmental organization or foundation operated) (1)	Customer	3	3	2	2	2	2
	Alarm	0	2	3	2	2	2
	Technical	0	0	0	3	2	0
	Network	1	2	2	2	2	2
Pilot project (1)	Customer	3	3	2	2	3	3
	Alarm	0	3	3	3	3	3
	Technical	0	1	1	3	2	1
	Network	2	3	3	3	3	2

Note: Weighting: 0 = Not applicable. This stage of analysis is not applicable to this type of information.
1 = Applicable but of lesser relevance; 2 = Applicable; 3 = Applicable and of particular relevance.

is included here. Each type of information was assessed by the relevant stages of analysis and all the information quality dimensions assigned to them.

An Example of Detailed Results: Timeliness of the Sources of Customer Information

Timeliness — the extent to which the age of information is appropriate for the task at hand — of the basis of customer information was found to require particular attention in safety telephone services. The basis of customer information is here understood as databases at call centres or corresponding units that answer alarm calls. The results showed that in large service systems, where each individual customer cannot be known, updating and supplementing customer information was poorly organized. Aging people's health condition may change quickly, and certain changes — for instance, if dementia comes out — even make the use of safety telephones difficult, if not impossible. Other types of information also change, such as telephone numbers of near relatives. The results indicated that these are not kept systematically up-to-date.

When the subscription is placed, the customer information is given on the form that is filled in. Changes have not, indeed, been communicated to the call centre. [...] We could have improved our practices there. There may be customers who do not get any type of service other than this safety telephone service ... if [the safety helper] does not know [the customer] and [the customer] has, for instance, a low blood sugar level — that the helper knows how to act ... (Employee of municipal home care service, nation-wide network)

The age of customer information may be from the time of safety telephone subscription, which may have taken place years ago. The results showed that procedures for updating and supplementing customer information have usually not been defined or are not sufficiently clear to the personnel. In one of the bigger networks investigated here, there is a system where the customers' files are regularly checked and subscriptions renewed once a year. In another smaller network, updates of information on customers' medication are systematically and regularly asked for, but the customers rarely return the form. Timeliness of the basis of customer information was shown to have a different weight in different kinds of networks. In internal safety telephone systems of institutions offering sheltered accommodation, timeliness of the basis of customer information was found to have a relatively small weight, as the personnel who helps the customers knows them. The results indicated that in a municipal system, again, collaboration partners sometimes benefit from access to other databases with up-to-date health-related information on the customers (for instance, databases of hospitals or health centres).

Summary Results

The rest of the results of the operationalization of the framework for information quality analysis are presented in the form of a summary table (Table 4). The full analysis including further illustrative quotations from the interviews may be read in Melkas (2004). Table 4 shows the structure of the analysis that was undertaken. For each stage of analysis, the relevant types of information are listed. For each type of information, the quality dimensions that were found to be particularly central in the analysis are written in bold. The quality dimensions of lesser importance are written in normal letters, and those of no importance are in brackets. The results are not summarized by type of network here. Although the type of network was found to affect many things, it also became evident that — apart from internal safety telephone systems of institutions offering sheltered accommodation — the problems and challenges in the operations are very similar. Differences between the networks investigated are in the scale of problems and challenges.

The operationalization led to useful results that can be utilized as guidelines when planning information-related matters in the case networks in the future. Particularly the dimensions written in bold deserve to be focused on. The summarized results also show that the utilization of this novel framework of analysis — in combination with the other steps of the comprehensive information quality analysis — results in a multi-faceted picture of the state of information quality. Although there was some overlap in the information quality dimensions investigated during the different stages of analysis, the importance of the various dimensions was discerned in a meaningful way (see, for instance, the results for customer information by stage of analysis).

There were altogether 48 dimensions assigned to the six stages of analysis. Six of those 48 were — according to the detailed analysis — not important for any type of information (analysis of basis: relevancy, objectivity, believability; analysis of content and instrument: reputation, traceability; analysis of routing: traceability) (Table 4). Table 1, the starting point, was thus reasonably correct, and the differences between the types of information were made visible. As to the dimensions that were excluded from the six stages of analysis, it is claimed that if something important had been omitted, it would have come up. Table 1 was both a "hypothesis" and based on an early assessment of the data collected. The dimensions that were not meaningful were excluded at an early stage already. The results were also discussed with the practitioners in many meetings, and these discussions support the conclusions made on the basis of the analysis.

It was thus possible to undertake a successful operationalization of the framework of analysis even in the complicated network environment. For utilization in practice for planning purposes, the summary table naturally needs to be read together with the full descriptions of the results.

Table 4. Summary results of the operationalization of the framework for information quality analysis

Stage of analysis	Type of information analyzed	Information quality dimensions investigated
Basis: the right source of information	Customer	(Relevancy), **timeliness, completeness, accuracy,** (objectivity), (believability), **accessibility, security**
	Network	(Relevancy), **timeliness, completeness, accuracy,** (objectivity), (believability), **accessibility,** (security)
Component: the right piece of information	Customer	**Relevancy,** value added, **timeliness, completeness,** appropriate amount of information
	Alarm	**Relevancy,** value added, timeliness, **completeness, appropriate amount of information**
	Network	**Relevancy, value added, timeliness, completeness,** appropriate amount of information
Content and instrument/ means: in the right form	Customer	**Accuracy** — (including accurate coding of message), objectivity, believability, (reputation), **interpretability, ease of understanding, concise representation, consistent representation, ease of operation,** (traceability), flexibility
	Alarm	**Accuracy** — including accurate coding of message, (objectivity), (believability), (reputation), **interpretability, ease of understanding, concise representation, consistent representation,** (ease of operation), (traceability), (flexibility)
	Network	**Accuracy** — (including accurate coding of message), (objectivity), (believability), (reputation), **interpretability, ease of understanding, concise representation, consistent representation, ease of operation,** (traceability), (flexibility)
Timing: at the right moment	Customer	**Timeliness, relevancy,** appropriate velocity
	Alarm	(Timeliness), (relevancy), **appropriate velocity**
	Technical	(Timeliness), (relevancy), **appropriate velocity**
	Network	**Timeliness, relevancy, appropriate velocity**

Table 4. continued

Stage of analysis	Type of information analyzed	Information quality dimensions investigated
Routing: in the right place	Customer	**Accessibility, security, relevancy, value added,** (traceability)
	Alarm	(Accessibility), (security), (relevancy), (value added), (traceability)
	Technical	(Accessibility), (security), (relevancy), (value added), (traceability)
	Network	**Accessibility,** (security), (relevancy), (value added), (traceability)
	Customer	**Accessibility — intellectual and physical, security, interpretability, ease of understanding, concise representation, consistent representation,** traceability, **cost-effectiveness, ease of operation, authority of person handling,** appropriate velocity, sustainability – costs, ethical aspects
Processing procedures: handled in the right way	Alarm	Accessibility — **intellectual** and physical, security, **interpretability, ease of understanding, concise representation, consistent representation,** (traceability), (cost-effectiveness), (ease of operation), (authority of person handling), **appropriate velocity,** sustainability – **costs,** (ethical aspects)
	Network	**Accessibility — intellectual and physical,** (security), **interpretability, ease of understanding, concise representation, consistent representation,** (traceability), **cost-effectiveness, ease of operation,** (authority of person handling), **appropriate velocity, sustainability –** costs, **ethical aspects**

Note: The summary results concern the nation-wide network. **Bold letters:** *The quality dimensions that were found to be particularly central in the analysis. Normal letters: The quality dimensions that are of lesser importance. (Normal letters in brackets): The quality dimensions that are of no importance.*

NETWORK COLLABORATION

As noted by Benassi (1993), network studies require a more holistic approach than just a review of alliances or partnerships of single organizations. In the present analysis, the network collaboration perspective complements the information quality perspective. The results of the analysis of information quality on the basis of the newly developed framework implied that network collaboration is a prerequisite for many of the improvements that could be done to information quality within safety telephone services. Network collaboration is a facilitator of management of information quality. Information quality considerations, on the other hand, may contribute to the creation of network identity and to socialization and institutionalization processes at the network level.

The comprehensive analysis continued after the operationalization of the information quality analysis framework to include the investigation of network collaboration as well as formulation of recommendations for practical development work in the case networks with regard to (1) information quality and (2) related general network collaboration (see Melkas, 2004, for the full description). After the analysis of information quality with the framework developed, the interviews were reanalyzed to gain additional understanding. This was mainly done through mind-mapping techniques. A corresponding methodology has been utilized by, for instance, Viitanen (1998) in a study of information management strategies in a global network organization.

The investigation of network collaboration was deliberately not as structured as, for instance, social network analysis (e.g., Wasserman & Galaskiewicz, 1994; Scott, 2000), due to its complementary character in relation to the operationalization of the information quality analysis framework.

The following themes were discerned as central with regard to the relationship between information quality and network collaboration:

- Personnel in safety telephone service networks (educational and professional background)
- Virtual networks and trust (development and existence of trust)
- Collaboration between public, private and third sectors (differences and barriers between sectors)
- Initiation into network operations and communication (beginning of collaboration between partners)
- Installation of safety telephone and guidance on its uses (customer's knowledge about the network)
- Monitoring of customer's condition (updated information to the network about the customer)
- Customers' regional equality (different local circumstances around Finland),
- Strategies of elderly care in the community (local authorities as part and supporter of the network)

The above list includes matters that were found to affect information flows and information quality. No correlations were studied. The comprehensive results are described in Melkas (2004).

FUTURE TRENDS

The emphasis in this chapter is on the framework for information quality analysis and its usability. This research opened up new insights into three directions: (1) analysis and management of information quality, (2) service networks based on virtualization and (3) the branch of safety telephone services. Literature studies had shown that qualitative tools to analyze information quality are needed, and that such analyses have not been undertaken in network environments.

The importance of finding out the views of personnel by means of interviews has recently been emphasized by Davidson, Lee, and Wang (2004). What made the case study of this chapter especially challenging was the relative ignorance of the interviewees about information-related matters and their role in those.

The framework introduced in the present chapter is, on the one hand, general in that it is argued to be well applicable in different organizational environments, and on the other hand, it was adapted here to the branch in which it was operationalized. The framework is thus flexible, and might well have good future potential in organizational research.

The environment of safety telephone services and their virtual networks was felt to be particularly challenging, as there were many completely different types of information transferred in multi-actor, multi-professional, multi-organizational, even multi-locality networks. Moreover, information flows form the basis for the operations in an especially clear way. In fact, the importance of information-related matters is claimed to be beyond comparison with many other branches. The demanding operationalization of the framework for information quality analysis in this environment succeeded. Having a combined framework with both the six stages of analysis and the information quality dimensions enabled a well-structured investigation of the complex information flows in the case networks. Undertaking the analysis implied that if the information quality dimensions had been used without the six stages, some issues might have remained unnoticed in the information processes.

Throughout the analysis as well as during the documentation of its results, the framework of analysis was continuously assessed. Several weaknesses were detected. It was often difficult to code the interview data so that different matters could be placed unambiguously under the relevant information quality dimensions. It was also felt to be difficult to document the results for this reason. Sometimes, it was even problematic to place matters under the six stages of analysis. The overlap in the stages of analysis, dimensions of information quality and presentation of the results was disturbing. However, coding checks were made, and after careful considerations of the usability of the framework, the conclusion was made that this was inevitable in an investigation of the present kind to get a comprehensive picture of a complicated phenomenon and things related to it.

In future studies, the number of information quality dimensions for the six stages of analysis could possibly be somewhat lower. The whole entity of information quality analysis as introduced — from the categorization of types of information to an investigation of bottlenecks of information flows — and from an assessment of the relevance of the different stages of analysis to undertaking the six stages of analysis — and finally, an investigation of network collaboration (and formulation of recommendations), is quite profound. Or, in its present multi-faceted scope, the information quality analysis may be better suited to an assessment of information quality in a smaller organizational context. Alternatively, the information quality analysis could be utilized in a study of a few service chains of customers of one virtual network (for example, subscription, installation, communication, alarm and repair chains) and/or of a few collaboration partners ("chains" of negotiations, closing of contracts, initiation of operations, alarms, communication and so forth).

CONCLUSION

It is argued that the above-mentioned shortcomings do not devalue the methodology developed. Numerous strengths were detected. The information quality analysis as introduced enables a versatile investigation, and it is regarded as a key to practical development work in organizations. Even the certain degree of repetition across the stages of analysis and information quality dimensions seemed meaningful, because at each stage of the operationalization, new insights were gained, and the area of information quality was thoroughly investigated. As information quality is a complicated topic, "encircling" problems and challenges helps in gaining a proper picture of the whole (cf., Pierce, Kahn, & Melkas, forthcoming, on quality measurements at different stages of information processes). The wealth of interview data and other materials on a very complicated environment were systematized to an extent where information quality planning by organization or network has become possible.

This research was the first attempt to study information quality in the branch of safety telephone services in Finland, or elsewhere, to the author's knowledge. Results of the information quality analysis could be utilized also in individual organizations' quality management systems. An information quality analysis could form one element of a general quality assessment at the organizational or network level. For suggestions on other avenues for future research and validation, readers are referred to Melkas (2004).

Although only partial results could be presented here, the investigation of network collaboration formed an important part of the information quality analysis. It highlighted issues that had not come up or had been merely touched upon in the earlier analysis. Yet, they affect information flows and quality. The network collaboration perspective also led to fuller use of all the valuable interview data and contributed to the basis for action and scientific recommendations. It is thus argued that the linking of previously distinct research areas — information quality, network collaboration and information flows — was useful.

The results of the operationalization of the methodology were branch-specific, so their wider applicability and significance remain to be seen. Their potential impact on the development of the branch in question is considerable. Interest towards information management was observed to increase in the case networks during the investigation. Training materials on information quality are being developed, and the results of this investigation were incorporated into general quality recommendations that were recently formulated for the whole branch of safety telephone services in Finland. Closely related branches developing distance care arrangements may also benefit from those.

REFERENCES

Benassi, M. (1993). Organizational perspectives of strategic alliances. In G. Grabher (Ed.), *The embedded firm* (pp. 95-115). London: Routledge.

Davidson, B., Lee, Y. W., & Wang, R. (2004). Developing data production maps: meeting patient discharge data submission requirements. *International Journal of Healthcare Technology and Management, 6*(2), 223-240.

Duarte, D. L., & Tennant Snyder, N. (2001). *Mastering virtual teams: Strategies, tools, and techniques that succeed.* San Francisco: Jossey-Bass.

EN 50134–7: 1996. (1996). *European Standard. Alarm systems — Social alarm systems. Part 7: Application guidelines.* Brussels: European Committee for Electrotechnical Standardization.

English, L. P. (1996). Help for data quality problems. *InformationWeek,* 600, 53-61.

English, L. P. (1999). *Improving data warehouse and business information quality: Methods for reducing costs and increasing profits.* New York: Wiley.

English, L. P. (2001). Information quality management: The next frontier. *Quality Congress: American Society for Quality's Annual Quality Congress Proceedings* (pp. 529-533). Milwaukee: American Society for Quality.

Handy, C. (1995, May-June). Trust and the virtual organization. *Harvard Business Review, 73*(3), 40-50.

Holton, J. A. (2001). Building trust and collaboration in a virtual team. *Team Performance Management, 7*(3/4), 36-47.

Huang, K-T., Lee, Y. W., & Wang, R. Y. (1999). *Quality information and knowledge.* Upper Saddle River, NJ: Prentice Hall PTR.

Jarvenpaa, S. L., Knoll, K., & Leidner, D. E. (1998, Spring). Is anybody out there? Antecedents of trust in global virtual teams. *Journal of Management Information Systems, 14*(4), 29-64.

Katzy, B. R., & Dissel, M. (2001). A toolset for building the virtual enterprise. *Journal of Intelligent Manufacturing, 12*, 121-131.

Kayworth, T. R., & Leidner, D. E. (2002, Winter). Leadership effectiveness in global virtual teams. *Journal of Management Information Systems, 18*(3), 7-40.

Kotorov, R. (2001). Virtual organization: Conceptual analysis of the limits of its decentralization. *Knowledge and Process Management, 8*(1), 55-62.

Lillrank, P. (1998). Introduction to knowledge management. In P. Lillrank & M. Forssén (Eds.), *Managing for knowledge: Perspectives and prospects* (Working Paper No. 17/1998/Industrial Management, pp. 3-28). Espoo: Helsinki University of Technology.

Lipnack, J., & Stamps, J. (1997). *Virtual teams: Reaching across space, time, and organizations with technology*. New York: John Wiley & Sons.

Melkas, H. (2004). *Towards holistic management of information within service networks: Safety telephone services for ageing people*. Doctoral dissertation. Espoo: Helsinki University of Technology, Department of Industrial Engineering and Management. Retrieved from http://lib.hut.fi/Diss/2004/isbn9512268868/

Miles, M., & Huberman, A. M. (1985). *Qualitative data analysis*. Beverly Hills, CA: Sage Publications.

Miles, R. E., & Snow, C. C. (1992). Causes of failure in network organizations. *California Management Review, 34*(4), 53-72.

Miller, B., Malloy, M. A., Masek, E., & Wild, C. (2001). Towards a framework for managing the information environment. *Information and Knowledge Systems Management, 2*, 359-384.

Molander, S. (2003). Call centeristä contact centeriksi: Turvapuhelinkeskus ikäihmisten tukena. In A. Serkkola (Ed.), *Turvapuhelinpalvelut ikääntyvän ihmisen elinympäristössä* (pp. 69-92). Lahti: Helsinki University of Technology Lahti Centre.

Pierce, E., Kahn, B., & Melkas, H. (forthcoming). *A comparison of quality issues for data, information, and knowledge*. Paper submitted to the Information Resources Management Association International Conference 2006. Washington, DC.

Provan, K. G., & Milward, H. B. (2001, July/August). Do networks really work? A framework for evaluating public-sector organizational networks. *Public Administration Review, 61*(4), 414-423.

Putnam, L. (2001, March/April). Distance teamwork: The realities of collaborating with virtual colleagues. *Online, 25*(2), 54-57.

Rouse, W. B. (1999). Connectivity, creativity, and chaos: Challenges of loosely-structured organizations. *Information & Knowledge Systems Management, 1*, 117-131.

Scott, J. (2000). *Social network analysis: A handbook* (2nd ed.). London: Sage Publications.

van der Smagt, T. (2000). Enhancing virtual teams: Social relations v. communication technology. *Industrial Management + Data Systems, 100*(4), 148-156.

Strong, D. M., Lee, Y. W., & Wang, R. Y. (1997a). Data quality in context. *Communications of the ACM, 40*(5), 103-110.

Strong, D. M., Lee, Y. W., & Wang, R. Y. (1997b). 10 potholes in the road to information quality. *IEEE Computer, 30*(8), 38-46.

van Berlo, A. (1998). How to enhance acceptance of safety alarm systems by elderly? In J. Graafmans, V. Taipale, & N. Charness (Eds.), *Gerontechnology: A sustainable investment in the future* (pp. 390-393). Amsterdam, The Netherlands: IOS Press.

van Hout, E. J. Th., & Bekkers, V. J. J. M. (2000). Patterns of virtual organization: The case of the National Clearinghouse for Geographic Information. *Information Infrastructure and Policy*, 6, 197-207.

Viitanen, J. (1998). *The information management strategies in the global network organization.* Publication of the Turku School of Economics and Business Administration, Series A-6: 1998. Turku: Turku School of Economics and Business Administration.

Voss, H. (1996, July/August). Virtual organizations: The future is now. *Strategy & Leadership*, 12-16.

Wang, R. Y. (1998). A product perspective on total data quality management. *Communications of the ACM, 41*(2), 58-65.

Wang, R. Y., Lee, Y. W., Pipino, L. L., & Strong, D. M. (1998, Summer). Manage your information as a product. *Sloan Management Review, 39*(4), 95-105.

Wang, R. Y., & Strong, D. M. (1996, Spring). Beyond accuracy: What data quality means to data consumers. *Journal of Management Information Systems, 12*(4), 5-34.

Wasserman, S., & Galaskiewicz, J. (Eds.). (1994). *Advances in social network analysis: Research in the social and behavioural sciences.* Thousand Oaks, CA: Sage Publications.

Yin, R. K. (1989). *Case study research: Design and methods.* Beverly Hills, CA: Sage Publications.

APPENDIX: DATA COLLECTION FOR THE OPERATIONALIZATION

The data collection for the operationalization of the methodology was made following the general principles of conducting case studies (Yin, 1989). The data included: (1) written material ranging from memoranda to formal reports; (2) organization charts, personal records, maps, graphs, service statistics, etc.; (3) open-ended and semi-structured interviews (the main data collection method), use of informants, and intraorganizational and interorganizational workshops, as well as (4) absorbing and noting details and actions in the field environment. Structured interviews and written questionnaires were seen as inappropriate for this research. It is not likely that they would unfold the care professionals' true views of the complicated phenomenon of information within the networks.

The semi-structured and open-ended interviews assumed a conversational manner, but the interviewer followed a pre-prepared set of questions that concerned the networks' characteristics and work practices, information flows and management as well as problems in these (for further details, see Melkas, 2004). The interviews were audiotaped and transcribed for analysis. At workshops and seminars, field notes were made. After reading, coding and analyzing the data, the results were sent to the interviewees for feedback and comments. The results were also discussed at several intraorganizational and interorganizational workshops, seminars or meetings.

The networks investigated represented several different types of safety telephone service networks in Finland, and one in Sweden. The branch is very fragmented. It is the duty of municipal authorities to give guidance on private safety telephone services, if the municipality in question does not have a system of its own. Many municipalities do have systems of their own, or they purchase the service from a private service provider (Figure A-1). Within one municipality, there may be several systems in operation at the same time; for instance, internal systems in institutions offering sheltered accommodation, a municipal system and several private systems.

The interviewees represented different types of safety telephone service systems of different sizes and operating in diverse localities (Figure A-2). Most of the interviewees (24) represented a nation-wide network offering safety telephone services around Finland. Seven interviewees were from municipal systems (three networks, of which two were Finnish and one Swedish). Four interviewees were from institutions offering sheltered accommodation (one system operated by a foundation and another by a cooperative). Three represented a system operated by a non-governmental organization, and four interviewees represented a pilot project testing mobile safety telephones.

The Finnish nation-wide network was the most interesting and challenging with regard to information-related issues and network collaboration. It received the most intensive attention in the study. Inclusion of the other types of networks for comparison increased the validity and reliability of the results. The bias in favour of the nation-wide system had an impact on some of the emphases, but challenges and development needs were largely the same in all kinds of safety telephone service networks — apart from the internal ones in very small institutions offering sheltered accommodation.

The study was undertaken in the period from August 2001 to May 2003, which included the study visits, test interviews, actual interviews, seminars, workshops and observation. The picture gained by the interviews around Finland was comprehensive, and the types of organizations and professional groups were representative of the branch. Municipalities (the social and health care sector) and companies were both represented by 12 interviewees. Altogether 16 interviewees represented non-governmental organizations, foundations and cooperatives. Half of the interviewees had a managerial occupation and the other half an employee occupation. There were 29 women and 11 men among the interviewees.

Figure A-1. Variety of actors involved in safety telephone services (examples)

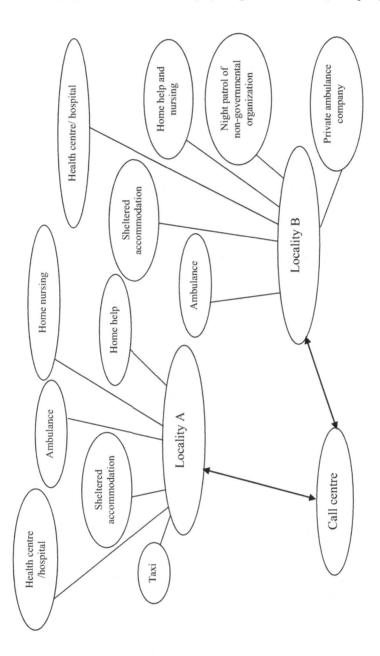

Figure A-2. Examples of alternative service chains of a safety telephone service customer in one locality

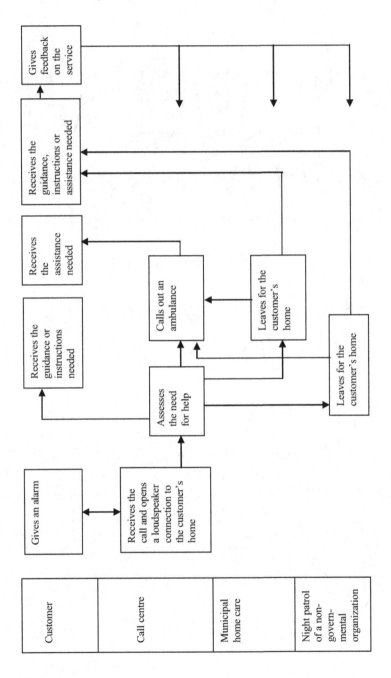

Chapter X

Quality Measures and the Information Consumer

Mikhaila S. E. Burgess, Cardiff University, UK

W. Alex Gray, Cardiff University, UK

Nick J. Fiddian, Cardiff University, UK

ABSTRACT

This chapter discusses the proposal for using quality criteria to facilitate information searching. It suggests that the information consumer can be assisted in searching for information by using a consumer-oriented model of quality. This is achieved by presenting the consumer with a set of relevant quality criteria from which they can select those of most importance to them at that present time, and allowing them to state preference values and importance weightings for each criterion. The consumer's quality profile can then be used to focus an information search onto relevant search domains, and produce a more focused output. The chapter presents our model of quality and shows that quality measures can be used to focus information searches by achieving statistically significant changes in the ordering of the obtained search results.

INTRODUCTION

In recent years the volume of data readily available to the information consumer has dramatically increased. It is now possible to search for information on an unlimited number of topics across a wide range of information environments, such as electronic library systems, corporate intranets and the Internet. Although plentiful, this information is also of varying levels of quality, with providers ranging from multi-national corporations to individuals with limited knowledge. This range of suppliers also results in a diverse variety of formats in which information is stored and presented.

With so much information available, quality has become an important discriminator when deciding which information to use and which to discard. However, problems such as information overload, specificity of database queries, and the requirement for users to be able to explicitly state their information need, can hinder their search for information that meets their current requirements.

Due to the mass of data now available to the information consumer, and being comparatively easy to access, an assumption could be made that finding information on a desired topic should be a straightforward task. However, due to the amount of information being so large, and of varying levels of quality, it is becoming increasingly difficult to find precisely what is required, particularly if the information consumer does not have precise knowledge of their information needs. The two hurdles that prevent the finding of relevant information are therefore "information overload" and "information quality." Our proposed solution to this problem, and thus the approach discussed in this chapter, consists of the development of a methodology for using quality criteria as an aid to information searching.

Research Premise

The hypothesis on which this work is based asserts that it is possible to create a hierarchical generic model of quality that can be used by the consumer to assist in information searching, by focusing the returned result set based on personal preferences.

The first part of this chapter introduces a number of definitions of quality. This is followed by a discussion about our consumer-oriented generic quality framework, and the domain-specific frameworks derived from this generic model. It then continues by discussing the experimental Information Search Environment created to demonstrate how the information consumer can use quality to focus information searches across a number of domains, and shows how changes in quality preferences produce different result-set ranking orders.

DEFINING QUALITY

Although people intuitively know what is meant by the term "quality," when asked to produce an explicit definition most will struggle. This is the principal problem that is encountered when discussing quality: everyone knows what it is but very few people can define it. This leaves us in a difficult position when wanting to incorporate quality in some computational system, as to be used in this type of environment an explicit definition, with quantitative representations of terms,

Table 1. Selection of current definitions of quality

PROJECT REFERENCE	QUALITY FRAMEWORK STRUCTURE
Software Quality Domain	
(Barbacci, Klein, Longstaff, & Weinstoch, 1995)	4 models for each of 4 primary attributes, with a total of 13 concerns
(Boehm, Brown, & Lipow, 1976)	Hierarchical tree structure comprising 10 categories and 15 metrics
(Dromey, 1995, 1996)	3 models, containing 17 attributes and 42 unique sub-attributes (repeated amongst the models)
(Hyatt & Rosenberg, 1996)	4 goals and 13 attributes
ISO 9126-1:2001 (ISO/IEC, 2001)	2 models: 1. "Internal & external software qualities" — 6 dimensions and 34 metrics. 2. "Quality in use" — 4 metrics
(Liu, Zhou, & Yang, 2000)	3 factors and 8 criteria
(McCall, Richards, & Walters, 1977)	3 classes, 11 factors, and 23 criteria
(Ortega, Pérez, & Rojas, 2002)	6 metrics
(Royce, 1990)	4 metrics
(Rubey & Hartwick, 1968)	7 attribute descriptions
Data Quality Domain	
(Abate, Diegert, & Allen, 1998)	4 categories and 15 dimensions
(Cykana, Paul, & Stern, 1996)	6 characteristics
(Gardyn, 1997)	5 dimensions
(Long & Seko, 2002)	5 dimensions and 24 characteristics
(Naumann, 2002)	4 dimensions and 22 metrics
(Redman, 1996)	3 categories and 27 dimensions
(Wang & Strong, 1996)	4 categories and 15 dimensions
Information Quality Domain	
(Bovee, Srivastava, & Mak, 2001)	4 criteria and 10 components
(Dedeke, 2000)	5 dimensions and 28 metrics
(Eppler, 2001)	4 quality levels and 16 criteria
(Matsumura & Shouraboura, 1996)	2 categories and 4 attributes
(Miller, 1996)	10 dimensions
Web Quality Domain	
(Aladwani & Palvia, 2002)	4 dimensions and 25 items
(Chen, Zhu, & Wang, 1998)	10 quality parameters
(Moustakis, Litos, Dalivigas, & Tsironis, 2004)	5 criteria and 24 sub-criteria
(Olsina, Lafuente, & Rossi, 2001)	Hierarchical model containing 100+ metrics
(Zhu & Gauch, 2000)	15 metrics

is essential. Therefore, before quality can be incorporated into such a system an explicit definition must be obtained.

Although quality is a difficult term to define, some research has been conducted in this area. Table 1 presents a variety of quality definitions and models that have been developed, focusing on the subject domains of: Information Quality, Data Quality, Software Quality and Web Quality. As can be seen in this table, although a great deal of research has been conducted in this area "no single definition or standard of quality exists" (Smart, 2002). However, although this table shows a variety of definitions, using different terminology (such as "attributes," "criteria" and "metrics"), all recognize:

- The importance of a definition of quality
- That quality is a multi-attribute entity

The majority also agree that the multiple attributes used to define quality can be grouped into related categories, and represented in a hierarchical structure.

The Information Consumer Perspective

Most of the work currently conducted in this area has looked at quality from the organisational or information producer perspective. The information consumer's perspective of quality differs from these in two important ways:

- The consumer has no control over the quality of available information.
- Their aim is to find information that matches their personal needs, rather than provide information that meets the needs of others.

This difference in focus means quality definitions that have been defined for use by information providers are not well suited to the information consumer.

The typical information consumer wants to find the best available information that meets their requirements, at that point in time, in their current domain of interest. This may not necessarily be the best possible result as the consumer often has restrictions, such as the time available to spend searching for information. For example, the consumer may need the information quickly and is unable to wait several hours while all possible sources of information are investigated to find the best result across all sources. In this case the consumer may be willing to accept the best possible results obtainable within a given restriction, such as immediately available data, data within their price range, or all data that can be obtained within a specified time limit.

A Consumer-Oriented Definition of Quality

Due to the lack of investigation into the quality requirements of information consumers, and thus also the lack of an appropriate model for defining quality from

*Figure 1. Hierarchical generic framework of quality, showing distinction between primary (**bold**) and secondary quality criteria*

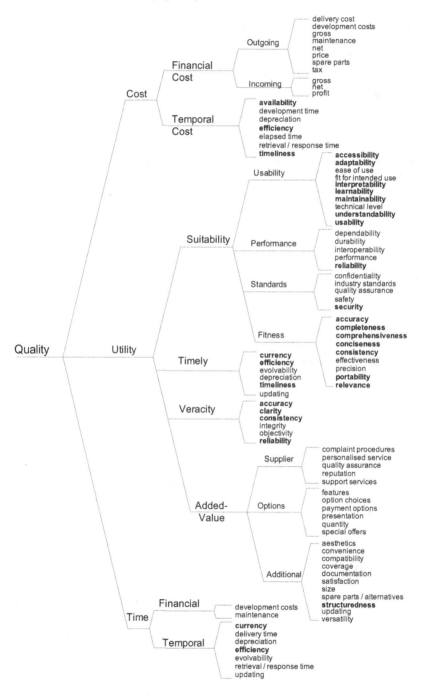

this perspective, the first stage of our work involved the creation of such a model. In this section we present our consumer-oriented model of quality and discuss how it was created.

The generic framework developed during this project can be seen in Figure 1. The criteria identified for incorporation in this model were based primarily on those identified during the investigation into previous definitions of quality, and features of quality stated as important by consumer representation organisations.

The principal features of this framework of quality are as follows:

- **Generic:** contains a set of quality criteria applicable to a range of subject domains.
- **Hierarchical:** allows criteria to be grouped into related categories and sub-categories.
- **Intuitive:** criteria are locatable by following an intuitive path through the hierarchy to ensure clarity, navigability and ease of use.
- **Flexible:** (1) provides facilities for the relocation of criteria within the hierarchy, (2) enables the selection of a set of criteria to create a personalised definition of quality.
- **Extensible:** provides facilities for the addition of new criteria and the deletion of unrequired criteria.

In the rest of this section we discuss the method used to develop our generic framework of information quality. After stating the aims of this model, and thus the desired objectives, this section continues by discussing the steps that were followed during framework creation, the identification of quality criteria, and how these criteria were organised into a set of quality dimensions. For further information about how this model was developed we refer the reader to Burgess, Gray, and Fiddian (2002, 2003), and Burgess (2003).

Clarification of Terminology

As can be seen in Table 1, there is a lack of consistency when discussing quality and its characteristics. Sets of quality characteristics are referred to as categories, domains, factors, goals and attributes. Individual quality characteristics are indicated by the terms criterion, attribute, metric, sub-factor and item. Due to this plethora of potential terms we need to define the terminology to be used in our quality framework, namely:

- **Criterion:** an individual quality characteristic (also referred to as attribute and metric).
- **Dimension:** a collection of criteria (also referred to as category).

Generally, the term "metric" refers to a measurable entity. However, as in the current quality literature it has been used to denote any features of quality, this less restrictive meaning has been maintained in this chapter.

Steps to Quality Framework Creation

To create our consumer-oriented framework of quality the following steps were followed:

1. Determine a set of quality criteria
2. Determine a set of quality dimensions
3. Hierarchically organise criteria and dimensions
4. Identify assessment methods for quality criteria

The identification of assessment methods is discussed later in this chapter. Steps 1 through 3 however are discussed next.

Selected Quality Criteria

The criteria of quality identified for incorporation into our generic model are based on those identified by other researchers during previous research projects, by consumer representation organisations, such as the UK consumer watchdog *Which?* (Which?Online, 2003), and other criteria including those that we, as consumers, feel are also of importance. The resultant set of criteria therefore also contains those quality criteria used by organisations when evaluating the quality of items and services not necessarily identified in previous research projects.

Primary Quality Criteria

The first phase of quality criteria determination was based on a review of 36 research projects across the domains of data, information, software and Web sites. Many of the projects identified during this stage of our research identified study-specific criteria that are only mentioned in a single project. These criteria are of limited use in a generic model, and so were discarded. The criteria selected for incorporation in our model as "primary" criteria were limited to:

*   **Generic quality criteria:** thus eliminating all domain-specific attributes; and
*   **Those occurring in multiple literature references:** the limit for this was decided upon as five or more references, thus eliminating all criteria that only appear in one to four previous research projects (this cut-off provides a coverage level of 16% of the total number of previously identified criteria).

These two restrictions reduced the number of criteria from 179 identified to 24 primary criteria, which appear in Figure 1 in bold font.

Secondary Quality Criteria

Alongside the primary criteria, a number of other criteria have been included as a result of research into those used by consumer representation organisations, discussions with potential users, and those attributes that we, as consumers ourselves, feel are important. These extra metrics constitute the secondary set of quality criteria, and are identified in Figure 1 as those criteria in normal font.

Categorisation of Quality Criteria

Having identified a set of quality criteria, the next step in the creation of a hierarchical framework was the categorisation of those criteria within a generic framework. The following three sections therefore focus on this criterion categorisation process.

Principal Quality Dimensions

Three main dimensions of quality were selected based upon the three characteristics of requirements engineering: *cost*, *time*, and *requirements*. Requirements engineering was chosen as a basis because it focuses on the development of some product, with the aim of meeting a customer's needs. During this process there are three main factors that need to be considered — all costs, item specifications and requirements, and either item development or procurement time.

The term *requirement* implies features that are essential in some product, but when discussing quality this is not necessarily the case. Features that are an additional benefit need also to be included to cater for the user who has an idea about the qualities they would like in a product, but which are not necessarily essential. The term *requirements* was therefore replaced by the more general term *utility*. This term implies a set of criteria that are equivalent to non-functional requirements, whereas cost and time refer to functional requirements.

Sub-Dimensions of Quality

Due to the potential number of criteria available for inclusion in our quality framework, and the need for simple framework navigation to enable users to easily locate desired criteria, further categorisation of criteria was required. The remaining dimensions selected for inclusion in the generic framework are as follows:

- **COST:** comprising the sub-dimensions Financial and Temporal Cost.
- **UTILITY:** comprising the sub-dimensions Suitability, Timely, Veracity, and Added-Value.
- **TIME:** comprising the sub-dimensions Financial and Temporal.

Having defined a set of dimensions, and sub-dimensions in which quality criteria can be located, each criterion was examined in turn to identify its most suitable location, or locations. To ensure ease of user navigation through this framework

Figure 2. Framework editing facility in the Quality Toolkit

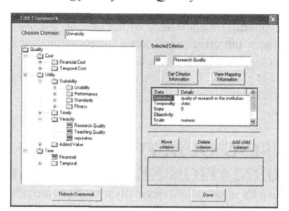

each criterion was placed in an intuitive position, thus modelling the natural categorisation of quality criteria. This approach results in some criteria appearing in multiple places within the hierarchy, ensuring each criterion can be easily found, but still representing the same real-world quality value.

The current framework position for each criterion is not, however, static. Framework flexibility is supported by the Quality Toolkit — an application designed for use by either a quality manager or a confident user, to facilitate framework maintenance and modification. Using this toolkit criteria can be relocated within the current framework, removed, and new criteria added. This flexibility also holds true for quality dimensions. Due to this flexibility of framework structure if criteria are not placed in a location where a user can find them by following an intuitive path, they can be moved to a new location to improve ease of framework navigation. The framework editing facility provided by the Quality Toolkit is illustrated in Figure 2.

Domain-Specific Frameworks of Quality

To be able to demonstrate how quality attributes can be used to assist in information retrieval the generic framework needs to be focused onto a real-world domain. This requirement results in the need for domain-specific quality criteria. Although these criteria could be incorporated into the initial generic framework, after the inclusion of just two or three different domains the number of criteria would become unmanageable.

Our proposed solution to this is the use of the generic framework as a blueprint for the development of separate, domain-specific frameworks. By using the structure of the generic framework as a starting point, relevant generic criteria can be selected followed by the inclusion of criteria specific to the chosen topic domain.

This domain-specific framework can then be used to facilitate a search for information within that topic.

As well as supporting maintenance of the generic framework, the Quality Toolkit also facilitates the creation of domain-specific quality frameworks. An example of a domain-specific framework based on our original generic model can be seen in Burgess et al. (2002), in which we present a quality framework for the domain of UK universities.

USING QUALITY TO FOCUS
INFORMATION SEARCH RESULTS

When searching for information, especially in multiple provider environments, the user can become inundated due to the vast number of potential results. This is

Figure 3. Potential for information overload in an information search

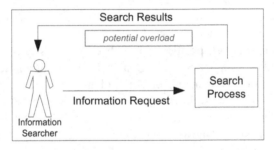

Figure 4. Information search focused according to quality requirements

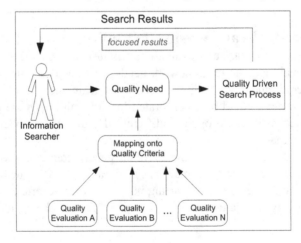

particularly the case when conducting a search on the Internet. As the number of information items available increases the consumer starts to suffer from information overload, where they are no longer able to effectively process that information, as illustrated in Figure 3.

We propose that by developing a model of quality that can be used to create a personalised definition of quality, according to the individual consumer, this quality profile can be used to focus an information search onto a relevant set of results, thus reducing information overload and increasing consumer productivity, as illustrated in Figure 4.

QUALITY CRITERIA EVALUATIONS

Before quality can be used as an aid to information searching, methods need to be defined for obtaining values for the identified quality criteria.

Classes of Quality Criteria Assessment

In his 2000 paper, Naumann (Naumann & Rolker, 2000) defines a set of classes for the assessment of information quality (IQ), and identifies methods developed for use in each class. The sources for quality criterion evaluation identified in his paper are the user, the information source, and the query process used when obtaining the information. These three sources are divided into the following classes of assessment:

- **Subject criteria:** when IQ scores can only be obtained from individual users, based on their personal views, experiences, and background
- **Object criteria:** when IQ scores can be obtained by analysing the information
- **Process criteria:** when IQ scores are determined by the query process

For each of these assessment classes Naumann presents a set of assessment methods that can be used to evaluate the quality of each information source:

- **Subject criteria:** user experience, user sampling, continuous user assessment
- **Object criteria:** contract of content quality, content parsing, content sampling, expert input, continuous assessment of content
- **Process criteria:** data cleansing, continuous assessment of process, structural parsing

For a comprehensive explanation of these methods of assessment, and illustrations regarding their usage, the reader is referred to Naumann's book, *Quality-Driven Query Answering for Integrated Information Systems* (Naumann, 2002).

Source vs. Information Quality

During Naumann's work the emphasis was on obtaining values for the quality of the information source, and the process used for accessing those sources, such as query processing quality. The thrust of our work was to ascertain the quality of the available information, rather than the source from which the information is obtained. Our work is therefore complementary to the work presented by Naumann and his colleagues: as whereas Naumann's approach looks at the coarse-grained aspect of source quality, ours focuses on the fine-grained aspect of the individual information items.

Due to the differing focus of our respective approaches the assessment methods described above are not immediately transferable to our research. To be of use in our work they must be modified, to consider quality of the information rather than the source from which it is obtained. However, this modification is only to the implementation of the assessment methods. Their definitions remain the same.

Frequency of Quality Criteria Assessment

An important issue when automatically obtaining IQ scores and storing them for use again at a later time is the frequency at which these values require updating. This is dependant on whether a criterion is static or dynamic in nature.

If a criterion is static then once a value is obtained and stored it will be possible to use that same value for some considerable period of time, and only check for changes after an appropriate time lapse. However, for dynamic criteria a judgement must be made as to how frequently these updates need to occur. If a criterion is dynamic over a period of weeks, then its value only needs to be updated after a predetermined number of weeks. If, on the other hand, the value can change in hours, minutes, or seconds — such as when considering values of stocks and shares — a frequent update cycle will be required, which has an elapsed time related to the time between expected changes.

The quality criteria used in our experimental research domains have been considered as static, in that once evaluated the values for these criteria do not change. Although in a real-world system a number of criteria would be dynamic, with evaluations requiring frequent updating, this dynamic nature was removed to ensure consistency of experimental results. The removal of dynamic criteria values does not adversely affect the results presented in this chapter as we are currently only concerned with static criteria. The inclusion of dynamic quality criteria is however an element due to be incorporated within future work.

Experimental Subject Domains

To demonstrate how quality can be used in the search for information within some data set, the generic quality framework was used as a basis for the creation of a set of domain-specific frameworks. Developing these sub-frameworks makes it possible to demonstrate the use of quality in real-world domains, with data obtained from real-world sources.

Two primary subject domains were selected for experimentation:

- UK universities
- Cars

The reason for the selection of these domains is to show how domain-specific quality frameworks can be developed and used when searching for a service (e.g., universities), and information on a tangible product (e.g., cars). Other subject domains have also been implemented for a number of tangible products including home freezers, luggage and cameras.

All of the data for each of these subject domains were acquired from Internet sources. The majority of these sources provide information via structured Web sites, so although the data was extracted manually for use in our experiments, it is also feasible to employ automatic parsing techniques to extract this data.

Although the initial driving force behind our work was the problem of the varying levels of quality of Internet-based information, to ensure the data used in our experiments remained under our control, and therefore so that the experiments were repeatable and comparable, this data was obtained from online sources but stored locally, off-line. This eliminated the dynamic nature of the information. If our experiments were conducted on data that was liable to change then reliable conclusions could not have been drawn. The next phase of our work will therefore move into this dynamic environment, with the first task of assessing the differences in working with static and dynamic data sources.

Mapping Quality Criteria to Available Data

To be able to calculate quality scores for available information items we need to know from where values are obtained for each quality criterion. This requires a mapping between quality criteria and the available data (i.e., values obtained from external sources which can be used to calculate quality scores for each item or piece of information). This mapping is currently created manually, using the Quality Toolkit. Using this tool each data field is mapped to the appropriate quality criterion, along with a ranking of its importance when calculating the criterion value. This is necessary due to each criterion score typically being based on a number of values, from more than one source. For example, in the UK university domain the criterion of "Teaching Quality" is based on teaching data values obtained from both of the chosen data sources: *The Times* (Times, 2003) and *The Guardian* (Guardian, 2003).

As this is currently a manual process the potential exists for further research into developing a semi-automatic process for creating criterion mappings. During this next stage in our research we also aim to incorporate further sources of quality rating data, including consumer feedback and automatic quality monitoring. However, the current data types and the method used for mapping criteria to available data does not affect how the information consumer uses quality to focus information searches.

For more information on the nature of the data obtained from these various Web sites, and a full list of the mappings between experimental data and the selected subject domains the reader is referred to Burgess (2003).

QUALITY-DRIVEN
INFORMATION SEARCHING

To demonstrate how quality criteria can be used to assist in information searching, the experimental Information Search Environment (ISE) was developed. This proof-of-concept application incorporates the ideas presented in this chapter, whereby quality criteria can be selected from within a chosen quality framework and then used to focus information search results.

Quality Preferences

A search for information using ISE comprises five stages:

1.   Selection of domain of interest
2.   Selection of set of quality criteria to focus the search
3.   Stating importance weightings for each selected criterion
4.   Stating preference values, if desired, for each criterion
5.   Stating importance rankings, if desired, for information providers

Figure 5. Selecting IQ criteria in the university domain

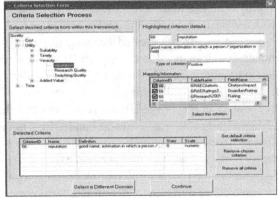

In this section we discuss each of these stages, and then conclude with a discussion on how results can be ranked based on user-specified quality preferences.

Selection of Subject Domain and Quality Criteria

A number of subject domains are currently available for selection by the user, in which to conduct an information search. The principal domains we have chosen for experimentation, as discussed above, are those of UK universities and new cars.

Once the user has selected their domain of interest they are presented with the corresponding domain-specific quality framework, from which they can select a number of quality criteria. Figure 5 shows the criteria selection process when the university domain has been chosen.

As well as selecting those criteria the user feels are important the user can also opt to select a default set of quality criteria. This feature enables popular quality criteria to be automatically selected for use in the current search, with the option for the user to remove any of these criteria and include others. In our demonstration environment default criteria are identified manually using the Quality Toolkit. However, this has been identified as an area requiring further research to enable these default criteria selections to be generated automatically based on previous user selections, user profiles and explicit user feedback.

Importance Weightings

Once a set of quality criteria have been selected, the user is then required to state weighting values for each criterion. These importance weightings are obtained from the user by presenting them with a graphical slider for each of their chosen criteria, such as that shown in Figure 6, and asking them to rate criterion importance using a percentage scale. They are then used by the ranking algorithm (see below) to find the best possible results, based on the importance of each criterion to the user, in their current situation.

Preference Values

As well as stating importance weightings the facility also exists for the user to state preferred values for each criterion. Although the highest value for a quality criterion might be assumed to be the most preferable, this is not always the case.

Figure 6. Example graphical slider

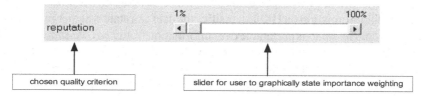

The user may not wish to search for the items that have the highest values for their chosen criteria. For example, they may wish to trade-off against cost and therefore search for some item valued up to a maximum price. These preference values are obtained from the user in the same way as importance weightings: via graphical sliders for each criterion.

User-Stated Source Preferences

Data for the two primary experimental subject domains were obtained from multiple sources:

- **UK universities:** two UK national newspapers — *The Times* (Times, 2003) and *The Guardian* (Guardian, 2003).
- **New cars:** the independent consumer organisations of Euro NCAP (EuroN-CAP, 2003), Parkers (Parkers, 2003), What Car (WhatCar, 2003), and Which (Which?Online, 2003).

When combining information from a variety of different sources, or multiple databases within a single environment, many difficulties arise. These include:

- Synonyms and homonyms
- Multiple formats of data representation and storage
- Data repetition
- Incorrect data
- Conflicting data

While obviously a problem when dealing with data in the real world, this is being investigated by other researchers and is a research area in its own right. Although the data used in our project has been obtained from multiple sources, it is stored in a local database and has gone through manual data checking to resolve the aforementioned difficulties.

This local storing of data also ensures consistency between experimental results. If the data were accessed directly from their original source we would have no control over that data. The information providers could potentially change their data, thus making it difficult to draw conclusions from our experiments into quality-oriented searching. Eliminating these limitations of the current search system is part of our planned further research.

The current version of ISE allows the user to state data source preferences when quality criteria evaluations come from multiple sources. For example, when searching for information on UK universities the user can state whether information obtained from *The Times* is preferable over information from *The Guardian* by setting the ranking orders to first and second respectively. It is also possible to eliminate undesired data sources by setting their ranking value to zero. These preference ranks are then used as a weighting value for data obtained from each source when calculating values for each quality criterion. Our future research includes plans to investigate the usage of information source quality ratings, as developed by Felix Naumann (Naumann, 2002), to enhance this aspect of ISE.

All of the data sources used in our experiments provide numerical quality ratings, on a variety of scales. Some values are on a percentage scale from 0 to 100, some are from 0 to 1, and others are on scales specific to the current topic. For example, *The Times* provides their values for university research ratings based on the UK academic Research Assessment Exercise, resulting in a scale of 1 to 6.4. All values that are required by the ranking algorithms are therefore scaled during use, to lie on the scale of 0 to 1.

Ranking of Search Results

To find the best results based on user stated criteria settings, from the available data, three ranking algorithms have been employed: SAW, TOPSIS and TOPSIS-GP.

Simple Additive Weighting (SAW)

SAW is the best-known and most widely used multi-attribute decision-making (MADM) ranking method (Hwang & Yoon, 1981). This algorithm comprises three basic steps:

- **Step 1:** Scale quality criteria values v and weights w using transformation functions.
- **Step 2:** Apply the scaled user defined weighting to each quality criterion.
- **Step 3:** Calculate quality score iq for each item S_i by summing scores for each criterion.

The final score for each data item is therefore calculated as follows:

$$iq\,(S_i) \rightarrow \Sigma\,w_j v_{ij}$$

When the items are then ranked according to this final score, items with high values for those criteria stated as being important by the user will appear towards the top of the ranked result set. Those items with lower values for the criteria stated as important will appear low in the ranked result set.

Technique for Order Preference by Similarity to Ideal Solution (TOPSIS)

The TOPSIS ranking method is based upon the concept that "the chosen alternative should have the shortest distance from the ideal solution and the farthest from the negative-ideal solution" (Hwang & Yoon, 1981).

The two solutions are defined as follows:

- **Ideal solution:** a potential solution composed of all best attainable criterion values
- **Negative-ideal solution:** a potential solution composed of all worst attainable criterion values

By calculating the difference between each information item's quality score across all criteria, and the ideal and negative-ideal solutions, TOPSIS ranks each item according to how closely they match these two solutions: those closest to the ideal and furthest from the negative-ideal being ranked highly, and those furthest from the ideal and closest to the negative-ideal receiving a low ranking. The final order of the ranked set of data items is therefore focused on those that best meet the stated needs of the user, based on their inputted weightings of importance for each criterion. The items ranked highly as a result of applying TOPSIS are those which are the closest available match to the user's requirement and are therefore considered the "best" items, and those ranked low are those considered the "worst" items against the user's requirement. The final set of ranked results is therefore focused according to the requirements of the user.

TOPSIS with Given Preferences (TOPSIS-GP)

The original version on TOPSIS does not take into consideration user preferences for ideal criteria values. We therefore created an updated version of this algorithm (first presented in Burgess, 2003) to incorporate user-specified preference values for each quality criterion, rather than the "best" available values.

The current version of ISE only provides a facility for stating positive ideal values. Expanding ISE to allow the stating of negative ideal, or worst, values for each criterion would be a relatively small step. However, at present negative values are assumed based on the following:

If the preferred ideal value for an IQ criterion is larger than the mean value, we assume the user prefers a high criterion value, so the negative-ideal is set to the lowest available value.

If the preferred ideal value for an IQ criterion is lower than the mean value, we assume the user prefers a low criterion value, so the negative-ideal is set to the highest available value.

Using these assumptions the preference negative-ideal solution is created complementary to the preference positive ideal. Both are then used in the TOPSIS method instead of the standard ideal and negative-ideal, thus increasing search focus based on user-desired preferences.

A full description of the TOPSIS and TOPSIS-GP ranking algorithms can be found in the Appendix to this chapter.

Table 2. Comparing SAW, TOPSIS and TOPSIS-GP

CONSIDERATION	SAW	TOPSIS	TOPSIS-GP
Criterion preference weightings	✓	✓	✓
Positive and negative criteria		✓	✓
Ideal values for criteria		✓	✓
User preference values for criteria			✓

Comparing Ranking Algorithms

Both the SAW and TOPSIS ranking algorithms were created to rank a set of data items into the best possible order, placing the "best" items at the top of the ranking order and the "worst" at the bottom. As can be seen however from the above discussions there are some major differences between the three algorithms. These differences are shown in Table 2.

The comparison of quality criteria features taken into consideration by these algorithms shows that both TOPSIS and TOPSIS-GP provide the opportunity for increased focusing of search results, to reflect the stated quality requirements of the user. By considering both positive and negative criteria, and ideal criterion values, TOPSIS ranks data according to how close each data item matches the user specified requirements across several criteria, based on criteria importance weightings. TOPSIS-GP increases ranking order focus by removing the assumption that the user is looking for the highest possible value for each criterion (or lowest for negative criteria), and ranks results according to both criteria importance weightings and how closely each criterion value is to the ideal value stated by the user.

Although these three algorithms are all available for use in ISE, TOPSIS-GP has been chosen as the primary algorithm due to its incorporation of user preferences. If no user preferences are stated then it defaults to the ideal values as used in the original TOPSIS algorithm. The decision between TOPSIS and TOPSIS-GP is therefore made dynamically as the search is executed, based on the user's decision to search on quality ratings alone or to incorporate preference values.

EXPERIMENTS IN QUALITY-ORIENTED INFORMATION SEARCHING

To evaluate the viability of using quality criteria to focus information searches a selection of simulations were conducted in the chosen subject domains. The purpose of these search simulations was to demonstrate the effects of changing quality preferences on the results obtained from an information search, and to ascertain if any statistically significant differences occur in the ranking order of the results when quality preferences are changed.

Figure 7. Search results presented in ISE — example of using the Research Quality (metric99) and Teaching Quality (metric100) metrics in the University domain with importance weightings of 100% and 80% respectively

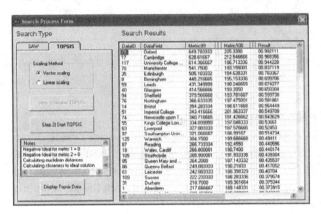

A typical result of a search conducted using ISE can be seen in Figure 7. This example shows the results when a search is conducted in the University domain, using the *Research Quality* and *Teaching Quality* criteria. As can be seen in this example a large amount of data is currently presented to the user. However, this is due to ISE currently being a research tool and thus required to show the results of each stage in the search process. The final version, as made available to consumers, would only show the final set of ranked results and would hide all values as calculated during the ranking process.

Results of Simulations

The results presented in this section were produced using our experimental Information Search Environment (ISE). There simulations were conducted to discover whether the ranking order of search results can significantly change in the following situations:

- Changing the selection of quality criteria
- Changing importance weightings for selected quality criteria
- Changing preference values for selected quality criteria
- Changing both importance weightings and preference values for selected quality criteria

To ascertain the significance of the differences, if any, between the search results we used the Wilcoxon signed ranks test for statistical significance (Crichton, 2003).

Next, we discuss each of these four experiment types and conclude with a summary of our obtained results.

Table 3. Results of varying quality criteria selection

DOMAIN	QUALITY CRITERIA	WEIGHTING	STATEMENT OF STATISTICAL SIGNIFICANCE
University	Research Quality	100%	Differences noted are very highly significant, to the 0.2% level.
	Facilities Spending	100%	
Cars	Drivability	100%	Differences noted are very highly significant, to the 0.2% level.
	Safety	100%	

Table 4. Results of selecting distinct sets of quality criteria

DOMAIN	QUALITY CRITERIA	WEIGHTING	STATEMENT OF STATISTICAL SIGNIFICANCE
University	The dimension of Financial-Incoming	80%	Differences noted are very highly significant, to the 0.2% level.
	The dimension of Veracity	80%	
Cars	Comfort, Drivability, Depreciation, Safety	100%	Differences noted are very highly significant, to the 0.2% level.
	Reliability Running costs Value for money Window visibility	100%	

Simulation Set 1: Changing Selected Quality Criteria

The first set of simulations focus on the selection of individual quality criteria for each domain, and compare the ranking order of the result set when the two searches were conducted. Two example results can be seen in Table 3. As the aim of simulation set 1 was not related to criteria importance weightings these were kept constant at 100%. Simulations were also conducted into selecting distinct sets of quality criteria, and are shown in Table 4.

Simulation Set 2: Changing Criteria Importance Weightings

The second set of simulations focus on the selection of two quality criteria for each domain, and compare the results of using both criteria to focus a search as their importance weightings are changed. Two example results from this set are shown in Table 5.

Table 5. Results of varying quality criteria importance weightings

Domain	Quality Criteria	Weighting	Statement of Statistical Significance
University	Teaching Quality Research Quality	10% 90%	Differences noted are very highly significant, to the 0.2% level.
	Teaching Quality Research Quality	90% 10%	
Cars	Reliability Running costs	90% 10%	Differences noted are very highly significant, to the 0.2% level.
	Reliability Running costs	10% 90%	

Table 6. Results of varying quality preference values, within identical criteria selection

Domain	Quality Criteria	Pref. Value	Weight	Statistical Significance
University	Research Quality	Max. possible value	100%	Differences noted are very highly significant, to the 0.2% level.
	Research Quality	Min. possible value	100%	
Cars	Depreciation	Max. possible value	80%	Differences noted are very highly significant, to the 0.2% level.
	Depreciation	Min. possible value	80%	

Table 7. Results of varying importance weightings and preference values, with identical sets of quality criteria

Domain	Quality Criteria	Pref. Value	Weight	Statistical Significance
University	Grad. Employment Dropout Rates	Max. possible value Min. possible value	100% 50%	Differences noted are very highly significant, to the 0.2% level.
	Grad. Employment Dropout Rates	Min. possible value Max. possible value	50% 100%	
Cars	Drivability Reliability	Average value Max. possible value	50% 100%	Differences noted are very highly significant, to the 0.2% level.
	Drivability Reliability	Max. possible value Average value	100% 50%	

Simulation Set 3: Changing Criteria Preference Values

The third set of simulations focus on the changing of quality criteria preferences values, while keeping all other settings constant. Example results from this set are shown in Table 6.

Simulation Set 4: Changing Criteria
Importance Weightings and Preference Values

The final set of simulations focus on changing both criteria importance weightings and preference values, while keeping the set of selected criteria constant. Example results from this set are shown in Table 7.

Results of Simulations

The results of these simulations, as presented in Tables 3 to 8, show that changing quality preferences can result in a highly statistically significant difference in the ranking order of the obtained result sets.

However, we must also be aware that such noticeable differences are not always obtained. For example, if conducting a search based on a single quality criterion, changing the importance weighting of that criterion alone will not result in a different result set ordering, as the same ranking will be obtained if the criterion is rated at 100% or 50%. The scores for that criterion for each information item will change, but this change will be the same for all items, thus resulting in an identical ordering. Also, no change will be noted if several criteria are selected, but their importance

Table 8. Examples of no statistically significant difference in ranking order of results

DOMAIN	QUALITY CRITERIA	PREF. VALUE	WEIGHT	STATISTICAL SIGNIFICANCE
University	Teaching Quality	Max. possible value	100%	No statistical significance is seen in this example
	Gradate Employment	Max. possible value	100%	
Cars	Reliability	Max. possible value	100%	No statistical significance is seen in this example
	Performance Drivability	Max. possible value Max. possible value	90% 50%	
Cars	Drivability Performance	None stated	100% 80%	Differences noted are significant to the 0.1% level (no statistical significance)
	Drivability Performance	None stated	80% 100%	

weightings change in the same direction. For example, if while searching in the university domain and the settings for the criteria Research Quality and Teaching Quality are changed from 100% and 80% to 50% and 40%, the ranking order will remain the same as importance values have not changed the relation between the selected criteria. Trivial changes in result ranking order are likely to be observed when making small changes to selected criteria preferences, such as when changing criteria preference values in minor steps. Examples of situations in which little or no statistical significance is observed can be seen in Table 8.

The results presented in this chapter, and Tables 3 to 8, therefore demonstrate that changes in the quality preferences of an individual consumer can result in a statistically significant difference in the ranking order of the result set, but that this is not necessarily always the case.

CONCLUSION

As stated in our research premise, the aim of this project was to ascertain whether it is possible to produce a hierarchical generic model of quality that can be used by the information consumer to assist in the information searching process, by enabling them to state their quality preferences and using this to focus information search results.

In this chapter we presented the work we have conducted thus far in this area, showing how the information consumer can use quality criteria to focus information searches, within a number of experimental subject domains. By conducting a set of simulations, using quality criteria to focus information searches, we have shown that changing quality preferences can result in a statistically significant difference in the ranking order of the returned results.

Having shown that it is possible to develop a consumer-oriented model of quality, and that quality criteria can be used successfully to focus information search results, further work must now be done that builds on this project. Potential exists for research into a number of areas, including, but not limited to:

- The use of quality preferences when searching for information in large, distributed and dynamic information environments
- Filtering information based on quality preferences, before result ranking
- Incorporating user feedback, both implicit and explicit, to improve default quality settings
- Semi-automatic mapping of quality criteria to available data
- Automatic relaxation of quality preferences to ensure results of the best available quality are returned when data is filtered based on (potentially unrealistic) quality preferences initially resulting in few, or no, results

The next phase of our work will therefore focus on investigating these potential areas, and others, to ascertain whether further development is most appropriate and in which direction to take this work, while keeping in mind the fundamental importance of the information consumer on the quality lifecycle. After all, "the customer or customers are the final arbiters of quality" (Redman, 1996).

ACKNOWLEDGMENTS

We would like to thank EPSRC (EPSRC, 2003) for supporting M. Burgess with a studentship (award number 99302270), and BT (BT, 2003) for providing additional funding.

REFERENCES

Abate, M. L., Diegert, K. V., & Allen, H. W. (1998). A hierarchical approach to improving data quality. *Data Quality, 4*(1), 365-369.

Aladwani, A. M., & Palvia, P. C. (2002). Developing and validating an instrument for measuring user-perceived Web quality. *Information and Management, 39*(6), 467-476.

Barbacci, M., Klein, M. H., Longstaff, T. A., & Weinstoch, C. B. (1995). *Quality attributes* (Tech. Rep. No. CMU/SEI-95-TR-021 ESC-TR-95-021). Software Engineering Institute, Carnegie Mellon University.

Boehm, B. W., Brown, J. R., & Lipow, M. (1976). *Quantitative evaluation of software quality.* Paper presented at the Proceedings of the 2nd International Conference on Software Engineering, San Francisco (pp. 592-605).

Bovee, M., Srivastava, R. P., & Mak, B. (2001). *A conceptual framework and belief-function approach to assessing overall information quality.* Paper presented at the Proceedings of the 6th International Conference on Information Quality (ICIQ-01), Cambridge, MA (pp. 311-324).

BT. (2003). *BT.* Retrieved May 1, 2003, from http://www.bt.com

Burgess, M. S. E. (2003). *Using multiple quality criteria to focus information search results.* PhD thesis, Cardiff University, Cardiff.

Burgess, M. S. E., Gray, W. A., & Fiddian, N. J. (2002). *Establishing a taxonomy of quality for use in information filtering.* Paper presented at the Proceedings of the 19th British National Conference on Databases (BNCOD 19), Sheffield, UK (pp.103-113).

Burgess, M. S. E., Gray, W. A., & Fiddian, N. J. (2003). *A flexible quality framework for use in information retrieval.* Paper presented at the Proceedings of the 8th International Conference on Information Quality (ICIQ-03), Cambridge, MA.

Chen, Y., Zhu, Q., & Wang, N. (1998). Query processing with quality control in the World Wide Web. *World Wide Web, 1*(4), 241-255.

Crichton, N. (2003). Wilcoxon signed rank test. *Journal of Clinical Nursing, 9*, 584.

Cykana, P., Paul, A., & Stern, M. (1996). *DOD Guidelines on data quality management.* Paper presented at the Proceedings of the 1996 Conference on Information Quality (IQ-1996), Cambridge, MA (pp. 154-171).

Dedeke, A. (2000). *A conceptual framework for developing quality measures for information systems.* Paper presented at the Proceedings of the 2000 Conference on Information Quality (IQ-2000), Cambridge, MA (pp. 126-128).

Dromey, R. G. (1995). A model for software product quality. *IEEE Transactions on Software Engineering, 21*(2), 146-162.

Dromey, R. G. (1996). Concerning the chimera. *IEEE Software, 13*(1), 33-43.

Eppler, M. J. (2001). *A generic framework for information quality in knowledge-intensive processes.* Paper presented at the Proceedings of the 6th International Conference on Information Quality (IQ-2001), Cambridge, MA (pp. 329-346).

EPSRC. (2003). *EPSRC.* Retrieved May 1, 2003, from http://www.epsrc.ac.uk

EuroNCAP. (2003). *European new car assessment programme.* Retrieved August 1, 2003, from http://www.euroncap.com

Gardyn, E. (1997). *A data quality handbook for a data warehouse.* Paper presented at the Proceedings of the 1997 Conference on Information Quality (IQ-1997), Cambridge, MA (pp. 267-290).

Guardian. (2003). *The Guardian Home Page.* Retrieved June 4, 2003, from http://www.guardian.co.uk

Hwang, C. L., & Yoon, K. (1981). *Multiple attribute decision making: Methods and applications.* New York: Springer-Verlag.

Hyatt, L. E., & Rosenberg, L. H. (1996). *A software quality model for identifying project risks and assessing software quality.* Paper presented at the Proceedings of the 8th Annual Software Technology Conference, Utah.

ISO/IEC. (2001). *Information technology — Software product quality* (Tech. Rep. No. ISO/IEC 9126-1:2001). International Organization for Standardization.

Liu, K., Zhou, S., & Yang, H. (2000). *Quality metrics of object oriented design for software development and re-development.* Paper presented at the Proceedings of the 1st Asian Pacific Conference on Quality Software, Hong Kong, China, (pp. 127-135).

Long, J. A., & Seko, C. E. (2002). *A new method for database data quality evaluation at the Canadian Institute for Health Information (CIHI).* Paper presented at the Proceedings of the 7th International Conference on Information Quality (ICIQ-2002), Cambridge, MA (pp. 238-250).

Matsumura, A., & Shouraboura, N. (1996). *Competing with quality information.* Paper presented at the Proceedings of the 1996 Conference on Information Quality (ICIQ-1996), Cambridge, MA (pp. 72-86).

McCall, J. A., Richards, P. K., & Walters, G. F. (1977). *Factors in software quality, Volumes I-III*. National Technical Information Service.

Miller, H. (1996). The multiple dimensions of information quality. *Information Systems Management, 13*(2), 79-82.

Moustakis, V. S., Litos, C., Dalivigas, A., & Tsironis, L. (2004). *Website quality assessment criteria*. Paper presented at the 9th International Conference on Information Quality (ICIQ-04), Cambridge, MA (pp. 59-73).

Naumann, F. (2002). *Quality-driven query answering for integrated information systems*. New York: Springer-Verlag.

Naumann, F., & Rolker, C. (2000). *Assessment methods for information quality criteria*. Paper presented at the Proceedings of the 2000 Conference on Information Quality (ICIQ-2000), Cambridge, MA (pp. 148-162).

Olsina, L., Lafuente, G., & Rossi, G. (2001). Specifying quality characteristics and attributes for web sites. In S. Murugesan & Y. Deshpande (Eds.), *Web engineering 2000* (pp. 266-278). Berlin, Germany: Springer-Verlag.

Ortega, M., Pérez, M. A., & Rojas, T. (2002). *A systemic quality model for evaluating software products*. Paper presented at the Proceedings of the 8th World Multi-Conference on Systemics, Cybernetics and Informatics (SCI 2002/ISAS 2002).

Parkers. (2003). *Parkers Web Site*. Retrieved August 15, 2003, from http://www.parkers.co.uk

Redman, T. (1996). *Data quality for the information age*. MA: Artech House.

Royce, W. (1990). *Pragmatic quality metrics for evolutionary software development models*. Paper presented at the Proceedings of the Conference on TRI-ADA '90, Baltimore, MD (pp. 551-565).

Rubey, R. J., & Hartwick, R. D. (1968). *Quantitative measurement of program quality*. Paper presented at the Proceedings of the ACM National Conference (pp. 671-677).

Smart, K. L. (2002). Assessing quality documents. *ACM Journal of Computer Documentation, 26*(3), 130-140.

Times. (2003). *The Times Online Newspaper*. Retrieved June 4, 2003, from http://www.timesonline.co.uk

Wang, R. Y., & Strong, D. M. (1996). Beyond accuracy: What data quality means to data consumers. *Journal of Management and Information Systems, 12*(4), 5-34.

WhatCar. (2003). *WhatCar Home Page*. Retrieved from the World Wide Web at: http://www.whatcar.com

Which?Online. (2003). *Which?Online Home Page*. Retrieved from the World Wide Web at: http://www.which.net

Zhu, X., & Gauch, S. (2000). *Incorporating quality metrics in centralized/distributed information retrieval on the World Wide Web*. Paper presented at the Proceedings of the 23rd Annual International ACM SIGIR Conference on Research and Development in Information Retrieval, Athens, Greece (pp. 288-295).

Figure A-1. Where A_i is the ith alternative, C_j is the jth criterion, and d_{ij} is the performance measure of the ith alternative in terms of the jth criterion.

	C_1	C_2	...	C_n
A_1	d_{11}	d_{12}	...	d_{1n}
A_2	d_{21}	d_{22}	...	d_{2n}
...	...	...	...	...
A_m	d_{m1}	d_{m2}	...	d_{mn}

APPENDIX

TOPSIS and TOPSIS-GP Ranking Algorithms

Step 1: Create the Decision Matrix

The first step taken within the TOPSIS ranking algorithm involves the creation of a decision matrix, representing all available data items and selected quality criteria, as illustrated in Exhibit 1 (with C = quality criterion, A = quality rating).

Step 2: Normalise IQ Criterion Values

Each value in the decision matrix must be placed on the same scale, typically 0 to 1, thus enabling cross-criteria comparisons. This normalises the decision matrix, and transforms it into the new normalised matrix R.

Step 3: Normalise Weightings

During this step user-specified importance weightings for each IQ criterion are scaled to lie on the scale 0 to 1. This results in the creation of a normalised set of weights W, where $W = (w_1, w_2, ...w_n)$.

Step 4: Construct the Weighted Normalised Decision Matrix

The set of normalised weights $W = (w_1, w_2, ...w_n)$ is then used in conjunction with the normalised matrix, to create the weighted normalised matrix V. This matrix is calculated by multiplying each column of the matrix R with its associated weights w_j. This is illustrated in Exhibit 2.

Step 5: Determine Ideal, and Negative-Ideal Solutions

As TOPSIS ranks scores according to how close they are to an ideal, and how far they are away from a negative-ideal, these two ideal scores must be calculated.

Figure A-2.

$$V = \begin{pmatrix} v_{11} & v_{12} & \cdots & v_{1j} & \cdots & v_{1n} \\ \cdots & \cdots & \cdots & \cdots & \cdots & \cdots \\ v_{i1} & v_{i2} & \cdots & v_{ij} & \cdots & v_{in} \\ \cdots & \cdots & \cdots & \cdots & \cdots & \cdots \\ v_{m1} & v_{m2} & \cdots & v_{mj} & \cdots & v_{mn} \end{pmatrix} = \begin{pmatrix} w_1 r_{11} & w_2 r_{12} & \cdots & w_j r_{1j} & \cdots & w_n r_{1n} \\ \cdots & \cdots & \cdots & \cdots & \cdots & \cdots \\ w_1 r_{i1} & w_2 r_{i2} & \cdots & w_j r_{ij} & \cdots & w_n r_{in} \\ \cdots & \cdots & \cdots & \cdots & \cdots & \cdots \\ w_1 r_{m1} & w_2 r_{m2} & \cdots & w_j r_{mj} & \cdots & w_n r_{mn} \end{pmatrix}$$

Virtual positive-ideal score: $IQ\ (A^+) : = (v_1^+, ..., v_m^+)$

Virtual negative-ideal score: $IQ\ (A^-) : = (v_1^-, ..., v_m^-)$
where

$$v_j^+ \Rightarrow \begin{cases} \max_i \lfloor v_{ij} \rfloor & \text{if criterion } j \text{ is positive} \\ \min_i \lfloor v_{ij} \rfloor & \text{if criterion } j \text{ is negative} \end{cases}$$

$$v_j^- \Rightarrow \begin{cases} \min_i \lfloor v_{ij} \rfloor & \text{if criterion } j \text{ is positive} \\ \max_i \lfloor v_{ij} \rfloor & \text{if criterion } j \text{ is negative} \end{cases}$$

Step 6: Calculate Euclidean Distances

The Euclidean distance between each score and the ideal and negative-ideal solution is calculated as follows:

$$S^{(+)}(S_i) \Rightarrow \sqrt{\sum_{j=1}^m \left(v_{ij} - v_j^{(+)}\right)^2} \quad \text{and} \quad S^{(-)}(S_i) \Rightarrow \sqrt{\sum_{j=1}^m \left(v_{ij} - v_j^{(-)}\right)^2}$$

Step 7: Calculate Relative Closeness to Ideal Solution

The relative closeness of each value to the positive ideal defines the ranking order. This closeness can be calculated as follows:

$$iq(S_i) = \frac{S^-(S_i)}{S^+(S_i) + S^-(S_i)}$$

Step 8: Rank the Preference Order

The final step in the TOPSIS algorithm is the ranking of the alternatives, be they products, information, data, etc., according to $iq(S_j)$. The result closest to the ideal solution will be ranked first, and the furthest from the ideal will be ranked last.

TOPSIS-GP

The TOPSIS-GP algorithm is the same as the normal TOPSIS algorithm, until Step 5. During this step the calculation of the ideal and negative-ideal values are replaced by user stated preferred ideal values, resulting in the following ideal scores:

Preferred ideal score: $IQ\,(A^+) := \left(v_1^+,...,v_m^+\right)$

Preferred negative-ideal score: $IQ\,(A^-) := \left(v_1^-,...,v_m^-\right)$

This refined version of the algorithm, TOPSIS-GP (TOPSIS with Given Preferences) can be used instead of the original when user stated preferred values for quality criteria are available. This modification results in a set of values which more closely meet user preferences as they are taken into consideration during result ranking rather than the assumed preferred values.

Chapter XI

DQ Options:
Evaluating Data Quality Projects Using Real Options

Monica Bobrowski, Pragma Consultores, Argentina

Sabrina Vazquez Soler, Pragma Consultores, Argentina

ABSTRACT

Data plays a critical role in organizations up to the point of being considered a competitive advantage. However, the quality of the organizations' data is often inadequate, affecting strategic and tactical decision-making, and even weakening the organization's image. Nevertheless it is still challenging to encourage management to invest in data quality improvement projects. Performing a traditional feasibility analysis based on return on investment, net present value, and so forth, may not capture the advantages of data quality projects: their benefits are often difficult to quantify and uncertain; also, they are mostly valuable because of the new opportunities they bring about. Dealing with this problem through a real options approach, in order to model its intrinsic uncertainty, seems to be an interesting starting point. This chapter presents a methodological framework to assess the benefits of a data quality project using a real options approach. Its adequacy is validated with a case study.

INTRODUCTION

Quality control and management have become competitive needs for most businesses today. Approaches range from technical, such as statistical process control, to managerial, such as quality circles. An analogous experience basis is needed for data quality.

Many of the problems that come up when using poor quality data are well-known to software engineers. The NEAT methodology (Bobrowski, Marre, & Yankelevich, 2001) provides a systematic way to determine data quality so as to develop an improvement plan. The output is a diagnosis of the present data quality condition and an improvement plan that comprises both corrective and preventive actions (in order to maintain the quality standards finally met). In particular, NEAT bases its approach on the goal question metric framework (Fenton & Pfleeger, 1997), GQM from now and on, a framework used for metrics definition.

However, there are no serious studies aimed at providing a framework to analyze the convenience of investing in data quality improvement. Many organizations come to action when they find they have very poor data (lawsuits filed by clients, returned posts, networks that do not match reality, etc.). The analysis is ad-hoc and, generally speaking, it aims at assessing the initiative cost alone, thus submitting the decision to the resulting amount (high or low) (Loshin, 2001; Trillium Software, 2002).

The question then is how to justify a preventive approach to these issues? The first approach would imply conducting a classic feasibility analysis, using standard techniques: net present value (NPV), profitability index (PI), and internal rate of return (IRR). Nevertheless, there are many limitations when applied to the analysis of quality investment projects: the benefits of this kind of projects are usually difficult to quantify economically, basically because they are not direct: they are related to the opportunities they bring about. In addition, part of the economic impact is associated with cost-saving resulting from prevented problems, which is difficult to measure and is not captured by traditional indicators.

Within this context, it seems interesting to use a real options approach (Brealey & Myers, 2000; Amran & Kulatilaka, 1999; Brach, 2002) to model the uncertainty that exists with respect to the subsequent decision. This model also allows capturing the essence of the NEAT methodology (Bobrowski, Marre, & Yankelevich, 2001), which presents the need of making a diagnosis to assess, based on its output, the convenience of implementing a corrective improvement action on the data and also to establish specific improvement expectations. This model would allow assessing the best investment that an organization can make to improve its data, considering the performance evolution of the quality investment and future benefit expectations.

There are records of the use of the real options model to assess different software engineering projects (Boehm & Sullivan, 2000; Sullivan, Chalasani, Jha, & Sazawal, 1999). However, their use to assess the benefits of quality investments has not been studied yet. We believe this model offers an interesting potential which is worth exploring.

The objectives of this section are:

- To define a methodological framework to assess the benefit of data quality improvement projects using the real options approach.
- To validate the model proposed by means of a case study.

In this work, we use data and information interchangeably, meaning we use both raw and processed data. Although there are some differences, they are of no significance within this context.

THE NEAT METHODOLOGY

We present the NEAT methodology (Bobrowski, Marre, & Yankelevich, 2001), based on theoretical models of the data lifecycle (Huang, Lee & Wang, 1999) as well as on our practical experience in many evaluations and controlled experiments (Bobrowski, Marre, & Yankelevich, 1999). The NEAT methodology is a framework for guiding data quality evaluation, consisting of six general stages: elicitation; planning; measurement; diagnosis; treatment; and maintenance.

Each step is composed of several tasks that must be carried out in order to achieve particular goals. This is a brief description, but we think that it covers the main components and ideas of the method.

First Step: Elicitation
(Data Life Cycle, Actual State and DQ Goals)

The first task during the elicitation step is the acquisition of the information on the data lifecycle in the organization.

During the second task of this step, we perform the evaluation of the state of the data in the organization. The outcome of this activity is a precise description of the actual state (a "snapshot") that will be used as a basis for many decisions during all steps.

Figure 1. NEAT steps

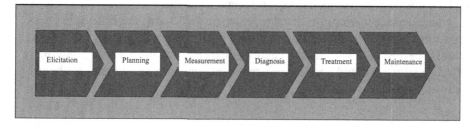

With the information of tasks 1.1 and 1.2, we can now establish which are the relevant quality dimensions for this particular project. Once these dimensions have been chosen, we must define the specific quality requirements for each dimension over different subsets of data. For each subset, we should establish two levels of quality: the target (optimum) level and the minimum level required.

Second Step: Planning

The second step is to develop a plan for assessment of quality. This step has a very concrete deliverable: a document, including the evaluation plan and how the plan is executed. The plan is defined at the very beginning of the step and the document is updated with each task.

Third Step: Measurement

The goal of this step is clearly to measure the quality of certain attributes. Thus, many tools and techniques are available: GQM tables, templates, data analysis tools, etc.

During this step, we perform the measurement, according to the measurement plan.

Fourth Step: Diagnosis

The outcome of this step is a document presenting the diagnosis of data quality. The step involves the interpretation of the measures, as well as reporting of findings. The document might be very useful by itself, but its main goal is to trigger actions that will change the status of data.

Fifth Step: Treatment — Corrective/Preventive

There are two main strategies to improve the quality of data. To improve existing data (through a corrective strategy, changing or deleting wrong data and including the data needed by the organization) or to improve the processes associated with data (data creation, consumption, updates, and so on). The latter prevents the injection of bad quality data into the system.

Sixth Step: Maintenance

When the desired quality goals are met, the project is still not over. We must find a mechanism to maintain the quality obtained.

Maintenance is strongly related to treatment, but clearly there are differences. Preventive actions should be used to prevent quality from decreasing in time, but it is also necessary to monitor the quality of data through time. This monitoring is based on systematic and periodic measurement, which in some cases can be partially automated.

This is an outline of the method used, which is descriptive enough to understand the following proposal and the case study, as well as discuss some conclusions.

IT PROJECT EVALUATION

Introduction

In 2000, Boehm and Sullivan published an article and advanced a new discipline called *software economics*. This field manages the analysis of improvements in software design and engineering, reasoning economically on matters related with products, processes, programs, portfolios and policies. They indicate that so far investigations have been mainly focused on costs, not on benefits.

Therefore, the value added by the investment has not been taken into consideration.

This lack of progress in the subject is based on several reasons (Benaroch & Kauffman, 1999), but the most important is:

- There are no suitable frameworks to model, measure and analyze the connection between technical characteristics, decisions and value creation. Central concepts of software engineering like concealment of information, architecture, spiral model, and so forth, have no clear relation with the value added to the organization.

It has been stated (Sullivan, Chalasani, Jha, & Sazawal, 1999) that the real options approach could help to establish some of these relations (staggered design decisions, staged development, etc.).

- Most designers and software engineers are not trained to analyze the concept of value creation as a goal, or to manage technical aspects to add value to the organization. Measurements are usually focused on technical characteristics.
- The set of technologies, the regulatory and tax framework, the market and other structures in which software is developed and used are inadequate. Designers are not able to make decisions that could help to increase the value created by products.

Evolution

In 1969, Sharpe (the "father" of software economics) presented the first application of information economics to software-related issues (cited in Benaroch & Kauffman, 1999). The work included subjects such as purchase, leasing or rent of information systems, definition of service prices and analysis of the scale as an economic aspect. The work includes a small section dedicated to costs, based on the SDC study. This study formulated a model of linear regression to consider software costs. Although not very accurate, it encouraged further research work that gave rise to better cost models in the 1970s and 1980s, some of which are still used nowadays, such as COCOMO, Estimacs, and so forth.

In his book *Software Engineering Economics*, Boehm (1981), in addition to the COCOMO model (Cost Constructive Model), presents a summary of the main concepts and macroeconomic techniques with some examples of their application to software development and software decision making (production functions, economies of scale, net value, present value, marginal analysis, etc.). Other contemporary works include a summary of cost estimates, costs comparisons of computational products and services, computer center management techniques, and so forth.

Some of the most important software engineering techniques implicitly include economic considerations (Benaroch & Kauffman, 1999):

- Software risk management uses principles of the theory of statistical decision to approach questions such as "how much formal verification is required" (to acquire data to reduce risk).
- Spiral or iterative life-cycles model use considerations on product value and risks to organize the increase in the capacity of applications.
- The notion of "design for change" is based on the recognition that a great part of the total product cost is incurred on its evolution (post production), and that a system that is not designed to evolve is going to incur enormous costs of maintenance (even limiting its capacity to adapt to new situations).

At the moment our capacity to analyze software costs exceeds our capacity to analyze its benefits. In recent years, there has been progress on the cost/benefit analysis of software projects, using all standard financial indicators to develop new case studies.

However, experience shows that it is difficult to evaluate a software project in the traditional manner, since they usually give negative numbers as a result. One of the greater problems is the definition of benefits. A great part of the advantages of investing in technology cannot be quantified directly (positioning, small improvements in response time which are of greatest value for the client, etc.) or they may work not as a direct source of income but as a means to open up new possibilities (technological infrastructure improvement that enables taking on more important projects, integrated systems that enable to plan unified, better directed campaigns, etc.)

As we see, there is still work to be done as regards the development of a comprehensive framework for the economic assessment of IT projects from the perspective of the value added to the business. This is clearly a multidisciplinary work. It cannot be performed only by technicians who do not know many business aspects, nor exclusively by businessmen, that may disregard the scope and impact of the technical characteristics when assessing which is the most suitable option within a certain context.

Quality Projects

In the last decades, software has become a vital part of most corporate products and services. As Kitchenham and Pfleeger (1996) indicate, such growth brings about the responsibility to establish the contribution of software to the organization. When a telephone company cannot implement a new service because the invoicing system cannot support it, software quality becomes a corporate issue. And these examples abound.

Nevertheless, very little has been made to investigate the relationship between software quality and business efficiency and effectiveness. One of the greater problems is to define the point where defect reduction or flexibility begin to threaten other desirable characteristics of software (time to market, performance, etc.) and cease to be a visible advantage (defects not noticed by users, products that are not going to be extended, etc.). Even in industrial sectors not related to software, returns on improvements in quality are decreasing (Slaughter, Harter, & Krishnan, 1998).

This type of analysis has not been seriously made in the software industry and, in fact, quality investment is usually a political or conjunctural decision (certifications, marketing, and differentiation) rather than economic. Organizations that decide to invest in quality on a systematic and constant basis are those that have experienced serious problems in the past. And, after some time, their expectations quite often decrease.

Some historical errors in software projects assessment go against the organization's goals. For instance, the cost of a software product has been traditionally considered (at least to decide upon its production or to choose among other alternatives) as the cost of its development up to its production, disregarding the statistics that indicate that maintenance (that is the tasks performed once the software is operative) uses 50% of the resources (cost) of a software project.

With a partial evaluation, no investment in quality will ever be justified, since the cost incurred until its operation (at least for the first time) will probably be greater in development than in activities of control and quality assurance. Nevertheless, this difference is compensated with the increase in maintenance-related savings (added to the improved image offered to the client) and to possible reductions of costs in future projects.

Let us remember that quality cost is the price paid for not doing things properly, and not the opposite. Therefore, a quality-oriented culture is going to focus on defining processes that come up rather than on fixing errors.

Quality cost (Slaughter, Harter, & Krishnan, 1998) is usually divided into two main categories: cost of conformity and cost of nonconformity. The conformity cost is the amount allocated to obtain quality products. It is then divided into evaluation and prevention costs.

Error prevention:
- Effort necessary to understand the root cause of the errors
- Process improvement activities
- Tools and quality training

Quality assessment:
- Inspections, peer reviews and testing
- Product quality metrics

The cost of conformity does not include all the expenses incurred when things go bad — Internal fault of the product (one that takes place before delivering the product to the client):

- Reproduction and fault diagnosis
- Reprocessing
- Requirement changes and program redesigns

External product fault (one that takes place in the client's facility):

- Guarantee (adjustment and replacement)
- Client support for products with faults or usability problems
- Complexity programs or documents
- Legal cost
- Damage cost

When trying to reduce quality costs and maximize benefits, the key is to determine how much and when it is worth investing in specific initiatives of software quality improvement.

If evaluating the benefits of software projects is complex, the case of quality investment is even more so. In a linear way of thinking, a product of better quality is better.

What about quantification? In general, some of the benefits associated to quality investment are:

- Better image before the client due to a smaller amount of errors (nevertheless, it is difficult to know which of the errors preventively eliminated had indeed been detected by the client)
- New projects (extensions, interphases with other systems, migrations)
- Reduce time in future projects (by greater knowledge and systematization of the development processes)

As it may be observed, these benefits are basically intangible and uncertain, which makes it difficult (or at least quite arbitrary) to use traditional indicators to evaluate them. What is clear is that software quality is an investment that must provide some financial return after the expenses incurred.

Slaughter, Harter, and Krishnan (1998) propose a series of indicators based on the most popular financial indicators to measure the return of investment of a quality initiative (specifically oriented to reduce the amount of defects in software), and to enable the comparison between different initiatives. They define measures for initial and recurrent costs and measure the benefits in terms of increase in sales (may be projected) or savings of costs considered. In order to apply their model, they compare different quality investment alternatives by means of an ex — post analysis of four initiatives carried out by a company.

Though interesting, this analysis has some limitations:

- It is made once the project is over and the initiatives implemented have been completed. They acknowledge this limitation and say that in order to use it a priori, there would have to be corporate information available as regards to reduction of defects in the products, statistics of defects, and so forth, as well as an estimate model to project improvements.
- When evaluating the obtained benefits, it is difficult to know what percentage can be attributed to quality initiatives.
- The analysis is limited to benefits that are perceived like directly bound to the improvement initiative.

The report shows that the return on quality investment is decreasing. This is particularly problematic when this model is used to compare initiatives that were already implemented sequentially (the effects of which are partially overlapped), since the last ones will be most affected in terms of their return.

Nevertheless, this work aims at understanding that quality-related actions, like investment, must be evaluated in terms of their costs and benefits (or contribution to the organization). The evaluation of data quality projects is much more precarious. There aren't any serious studies that may serve as a framework to analyze the convenience of investing in data quality improvement. Organizations come to action when they find they have very poor data (lawsuits filed by clients, returned posts, networks that do not match reality, etc.) and try to correct such data because they have no other choice (or they stop using them if they are irreparable).

The analysis is ad-hoc and, generally speaking, it aims at assessing the initiative's cost alone, thus submitting the decision to the resulting amount (high or low). Not only does this philosophy hinder the possibility of associating data improvement to the accomplishment of other projects, but it also goes against preventive investment in data quality — it only deals with incorrect data, without trying to identify the root cause of the problems.

Loshin (2001) shows a series of tactical missions of bad data quality and the cost incurred by the organizations. The author proposes the implementation of a

Data Quality Scorecard, by means of which it is possible to assess the data's current condition and identify the greater causes of problems as potential improvement areas. Nevertheless, this approach is entirely focused on costs related to poor quality, without providing a framework to analyze if the cost of the improvement is justified (considering that the benefits are uncertain). It only aims at trying to achieve greater benefit with less investment, without describing how this may be done.

The ROI of data quality (2002) shows six cases in which corrective improvement measures are applied to data and tries to calculate the return on investment of these initiatives. Nevertheless, it does not provide a framework to evaluate data quality projects a priori and, within this context of scope uncertainty, it is not possible to define an improvement initiative (this evaluation can only be done a posteriori). In addition, it only contemplates direct benefits (that could not justify the investment) and it aims at corrective and no-preventive improvement.

REAL OPTIONS

Introduction

What is an Option?

An option is the right, but not the obligation, to take an action in the future. Options are valuable when there is uncertainty. For example, one option contract traded on the financial exchanges gives the buyer the opportunity to buy a stock at a specified price on a specific data and will be exercised (used) only if the price of the stock exceeds the specified price. Many strategic investments create subsequent opportunities that may be taken, and so the investment opportunity can be viewed as a stream of cash flow plus a set of options. (Brealey & Myers, 2000)

What are Real Options?

In a narrow sense, the real options approach is the extension of the financial option theory to options on real (nonfinancial) assets. While financial options are detailed in the contract, real options embedded in strategic investments must be identified and specified. Moving from financial option to real options requires a way of thinking, one that brings the discipline of the financial markets to internal strategic investment decisions.
The real options approach works because it helps managers, with the opportunities they have to plan and manage strategic investments. (Brealey & Myers, 2000)

A real option is an option "related to things" (Brach, 2002). Strategic investment and budget decisions are decisions to acquire, exercise, abandon, or let a real option expire. Managerial decisions create put and call options over real assets, which give management the right, but not the obligation, to use those assets in order to achieve strategic goals, and, consequently, maximize the organization's value.

An investment decision is rarely a "now or never" decision, nor a decision that cannot be abandoned or modified during the project. The decision can at least be delayed or accelerated, and it is often organized as a sequence of steps encompassing decision points. All these choices have an impact on the investment value, and constitute real options.

Stewart Myers coined the term "real option" when developing the idea that financial investments generate real options (Brach, 2002). Myers claimed that the valuation of investment opportunities using the DCF traditional approach disregarded the value of options arising in risky and uncertain projects. This idea was later expanded to any kind of investment decision and corporate budgeting.

According to Amran and Kulatilaka (1999), the real options model is a line of thought which comprises three main components rather useful to managers:

- Options are contingent decisions: an option is the opportunity to make a decision once an individual sees how events are taking place.
- Options valuation is aligned with financial markets valuation: the approach uses data and concepts from financial markets to assess complex payments in various kinds of real assets.
- Thinking about options may serve to design and manage strategic investments proactively.

As a matter of fact, the real options approach cannot be used for all investment decisions (Amran & Kulatilaka, 1999). In some cases, the investment is clearly good or bad, and an analysis based on real options would not change that decision. However, many of such decisions fall into a grey area that requires thorough assessment. A real option analysis becomes necessary when:

- There is a contingent investment decision
- Uncertainty is such that it is convenient to wait and gather more information
- Value seems to lie on future growth possibilities rather than on direct cashflows
- Uncertainty is such that flexibility becomes important
- Updates will take place during its development

The six basic real options which derive from managerial options are (Brach, 2002):

- **Defer:** wait until further information reduces market uncertainty
- **Abandon:** dispose of an unprofitable project
- **Switch:** change input/output parameters or modus operandi
- **Expand/Contract:** alter capacity depending on market conditions
- **Grow:** consider future-related opportunities
- **Stage:** break up investments into incremental, conditional steps

Real Options Valuation

In the beginning, real options valuation models assumed that costs were deterministic, while in practice, costs, as benefits, tend to be uncertain. The time necessary to complete the project is usually uncertain as well. These features are characteristics of the real options model, the valuation of which must incorporate static product life cycles and variable cost structures.

The application of the real options valuation has expanded to appraise intangible assets investments, such as acquisition of knowledge or information and intellectual property, which are usually called virtual options.

Brach (2002) presents an analogy between financial options and real options concepts (see Table 1).

Let's see the assumptions of the Black and Scholes model that are not met in the case of real options:

- The project's volatility is not constant throughout time
- There is no final expiration date for the option
- Both the underlying asset value and the exercise price (i.e., the project's development cost) behave stochastically
- Payoffs are not normally distributed
- Real assets do not follow a "random walk"

Given its discrete nature, in the case of the binomial model, the evolution of parameters can be monitored on a step-by-step basis while "unforeseen" changes

Table 1.

Financial Option	Variable	Real Option
Exercise price	K	Cost to acquire the asset
Stock price	S	PV of future cash flows from the asset
Time to expiration	t	Length of time option is viable
Variance of stock returns	Var	Riskiness of the asset, variance of the best- and worst-case scenario
Risk-free rate of return	r	Risk-free rate of return

can be observed. However, this also hinders the application of the model since, given the stochastic nature of many of its parameters in the case of the real options, it may be necessary to analyze several periods, making the construction of the binomial tree difficult.

Real Options in IT Projects

The application of real options to the information technology field has increased in recent years, the main reasons being twofold:

- A renewed need to justify the convenience of investing in IT.
- The boundaries of traditional project assessment techniques to model an IT investment properly.

Sullivan, Chalasani, Jha, and Sazawal (1999) present an approach to assess design decisions within the context of software development. Authors suggest assessing these principles integrally within the framework of an options analysis, to appreciate their contribution to the project's value. Benaroch (2002) suggests managing IT investment risk within the framework of real options. The author, together with Kauffman (Benaroch & Kauffman, 1999), presents the application of the real options valuation method on an IT investment project: the analysis of the right time to install POS (point of sale) debit services in the Yankee 24 banking network in New England. Schwartz and Zozaya-Gorostiza (2003) propose two models to assess IT projects based on whether they imply infrastructure acquisition or development. The authors also suggest a homogeneous framework to incorporate both types of projects.

Staged Options

Many projects are divided into a number of sequential stages where each step is based on the successful completion of the previous step and the management's possibility to assess the project in each stage (Brach, 2002). The benefit of a staged option will only be appreciated once all its stages have been fulfilled. Some examples are: investments in new technologies and in R&D. Both share the uncertain nature of staged investments, as long as the two main risk sources: private or technical risk (ability of the firm to effectively develop a successful project), and market risk (uncertainty of future demand). Key features of flexibility in a sequential project include the possibility to abandon it once more information is available at each step.

The assessment of this kind of option depends on the knowledge of the costs and benefits' stochastic processes:

- If they are known (or assumed), known closed-form valuation methods may be used.

- If they are unknown, the binomial model offers a viable assessment option. This means:
  - ○ Defining milestones and decision-making points
  - ○ Identifying sources of uncertainty
  - ○ Estimating the costs of each stage
  - ○ Estimating the time needed for the completion of each stage
  - ○ Estimating the success probability of each stage
  - ○ Estimating the best and worst net present value (NPV) case scenarios for the related project.

ASSESSMENT OF DATA QUALITY PROJECTS USING REAL OPTIONS

We present a methodological framework to apply the real options approach to the assessment of data quality projects. We will use the NEAT methodology to illustrate this approach, identifying its various stages.

There are different types of assessments that can be performed on a project of these characteristics:

- To assess the convenience of a specific investment
- To assess the maximum convenient investment within certain framework
- To analyze different scenarios to establish which one justifies an investment

To apply the real options model, it is essential to identify the sources of uncertainty typical of this type of projects:

- State of data — theoretical scope of the improvement
- Cost of the improvement
- Real improvement
- Contingent projects — some projects may depend on the actual quality achieved and therefore, may not be convenient if the improvement does not reach certain levels
- Potential benefits from projects to be implemented

Although the numerical analysis is vital to draw a conclusion, we do not disregard the fact that many of the values used are predictions (with a higher or lower degree of certainty), estimates and even desires. Hence, we will focus on establishing a homogeneous comparison framework of investment alternatives based on the use of real options.

Why Use Real Options?

As mentioned in previous sections, it is difficult to assess the convenience of a quality investment project (whether of software or data) just by looking at the cash-flow directly associated to it. In data quality projects we can highlight the following features:

- They help the organization be ready to perform actions they would otherwise be unable to.
- A great part of the benefits is qualitative and difficult to quantify (what is the value of a robust application?).
- Benefits are not always direct; quality improvement projects establish the starting point to many different initiatives that may or may be not carried out, and they open up new opportunities to organizations that were not even considered before. For instance, a flexible software design allows considering software evolution, which would otherwise be costly or even impossible.
- Although they open up new opportunities, the benefits are still uncertain (quality may not reach the expected level, timing may be wrong, etc.).
- There are some economic issues to consider when investing in quality. Not all investments are cost-effective.

In addition, traditional techniques (discounted cash flow, net present value, return of investment, and internal rate of return) are limited:

- They do not capture the possibility to change the investment sequence.
- They do not consider the option to abandon a project.
- They deal with deterministic and known costs (which is not always the case).
- The discount rate and future cash flows may be arbitrarily determined, thus affecting the accuracy of the computation.

These factors make the real options approach seem a natural alternative for these projects.

Methodological Framework

We propose the *life cycle of a DQ project assessment.* Figure 2 shows a graphic representation where:

- **Problem specification:** Informal description of the project; evaluation goals; sources of uncertainty; sources of benefits and option type (default: staged option).
- **Solution design:** Real option/s and its components, valuation model and key parameters.

Figure 2. Life cycle

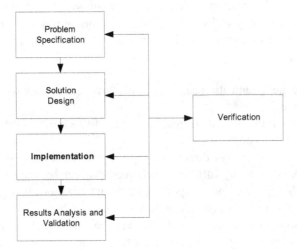

- **Implementation:** Assigning values to parameters and computing option price.
- **Results analysis and validation:** Comparison with former projects, sensitivity analysis and results recording.
- **Verification:** tasks are performed during the whole process in order to assess consistency among stages.

This methodology is absolutely simple and general. However, we have listed some basic considerations to make its application successful:

- As in every IT project, the key issue is to understand all requirements properly. In this case, this means understanding the project to be assessed, which components follow stochastic processes and which are deterministic, and identifying all the possible sources of benefits.
- Future benefits are associated to projects, the costs of which are independent from data improvement costs.
- The solution design must contemplate the possibility of assessing more than one option, due to different future projects, diverse investment alternatives, different stages, and so forth.
- The choice of the assessment model is important to ensure the accuracy of the analysis. Nevertheless, given a highly uncertain context with little experience in the use of the technique, it is convenient to promote less complex models (considering their limitations) and, based on the experience, search for models that can better adjust to the problem that is being addressed.

- Analyzing the results is vital, not only for the project under assessment but also for the lessons learned which will enable to improve the application of the model in the future.
- It is convenient to repeat the analysis as you make progress on the project and gain more certainty so as to improve the decision-making process.

EVALUATING DQ PROJECTS USING REAL OPTIONS

To avoid presenting the proposed methodology in rather abstract manner, considering that we are presenting it for a specific type of project (NEAT projects), in this section we will describe how a real option with these characteristics should be produced. However, this does not mean that under different circumstances another type of option could be more convenient. This section may be considered *a partial instance* of stages 1 and 2 of the methodology presented.

Some considerations:

- For the sake of simplicity, this last stage of the methodology, monitoring, is not included in the scope of the projects to be assessed.
- The benefits obtained from this type of project are associated to future projects, which have their own cost.
- An improvement plan may consist of several tasks that are optional to the organization, each of them with its corresponding cost and improvement expectation.
- In the case of poor quality data, the company may be losing money for that reason (as we will show in the case study). In this case, the benefit of the data improvement will be to prevent such loss and therefore it will be direct and positive.

At this point, we will present a two-stage analysis by means of which it is possible to make a preliminary assessment so as to determine if it is worth implementing a data quality improvement project within the NEAT framework, and then, a more detailed analysis that covers specific tasks to be carried out. The application of the model adds a few requirements to the methodology which will be explained later. In the next section, a complete case study is presented.

First Stage

Before elaborating the diagnosis, it may be necessary to consider under what circumstances diagnosis may be justified. That is to say, assessing different possibilities with various probabilities, even without knowing the improvement cost, as wells as considering the success probability of the improvement and considering different contingent projects. In this case, and to make matters simple, the binomial valuation model is recommended as well as creating an option for the cost of each improvement plan.

Questions that should be addressed during this stage:

- How much is it worth to invest in data quality?
- Is it worth to proceed with the diagnosis phase?

Solution design consists partially of identifying the set of questions to be answered. In fact, design is driven by these questions. We need to establish (or at least estimate):

- Cost, duration and success probability of the improvement: recorded information regarding previous experiences can be used.
- Cost, benefits, duration and success probability of the different projects: future project cash flow pessimistic and optimistic estimates
- Project volatility: inferred from the scenarios presented, based on the success probability of the project (if project expected value (E(S)) is $E(S) = S_{max} * q_{max} + S_{min} * q_{min}$ then $Var(S) = (S_{max} - E(S))^2 * q_{max} + (S_{min} - (E(S))^2 * q_{min}$ and $\sigma = Var(S)^{1/2}$) (see Table 2)

- Diagnosis cost and duration
- Risk-free rate of return (company data)
- WACC or rate of return uses for NPV computations

Additional requirements imposed over the NEAT methodology:

- If this stage takes place before the diagnosis phase, there are no additional requirements
- If it is performed again after the diagnosis, second stage requirements apply

Table 2.

Variable	Real Option
K	Cost to acquire the asset
S	PV of future cash flows from the asset
t	Length of time option is viable
Var	Riskiness of the asset, variance of the best and worst case scenario
r	Risk-free rate of return
E	Expected Value
q	Probability
σ	Variance

In order to be worthwhile, the resulting price should be equal to or lower than the diagnosis cost. If more than one option is defined, a more detailed analysis is needed.

Second Stage

The second stage aims at conducting an in-depth analysis to determine the suitability of the improvement. The steps to follow are similar to those of the first stage, with the exception that the improvement has already been broken down and various tasks may be combined. It is necessary to determine:

- Different improvement configurations (if any)
- Cost and success probability of each improvement configuration
- Possible cost and success probability of the project/s and minimum quality requirements, to establish under which improvement configuration they are feasible.
- Benefits of the project/s

Questions to answer:

- Is the improvement process worthwhile?
- Which projects and improvement tasks should be performed?

Data required:

- Diagnosis cost and duration
- Improvement plan: including, for each task
  - Activity
  - Cost
  - Success probability
  - Duration
  - Relation to other tasks

- Future projects:
  - Project
  - Optimistic cost and benefits (Net Present Value, expected cash flow, etc.)
  - Pessimistic cost and benefits (Net Present Value, expected cash flow, etc.)
  - Pessimistic scenario probability
  - Optimistic scenario probability
  - Duration

- ◦   Previous activities required
- ◦   Volatility

- •   Different combinations of future projects (to construct different scenarios)
- •   Risk-free rate of return
- •   Weighted-average cost of capital (WACC) or discount rate used for net present value (NPV) calculations

Additional requirements over the NEAT methodology:

- •   Success probability of the improvement plan
- •   Success probability of the improvement tasks
- •   Evaluation criteria (to assess whether or not activity goals have been accomplished)
- •   Quality requirements for each contingent project
- •   Dependencies among tasks
- •   Worst- and best-case scenario for each future project; probability of each scenario

Option Valuation Model

For this assessment, we also suggest using the binomial model as proposed by Brach (2002). It is worth pointing out that, though simple, this approach poses an essential constraint: it does not contemplate that the success of an improvement action (or of the plan as a whole) may be partial. However, it is a useful approach, a trade-off between simplicity and clarity. The valuation model should be further improved in the future.

We present a simple application of the binomial valuation model.

Figure 3. First stage analysis

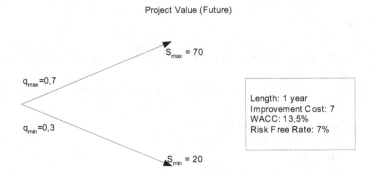

Take the scenario in Figure 3 for a first stage analysis. We can compute (Brach, 2002):

Project expected value:

$$V = (q_{max}*S_{max}+q_{min}*S_{min})$$
$$V = (0.7*70+0.3*20)=55$$
$$\sigma= 40.31$$

Risk-free probability (Brach, 2002) uses this formula to compute p because it is less complex than the one used to valuate financial options and comprises all the properties p should have (i.e., be a probability and represent the value q would have in equilibrium in a risk-free scenario. That is why we are using it here, too).

$$p = ((1+r_{free}*V)- S_{min}) / (S_{max} - S_{min})$$
$$p = ((1.07*55)-20) / (70-20) = 0.777$$

Option value:

$$C = ((p * S_{max} + (1-p)* S_{min})/ (1+r_{free})^t) -K*(1+r_{wacc})^t)= 47.055$$

Where K is the improvement cost, t is the diagnosis duration + improvement
$$C = ((0.777*70 + (1-0.777)*20)/1.07) -7*1.135= 47.055$$

The option value is calculated after the improvement has been performed, but before the so-called future project is executed. That is why the future project's NPV is subtracted and the improvement cost is to be considered in the future (we are assuming it to be one year).

If we plan to spend 7 in improvement tasks, and the diagnosis cost is below 47.055/1.135 (and it requires a very short time), the investment is worthwhile (notice that data here is only presented to exemplify the valuation method). If we want to compute the critical investment level K, we should solve the last equation making it 0 and leaving the improvement cost variable. The result would include diagnosis plus improvement costs.

Assuming that the diagnosis and improvement last a year, at most:

$$C = ((0.777*70 + (1-0.777)*20)/1.07) - K*1.135= 0$$

or:

$$(((0.777*70 + (1-0.777)*20)/1.07)) /1.135 = K$$

so K = 48.458

So diagnosis and improvement costs together have to be at most 48.458.

Knowing the diagnosis cost in advance, this analysis becomes a crucial input for stage 2, because it helps to determine whether to implement the improvement plan completely or partially, even before a detailed analysis is made.

CASE STUDY

In this section, we will apply the methodology to evaluate a real DQ project, as described in earlier sections. At present, the project is in the "lessons learned" phase, so the analysis allows the upper management to assess its progress.

Actual names and figures were changed in order to preserve confidentiality. These changes do not affect the results of the analysis.

Problem Specification

International Petroleum is implementing an information quality assurance program on its geology and geophysics (G&G) information. This program relates with a parallel project that aims at classifying physical data.

The aims of the project are: perform an information diagnosis; ensure that the classification of information meets minimum quality standards; ensure that the tools that are being used are adequate; standardize the input data of all applications; and implement a data quality improvement process.

Solution Design

To evaluate the case, we will apply both stages proposed. In this section we will design the components to be included in each of the evaluations.

The variables risk-free ratio (7%), WACC — capital cost — (13.5%), diagnosis' cost ($0.1) and diagnosis' length (2 months) are required for both stages (money figures in MM US dollars).

The company only identified the physical data classification project. This is a high yield project. However, the project success depends on the availability of high quality information.

The general **Project** variables are the *diagnosis' cost* ($0.1), *length* (5 years), *scenario probability* (50%) and *total cost* ($4.21).

For the **Project Yield**, the optimistic variables were defined as *NPV* -$9 and *revenue* — $15; and the pessimistic scenario were defined as *NPV* — 0.5% and *Revenue* — $5.35.

First Stage

In this stage of the analysis we need to know the kind of data quality investment the company is planning to make. This level of investment will enable to assess

Figure 3. Project feasibility

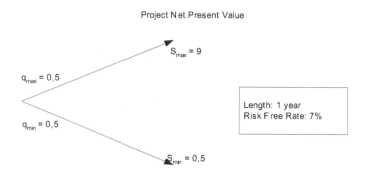

Project Net Present Value

the project's feasibility, even if the total cost of the data improvement program still remains unknown.

The variables of the **Improvement Project** are *length* (diagnosis + improvement): 1 year and *success probability*: 60%.

Second Stage

This analysis is done after the diagnosis is completed and the improvement plan tasks are identified and estimated.

This first analysis will be similar to the previous one, with the addition of the improvement cost and success probability. A subsequent analysis will identify sequential tasks.

The required data for the First Stage are *length, cost and success probability*; and for the Second Stage are *improvement plan (activity-based)* and *dependencies among tasks*.

Diagnosis Result

The following issues were detected during the analysis: problems in the definition of roles and responsibilities; lack of definitions for data loading criteria; and Data inconsistencies among different applications.

Improvement Plan

The *cost* of improvement plan for data loading criteria definition and implementation is *$1.2*; the *success probability 70%* and *length 4 months*.

The *cost* of the data-cleansing activities is *$1.5*, the *success probability*: 50% and the *length: 3 months*.

Figure 4. Overall improvement

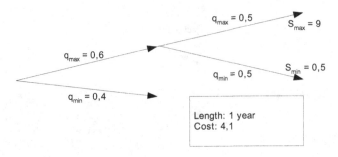

Global Improvement Plan

The *cost* of the Global Improvement Plan is *$4*, the *success probability*: 60% and the *length: 10 months*. (Success of the improvement plan depends on the success of the data cleansing process, as well as on the success of the remaining tasks.) The diagram in Figure 4 shows the design of the first stage.

This graph represents the overall improvement project: The first node shows that the improvement will have a 60% success probability. If the improvement fails, the overall project will be abandoned. If it is successful, then the physical data classification project will be implemented, with a 50% success probability.

Implementation

To calculate the value of the options a binomial model was used. All the necessary functions were defined in a Microsoft Excel spreadsheet.

First Stage

Project NPV

$$V = (q_{max}*S_{max}+q_{min}*S_{min})$$
$$V = (0.5*9+0.5*0.5)=4.75$$
$$\sigma= 4.25$$

Risk-free probability:

$$p = ((1+r_{free}*V)- S_{min}) / (S_{max} - S_{min})$$
$$p = ((1.07*4.75)-0.5) / (9-0.5) = 0.539$$

Critical investment level:

$$K = ((p * S_{max} + (1-p)* S_{min})/ (1+r_{free})^t) - K*(1+r_{wacc})^t) = 0$$
$$K = ((0.539*9 + (1-0.539)*0.5)/1.07) / 1.135 = 4.18$$

Second Stage

We will use these formulae to assess the staged options.

- **First analysis:** The previous node evaluation is completed in the same way. First we calculate the node NPV assuming that the immediate node was successful, subtracting the maximum value for the WACC for the number of periods (15 in this case). The minimum value is always 0, because if the task fails the project is abandoned). The expected value is calculated using the success probability. To see details of this case, refer to Table 3.

Max Value:

$$S_{max} = S_{max'}/(1+r_{wacc})^t$$
Where $S_{max'}$ is the maximum value of the immediate node
$$S_{max} = 15/1.135 = 13.2$$

Project NPV:

$$V = (q_{max}*S_{max} + q_{min}*S_{min})$$
$$V = (0.6*15 + 0.4*0) = 5.4$$

Risk-free probability:

$$p = ((1+r_{free}*V)- S_{min}) / (S_{max} - S_{min})$$
$$p = (1.07*5.4) / (13.2) = 0.435$$

Table 3.

Stage	NPV	q (success)	length	Cost	Option Value	P
Project	15 (max) 5.35 (min) 10.175 (exp)	0.5	1 year	4.21	5.96	0.573
Improvement + diagnosis	13.2 (max) 0 (min) 5.4 (exp)	0.6	1 year	4.1	1.27	0.435

Table 4.

Stage	NPV	q (success)	length	Cost	Option Value	P
Project	15 (max) 5.35 (min) 10.175 (exp)	0.5	1 year	4.21	5.965	0.573
Data cleansing	13.2 (max) 0 (min) 4.48 (exp)	0.5	3 months	1.5	3.225	0.363
Dataflow, roles & responsibilities	12.78 (max) 0 (min) 2.76 (exp)	0.7	4 months	1.3	1.6	0.231
Data loading criteria	12.22 (max) 0 (min) 1.95(exp)	0.8	3 months	1.2	0.734	0.171

Option Value:

$$C = ((p * S_{max} + (1\text{-}p)* S_{min})/ (1+r_{free})^t) - K$$
$$C = ((0.435*13.2 /1.07) -4.1 = 1.27$$

- **Second analysis:** Refer to Table 4.

Analysis

After the first stage we can conclude that diagnosis is worthwhile and, if improvement costs are below 4, it is convenient to proceed.

The second stage gives us a more detailed view. We observe that it is still convenient to perform the improvement, but also we can see how the option value increases as long as intermediate milestones are met and uncertainty is reduced.

A sensibility analysis shows that if the estimated probabilities are modified, the results can be substantially affected. Having in mind the fact that those values are estimations, a close tracking of the tasks involved may help improving the model calibration.

In this particular example we haven't obtained negative values. If that was the case, a tasks subset could have been chosen, in order to maximize the option value but, at the same time, achieving project quality requirements.

Our model also facilitates the process of staging the improvement project, defining checkpoints to decide whether to abandon the project or not, thus reducing any potential loss.

Conducting a NPV analysis (setting the expected DCF):

$$NPV = -4.1 + (4.75/ 1.135) = 0.08$$

Although the NPV is positive (which is not always the case), based on this number alone we would not be able to decide to abandon the project if one of the stages fails. In addition, since the value is relatively low, we could be tempted to terminate the project. We see that the NPV analysis may force us to abandon valuable projects, but also to proceed with a project without reviewing the decision. Finally, the option value is significantly higher than the NPV, because the option analysis captures the "time flow" that reduces uncertainty and helps to decide whether to abandon the project or not.

Conclusion

After developing the case study we may conclude:

* The proposed analysis gives us a global view of the overall project and how much we would be willing to invest in it, considering future expectations.
* The binomial valuation model facilitates the definition of simple spreadsheets to perform the calculations, even when specific software may not be available. However, tracking the valuation is a complex process.
* The proposed model facilitates the definition of go/no go stages, which add flexibility to the management decision process, enabling to take risks and delay decisions in a controlled framework.
* It would be valuable to enrich the model by adding sensitivity analysis, scenario analysis, project combinations, investment portfolios, etc.
* The proposed model shows some advantages over traditional indicators, showing some limitations of the classical view. However, further research on this field is required.
* The chosen valuation method considers neither partial success, nor the possibility to paralyze stages. The steps are sequential and the results are either success or failure.
* More experimentation with complex cases is needed.
* **Comparison with NPV:** the results obtained with the most traditional analysis were compared using NPV, thus giving clear proof of their own limitations.
* **Support tools:** although the model can be applied, the use of support tools is critical to extend the scope of the evaluation.
* **Complexity of the case:** Since a simple case was used, it is essential to experiment with situations of greater complexity.
* **Time management:** for short-duration tasks, time management makes the use of discount rates more complex.

Detailed Calculations

Tables 5 through 8 show the spreadsheets used for these calculations. The nodes are numbered in their evaluation order (in reverse chronological order).

Table 5.

First node		
Concept	**Value**	**Formula**
qmax	0,5	Data
qmin	0,5	Data
Smax	15	Data
Smin	5,35	Data
rfree	0,07	Data
rwacc	0,135	Data
Length (t)	1	Data
Stage Cost (K)	4,21	Data
V expected	**10,175**	qmax*Smax+qmin*Smin
p free	**0,574**	((1+rfree *Vesp)- Smin) / (Smax- Smin)
Vop	**5,965**	((p * Smax + (1-p)* Smin)/ (1+rfree)t) –K

Table 6.

Second Node		
Concept	**Value**	**Formula**
qmax	0,5	Data
qmin	0,5	Data
Smax	**13,216**	Smax = 15 /(1+rwacc)
Smin	0	Data
rfree (monthly)	0,005	Data
rwacc	0,135	Data
Length (t)	3	Data (months)
Stage Cost (K)	1,5	Data
V expected	**4,482**	V esp= (qmax*Smax+qmin*Smin)
p free	**0,363**	p = (1+rfree*Vesp) / Smax
Vop	**3,225**	(p * Smax / (1+rfree monthly)t) –K
rwacc (monthly)	0,011	Data
rfree	0,07	Data

Table 7.

Third Node		
Concept	**Value**	**Formula**
qmax	0,7	Data
qmin	0,3	Data
Smax	**12,780**	13.216 /(1+rwacc monthly)3
Smin	0	Data
rfree (monthly)	0,005	Data
rwacc	0,135	Data
Length (t)	4	Data(monthly)
Stage Cost (K)	1,3	Data
V expected	**2,764**	Vesp = qmax*Smax+qmin*Smin
p free	**0,231**	(1+rfree*Vesp) / Smax
Vop	**1,600**	(p * Smax/ (1+rfree monthly)t) –K
rwacc (monthly)	0,011	Data
rfree	0,07	Data

Table 8.

Fourth Node		
Concept	**Value**	**Formula**
qmax	0,8	Data
qmin	0,2	Data
Smax	**12,220**	12.780 /(1+rwacc monthly)4
Smin	0	Data
rfree(monthly)	0,005	Data
rwacc	0,135	Data
Length (t)	5	Data (monthly)
Stage Cost (K)	1,3	Data
V expected	**1,949**	Vesp = qmax*Smax+qmin*Smin
p free	**0,171**	(1+rfree*Vesp) / Smax
Vop	**0,734**	(p * Smax/ (1+rfree monthly)t) –K
rwacc (monthly)	0,011	Data
rfree	0,07	Data

FUTURE TRENDS

We believe the proposed model is not only useful to evaluate data quality projects, but to help organizations to analyze and optimize systematically quality investments in general. In order to achieve that goal several issues have to be cover:

- Validate the suitability of the model by applying it to more case studies in different industries
- Extend the proposal to other quality investment projects (i.e., apply this methodology to other fields, not only data quality). It will only be necessary to review how to define some stages, since the methodological frame is the same.
- Develop tools to automate the estimation process and the recording of results.
- Consider the analysis of the combination of future projects, avoiding the simplifications presented in this work.
- Study how to incorporate intangible benefits to the analysis in systematic manner, considering the frequency of its appearance in this type of projects.
- Systematize the scenario analysis and facilitate comparisons.
- Consider other valuation models
- Extend the model to consider different quality investment combinations (software + data).
- Incorporate additional requirements to the NEAT methodology.

CONCLUSION

This chapter was aimed at defining a methodological framework to assess the benefit of a data quality improvement project using real options and to validate the proposal with a case study. We have drawn the following conclusions:

- Despite the fact that information is highly important, it is difficult for organizations to find an economic justification to invest in data improvement.
- Traditional techniques are very limited, since they do not consider the possibility of changes in investment sequences, they consider deterministic and already known costs, and may be somewhat arbitrary in the choice of a discount rate, in addition to the determination of future flows.
- Real options are a suitable approach for quality projects in general and data quality in particular, since they allow to consider uncertainties in terms of costs and benefits, flexibility to decide whether to continue with a project or not, different open opportunities, etc.
- We have proposed a methodological framework to use real options for the assessment of data quality projects. The framework is general and we have instantiated it for this type of project specifically. We have not made emphasis

on the valuation method, since we'd rather prioritize the underlying reasoning model.

- Applying this methodology to a concrete case enabled to prove its simplicity, its swift implementation and also some of its constraints (binary result of activities, arbitrary estimation of some probabilities, etc.).
- The methodology proposed does not solve the difficulties that arise when trying to quantify benefits and opportunities. Moreover, though possible, the analysis of different scenarios may be highly complex and bothersome.

ACKNOWLEDGMENTS

We'd like to thank Daniel Yankelevich and Martin Patrici for their helpful comments.

REFERENCES

Amran, M., & Kulatilaka, N. (1999). *Real options: Managing strategic investment in an uncertain world.* Boston: Harvard Business School Press.

Benaroch, M. (2002). Managing information technology investment risk: A real options perspective. *Journal of MIS, 19*(2), 43-84.

Benaroch, M., & Kauffman, R. J. (1999). A case for using real options pricing analysis to evaluate information technology project investments. *Information Systems Research, 10*(1), 70-87.

Bobrowski , M., Marre, M., & Yankelevich, D. (1999, November). *An homogeneous framework to measure data quality.* Paper presented at the Information Quality Conference, Boston.

Bobrowski, M., Marre, M., & Yankelevich, D. (2001). A NEAT approach for data quality assessment. In M. G. Piattini, C. Calero, & M. Genero (Eds.), *Information & database quality* (pp. 135-162). Norwell, MA: Kluwer Academic Publishers.

Boehm, B., & Sullivan, K. (2000, June). *Software economics, a roadmap.* Paper presented at the 22nd International Conference on Software Engineering, Limerick, Ireland.

Brach, M. (2002). *Real options in practice.* Hoboken, NJ: Wiley & Sons.

Brealey, R. A., & Myers, S. C. (2000). *Principles of corporate finance* (6th ed.). Boston: Irwin McGraw-Hill.

COCOMO. (2005). Retrieved January 20, 2005, from http://sunset.usc.edu/research/COCOMOII/

Fenton, N., & Pfleeger, S. (1997). *Software metrics, a rigorous and practical approach* (2nd ed.). London: PWS Publishing.

GQM. (2005). Retrieved February 10, 2005, from http://sel.gsfc.nasa.gov/website/exp-factory/gqm.htm

Huang, K., Lee, Y., & Wang, R. (1999). *Quality information and knowledge.* Englewood Cliffs, NJ: Prentice Hall.

Kitchenham, B., & Pfleeger, S. L. (1996). Software quality — the elusive target. *IEEE Computer, 13*(1), 12-21.

Loshin, D. (2001, June). The cost of poor data quality. In *DM direct Newsletter.* Retrieved November 21, 2001, from http://www.dmreview.com

McKnight, W. (2003). *Overall approach to data quality ROI* (white paper). Retrieved October 20, 2003, from http://www.firstlogic.com/papers

PI. (2005). Retrieved January 18, 2005, from http://www.investopedia.com

Redman, T. D. (2001). *Data quality: The field guide.* Boston: Butterworth-Heinemann.

ROI. (2005). Retrieved February 3, 2005, from http://www.mrlease.com/leasedict.htm

Schwartz, E. S., & Zozaya-Gorostiza, C. (2003). Investment under uncertainty in information technology: Acquisition and development projects. *Management Science, 49*(1), 57-70.

Slaughter, S. A., Harter, D., & Krishnan, M. S. (1998): Evaluating the cost of software quality. *Communications of the ACM, 41*(8), 67-73.

Sullivan, K. J., Chalasani, P., Jha, S., & Sazawal, V. (1999). Software design as an investment activity: A real options perspective. In L. Trigerorgis (Ed.), *Real options and business strategy: Applications to decision making* (pp. 215-261). London: Risk Books.

The ROI of data quality. (2002). Retrieved October 15, 2002, from http://www.trilliumsoftware.com

WACC. (2005). Retrieved January 15, 2005, from http://www.invesco.com.au

GLOSSARY

COCOMO: "is a model that allows one to estimate the cost, effort, and schedule when planning a new software development activity. It consists of three submodels, each one offering increased fidelity the further along one is in the project planning and design process. Listed in increasing fidelity, these submodels are called the Applications Composition, Early Design, and Post-architecture models." (COCOMO, 2005)

expected rate of return: "The weighted arithmetic average of all possible returns on an asset or portfolio, where the weights represent the probabilities that the outcomes will occur. It is the expected value or mean of a probability distribution." (WACC, 2005)

expected value: "A statistical term denoting a predicted value of a variable in the future." (WACC, 2005)

GQM: "The Goal-Question-Metric (GQM) method is used to define measurement on the software project, process, and product in such a way that:

- Resulting metrics are tailored to the organization and its goal.
- Resulting measurement data play a constructive and instructive role in the organization.
- Metrics and their interpretation reflect the values and the viewpoints of the different groups affected (e.g., developers, users, operators).

GQM defines a measurement model on three levels:

- **Conceptual level (goal):** A goal is defined for an object, for a variety of reasons, with respect to various models of quality, from various points of view, and relative to a particular environment.
- **Operational level (question):** A set of questions is used to define models of the object of study and then focuses on that object to characterize the assessment or achievement of a specific goal.
- **Quantitative level (metric):** A set of metrics, based on the models, is associated with every question in order to answer it in a measurable way." (GQM, 2005)

internal rate of return (IRR): "The rate of interest that needs to be applied to make the net present value of an investment equal to the price paid." (WACC, 2005)

net present value (NPV): "The current value of a stream of income and principal (if any) discounted by an interest rate over the period of an investment." (WACC, 2005)

profitability index (PI): "An index that attempts to identify the relationship between the costs and benefits of a proposed project through the use of a ratio calculated as:

$$= \frac{\text{PV of Future Cash Flows}}{\text{Initial Investment}}$$ " (PI, 2005)

return on investment (ROI): "The yield. The interest rate earned by the lessor in a lease, which is measured by the rated at which the excess cash flows permit recovery of investments. The rate at which the cash flows not needed for debt service or payment of taxes amortize the investment of the equity participation." (ROI, 2005)

risk-free rate of return: "A theoretical return that is earned with perfect certainty; it is without risk. In Australia, the risk-free return is generally the government bond rate." (WACC, 2005)

weighted average cost of capital (WACC): "Expected return on a portfolio of all the firm's securities. Used as hurdle rate for capital investment" (WACC, 2005).

yield: "(a) The return on an investment expressed as a percentage; (b) the profit or income that an investment or property will return; (c) the money derived from any given business venture, usually expressed as an annual percentage of the initial investment. Straight yield (or running yield) relates cash flow to price paid and does not take into account any gain or loss of principal. Redemption yield relates to the sum of both cash flow, for example interest payments, over the life of the security and any gain or loss at maturity on the initial amount invested." (WACC, 2005)

Chapter XII

Purpose-Focused View of Information[1] Quality:
Teleological Operations Research-Based Approach

Zbigniew J. Gackowski, California State University Stanislaus, USA

ABSTRACT

This chapter presents a logical technology-independent fully content-focused inquiry into the operations quality problems of any symbolic representations of reality. This teleological operations-research-based approach demonstrates that a purpose-focused view, natural within the operation-research (OR) methodology, facilitates faster progress in identifying the fundamental relationships of more lasting validity for business, public administration, and military purposive operations. Products of the Information Quality Programs and Initiatives at MIT (MITIQ Program) serve as recognized research references. It contains definitions of: (1) a tentatively universal hierarchical taxonomy of the entire universe of quality requirements, (2) the definitions of the first five tentatively universal operations quality requirements for any situation, (3) an economic sequence of their examination, and (4) the first seven tentatively universal principles in this domain. This quality framework may assist researchers in further studies and assist practitioners in understanding the intricate relationships among operations quality attributes. The chapter presents the tentative results of the author's research in progress.

INTRODUCTION

This chapter presents a logical technology-independent fully content-focused inquiry into quality problems with data and information. Current research supports such a view. Huang, Lee and Wang (1999, p. 4) say, "Many best-practice reports witness that information technology alone is not the driver for knowledge management in companies today ... Information and knowledge experienced by members of an organization should be the focus, not the system or technology per se. Technology and systems ... are facilitators." Most authors use the terms *data* and *information* interchangeably, however, the purpose-focused, operations-research-based perspective requires considering data and information as two disjunctive sets of symbolic representations with common quality attributes but distinctively different quality problems, as it will be later explained.

It is a theoretical teleological operations-research (OR)-based content-focused approach to quality problems. It provides the examiner with an intimate insight into the fundamental relationships that:

- Directly link business, public administration, and military operations to the content quality of data and information used in conduct of such operations, and
- Exist within, and pervade throughout the entire universe of all quality attributes per se in a complex interplay.

Products of the Information Quality Programs and Initiatives at MIT (MITIQ Program) serve as a recognized research references. Among them are "Quality Information and Knowledge" by Huang, Lee, and Wang (1999) and "AIMQ: A Methodology for Information Quality Assessment" by Lee, Strong, Kahn, and Wang (2002).

This study of the operations quality attributes of the content of symbolic representations of reality such as data and information with the exclusion of knowledge meant as rules of reasoning that emerge when purposive operations are performed (Gackowski, 2004). One assumes that based on the available representation values pertinent decisions are made, respective actions are taken, and the results of operations are measurable or at least identifiable. This approach: (1) complements and accommodates some earlier findings, (2) overcomes the deficiencies and inconsistencies of the conceptual data quality framework derived from studies that used marketing research of data users considered as data consumers (Wang & Strong, 1996), (3) decisively reduces the need for empirical, particularly survey-based studies and limits them mainly to attributes that unquestionably depend on user personal preferences, and (4) overcomes the inherent limitations of the PSP/IQ model in AIMQ methodology (Lee et al., 2002).

The main objective of this chapter is to demonstrate that:

- A tentatively universal hierarchical result-oriented taxonomy of operations quality requirements can be defined
- Logical interdependencies among them can be identified
- A simpler economical sequence for their examination can be determined

This is an outline of a theoretical framework, which hopefully will:

1. Produce results of a more lasting validity,
2. Assist researchers in designing further studies in this domain, and
3. Assist practitioners in understanding the intricate relationships among operations quality requirements and the ultimate results of operations that depend on the operations quality of the data and information values used in making decisions.

The chapter presents the first tentative results of the author's current research in progress.

BACKGROUND AND RELEVANT LITERATURE

Huang et al. (1999, p. 13), unless specified otherwise, use the term "information" interchangeably with "data." After they reviewed three approaches used in literature and in business practice to study information quality (IQ) (**intuitive, system,** and **empirical**), they decided to use a system definition anchored in an ontological, logical foundation (Wand and Wang, 1996, pp. 86-95), and an empirical definition derived from the information consumer's perspective. Later, based on the previous research, Lee, Strong, Kahn, and Wang developed AIMQ: A Methodology for Information Quality Assessment (2002).

The System and Ontological Approach

The system definition of information quality concentrates on the internal view intrinsic to system design and data production, is use-independent, enables comparisons across applications, and may guide the design of information systems by information quality objectives (Wand & Wang, 1996, pp. 86-95).

The fundamental role of an information system is to provide a representation of an application domain (real-world system) as perceived by the user. Representation deficiencies are defined in terms of the differences between the view of the real-world system as inferred from the information system and the view that is obtained by directly observing the real-world system. From various types of representation deficiencies, a set of information quality dimensions is derived. Huang et al. (1999, pp. 39-40) identified four potential representation deficiencies with regard to four intrinsic information quality dimensions (complete, unambiguous, meaningful, correct), associated them with two sources of deficiencies (design and operation failure), and with some observed information problems.

Comment: There is a problem with **completeness** defined as no missing information system states. Despite professing the ontological approach, Wand and Wang (1996) did not address the most acute problem of completeness in real life situations. Every business manager, field commander, and scientist is aware that completeness of information in the real world is mostly unattainable. It is not simply a design failure. It is the result of the limitations of human cognition in science, and the limitations of intelligence in business and military operations. In business organizations, in cutthroat competition, and in warfare, the critical blow most frequently comes from a danger, direction, or factors not recognized in time.

Other dimensions such as **unambiguous, meaningful, correct** are defined within the strict context of mapping, but that constitutes only the first part of the problem. Even with perfectly meaningful and correct mapping, as defined by the authors, another type of mapping follows immediately — the mapping of the information system state to the decision maker's mindset. At that time, other serious distortions cannot be entirely avoided. Only, by careful design of proper organizational procedures, decision-making procedures, and proper checks and balances, can they be minimized to some degree. Hence, they should not be ignored in discussions.

The Empirical Approach from Information Consumer Perspective

Here, the empirical definition of information quality is based on the information consumer's perspective, and on the total quality management (TQM) literature. In this view, information quality should not be defined by providers or custodians of information, but instead, by information consumers. Information quality is defined as information that is *fit for use* by information consumers. Information is treated as a product. While most information consumers do not purchase information, they choose to either use or not use information (Huang et al., 1999, pp. 42-43).

Huang et al. (1999, p. 44), using qualitative analysis, examined 42 information quality projects from three leading-edge data-rich organizations that are leaders with regard to attention to information quality. Each project served as a mini-case, and was analyzed using the framework developed by Wang and Strong (1996) with four **information quality categories** (**intrinsic, contextual, representational, accessibility**), and with two or more associated **information quality dimensions** (**attributes**). The authors refer to a "case study" as an empirical inquiry that investigates a contemporary phenomenon within its real-life context. They emphasize that the study was done within a "larger information system's context" to cover the organizational processes, procedures, and roles employed in collecting, processing, distributing, and using data.

Intrinsic information quality denotes that information has quality in its own right. Accuracy is merely one of the four dimensions underlying this category. **Contextual information quality** highlights the requirements that information quality must be considered within the context of the task; it must be relevant, timely, complete, and appropriate in terms of amount to add value. **Representational** and **accessibility information quality** emphasize the importance of the delivery system. It must be accessible but secure. It must present information in a way that is interpretable, easy to understand, concise, and consistently represented. Huang et al. (1999, p. 56) claim that they defined the concepts of information quality objectively and subjectively, provided the essential vocabulary for identifying IQ problems, and formed the foundations for measuring, analyzing, and improving information quality in a continuous cycle.

Comment: The first inconsistency is that completeness is listed twice. First, it is defined as a mapping or design feature and listed as an independent intrinsic dimension of information in Wand and Wang (1996). Second, it is not defined explicitly, but is listed separately as a contextual dimension of information quality in Wang and Strong (1996).

The glossary of the text *does not* contain a definition of **completeness**. One can find a definition of *incompleteness*, but it pertains only to incompleteness of mapping, which is not of contextual nature. Later, in the text, **contextual incompleteness** is explained as missing data due to operational problems within the boundaries of the mini-case. Even within the contextual category, the purely empirical approach neglects the difficult strategic aspect of information completeness — the deficiency of business intelligence.

The authors are aware of inevitable limitations of such studies when they emphasize, "the disadvantage of empirical approach is that the correctness or completeness of the results cannot be proven based on fundamental principles" (Huang et al., 1999, p. 34).

AIMQ: A Methodology for Information Quality Assessment

Probably the broadest overview of academics' and practitioners' views on IQ dimensions is in Lee et al. (2002). The authors admit, "Despite a decade of research and practice only a piece-meal, ad-hoc techniques are available for measuring, analyzing and improving IQ" (p. 133). They claim, "We developed a methodology called AIM Quality (AIMQ) that provided a rigorous and pragmatic basis for IQ assessment" (p. 134). The foundations of AIMQ methodology are a model, and a set of IQ dimensions, which covers aspects of IQ that are important to information consumers. For defining the IQ concepts, and ensure complete coverage, the authors use again the concepts derived empirically from studying consumers preferences (Wang & Strong, 1996). The first essential component of the methodology is the PSP/IQ model, which considers four situations derived from the combination of two factors: whether one deals with an information product or information service, and whether one is concerned with meeting specifications or expectations of information users.

Comment: It seems to be a strong model within the confines of TQM principles until, however, one realizes its inherent limitations. It is limited to products or services, and to given specifications or preferences of information users. These limitations are substantial when one becomes aware of the consequences:

- Products or services are not identical with purposes, goals, and objectives of operations entities.
- Specifications provided by a contracting entity may be sacred to contractors, but they may be substantially deficient in meeting the actual operations purpose.
- Preferences of information users within a business entity may deviate considerably or even be in conflict with operations purposes of the entity they serve or work for.

THE SUGGESTED APPROACH

About 150 years ago in his opus vitae "The World as Will and Representations," Schopenhauer presented a consistent framework based on the premise that human acts are rooted in the will (including all the urges and drives) and the representations of the world in human mind (Hamlyn, 1980). Today, in most cases, **data**, **information**, and **knowledge** stored, processed, and presented by computers to users constitute these representation of the **operation reality** the management deals with. There may be and usually exists a substantial gap between the actual reality and all its representations. This is the main quality problem of all symbolic representations of any reality. This chapter deals with quality problems of data and information values, with the exclusion of rules of reasoning stored in knowledge bases. Although, it seems that most of the results and conclusions presented here may pertain equally to the rules of reasoning, as well.

In business and public administration, on one hand, data values about the past and present are collected and stored to satisfy the established accountability requirements, whether for legal, tax, and auditing purposes, and as an important input for their further processing. On the other hand, some of the data values together with the additional indispensable incoming information values are used to cope with the present and future problems of organizations. They are used in decision making at the non-managerial, operational, tactical, and strategic level. This approach fully focuses on the quality of the content of data and information while assuming that their values are formally correct as stored in respective common databases.

Quality requirements for data that satisfy accountability requirements are defined in General Accepted Accounting Principles (GAAP) and be the Financial Accounting Standard Board (FASB). Data used for managerial accounting, daily operations and planning are not subject to those requirements. Usually they are defined within the scope of specific applications, for they are task — and situation-specific. When considering the quality of any representations, the main focus should be on their use for effective operations. The ultimate assessment of their quality should be derived by observing and measuring how any aspect of their quality affects the ultimate purpose of the operations under consideration. On the one hand, empirical survey-based studies may substantially assist in improving the current precarious situation with regard to the quality of those representations but they are ineffective in producing research results of more lasting validity. On the other hand, the ontological studies on intrinsic aspects of the quality within the confines of the assumptions[2] used, produce quality "attributes that have crystal-clear definitions and a theoretically sound justification, but they constitute only a small subset of known attributes leaving the rest unspecified" (Liu & Chi, 2002, p. 294).

One needs to turn attention to alternative approaches that promise better rewards. Any organized human action is by nature purposive, hence in business, public administration, and military operations the selected research methodology should emphasize less the ontological but more the teleological perspective of the quality of those representations. Within this context, the most natural, adequate and promising seems to be the operations research methodology, which emerged and was developed in direct response to the need of improving the performance of massive organized military, governmental, commercial, and industrial processes. It attempts to provide those who manage such systems with an objective and quantitative bases for decisions. A wide body of experience has been accumulated.

The Selected Point and Frame of Reference

The purpose-focused framework (Gackowski, 2004), selected for a logical inquiry into the problems of the representations' quality, takes the teleological operations-research-based (OR) approach and refers to the decision situations it serves. One tentatively assumes:

- A relatively complete qualitative cause/effect diagram, known also as a fishbone diagram, is available or can be drawn. It identifies the major factors affecting the situation itself, the required actions to implement the decisions made, and the expected results. Based on the representations of the reality available users make pertinent decisions and take subsequent actions. The results of the operations can be measured as functions of the operations quality of the representations used.

- An analysis can reveal the relative strength of each factor by its impact on the main operations' purpose. In business, various criteria are used to measure the main purpose of its operations such as net income after taxes, retained earnings, return on investment, return on equity, and so forth. In public administration and military operations different measures are used.
- One can develop a symbolic model of the decision situation under consideration by taking inventory of what is already known, and what still must be acquired. That what is known, given, or available constitutes the **data component** of the model. Anything that is not yet available, is still missing, thus must be acquired by proper intelligence constitutes the **informational component** of the model.

The **data component** of the model is here the set of variable values that symbolically represent what is already known (objects, events, and their states) about the situation. The **informational component** *is* here the set of variable values that symbolically represent what is not yet known (objects, events, and their states) about the situation and must be acquired, gathered, measured, counted, and so forth. **Information values**, if only of significant impact, change the **decision situation**. Such a framework enables a logical examination of quality of the representations used.

The operations quality requirements of all types of symbolic representations change with the changing purpose and circumstances of operations. Thus, they are relative to them. The main purpose of operations will serve as the main point of reference and the circumstances of operations will serve as the main frame of reference. By the law of relativity, they automatically determine all operations' quality requirements for the representations necessary to conduct the operations.

Within a well-defined frame of reference, one may embark upon a truly purpose-focused examination of every variable value with regard to its practical usefulness. A good analytical example of this approach is desirable to elucidate all of its components. This, however, would exceed the acceptable size of this chapter. The appendix attached to this chapter contains a simplistic example of this kind of reasoning for illustrative purposes only.

Data Values vs. Information Values in Representations

- Data values symbolically represent aspects of reality that are known, given, or assumed true, hence their impact has already been discounted or taken into considerations.
- Information values symbolically represent aspects of reality that are unknown and must still be obtained. Only they change the decision situation per se and/or the necessary actions and/or the results.
- Data and information values are two separate disjoint sets of values with no overlapping elements. They are distinctively different.

- Any data value when available never changes, a relevant information value always changes the situation qualitatively and quantitatively.
- Data values never increase the operations completeness. An incoming information value, if only of significant impact, always increases completeness.
- All values of quality attributes of data and information values share the same multidimensional space, but differ substantially. Usually they are at the opposing ends of their respective spectra.

Usefulness of Representations

In operations, only *useful* values are worth considering. **Usefulness**, however, is contextual, depends heavily on the situation. How may usefulness be perceived in different situations?

- For *general education* any representation that broadens the students' intellectual horizons is useful.
- For *designers of decision support systems* only representation values that change the outcome of a decision situation under consideration are useful.
- For *operations research* only these representation values are useful that change the decision situation by itself, and/or change the actions that implement the decisions made and/or change the results of operations. Here, however, only significantly relevant information values are capable of doing it.

Hence, in any results-oriented environment, **usefulness of data values** for accountability and operations and **information values** for operations only should be of foremost interest, and the focus of discussions about **quality of representations**. *Currently it is not.* MIS textbooks and other publications rarely, if at all, cover fundamentals of how to define usefulness of representations in operations and how to articulate the attributes of their quality that determine it or contribute to it. In this chapter it is assumed that the *single most important cumulative measure* of **usefulness of any representation** is its **expected cost-effectiveness** assessed from the viewpoint of the purpose of the operations it serves. This fundamental tenet of economically purposive operations, however, was eliminated by Wang and Strong (1996) from their frequently cited conceptual model of data quality. It was derived from their empirical survey-based study of consumers' preferences with regard to data quality. They did it for trivial statistical reasons.

Tentatively Universal Taxonomy of Operations Quality Requirements

Most textbooks and the cited empirical studies list under different names a plethora of quality attributes or dimensions for consideration. Wang and Strong (1996) list 179 potential quality attributes derived from an empirical survey-based study about data consumers' views on data quality. The major question is, however, how to examine those attributes in real life situations.

Which of them affect the operations results directly or indirectly, are primary or secondary, mandatory or optional, should be examined first, or which are not fully attainable? One must also learn to act with only some acceptable level of quality. This leads us to a tentatively universal taxonomy of the entire universe of operations quality requirements. The taxonomy is **hierarchical, impact-determined** and defined as follows (Gackowski, 2005a) (see Table 1):

1.   One can subdivide the universe of all operations' quality requirements into direct and indirect ones. Changes to the values of **direct attributes** directly affect the operations, while changes to values of **indirect attributes** affect the operations only via the direct ones.

2.   The direct operations' quality requirements can be further subdivided into primary and secondary ones. Changes of the values of the **primary** ones result in *qualitative* changes to the decision situations under consideration, while changes to values of **secondary** ones *quantitatively* change the operations. The latter are mostly of economic nature. In business, they become mandatory too, otherwise the use of any symbolic representations that does not meet the economic requirements would not make business sense.

3.   Within the primary operations' quality requirements, one must distinguish those of **universal nature** vs. the **situation-specific** ones. The **direct primary tentatively universal quality requirements** apply to each representation; the **situational-specific** ones pertain only to some quality attributes of some representations under certain circumstances.

Analyzing the existing logical interdependencies among at least the direct primary quality attributes, one arrives at a tentative economical sequence of their examination. This offers not only a better understanding of the phenomenon of quality, but also yields a tangible practical benefit for all who analyze it, whether theoretically or practically. It seems to be a significant progress in comparison to

Table 1. The universal hierarchical disjoint impact-oriented taxonomy of operations quality requirements of any symbolic representations — a schema

Direct impact			Indirect impact
Primary mandatory		Secondary on economy	....
Universal	Specific	....	....
		....	....
....	....		

the known publications on this subject by other authors. It accommodates any quality dimensions — those already identified and known and also any other that may emerge. It overcomes the limitations of the PSP/IQ model in AIMQ methodology (Lee et al., 2002). It immediately focuses the attention of analysts on what should be considered first and provides them with a reference point to how much attention should be given to each value. Most authors do not go beyond eclectic piecemeal enumeration of some quality attributes and the sequence of their enumeration is usually of undefined logic.

Direct Primary Tentatively Universal Quality Requirements

They apply to each value in all tasks, are *mandatory*, and must be met *unconditionally* in all situations. Changes to the values of the respective direct primary operations quality requirements result in qualitative changes in the decision situations under consideration (Gackowski, 2005b).

(1) *Interpretable During Acquisition*

Messages or composite representations may consist of one or more values. For them to be usable at all, they must be **interpretable** within the process of their acquisition. In practice, interpretability means whether the received value matches any state with some attributed or associated meaning in the mind of the receiving individual, or any state that automatically triggers a designed sequence of state transitions in the receiving numerically controlled device. Most authors omit it as obvious. When for any reason the targeted individual or the receiving device is unable to interpret a value, it is lost and it must be excluded from further examination. This is a **tentatively universal direct primary operations quality requirement for any value and is the prerequisite for examining all other quality requirements for this value**.

Interpretability is contextual; a more educated receiver, a conditioned one, a trained one, or a different receiving device may still be able to interpret it. The information carrying signals must be noticeable to senses or sensors, discernible, recognizable, or identifiable. The latter are examples of **indirect attributes**. These considerations are of major concern for users and disseminators. The interpretability of information values during their acquisition should not be confused with their presentational interpretability for users/clients.

More complex conditions and circumstances must be considered by information disseminators. A plethora of factors here comes into play. Many of them of a very subtle psychological nature how to effectively and gainfully reach the targeted client by employing the many findings, skills, and tricks offered by the art of communications, psychology, marketing, advertising, and so forth, which intersect here. They are subject of studies how effectively attract others' attention and how to persuade them into desired actions.

(2) *Of Significant Impact, Relevance by FASB (1983), and by Wang and Strong (1996)*

The content, subject, or meaning of individual values or any combination thereof must make a *significant* impact on the situation under consideration. Its **impact** should be assessed by the scope of changes made in the situation itself and/or in the results of operations, and/or the actions taken to implement the decisions made. **The impact a task-specific value makes lends importance to all other attributes of its quality**. This is a tentatively universal principle to which all operations' quality attributes of a task-specific value of significant impact are subject when viewed from the teleological perspective. This is **the principle of pervasiveness of the significant impact on operations of any task-specific value over all other quality attributes of that value**. This attribute dominates over all other possible operations' quality attributes of the same value when viewed from the operations' perspective. If the impact is insignificant from the perspective of disseminators and/or clients, the remaining attributes of the value are irrelevant, too. For any value to be usable its **significant impact is another direct primary tentatively universal quality requirement, which dominates and pervades all of its remaining quality requirements**.

Impact can be quantified or at least ranked either from the viewpoint of information disseminators or information users. One may ask how the payoff or added benefit depends on the use of any value, whether its impact is *significant* enough to warrant consideration. In a more rigorous manner, one may say that a situation-specific value may be qualitatively relevant but quantitatively irrelevant when its impact is practically negligible. If so, one should cease further examination of its remaining quality attributes.

It may happen that the size of the impact depends also on other factors such as the type of availability of the value: whether restricted only to a specific decision-maker, fully unrestricted or anything in between. Restricted availability gives advantage to some decision makers over their competitors. Unrestricted availability of a value may reduce that advantage to insignificance. These considerations are situation specific and are examples of **indirect operations quality requirements** affecting a direct primary one. (See also "actionably timely available.")

One must also be aware of a very frequent case that a value of a zero payoff or **added benefit** may still be of significant impact on the ultimate outcome. This takes place when it is a required companion of another value that is associated with a significant added benefit. For instance, emergency calls for roadside assistance may yield a well-defined payoff. Nevertheless, the call must be accompanied by information values about the location. Without the latter, such calls cannot be effectively handled on theirs own. The definitions of relevance referred to in the above sub-title are too narrow from the operations research (OR) view.

(3) *Operationally Timely Available, Timeliness by FASB (1983), and Accessibility by Wang and Strong (1996)*

Once all values of significant impact are identified, the next direct primary quality attribute is "operationally timely available" before they lose their capacity to make a significant impact. It pertains to individual values or any combination thereof. If the value is not on time to meet the need, why bother about other requirements? In ever-changing reality, time is of the essence. Even with all remaining requirements met perfectly, if timely availability cannot be assured, the impact of late values may be null. For any value of significant impact to be usable at all "**operational timely availability**" **is the third direct primary tentatively universal quality requirement.**

The "actionable timely availability" may also be viewed differently. For instance, whether the value under consideration is available exclusively to a single interested individual. Here, one deals with two extremes: with restricted or unrestricted availability. Within the logical interdependencies among quality attributes, one can see here an interesting case of circular interdependence. In order to consider the "actionable timely availability" of any value, it must be of "significant impact." In a competitive environment, however, the significant impact of a value may depend entirely on its restricted availability. The latter is an example of situation-specific requirements that are task-specific, mandatory, but not universal. This again is an example of an **indirect operations quality requirement** affecting a direct one.

(4) *Actionably Credible, Reliable by FASB (1983), Believable by Wang and Strong (1996)*

Messages declared of significant impact and actionably timely available imply they were interpretable during acquisition. Users/clients should test them for **credibility**, whether they are true, whether they can be relied on. The adjective **true** means consistent with reality. While probing for veracity, users/clients face dramatic options: whether they received disinformation, misinformation, or valid information.

- **Valid information** faithfully represents or reflects reality. To this end, it should be well-defined, objective (unbiased), accurate (error free), precise, and current (up to date). Usually this is assumed, when information is of proven authorship, from a reputable source, can be independently replicated, confirmed otherwise, or traced back to a responsible originator, and the level of responsibility is commensurate to the potential consequences of possible errors.

- **Misinformation** unintentionally misrepresents reality. It may be distorted at its acquisition, communication, storing, processing, presentation and the interpretation by itself. It may be of lesser or higher materiality as defined and required by FASB (1983).

- **Disinformation** intentionally misinforms. On one hand, in simple cases, it may not be clear who the originator is. It may be due to omission of contact addresses, when it was originated or updated, how it was defined, what methods of collection or acquisition were used, etc. On the other hand, all the above may be available. Now, however, the user or client faces another two extremes of **deception** with many possibilities in between. All the above listed indicators of validity are given: (1) To appear legitimate, but one or more of them are false, or (2) Are true, and usually presented in a very motivational manner, but actually the intent of the message is deliberately malicious, criminal, aimed at trapping the gullible.

Credibility of data/information values is a complex function of many indirect attributes of quality such as the **credibility of the source** they are derived from, the **variety of independent sources** available, the **quality of their mapping** within the delivery system and the **credibility of their presentation** in indirect informing. These attributes are **indirect attributes of the first order**. **Reputation of a D/I source**, which lends source-specific credibility to the yielded values, depends on a multitude of external preconditions (**traceability** — rejected in [13], **availability** of **communication channels** — **communicable** sources, **alignment of attitudes and alignment of interests**) that enable or preclude its further examination. The remaining factors are more intrinsic to the source. Some of them *increase* its reputation by offering information services that are **reliable, verifiable, replicable**, and even with some **warranty**. Other factors *impair* the reputation due to deficiencies in data **definition, variability, objectivity, accuracy, precision**, and **currency**.

The latter deficiencies form hierarchies of linear downward directed pervasiveness of quality impairments. If, at any level of their hierarchy, a quality requirement cannot be met, testing for quality-requirement compliance at lower levels is redundant. Further examination should be aborted. An impairment of a quality requirement incurred at a higher level of the hierarchy cannot be compensated at any lower level. In reverse order, any quality impairment at lower level of the hierarchy affects upward directly the credibility of the concerned value to their **currency,** and then even satisfactory objectivity, accuracy, and **precision** is wasted. Credibility of presented D/I values will suffer again.

Since credibility is rarely-to-never fully attainable, in many situations, users must act with only an acceptable level of credibility labeled here **actionably credible.** For practical purposes, **actionably credible** can be defined as the degree of credibility of an information value at which the user or decision-maker is willing to take action. The definition is precise, but the actionable level of credibility again is a function of the decision situation, including the personality of the decision maker in particular. For any available information value to be usable at all, **actionable credibility is the fourth direct primary tentatively universal operations quality requirement**.

The previously described four direct primary quality requirements seem to define by enumeration the minimum of the tentatively universal quality requirements for **task-specific usability of any single information value** in all situations of **direct informing** (no intermediaries between the source and the user/client). It is another **tentatively universal principle of task-specific usability of single values**. In many cases, so defined usability is sufficient. Some situations, however, impose additional mandatory requirements such as the previously discussed restricted availability of values. Usability in its own right indicates that a value may be used but not necessarily used effectively.

In most organizations, however, due to division of labor the acquisition of values and their use are completely separated. Thus **indirect informing** is nearly a standard mode in IT operations. In such situations, users must be presented with value that is interpretable and understandable for them (e.g., legible, in their preferred language, measurement units, conventions, etc.). Then the value must also be **presentation interpretable** and it becomes another direct primary mandatory quality requirement, but not a universal one.

(5) *Operations Triggering Completeness*

Completeness of representations pertains to a set of identified potential, task-specific factors of significant impact on operations that is on the decision situation itself, and/or on the operations results, and/or at least on the actions necessary to implement the decision made. Once one arrived at a task-specific set of usable values, one can test their completeness with regard to the situation under consideration. Completeness of values in decision-making, in contrast to their mapping while storing, processing and presenting them is more complex than it appears on its surface. It is strongly related to their impact as defined earlier. One must distinguish at least two types of completeness: **operational completeness** and **cognitive completeness**.

Within the context of decision situations, *operational completeness* may measure the degree to which the usable values are available. Operational completeness may be measured in percentage points (1 - 100%) as the ratio of the sum of all results that can be attributed to the corresponding values available and the sum of the results that might be attained with perfect completeness. In real-life situations, usually, some residual operational results remain unaccountable. This means it is not possible to attribute them to any previously identified factors. They may be used as a relative or absolute measure how incomplete the impact analysis is. Figure 1 illustrates the general interdependence between **impact** and **operational completeness** of values. The relevant factors are listed on the horizontal axis of the graph by their diminishing impact outwards, whether positive or negative, until their value falls below the defined threshold level of significance.

Murkier is the qualitative or **cognitive** aspect of **completeness** of values in a situation under consideration. In real-life situations, in the fight for survival, on a

Figure 1. The relationship between significant relevance and operational completeness of data or information items pertaining to the corresponding factors that determine and contribute to the total value of the expected results in a decision situation under consideration

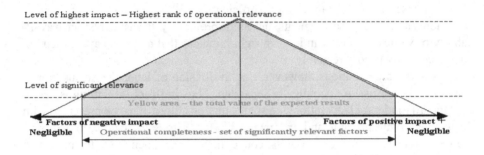

Figure 2. Relevance of data/information items about identifiable potential factors pertaining to a decision situation under consideration and the unattainable notion of their congnitive completeness

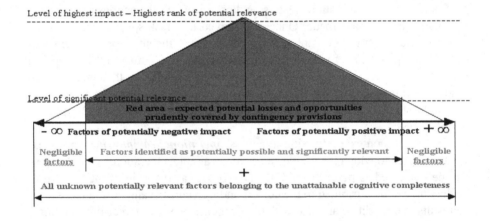

battlefield or in global business competition, one may never be certain whether all relevant success factors or dangers are identified and evaluated. Prudence requires gathering more information to inform interested decision-makers so that they may assess all the maybe not yet perceivable but potentially possible critical factors for planning of counter measures and contingency provisions. Most frequently, the critical blow comes from a danger or direction not identified and recognized in time. It cannot be considered mandatory on its own merit, for it is rarely-to-never fully attainable. Figure 2 illustrates the general interdependence between **impact** of values about all identified hypothetical factors pertaining to a decision situation under consideration and the fuzzy notion of their **cognitive completeness**.

Both Figures 1 and 2 illustrate how the quantified impact of values determines the operational and cognitive completeness of the totality of factors pertaining to a specific situation. Since both are rarely-to-never fully attainable, managers must frequently act based on an incomplete set of values. Like credibility, completeness is measured by a continuum of degrees. From the purely pragmatic viewpoint, there is at least one important degree of operational completeness, when it becomes **motivationally sufficiently effective** to trigger operations.

Character of an individual, business policy, administrative policy or military doctrine usually determine in general, and within organizations the then executive decision-makers determine in particular the time and situation specific level of sufficiency of the reason for triggering operations. About 200 years ago, Schopenhauer defined the will as the fourth form of sufficient reasons of being, changing, knowing, and acting, hence for **operations**. Here, the will is motivated by the potential effectiveness and success of the planned operations. In a very gross manner, one may distinguish about four major types of effectiveness.

When economy of operations is second to operational effectiveness, one may be satisfied with **sufficiently effective operational completeness** to trigger operations. Effective operational completeness pertains to situations of an all out effort to attain the stated goal by whatever it takes when at least temporarily economy is a secondary concern. Only then all the direct secondary requirements of quality discussed later need *not be tested*.

When economy takes precedence over the bare-bones effectiveness of operations, it becomes the all "pervasive constraint: benefits > costs" (FASB, 1983, p. 44). Then all the later discussed direct secondary quality requirements become mandatory, as well. One may distinguish:

- **Economical operational completeness:** attained when the sum of all added benefits sufficiently exceeds the sum of all costs of the operations under consideration
- **Cost-effective operational completeness:** attained when the ratio of the sum of all added benefits divided by the sum of all operations costs exceeds the sufficient level
- **Expected cost-effective operational completeness:** computed as above, but as a function of expected added benefits and expected costs

There is, however, a legitimate question how the operations triggering completeness of motivationally sufficient effectiveness manifests itself in operations. In project management one decomposes complex operations into relatively simple activities as required by the Project Evaluation and Review Technique (PERT)

(Moder, 1983). The simple activities are linked into a project graph connecting its starting node and its closing node. The latter represents the accomplished final state and the purpose of the project. Each simple activity requires the use of specified resources. Among them, one may find the indispensable values, if the outcome of the activity is also a function of a set of such usable values. Only such cases are the subject of this inquiry.

For an activity to be successfully accomplished, the required indispensable usable values must be effectively complete. They usually appear in clusters. For any activity-related cluster to be **effectively complete** it must consist of one or more values of significant added-benefit to the activities' outcome and all its/their indispensable companions. For instance, an emergency call for road-side assistance (here an information value) must be accompanied by data or information values that represent the time and location of emergency, the identity and look of the car, and about the party guaranteeing the payment. If any of these values is missing road-side assistance cannot be effectively accomplished.

The **operations state transistion triggering completeness** of values is more demanding; it requires that all added benefits and costs computed as functions of the values used for the completed activities over the entire operations project or campaign become motivationally sufficiently effective to act or not.

Operational and cognitive completeness must be considered mainly by information users or clients. However, these should not be completely ignored by information disseminators. The latter, in their messages, ought also to consider the *potentially* possible concerns of clients. Thus, **the operation triggering completeness of a set of usable values is the fifth direct primary tentatively universal operations quality requirement**.

Tentatively Universal Principles of Operations Quality

Now, within the realm of purposive operations, one may tentatively summarize that the operations quality attributes of all task-specific values viewed from the teleological perspective are subject to at least the following tentatively universal principles:

1. **The principle of *relativity* of all aspects of representations.** Their quality requirements are determined by the purpose and circumstances of operations where they are used. It pertains to all types of representations of the real-world states (data, information, and rules of reasoning).

2. **The principle of *pervasiveness* of the significant impact a value may exert** (on the decision situation itself, and/or the results of operations, and or the actions to implement the decisions made) on other attributes affecting the value's quality. The importance of impact a data or information value exerts on operations lends importance to attributes affecting that value.

3. **The principle of** *equivalency of a lost or otherwise unavailable data value and an unavailable information value*, **if they exert equivalent impact on operations.**

4. **The principle of** *usability* **of values.** A value becomes usable when all the universal (acquisition interpretability, of significant impact, operationally timely available, and actionable credible) and the situation-specific mandatory requirements are jointly met. Usability does not imply effective usability; it is only a necessary or mandatory requirement.

5. **The principle of** *operational usefulness of a usable value*. A usable value can become operationally useful only as a member of an operationally effectively complete activity-specific cluster of required usable values.

6. **The tentative principle of task-specific effective operational** *completeness*. An activity-specific cluster of indispensable usable values to be effectively operationally complete must consist of one or more task-specific, benefit-adding values and all of its/their mandatory usable companion values.

7. **The principle of** *degradation* **of decision situations by declining quality of usable values.** It says, if the quality of a usable value affecting a certain part of a decision situation:
   a. **Is certain**, the decision-maker deals with a **deterministic situation** at least within the affected area
   b. **Is only** probable (the most likely case), the decision-maker deals with a **stochastic situation** to the same extent as above
   c. **Is not usable**, for instance when the value is not timely available or not actionable credible, the decision-maker **games** to the same extent. It may be the case even when operations are not triggered, for instance when threats are ignored.

This discussion closes also the list of the five direct primary tentatively universal operations quality requirements for all task-specific quality values. Sometimes, there may be other additional situation specific quality requirements such as the before-mentioned exclusive or restricted availability. However, they are not universal. What follows is a discussion of the direct but secondary attributes of quality, which are of economic nature. In business, where cost-effective projects are required, meeting all the direct secondary quality requirements makes them economically useful, and then they become mandatory, too.

Direct Secondary Operations Quality Requirements (Economical)

Changes in values of the respective operations quality requirements result mainly in quantitative changes in operations results (Gackowski, 2005b)

One may ask how sensitive a situation is to the use of any specific value, whether it has a significant impact on results that is worthy of consideration. The quantified and ranked impact carries all of the gross added benefits possible to attain and provides the examiner with a **situational reference scale**. It suggests how much attention one should pay to each value relative to the other with regard to the three remaining primary attributes of their quality. Hence, one must test the economic level of **acquisition interpretability**, **actionable timely availability**, **actionable credibility**, their **presentation interpretability** (where applicable), and finally the economic level of their **effective operational completeness**.

Changes in these requirements are additive. Therefore, the sequence of their examination is formally irrelevant. Nevertheless, all values can be economically evaluated only after their proper ranking during a completeness check. In operations, however, values, separately or collectively in composite combinations of them, must also be economically useful. Therefore, in business, the direct secondary quality requirements are mandatory, too. For instance, when a single or a composite value cannot be economically acquired, one should cease examining the remaining direct secondary attributes. The same applies to the remaining direct secondary attributes of quality.

(1e) *Economically Interpretable During Acquisition*

There is no doubt that interpretability of incoming information values during their acquisition is the first direct primary tentatively universal and mandatory requirement that must be met in order to trigger the chain of further examinations. In certain situations, however, it may be attainable only at a prohibitively high cost in comparison to the associated added benefit so that it is not worth the effort. This cost may entail the cost of decoding, translation, maintaining a system of early detection and warning about dangers (tsunami, earthquake, missile attack, etc.). Therefore, the first question to ask is whether it is technologically possible at all. Only after all mandatory requirements are met one should ask whether those requirements can be met economically as it is required in business environments.

In business environments, economy is mandatory. Only when interpretability of information values during their acquisition is economically attainable, it opens the door for examination of the remaining direct secondary requirements. On the other hand, when the stakes of national security, for instance, are higher than the established economical criteria, the concerned information values still remain effectively usable (however, not economically).

(2e) *Economically Actionably Timely Available*

Meeting the universal and the situation-specific quality requirements usually does not add value; it only makes the value usable. In business, however, the cost of making a value timely available should not exceed the associated payoff. In addition, timely availability is scalable. One may receive the necessary values not only on time, but also more or less in advance. The cost of rendering them sooner "actionably available" should also not exceed the associated projected additional benefits. The additional time may be used for making decisions with less haste, and/or for better preparation of operations. Hence, one may also obtain better results when additional time is available. Providing additional time may add value, but it may cost more. On the other hand, excessive additional time can cause a deterioration of operations results due to human forgetfulness or possible distractions between the time of early warning and time for action. Up to now, there is no analytical formula to estimate it. However, in specific situations it may be possible to determine experimentally the best timing. Whether additional time is worth it depends on the difference in results it makes and on how much it will cost to accelerate the informing process or increase its frequency.

(3e) *Economically Actionably Credible*

Actionable credibility may be compromised by deficiencies in several other **indirect** quality attributes — for instance, by deficiencies in its **definition, objectivity, accuracy, precision** and **currency**.

Loss of **objectivity** (meant as free from bias) may happen in the process of acquisition due to the approaches and methods used in selecting the primary sources, measuring points, observation points, and finally, when collecting, processing and presenting the values. The resulting bias may be either unintended due to ignorance or introduced intentionally. In both cases, the results of such distortions may be significant, and in the latter case, deceptive and damaging. To rectify the bias and compensate for it may require engagement of substantial additional resources. Whether it is economically justified, it can be estimated only when the size of its impact on the results is significant enough.

Another problem is **accuracy** (meant as free from errors, including random errors). One encounters them in all situations. Usually accuracy is indicated indirectly by inaccuracy of values, which is the complement to one of accuracy. Accuracy equals one minus inaccuracy. A gross measure of **inaccuracy** in this sense may be the **error rate**. One calculates it by dividing the number of values in error by the total number of values gathered. In practice, a more useful measure of inaccuracy due to different kind of errors is the **expected cost of dealing** with their consequences. One may calculate it by multiplying the number of values by the probability or frequency of each type of error by the average cost of rectifying them and dealing with each type of them. This consequence-weighted measure of **inaccuracy** provides the clients with a better idea how serious the consequences of each type of error are. Such a consequence-weighted inaccuracy is conceptually much closer to the concept of **materiality** as defined and required by FASB (1983). One may reduce many of the errors by using check digits, error self-detection codes, error self-correcting codes, and so forth. Another example is the use of bar code readers that considerably reduce many types of errors with the exception of completeness.

Clients/users of information systems, even business systems analysts, need not be experts in dealing with such situations, but they should be taught to recognize the need for those provisions.

One may also encounter low **precision** in the representation of the reality. For numerical values, *precision* is measured by the number of significant digits used. One measures the precision of pictures and images by the number of dots per inch. This unit is commonly used to describe the precision of printers, computer screens, scanners, etc. Insufficient precision of values may compromise the results obtained.

There is a trap associated with accuracy and precision. Generally, they are over-rated (Wang & Strong, 1996). Unchecked efforts to increase the level of accuracy and/or precision of any data and information value can become counterproductive. The ultimate determination of the indispensable and economically justified level of any of them strongly depends on its utility value.

Figure 3 illustrates graphically how the net operations utility value of information changes as a function of its accuracy. One can see there two graphs plotted as functions of the level of **accuracy (A)** in percentage points (1 - 100%), for its level affects both the numerator and the denominator of the cost effectiveness ratio.

The first graph represents the **operations utility value V (I)** of information **I** as a function of **accuracy A** in percentage points, that is **V (I) = f(A).** There is an assumption that the utility value of value of unknown accuracy is equal to zero. First, the graph line of utility value rises relatively fast then it slows down with increasing accuracy until it reaches its full value according to the definition **V (I) = V (D + I) – V (D),** where **D** represents the data already known to the decision maker and **I** represents the information under consideration. Close to the end, any increase in accuracy yields a lesser and lesser marginal increase in the data or information's operations utility value. The graph is similar to the graph of a logarithmic function.

Figure 3. Optimum level of accuracy A as function of net utility V_N of information I

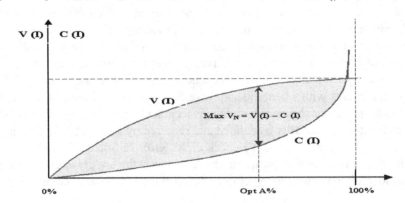

On the other hand, the second graph represents the **procurement cost C (I)** of **information I** again as a function of **accuracy A**, that is **C (I)** = f(**A**). Usually, one may assume that the cost of information of zero accuracy is equal to zero. One can get it free as gossip or rumor, for instance. At the beginning, the graph line rises slowly with increasing accuracy, then the rise accelerates, and before the end, the rises becomes steeper and steeper to reach infinity, whenever one attempts to attain 100% accuracy. In mathematics, this kind of rise is referred to as **asymptotical**. Hence, the first conclusion is that when one pushes too hard for increased accuracy, the **procurement cost C (I)** becomes *prohibitively high*. Attaining higher levels of accuracy requires end-users to incur ever-higher costs of research, measurement, additional observations, expensive instruments, and so forth.

Before reaching 100% accuracy, the steep rise in cost and marginally slower rise of utility value causes both graph lines to intersect. In contrast to the prevailing initial perception of business students, in business one never gets rich or enriches others by incurring costs equal to the value of results. The optimum level of accuracy in the business environment lies where both graphs are the furthest apart. This is the point where the **net utility value of information V$_N$ (I)** reaches its maximum. One can count on *maximum operations benefits* from using representations only at their *optimum level of accuracy and precision*.

Currency of values means here whether it is adequately up-to-date. It was labeled timeliness by Wang and Strong (1996) and defined as, "The extent [to which] the age of the data is appropriate for the task at hand" (p. 32). The label timeliness is used there in conflict with the terminology used by FASB (1983) and subsequently by CPAs for timely availability. It causes unnecessary confusion. The frequency of updates should be optimized, where possible, for either insufficient frequency or too frequent updates are detrimental to the cost effectiveness of the informing delivery system.

Maximum benefits of operations when using values can be attained only at their *optimum level of objectivity, accuracy, precision*, and *currency*. Finding this optimum is not easy, but the truth is that it lies somewhere between the low and high level. For instance, whenever information technology professionals tempt clients with higher accuracy, precision, or currency than they had before, they should ask bluntly, "What will be the additional benefits and at what additional cost?" When one has no indication that their increased level leads to higher cost effectiveness, forget it. To the surprise of many, one thing is sure: the *examination of their economic level should be postponed nearly until the very end*.

Tentative Examination Sequence of Operations Quality Requirements

The sequence of examining the tentatively universal direct primary and the direct secondary operations quality requirements as suggested above seems to be the most economical one in any situation of direct informing. **Direct informing** takes place when signals conveying information flow directly between information sources and users/clients (Gackowski, 2005a). In such situations the information values acquired are relatively new to users/clients and must be examined thoroughly, when acquired for the first time.

Once the role of the data values is relatively well-known and their values are stored in common databases and data warehouses to be shared with many users /clients, one deals with indirect informing. **Indirect informing takes place** when intermediary storing and processing of information takes place between information sources and users/clients. In technologically advanced environments, data are usually organized in databases or data warehouses. These may be run by information providers or by client organizations for themselves. In such a situation, data or information acquisition, entry, verification, validation, storing, making them available, and converting them into **presentation interpretable** format develop into separate, specialized business processes. Then, testing of values for actionable credibility, reliability by FASB (1983), or believability by Wang and Strong (1996) is performed not by the users/clients, but by specialized personnel during acquisition using specialized techniques on behalf of all authorized users.

The ultimate goal of examining values for the above-discussed quality requirements is to arrive at a **set of task-specific usable values that its task-specific operational completeness becomes effective enough to trigger state transition of operations**. When not only effectiveness but also economy is required, one wants such sets to be also effective economically, cost effectively, or even exceed the required level of expected cost effectiveness. Then of course, all the direct secondary quality requirements, which are of economical nature, are mandatory, as well.

Differences in Assessing Data and Information Quality

The previously presented tentatively universal direct primary and direct secondary operations quality requirements were discussed mainly within the context of their first assessment. In routine operations, the dominant problem is the operation's quality of *data*, much less than the operation's quality of *information* (as defined before). Routine assessment of data quality is not easy, but much simpler. Now, the assessment of data and information quality is viewed differently. One deals mainly with acquisition of data values, much less of information values and most of the data already play a well-established role in operations. For instance:

1.   The requirement of **acquisition interpretability** of data is much less of a problem, considerably reduced, and not as acute as with a newly acquired information value when extracted from the real world for the first time, of entirely unknown quality, and from unknown sources.
2.   The requirement of **significant impact** has lost its punch, for the need for data values was well established usually by multiple users/clients or applications.

3.   The requirement of **operational timely availability** of data stored in shared databases is reduced mainly to the problem of technical authorized accessibility and the reliability of the delivery system. This is not anymore the real-life problem, whether the necessary information must be timely extracted from the real world, sometimes a very adversary one, and become available on time.

4.   The requirement of **actionable credibility** of data values in routine operations is by no means less important, but it is of lesser concern to individual internal users. It so because in such well organized business environments, all data should be now subject to established rigorous procedures that assure their integrity during acquisition, entry, storing, making available, and even their presentation. It is done on behalf all data-sharing users.

5.   The requirement of **task-specific effective operations state transition triggering completeness** usually boils down to careful design of a corresponding *subschema* for application processing and predefined database inquiries.

6.   Usually a division of labor and separation of information acquisition and presentation takes place — resulting in *indirect* informing. When users and acquisitors are different entities, a new problem emerges. It is the problem of **presentation interpretability** by different users in different locations, of different cultures, languages, and so forth.

Thus operations' quality problems with information values are incomparably more acute than with data values of usually well established roles and use. Similarly data and information content-related operations quality problems should be considered as of primary importance over the important but secondary issues of formal correctness, completeness and internal integrity of data values stored in common databases. Current research, to the contrary, is mainly concerned with the latter.

Operationally Presentation Interpretable
In most organizations, due to the division of labor, acquisition of information and its use are separated. Thus, ***indirect informing*** takes place. In such situations, users must be presented with data and information that is interpretable and understandable. (For instance, it must be legible, in their preferred language, measurement units, conventions, etc.) At least, it must be operationally usable — however, not necessarily economically feasible. Thus, **presentation interpretability** of values becomes another direct primary operations quality requirement, but not a universal one. It is imposed by the organizational circumstances within which data are used. Presentation of data and information values may be done more (but not less) conveniently. This presents a new economical issue, how far one should go when improving the convenience of data and information presentation.

Economically Presentation Interpretable

Ease and comfort, even enjoyment of the use of values in educational services or computer games is related to their form, format, and mode of delivery. It may affect how fast users read, perceive, interpret, comprehend, analyze, absorb, draw conclusions, react, and finally act upon it. Within this category, one considers clarity, consistency, order, media used, level of summarization, user-preferred type of presentation such as text, graph, diagram, picture, esthetics, and so forth. In the case of composite representations, these properties are determined not only by its components, but also by the way the components are combined. Some deficiencies in this respect rarely preclude use of the presented values. These **indirect quality attributes** may increase or decrease the convenience of the use of those values and their procurement cost, hence subsequently their expected cost-effectiveness.

When values are presented to users/clients via a complex delivery system, a new aspect of actionable credibility arises. Besides, of the previously mentioned unambiguous definitions (objectivity, accuracy, precision, currency), another indirect quality requirement of faithful mapping, as defined by Wand and Wang (1996), becomes a prerequisite.

Rarely does anything useful come at no cost and at no risk. Hence, the real cumulative measure of usefulness should be the **expected cost-effectiveness** of the operations assessed from the viewpoint of the purpose they serve. It can be evaluated by either objective criteria, when an adequate model of the decision situation exists or post-*facto*, after deployment of an information system. The ultimate goal of examining values for the above-discussed quality requirements is to arrive at a **set of task-specific usable values of operational completeness that is effective enough to trigger operations**. When not only effectiveness, but also economy is required one wants such sets to be also effective economically, cost effectively, or even wants them to exceed a required level of expected cost-effectiveness. Then of course, all the direct secondary quality requirements, which are of economical nature, will become mandatory, as well.

When summarized, all the direct secondary quality requirements determine the economic usability of the values concerned, and ultimately the cost-effectiveness of the delivery system and the entire set of operations. The same aspects, when considered from the viewpoint of information disseminators, carry more weight. Even subtle differences in these aspects may decide whether clients respond at all, and/or how they respond. One must also avoid a one-sided assessment of the cost-effectiveness of informing that is only from the disseminators' or only from the clients' viewpoint. In an ideal solution, it should be cost-effective for both sides. This is what makes a business relationship lasting and successful.

Examples of Predictive and Explanatory Aspects
of the Framework

"The purpose of science is to develop theories, which can be defined as sets of formulations designed to explain and predict phenomena" (Mason & Bramble, 1978, p. 3). For the sake of brevity only a few examples of some of the predictive and explanatory aspects of the proposed theoretical framework and model for operations' quality of data or information will be given.

It seems it will be difficult, if possible at all, to find any example or argument to the contrary (indirect proof) that *all identified and also not yet identified operations' quality requirements of data and information values exist.* The inherent relativity (with regard to the purpose and circumstances of operations) of how attributes of operations' quality of data/information values are viewed, perceived, and evaluated explains why even highly educated subjects of empirical, in particular, survey-based studies, are inherently incapable of coherently and consistently responding to questions about those attributes (if the decision situation of the operations is not defined as in Wang and Strong, 1996), for instance:

- The universal direct primary quality requirements are of the highest importance; hence, always all of them should be ranked 1st.
- Effective operational completeness is an extreme example of a universal requirement of the highest importance, ranked 5th by priority in a sequence of examination, and ranked only 10th out of 20 in Wang and Strong (1996).
- The mandatory requirement of acquisition interpretability of data/information was not even considered. For instance, consider an example when the stakes are high, as the USA is experiencing just now, or the anguish of the three Polish mathematicians who cracked the Nazi Germany military code and passed it successfully to the British at the brink of WWII. Those without such experience find it difficult to develop a feeling for the enormous difference between *acquisition of data* that, in most cases, are practically waiting to be collected, and *acquisition of information* of real utility value that changes our thinking about a situation, and/or the results of operations, and or the conduct of operations and business. Current MIS textbooks are unhelpful in this respect.
- Similarly, "accessibility" of data is mandatory for any action, and is unquestionably of the highest importance, ranked 3rd by priority in a sequence of consideration, and ranked a low 7th by importance by the subjects of the empirical study in Wang and Strong (1996). Thus, if rational thinking could be applied, although the questions in the empirical survey make it impossible, accessibility should come before anything else, except for relevancy. Hence, accessibility should be ranked 4th instead of 7th, because if not met, it renders irrelevant bothering about any other quality attributes of the same value, etc. Usually in empirical studies, no one expects that the answers given by sub-

jects will be derived by rational thinking. The actual responses, here again, demonstrate that the subjects did not experience the anguish of extracting important information from the real world of undeclared war when one must race against time to avert disaster, and so forth, because their main experience was based on accessing carefully prepared data from a database, which is an oversimplification of real-life situations.

What does it mean? With hindsight, of course, one may dare to guess that those subjects actually were answering a different question — "How do you perceive the importance of the problems you were experiencing at your workplace with regard to the following dimensions (a list follows with respective definitions in an appendix)?" Consider the implications of answering that question instead of the actually asked question "to rate the importance of each data quality attribute for their data on a scale from 1 to 9, where 1 was extremely important and 9 not important" (Wang and Strong, 1996, p. 12). Otherwise, in real life, accessibility and completeness could never end up with the importance 7 and 10 respectively. One simply cannot act when pertinent data are not accessible and complete, as required by the task — unless one gambles.

For a framework to be sound and complete, much more has to be taken into account than the experience gathered from using data taken from shared common databases. There are important problems as well, but these are rather technical problems. The above list of comments could be much longer, but for the sake of brevity, these few examples must suffice.

FUTURE TRENDS

In general, in business and public administration, data about the past and present are collected and stored to satisfy the established accountability requirements, whether for legal, tax, and auditing purposes, and as an important input for all other information processing. Some of the data, together with the additional indispensable information, are used to cope with the present and future of organizations. They are used in decision-making at the non-managerial, operational, tactical, and strategic level.

The operations' research approach to data quality can easily be started on a small scale with simple tasks performed on a massive scale, where the quality of available data and acquired information directly affects measurable results with the immediate goal to maximize the results, minimize the cost, or both, and increase the overall cost effectiveness of those tasks. One may easily argue and demonstrate that by examining a series of calls for roadside assistance or 9-1-1 calls in emergencies, one may more quickly arrive at a much clearer perception of the fundamental quality requirements of lasting and universal validity than by conducting tedious empirical survey-based studies of user preferences in an *undefined situational context*. Gradually one may take up more complex tasks, gather more experience, while at the same time develop adequate data quality analysis systems such as a decision-support system or expert system. More ambitious projects might entail information quality analysis including the evaluation of the quality of intelligence services applicable at all levels of decision-making, including the strategic level.

Operations' research-based approach is more promising in yielding both a real qualitative insight into the theoretical and practical intricacies of quality and real, quantitatively measurable practical results. The latter, under shrewd management may become so substantial that the operations' research approach may become the foundation for developing an entire line of Data Quality, or Information Quality Consulting Services of significant commercial value. Research at MIT was known for its ability to generate seeds of operations initiatives with the potential for mature business projects. Of course, there is room for empirical (both exploratory and confirmatory, and even survey-based) studies of various quality aspects of user-machine interfaces offered on the market for real consumers with real purchasing power, such as Web site quality (Mustakis, 2004). This is clearly the domain of individual or group preferences in using data and information values, where other research tools are not so effective.

RESULTS AND CONCLUSION

This is a summary of the results and conclusion (see Table 2) from this technology-independent inquiry into the interdependencies among the operations quality attributes of any symbolic representation with the emphasis on data and information values, while applying the teleological operations-research-based approach and viewing them from a purpose- and content-focused perspective.

1. A **teleological operations' research-based** framework of reference for examination of operations' quality requirements was defined.
2. A **purpose- and content-focused perspective** for assessment of quality was applied.
3. A tentatively **universal hierarchical impact-determined taxonomy** of operations quality requirements was defined.
4. **Five direct primary tentatively universal quality requirements** were defined and briefly described.
5. A tentative **economical order** of examination of operations quality requirements was defined by exploiting the logical interdependencies among them and providing the analyst with a point of reference to how much attention they deserve.
6. The first seven tentatively **universal principles** of operations quality were formulated and not yet challenged.

Table 2. Examples of operations quality requirements of symbolic representations within a tentatively universal hierarchical disjoint impact-determined taxonomy in an economic sequence of their examination (Source: Gackowski, 2005a)

					Direct Attributes	*Indirect* Attributes
Sequence of examination	Formally irrelevant	*Primary Attributes*	Universal Mandatory		Acquisition interpretable	Discernible, recognizable, identifiable
					Of significant impact or relevance	Adds value, mandatory companion, admissible, restricted access
					Operationally timely available	Mode of decision-making (individual, collective)
					(Presentation interpretable)	Legible, understandable, conventions, measurement units, etc.
					Actionably credible	Disinformation, misinformation, valid, traceable, faithfully mapped
					Task-specific operations triggering complete set of values[1]	Decision-maker's traits: risk averse, cautious, prudent, motivated, jumpy
		Secondary attributes	Mandatory when economy is the primary issue	Economically	Acquisition interpretable	Requires decoding, translation
					Timely available	How much in advance
					Actionably credible	Objective, accurate, precise, current
					(Presentation interpretable)	Summarized, detail, text, graph, diagram, picture, media, clarity, order, consistency, mode of delivery
					Task –specific operations triggering complete set	Expected payoffs, expected cost

Note: Operations' quality attributes that are not universally applicable for they are situation-specific but occur frequently are placed in parentheses.

It is an attempt at formulating a theoretical framework for examining and assessing the operations quality of data and information. The purpose was to arrive at an explanatory theory and results of more lasting validity. The model is based on the fundamental principles of human purposes and subsequent actions, which are the subject of **teleological methods** (Mende, 2005, p. 202). The method of **thought experiments** was applied to generate the outline of the model by imagining the situation and using its features as premises for deductive arguments (Mende, 2005, p. 202) that enable the formulation of the first seemingly universal principles in this domain. The presented framework is a purpose- and content-focused, operations' research-based approach to a logical inquiry into the universe of all operations' quality requirements. By the law of relativity they are always determined by the purpose and circumstances of purposive operations. Those attributes are in many ways logically **interdependent**.

The most interesting conclusion, however, emerged at the very end. It seems, that all the finding of tentatively universality (taxonomy, requirements, and principles) **remain valid** not only in information systems and informing science, but literally **in all disciplines dealing with operations conducted by autonomously purposively acting humans, their organizations, systems controlled by artificial intelligence (robots), and any combinations thereof**. Among others, all those disciplines have at least one thing in common that pertains to the presented subject — they study effectiveness of **actions based upon available data and obtainable information**. Without claiming completeness, one may list here: operations' research in all its main areas (business, public administration, and military operations), decision science, management science, economics, medical science, political science, sociology, psychology, etc., and systems science/cybernetics.

This is a research in progress. Of course, this first attempt of outlining and presenting such a framework is simplified, because it implicitly assumes a single main purpose with no conflicting requirements and constraints imposed upon decision-makers. This fact immediately opens many further research opportunities to expand and refine the framework so that it can accommodate cases that are more complex. It facilitates an elevation of operations' quality assessment of any symbolic representations from the operational to the *strategic level* of applications in business and administration, including applications related to national security.

REFERENCES

Financial Accounting Standard Board (FASB). (1983). *Accounting standard: Statement of financial accounting concepts.* McGraw-Hill.

Gackowski, Z. J. (2004). Logical interdependence of data/information quality dimensions — a purpose-focused view on IQ. In *Proceedings of the 9th International Conference on Information Quality (ICIQ 2004)*, Massachusetts Institute of Technology (MIT), Cambridge, MA. Retrieved from http://www.iqconference. org/Documents/IQ Conference 2004/Papers/LogicalInterdependence.pdf

Gackowski, Z. J. (2005a). Informing systems in business environment: A purpose-focused view. *Informing Science Journal*, 8, 101-122. Retrieved from http://inform.nu/Articles/Vol8/v8p101-122Gack.pdf

Gackowski, Z. J. (2005b). Operations quality of information: Teleological operations research-based approach, call for discussion. In *Proceedings of the 10ᵗʰ Anniversary International Conference on Information Quality (ICIQ-05)*, Massachusetts Institute of Technology (MIT), Cambridge, MA

Garvin, D. A. (1987). Competing on the eight dimensions of quality. *Harvard Business Review, 65*(6), 101-109.

Gleim, I. N. (2004). *CPA review financial* (12ᵗʰ ed.). Gleim Publications.

Hamlin, D. W. (1980). *Schopenhauer — The arguments of the philosophers*. London: Routledge & Kegan Paul.

Huang, K., Lee, Y. W., & Wang, R. Y. (1999). *Quality information and knowledge*. NJ: Prentice Hall.

Lee, Y., Strong, D., Kahn, B., & Wang. R. (2002). AIMQ: A methodology for information quality assessment. *Information & Management, 40*(2), 133-146. Retrieved from http://www.iqconference.org/documents/publications/TDQM-pub/AIMQ.pdf

Liu, L., & Chi, L. N. (2002). Evolutional data quality: A theory-specific view. In *Proceedings of the 7ᵗʰ International Conference on Information Quality (ICIQ-02)*, Cambridge, MA (pp. 292-304). Retrieved from http://www.iqconf erence.org/iciq/iqdownload.aspx?ICIQYear=2002&File=EvolutionalDataQu alityATheorySpecificView.pdf

Mason, E. J., & Bramble, W. J. (1978). *Understanding and conducting research*. New York: McGraw-Hill.

Mende, J. (2005). The poverty of empiricism. *Informing Science Journal, 8*, 180-210.

Moder, J., Phillips, C., & Davis, E. (1983). *Project management with CPM, PERT, and precedence diagramming* (3ʳᵈ ed). New York: Van Nostrand Company.

Moustakis, V. S., Litos, C., Dalivigas, A., & Tsironis, L. (2004). Website Quality Assessment Criteria. *Proceedings of the 9ᵗʰ International Conference on Information Quality (ICIQ-04)*, Cambridge, MA (pp. 59-73). Retrieved from http://www.iqconference.org/iciq/iqdownload.aspx?ICIQYear=2004&File= WebsiteQualityAssessmentCriteria.pdf

Wand, Y., & Wang, R. Y. (1996). Anchoring data quality dimensions in ontological foundations. *Communications of the ACM, 39*(11), 86-95.

Wang, R. Y., & Strong, D. M. (1996). Beyond accuracy: What data quality means to data consumers, *Journal of Management Information Systems (JMIS), 12*(4), 5-34.

ENDNOTES

[1]   Most authors use the term **data** and **information** interchangeably, however, the purpose-focused, operations-research-based perspective requires considering data and information as two disjunctive sets of symbolic representations with common quality attributes but distinctively different quality problems, as it will be explained.

[2]   **The Internal View assumptions:** Issues related to the external view such as why the data are needed and how they are used is not part of the model. We confine our model to system design and data production aspects by *excluding issues related to use and value of the data* (Wand & Wang, 1996, p. 89) (emphasis added).

[3]   Pertains to **sets** of usable values, not to single values.

About the Authors

Latif Al-Hakim is a senior lecturer of supply chain management in the Department of Economics and Resources Management, Faculty of Business at the University of Southern Queensland, Australia. His experience spans 35 years in industry, research and development organizations and in universities. Al-Hakim received his first degree in mechanical engineering in 1968. His MSc (1977) in industrial engineering and PhD (1983) in management science were awarded from University of Wales, UK. Al-Hakim has held various academic appointments and lectured on a wide variety of interdisciplinary management and industrial engineering topics. He has published extensively in facilities planning, information management and systems modelling. Research papers have appeared in various international journals and have been cited in other research and postgraduate work. Al-Hakim is the editor of the *International Journal of Information Quality*

* * * *

Monica Bobrowski works as project management manager at Pragma Consultores, Argentina. She has a degree in computer science from ESLAI, Argentina, and an MBA from Universidad Torcuato Di Tella, Argentina. She has been a professor with the Computer Science Department at the University of Buenos Aires. Her main interest areas include data quality, project evaluation, and project management.

Mikhaila Burgess is a lecturer in the School of Computer Science at Cardiff University, UK. Having received a BSc in computer science from Cardiff University in 1998 she worked for a year as a programmer, returning to Cardiff in 1999 as a PhD researcher. Since gaining her PhD in 2004 she has worked as a researcher on a number of projects including FASTER (feasibility study for an advanced systematic documentation, information and communication tool in the field of ethical issues in science, research and technology) and BiodiversityWorld. Her current research interests include using quality measures in information retrieval, ontology languages and tools, and the use of ontologies in information retrieval.

Tamraparni Dasu graduated with a PhD in statistics from the University of Rochester in 1991 and joined AT&T Bell Laboratories. Her interests include point processes, data mining and data quality. Her most recent publications include a book published by Wiley in 2003, *Exploratory Data Mining and Data Cleaning* with T. Johnson.

Nick J. Fiddian is head of school and professor of computer science at Cardiff University, UK. He was educated at London (LSE and ULICS) and Southampton Universities. His current research interests lie in the field of meta-translation—meta-programmed automatic translation between syntactically diverse but semantically similar programming languages in specific areas of computer application, particularly data/knowledge-base system interoperation. He has served as a member of numerous committees and working groups of Cardiff University including academic quality, teaching and learning, personnel/human resources and information services committees, standing committee of senate, council and court.

Zbigniew J. Gackowski has extensive experience in industry, public administration, and universities. His teaching and research bridge the gap between Central European and U.S. experience in computer information systems: Warsaw Polytechnic; University of Michigan (*Fulbright Research Scholarship*); Purdue University; Baruch College; CSU, Stanislaus; and University of Melbourne (visiting). While in Poland, he published more than 120 items, among them four books. He presented many papers across Europe, the United States, the Middle East, and South America. He is a member of ACM and DSI, and a charter member of the *Association for Information Systems* and *the Institute of Informing Science.*

Les Gasser, an associate professor of library/information science and computer science at the University of Illinois, has been studying socio-technical aspects of information systems — "Social Informatics" — for over 25 years. His research teams are currently investigating distributed continuous design and knowledge management processes in open source software projects (leading a 7-University U.S./French/EU collaboration), and computational models of language evolution in multi-agent systems, under multiple grants from NSF, industry, and the University of Illinois, USA.

W. Alex Gray is a professor of advanced information systems in the School of Computer Science at Cardiff University, UK, where he leads the school's Knowledge and Information Systems research group. He is also deputy director of WeSC — the Welsh e-Science Centre, which is one of 8 Regional Grid facilities in UK academia. He was educated at Edinburgh and Newcastle upon Tyne Universities. His current research is in interoperability of distributed data and knowledge based systems with a particular interest in how knowledge and semantics can be exploited to enrich the interoperation process and allow users to have different perspectives of data linkage. This research is conducted in application areas such as concurrent engineering and bioinformatics, especially in the WeSC/Grid context.

Kimberly Hess is a product manager for Acxiom Corporation supporting Acxiom's core linking product AbiliTec. Since 1999 she has worked at Acxiom in various capacities from the initial rollout of AbiliTec to implementing corporate quality initiatives including participating in a joint venture with Acxiom and MIT and the MIT ICIQ conference. Her current focus is around the internal and external support of data integration initiatives including new products.

Eric Infeld is director of Ingenix's Shared Data Warehouse group with responsibility for business analysis, data quality, and end-user support functions. He was instrumental in defining Galaxy's data quality strategy when the warehouse was launched. He has delivered papers at MIT's International Conference on Information Quality and was an invited speaker at the Information Quality for Executives seminar in 2004. Infeld holds a Master of Science in nursing from Pace University, Pleasantville, NY, and a Bachelor of Science in biology/psychology from the University of Connecticut. He also holds a certificate in information quality from MIT.

Andrea Krejza holds a licentiata philosophiae degree in political science of the University of Zurich, Switzerland, since 2004. She has specialized in terrorism and guerilla warfare. From 1999-2004 she worked at IBM Switzerland where she realized several knowledge management projects within the Consulting Group. In 2005 she transferred to the Investigation & Inquiries Unit of Credit Suisse in Zurich as a junior project manager.

Daniel Maier holds a PhD in genetics and worked as a postdoctoral fellow at the Neurosurgery University Clinics of Basel, Switzerland, before he started at Credit Suisse in 2000. As a project manager he was initially involved in several business process re-engineering projects with focus on operational risk and knowledge management. At present he is the head of the Investigation & Inquiries section and responsible for the operational management of legal investigations within the Legal & Compliance Department at Credit Suisse.

Helinä Melkas works as a senior researcher and project manager at Helsinki University of Technology, Lahti Centre, Finland. She holds a degree of doctor of science in technology from Helsinki University of Technology, Department of Industrial Engineering and Management (2004). She has earlier degrees in social sciences from University of Helsinki and Åbo Akademi University, Finland. She worked previously as a government official and researcher at Finnish Ministry of Labour; World Institute for Development Economics Research, Helsinki (part of United Nations University), and International Labour Office, Geneva (also a United Nations organization). Besides on information quality, she has written on subjects such as knowledge management, gerontechnology as well as various employment and labour market issues.

Thomas Muegeli studied modern Swiss history at the University of Bern, Switzerland, graduating 1995 with a licentiata philosophiae in history. Starting 1997 at Credit Suisse he was responsible for reconstructing a database of closed accounts to facilitate the research of Credit Suisse's role during the Second World War. In addition he also realized the implementation of several search engines and fuzzy logic databases for the Central Corporate Archive. In 2001 he joined Arthur Andersen, focusing on intelligent ways to treat unstructured information as well as anti-money laundering solutions. Returning to Credit Suisse in 2002 he realized several IT projects involving name-searching and name-matching for investigative and anti-moneylaundering purposes. At present he is a senior project manager for Investigations & Inquiries at Legal & Compliance in Zurich.

Felix Naumann received a diploma degree in mathematics from the University of Technology, Berlin, in 1997 and a doctoral degree in computer sciences from Humboldt-University of Berlin, Germany, in 2000. From 2001 to 2002 he was visiting researcher at the IBM Almaden Research Center, working on the Clio project. Since 2003 Felix Naumann heads the information integration group at Humboldt-University in Berlin as an assistant professor.

Elizabeth M. Pierce is a professor in the MIS & Decision Sciences Department at the Eberly College of Business and Information Technology at Indiana University of Pennsylvania. Since 1997, she has been actively involved with the Conference on Information Quality sponsored by MIT. Her research focuses on data, information, and knowledge quality. Pierce received her PhD from the University of Michigan.

Mary Roth is a senior architect for WebSphere Information Integration Solutions at IBM's Silicon Valley Lab, USA. She has more than 15 years of experience in database research and development. As a researcher at the IBM Almaden Research Center, she contributed key advances in heterogeneous data integration techniques and federated query optimization techniques. Roth is currently a leading a team of developers to deliver the next generation of metadata-driven discovery and integration capabilities for the Websphere Information Integration Solutions platform.

Laura Sebastian-Coleman is the data quality manager for the Galaxy Shared Data Warehouse operated by UnitedHealth Group's Ingenix business unit. She is responsible for monitoring and measuring data quality. She has delivered papers at MIT's International Conference on Information Quality and was an invited speaker at the Information Quality for Executives seminar in 2004. Sebastian-Coleman earned a bachelor's degree from Franklin & Marshall College and a PhD from the University of Rochester, New York. She also holds a certificate in information quality from MIT.

Besiki Stvilia is an assistant professor of the College of Information, Florida State University, USA. His research interests include information and metadata quality, digital library design and assessment, knowledge management, and recommender systems.

John R. Talburt is the leader for New Products and Solutions for Acxiom Corporation and Director of the Acxiom Laboratory for Applied Research. He led the team that developed the Acxiom Data Toolkit and the Acxiom Data Quality Scorecard Solution. Before going to Acxiom, Talburt was professor and chair of the Computer and Information Science Department at the University of Arkansas at Little Rock, USA. He has authored numerous publications in areas of information quality, data management, knowledge representation, and intelligent systems.

Michael B. Twidale is an associate professor of the Graduate School of Library and Information Science, University of Illinois at Urbana-Champaign, USA. His research interests include computer supported cooperative work, computer supported collaborative learning, user interface design and evaluation, error analysis, information quality, and museum informatics. Current projects include over the shoulder learning, extreme evaluation, collaborative techniques for improving quality in databases, and the usability of open source software.

Sabrina Vazquez-Soler works as project management office manager at Pragma Consultores, Argentina. She has a degree in computer science from Universidad de Buenos Aires, Argentina, and she is currently finishing her MOT studies at the University of San Andres Argentina. She is a professor at the Universidad Catolica Argentina. Her main interest areas include data quality, project evaluation, and project management.

Gregg T. Vesonder is director of the Communication Software Research Department at AT&T Labs - Research, USA. He also is an adjunct professor of computer and information science at the University of Pennsylvania, and an adjunct professor of computer science at Stevens Institute of Technology. Vesonder has developed and managed software systems supporting operations, e-commerce, sales support and data mining. He has been involved in software tool development for speech recognition, C++ compilers, artificial intelligence and software design and analysis. At Bell Labs Software Technology Center, Vesonder served on software architecture review boards and focused on software process improvement using object oriented and agile process methodologies. He is both a Bell Labs and an AT&T fellow. Vesonder received a BA in psychology from the University of Notre Dame and an MS and PhD in cognitive psychology from the University of Pittsburgh.

Jon R. Wright received a PhD in experimental psychology from Rice University in 1978, and joined Bell Telephone Laboratories shortly afterwards. He first worked as a human factors expert and later became interested in expert systems and various applications of artificial intelligence. He received the distinguished member of technical staff award from Bell Labs in 1985. In 1996, he joined AT&T Labs - Research, USA, as a principal member of Technical Staff, where he continues to pursue applications of the most recent trends in artificial intelligence research.

Index

D

database administrator 116
database management system (DBMS)
115, 117, 119, 120, 122, 130
data life cycle 245
data mining 136
data quality 1, 53, 243
data storage 115
data stream 136, 138, 140, 144
data stream management 140
data transfer 139
data value 284
data warehouse 1, 2, 66, 67, 96, 124, 300
developer 120
digital library 154, 155, 166
direct attribute 286
direct mail marketing 100
domain 221
Dublin Core 157
durability 119

E

electronic library system 214
enterprise network 189
ephemeral data 138
extract, transformation and load (ETL) 67

F

flexibility 98, 105, 111, 192, 221, 255
foreign key 4, 5, 7, 19

G

Galaxy 1, 2, 5, 12
general education 285
generic quality 219

H

health care 1, 188
hospital 29

I

indirect attribute 286
information behaviours and values (IBV) 37
information chain 3
information consumer 213, 216
information function deployment (IFD) 40
information management practices (IMP) 37
information needs 78
information orientation (IO) 36, 38, 46
information product manager 78
information quality (IQ) 26, 30, 99, 115, 160, 187, 190, 277, 280
information searching 213
information seeking 155
information system (IS) 28, 53, 78, 188
information technology (IT) 27, 28
information technology practices (ITP) 37
information value 284
internal rate of return 244
Internet 102, 106, 214, 223, 225
intranet 214
intrinsic quality 81
investment error 53
ISBN 160
isolation 119

K

knowledge 19, 34, 99, 146, 282

L

large-scale data mining 136
low quality metadata 155

M

maintenance 246
metadata 22, 126, 130, 154, 155, 158, 161, 163, 177

U

UnitedHealth Group 1, 3, 8
usability 155
user interface 66

V

value-added feature 91
virtualization 188
virtual network 187, 204